WCF Multi-tier Services Development with LINQ

Build SOA applications on the Microsoft platform in this hands-on guide

Mike Liu

BIRMINGHAM - MUMBAI

WCF Multi-tier Services Development with LINQ

First published: December 2008

Production Reference: 1261108

Published by Packt Publishing Ltd.
32 Lincoln Road
Olton
Birmingham, B27 6PA, UK.

ISBN 978-1-847196-62-0

www.packtpub.com

Cover Image by Parag Kadam (Paragvkadam@gmail.com)

Credits

Author
Mike Liu

Reviewers
Jeff Sanders
Yingwei Yang

Senior Acquisition Editor
David Barnes

Development Editor
Nikhil Bangera

Technical Editor
Dilip Venkatesh

Copy Editor
Sumathi Sridhar

Editorial Team Leader
Akshara Aware

Project Manager
Abhijeet Deobhakta

Project Coordinator
Rajashree Hamine

Indexer
Monica Ajmera

Proofreader
Dirk Manuel

Production Coordinator
Shantanu Zagade

Cover Work
Shantanu Zagade

About the Author

Mike Liu was born in 1966 in China. He studied Mathematics at Nanjing University between 1984 and 1988. After graduating with a Bachelor's degree, he worked as a Programmer / Senior Software Engineer / Architect under Unix and DOS using C/C++, DBase and Oracle. In 1995 he moved to New Zealand and studied Business Computing at the Auckland University of Technology in 1996. During his 5 years New Zealand, he worked as a Senior Software Engineer under Unix and Windows using C/C++, Java, FoxPro, Informix, Oracle and SQL Server. He moved to the United States in 2000, and since then has been working as a Web Developer / Senior Software Engineer / Principal Software Engineer under Unix and Windows using C/C++, C#, Visual Basic, Java, ASP, ASP.NET, Oracle and SQL Server. While working in the United States he studied Software Engineering at Brandeis University, and graduated in 2005 with a Master's degree.

Mike Liu had his first book (*MITT: Multi-user Integrated Table-processing Tool Under Unix*) published in 1993, and had his second book (*Advanced C# Programming*) published in 2003. He became a Sun Certified Java Programmer (SCJP) in 2000, a Microsoft Certified Solution Developer (MCSD) for Visual Studio 6.0 in 2001, and an MCSD for .NET in 2004.

Many thanks to the editors and technical reviewers at Packt Publishing. Without their help, this book won't be of such high quality. Thanks also to my wife, Julia Guo, and my two sons, Kevin and James Liu, for their patience and support while I was working on this book.

About the Reviewers

Jeff Sanders is a 16 year IT industry veteran with extensive experience in Solutions Architecture, BizTalk, SharePoint Server, and the .NET framework. Jeff's interests lie in design patterns of message-based architectures and connected systems design, EAI, workflow, WCF, and reducing complexity.

Jeff is a Group Manager and Solution Developer for Avanade Inc., a global IT consultancy specializing in solutions based on the Microsoft Enterprise platform that help to achieve profitable growth. He proudly works out of the East Region with some of the most talented and customer-obsessed professionals he has ever met.

Jeff also independently consults as a BizTalk Solutions Architect, Technical Lead, and Microsoft Certified Trainer for DynamicShift. He speaks at regional and local user groups on Microsoft technologies and industry-related topics.

With a deep interest in Business Intelligence (BI) and a passion for all things BizTalk, Jeff currently is writing *BizTalk 2009 Business Intelligence*, to be published in May 2009. He is also serving as a Technical Editor on a number of other books.

I would like to thank the most important person in my life, Lisa, for her well of unlimited patience and support that never runs dry. I'm definitely in love with Italian food.

Yingwei Yang joined Microsoft recently. Before that, he worked for ITG and Redcats USA. Yingwei enjoys working with .NET technology and is a big fan of Service Oriented Architecture, Silverlight, and High Performance Computing. He always thinks that Web Services/Software as a Service brings endless opportunities and possibilities.

Table of Contents

Preface

WCF is Microsoft's unified programming model for building service-oriented applications. It enables developers to build secure, reliable, transacted solutions that integrate across platforms and interoperate with existing investments.

If you are a C++/C# developer looking for a book to build real-world WCF services, have probably run into the huge reference tomes currently available in the market. These books are crammed with more information than you need, and most build only simple one-tier WCF services. And if you plan to use LINQ in the data access layer, you will probably need to buy another volume that is just as huge, and just as expensive.

This book is the quickest and easiest way to learn WCF and LINQ in Visual Studio 2008. It is the first book to combine WCF and LINQ in a multi-tier real-world WCF service. Multi-tier services provide separation of concerns and better factoring of code, which gives you better maintainability and the ability to split layers out into separate tiers, for better scalability. WCF and LINQ are both powerful yet complex technologies from Microsoft, but this book will get you through. The mastery of these two topics will quickly get you started on creating service-oriented applications, and will allow you to take your first steps into the world of Service Oriented Architecture, without getting overwhelmed.

This book is a step-by-step tutorial with clear instructions and screenshots to guide you through the creation of a multi-tier real-world WCF service solution. It focuses on the essentials of using WCF and LINQ, rather than providing a reference to every single possibility. It leaves the reference material online where it belongs, and concentrates instead on practical examples, code, and advice.

What This Book Covers

- Creating, hosting, and consuming your first WCF service, in just a few minutes
- Exploring and learning different hosting and debugging options for a WCF service
- Building a multi-tier real-world WCF service from scratch to understand every layer of a WCF service, and applying it to your real work
- Adding exception handling to your WCF services
- Accelerating your WCF service development with Service Factory by applying best practices
- Understanding basic and advanced concepts and features of LINQ and LINQ to SQL
- Communicating securely and reliably with databases by rewriting the data access layer of your WCF service with LINQ to SQL
- Controlling concurrent updates to the databases and adding distributed transaction support to your WCF services

What You Need for This Book

To run the examples in this book, you need to have Visual Studio 2008 installed on your computer. As a result, all pre-requisites of Visual Studio 2008 should be installed as well.

In Chapter 7, you will be guided to download and install Microsoft Web Service Software Factory. This Service Factory will be used to model all of the WCF services starting from this chapter.

You need an SQL Server database engine, and in Chapter 6 you will be guided to download and install the Microsoft sample database Northwind to this database engine. This sample database will be used for all of the data access layers used in this book.

You need a second SQL Server database engine on a different computer to hold another sample database. This database will be used to run examples for the distributed transaction support of the WCF services described in Chapter 13.

Who is This Book For

This book is for C# and C++ developers who are eager to get started with WCF and LINQ, and who want a book that is practical and rich with examples from the very beginning. Developers and architects evaluating SOA implementation technologies for their company will find this book particularly useful because it gets you started with Microsoft's tools for SOA, and shows you how to customize our examples for your prototypes.

This book presumes a basic knowledge of C# or C++. Previous experience with Visual Studio will be helpful but is not required, as detailed instructions are given throughout the book.

Conventions

In this book, you will find a number of styles of text that distinguish between different kinds of information. Here are some examples of these styles, and an explanation of their meaning.

Code words in text are shown as follows: "At this point, we will use the raw `SqlClient` adapter to do the database work."

A block of code will be set as follows:

```
[DataContract]
public class ProductFault
{
    public ProductFault(string msg)
    {
        FaultMessage = msg;
    }

    [DataMember]
    public string FaultMessage;
}
```

When we wish to draw your attention to a particular part of a code block, the relevant lines or items will be made bold:

```
<?xml version="1.0" encoding="utf-8" ?>
<configuration>
<appSettings>
  <add key="NorthwindConnectionString"
       value="server=your_db_server\your_db_instance;
       uid=your_user_name; pwd=your_password;
       database=Northwind"/>
```

```
</appSettings>
  <system.web>
    <compilation debug="true" />
  </system.web>
```

New terms and **important words** are introduced in bold-type font. Words that you see on the screen, in menus or dialog boxes for example, appear in our text like this: "clicking the **Next** button moves you to the next screen".

[ Warnings or important notes appear in a box like this.]

[ Tips and tricks appear like this.]

Reader Feedback

Feedback from our readers is always welcome. Let us know what you think about this book—what you liked or may have disliked. Reader feedback is important for us to develop titles that you really get the most out of.

To send us general feedback, simply drop an email to `feedback@packtpub.com`, and mention the book title in the subject of your message.

If there is a book that you need and would like to see us publish, please send us a note in the **SUGGEST A TITLE** form on `www.packtpub.com` or email `suggest@packtpub.com`.

If there is a topic that you have expertise in and you are interested in either writing or contributing to a book on, see our author guide on `www.packtpub.com/authors`.

Customer Support

Now that you are the proud owner of a Packt book, we have a number of things to help you to get the most from your purchase.

Downloading the Example Code for the Book

Visit `http://www.packtpub.com/files/code/6620_Code.zip` to directly download the example code.

The downloadable files contain instructions on how to use them.

Errata

Although we have taken every care to ensure the accuracy of our contents, mistakes do happen. If you find a mistake in one of our books—maybe a mistake in the text or in the code—we would be grateful if you would report this to us. By doing this you can save other readers from frustration, and help to improve subsequent versions of this book. If you find any errata, report them by visiting `http://www.packtpub.com/support`, selecting your book, clicking on the **let us know** link, and entering the details of your errata. Once your errata are verified, your submission will be accepted and the errata added to any list of existing errata. The list of any existing errata can be viewed by selecting your title from `http://www.packtpub.com/support`.

Piracy

Piracy of copyright material on the Internet is an ongoing problem across all media. At Packt, we take the protection of our copyright and licenses very seriously. If you come across any illegal copies of our works in any form on the Internet, please provide the location address or website name immediately so we can pursue a remedy.

Please contact us at `copyright@packtpub.com` with a link to the suspected pirated material.

We appreciate your help in protecting our authors, and our ability to bring you valuable content.

Questions

You can contact us at `questions@packtpub.com` if you are having a problem with some aspect of the book, and we will do our best to address it.

1

SOA—Service Oriented Architecture

In this chapter, we will explain the concepts and definitions related to SOA, and clarify some confusions regarding SOA. Let's discuss each of the following in detail:

- What is SOA?
- Why do we need SOA?
- What are the various approaches to implementing SOA and what are the key differences between them?
- What is a web service and how is it related to SOA?
- What standards and specifications are there for web services?

What is SOA?

SOA is the acronym for Service Oriented Architecture. As it has come to be known, SOA is an architectural design pattern by which several guiding principles determine the nature of the design. Basically, SOA states that every component of a system should be a service, and the system should be composed of several loosely-coupled services. A service here means a unit of a program that serves a business process. "Loosely-coupled" here means that these services should be independent of each other, so that changing one of them should not affect any other services.

SOA is not a specific technology, nor a specific language. It is just a blueprint, or a system design approach. It is an architecture model that aims to enhance the efficiency, agility, and productivity of an enterprise system. The key concepts of SOA are services, high interoperability and loose coupling.

Several other architecture/technologies such as RPC, DCOM, and CORBA have existed for a long time, and attempted to address the client/server communication problems. The difference between SOA and these other approaches is that SOA is trying to address the problem from the client side, and not from the server side. It tries to decouple the client side from the server side, instead of bundling them, to make the client side application much easier to develop and maintain.

This is exactly what happened when object-oriented programming (OOP) came into play 20 years ago. Prior to object-oriented programming, most designs were procedure-oriented, meaning the developer had to control the process of an application. Without OOP, in order to finish a block of work, the developer had to be aware of the sequence that the code would follow. This sequence was then hard-coded into the program, and any change to this sequence would result in a code change. With OOP, an object simply supplied certain operations; it was up to the caller of the object to decide the sequence of those operations. The caller could mash up all of the operations, and finish the job in whatever order needed. There was a paradigm shift from the object side to the caller side.

This same paradigm shift is happening today. Without SOA, every application is a bundled, tightly coupled solution. The client-side application is often compiled and deployed along with the server-side applications, making it impossible to quickly change anything on the server side. DCOM and CORBA were on the right track to ease this problem by making the server-side components reside on remote machines. The client application could directly call a method on a remote object, without knowing that this object was actually far away, just like calling a method on a local object. However, the client-side applications continue to remain tightly coupled with these remote objects, and any change to the remote object will still result in a recompiling or redeploying of the client application.

Now, with SOA, the remote objects are truly treated as remote objects. To the client applications, they are no longer objects; they are services. The client application is unaware of how the service is implemented, or of the signature that should be used when interacting with those services. The client application interacts with these services by exchanging messages. What a client application knows now is only the interfaces, or protocols of the services, such as the format of the messages to be passed in to the service, and the format of the expected returning messages from the service.

Historically, there have been many other architectural design approaches, technologies, and methodologies to integrate existing applications. EAI (Enterprise Application Integration) is just one of them. Often, organizations have many different applications, such as order management systems, accounts receivable systems, and customer relationship management systems. Each application has been designed and developed by different people using different tools and technologies at different times, and to serve different purposes. However, between these applications, there are no standard common ways to communicate. EAI is the process of linking these applications and others in order to realize financial and operational competitive advantages.

It may seem that SOA is just an extension of EAI. The similarity is that they are both designed to connect different pieces of applications in order to build an enterprise-level system for business. But fundamentally, they are quite different. EAI attempts to connect legacy applications without modifying any of the applications, while SOA is a fresh approach to solve the same problem. And in the following chapters, you will come to understand why SOA is a better designed approach.

Why SOA?

So why do we need SOA now? The answer is in one word—agility.

Business requirements change frequently, as they always have. The IT department has to respond more quickly and cost-effectively to those changes. With a traditional architecture, all components are bundled together with each other. Thus, even a small change to one component will require a large number of other components to be recompiled and redeployed. Quality assurance (QA) effort is also huge for any code changes. The processes of gathering requirements, designing, development, QA, and deployment are too long for businesses to wait for, and become actual bottlenecks.

To complicate matters further, some business processes are no longer static. Requirements change on an ad-hoc basis, and a business needs to be able to dynamically define its own processes whenever it wants. A business needs a system that is agile enough for its day-to-day work. This is very hard, if not impossible, with existing traditional infrastructure and systems.

This is where SOA comes into play.

SOA's basic unit is a service. These services are building blocks that business users can use to define their own processes. Services are designed and implemented so that they can serve different purposes or processes, and not just specific ones. No matter what new processes a business needs to build or what existing processes a business needs need to modify, the business users should always be able to use existing service blocks, in order to compete with others according to current marketing conditions. Also, if necessary, some new service blocks can be used.

These services are also designed and implemented so that they are loosely coupled, and independent of one another. A change to one service does not affect any other service. Also, the deployment of a new service does not affect any existing service. This greatly eases release management and makes agility possible.

For example, a `GetBalance` service can be designed to retrieve the balance for a loan. When a borrower calls in to query the status of a specific loan, this `GetBalance` service may be called by the application that is used by the customer service representatives. When a borrower makes a payment online, this service can also be called to get the balance of the loan, so that the borrower will know the balance of his or her loan after the payment. Yet in the payment posting process, this service can still be used to calculate the accrued interest for a loan, by multiplying the balance with the interest rate. Even further, a new process can be created by business users to utilize this service if a loan balance needs to be retrieved.

The `GetBalance` service is developed and deployed independently from all of the above processes. Actually, the service exists without even knowing who the client will be or even how many clients there will be. All of the client applications communicate with this service through its interface, and its interface will remain stable once it is in production. If we have to change the implementation of this service, for example by fixing a bug, or changing an algorithm inside a method of the service, all of the client applications can still work without any change.

When combined with the more mature Business Process Management (BPM) technology, SOA plays an even more important role in an organization's efforts to achieve agility. Business users can create and maintain processes within BPM, and through SOA they can plug a service into any of the processes. The front-end BPM application is loosely coupled to the back-end SOA system. This combination of BPM and SOA will give an organization much greater flexibility in order to achieve agility.

How do we implement SOA?

Now that we've established why SOA is needed by the business, the question becomes—how do we implement SOA?

To implement SOA in an organization, three key elements have to be evaluated—people, process, and technology. Firstly, the people in the organization must be ready to adopt SOA. Secondly, the organization must know the processes that the SOA approach will include, including the definition, scope, and priority. Finally, the organization should choose the right technology to implement it. Note that people and processes take precedence over technology in an SOA implementation, but they are out of the scope of this book. In this book, we will assume people and processes are all ready for an organization to adopt SOA.

Technically, there are many SOA approaches. At certain degrees, traditional technologies such as RPC, DCOM, CORBA, or some modern technologies such as IBM WebSphere MQ, Java RMI, and .NET Remoting could all be categorized as service-oriented, and can be used to implement SOA for one organization. However, all of these technologies have limitations, such as language or platform specifications, complexity of implementation, or the ability to support binary transports only. The most important shortcoming of these approaches is that the server-side applications are tightly coupled with the client-side applications, which is against the SOA principle.

Today, with the emergence of web service technologies, SOA becomes a reality. Thanks to the dramatic increase in network bandwidth , and given the maturity of web service standards such as WS-Security, and WS-AtomicTransaction, an SOA back-end can now be implemented as a real system.

In this book, we will discuss how to implement SOA with web services, particularly with **WCF services**. We will discuss how to create, host, and consume a WCF service. Beneath the WCF service, we will use LINQ to SQL as the ORM to manage the relationships between WCF and the databases.

SOA from different users' perspectives

However, as we said earlier, SOA is not a technology, but only a style of architecture, or an approach to building software products. Different people view SOA in different ways. In fact, many companies now have their own definitions for SOA. Many companies claim they can offer an SOA solution, while they are really just trying to sell their products. The key point here is—SOA is not a solution. SOA alone can't solve any problem. It has to be implemented with a specific approach to become a real solution. You can't buy an SOA solution. You may be able to buy some kinds of products to help you realize your own SOA, but this SOA should be customized to your specific environment, for your specific needs.

Even within the same organization, different players will think about SOA in quite different ways. What follows are just some examples of how different players in an organization judge the success of an SOA initiative using different criteria. [*Gartner, Twelve Common SOA Mistakes and How to Avoid Them*, Publication Date: 26 October 2007 ID Number: G00152446]

- To a programmer, SOA is a form of distributed computing in which the building blocks (services) may come from other applications or be offered to them. SOA increases the scope of a programmer's product and adds to his or her resources, while also closely resembling familiar modular software design principles.

- To a software architect, SOA translates to the disappearance of fences between applications. Architects turn to the design of business functions rather than to self-contained and isolated applications. The software architect becomes interested in collaboration with a business analyst to get a clear picture of the business functionality and scope of the application. SOA turns software architects into integration architects and business experts.
- For the Chief Investment Officers (CIOs), SOA is an investment in the future. Expensive in the short term, its long-term promises are lower costs, and greater flexibility in meeting new business requirements. Re-use is the primary benefit anticipated as a means to reduce the cost and time of new application development.
- For business analysts, SOA is the bridge between them and the IT organization. It carries the promise that IT designers will understand them better, because the services in SOA reflect the business functions in business process models.
- For CEOs, SOA is expected to help IT become more responsive to business needs and facilitate competitive business change.

Complexities in SOA implementation

Although SOA will make it possible for business parties to achieve agility, SOA itself is technically not simple to implement. In some cases, it even makes software development more complex than ever, because with SOA you are building for unknown problems. On one hand, you have to make sure that the SOA blocks you are building are useful blocks. On the other, you need a framework within which you can assemble those blocks to perform business activities.

The technology issues associated with SOA are more challenging than vendors would like users to believe. Web services technology has turned SOA into an affordable proposition for most large organizations by providing a universally-accepted, standard foundation. However, web services play a technology role only for the SOA backplane, which is the software infrastructure that enables SOA-related interoperability and integration.

The following figure shows the technical complexity of SOA. It has been taken from *Gartner, Twelve Common SOA Mistakes and How to Avoid Them,* Publication Date: 26 October 2007 ID Number: G00152446.

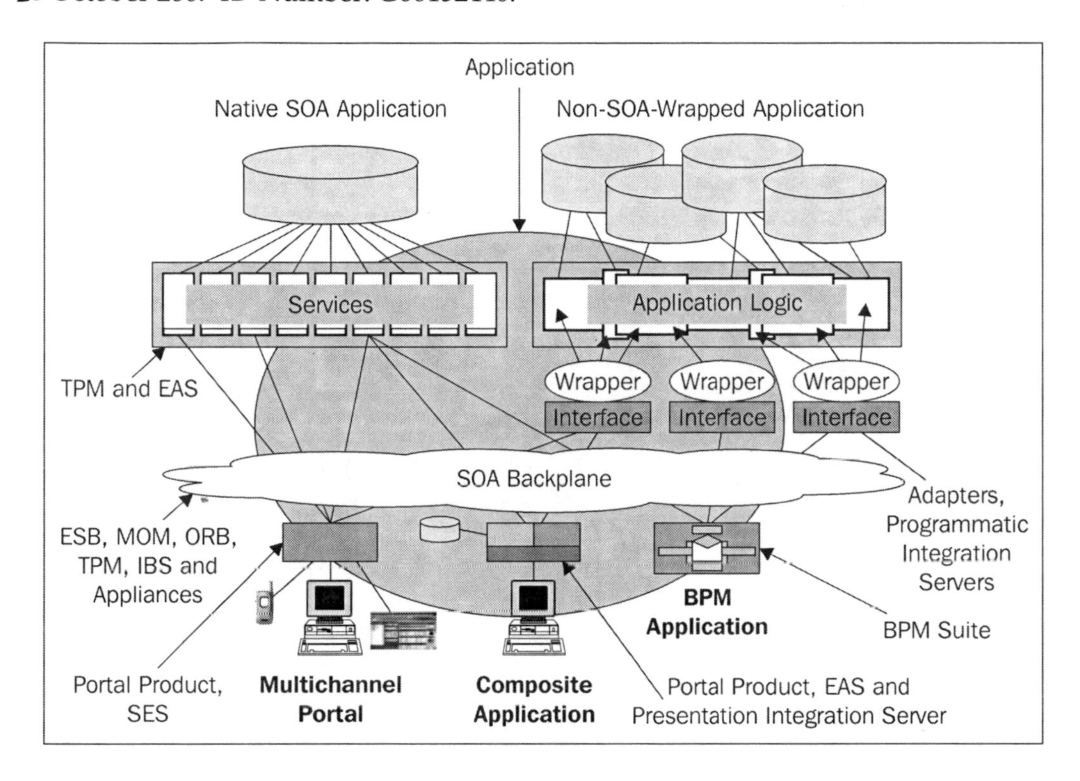

As Gartner says, users must understand the complex world of middleware, and point-to-point web service connections only for small-scale, experimental SOA projects. If the number of services deployed grows to more than 20 or 30, then use a middleware-based intermediary—the SOA backplane. The SOA backplane could be an Enterprise Service Bus (ESB), a Message-Oriented Middleware (MOM), or an Object Request Broker (ORB). However, in this book, we will not cover it. We will build only point-to-point services using WCF.

Web services

There are many approaches to realizing SOA, but the most popular and practical one is—using **web services**.

What is a web service?

A web service is a software system designed to support interoperable machine-to-machine interaction over a network. A web service is typically hosted on a remote machine (provider), and called by a client application (consumer) over a network. After the provider of a web service publishes the service, the client can discover it and invoke it. The communications between a web service and a client application use XML messages. A web service is hosted within a web server and HTTP is used as the transport protocol between the server and the client applications. The following diagram shows the interaction of web services:

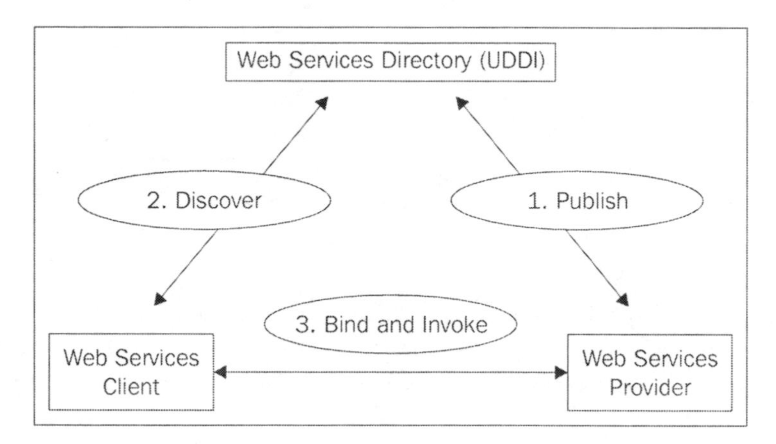

Web services were invented to solve the interoperability problem between applications. In the early 90s, along with the LAN/WAN/Internet development, it became a big problem to integrate different applications. An application might have been developed using C++, or Java, and run on a Unix box, a Windows PC, or even a mainframe computer. There was no easy way for it to communicate with other applications. It was the development of XML that made it possible to share data between applications across hardware boundaries and networks, or even over the Internet.

For example, a Windows application might need to display the price of a particular stock. With a web service, this application can make a request to a URL, and/or pass an XML string such as `<QuoteRequest><GetPrice Symble='XYZ'/></QuoteRequest>`. The requested URL is actually the Internet address of a web service, which, upon receiving the above quote request, gives a response, `<QuoteResponse><QuotePrice Symble='XYZ'>51.22</QuotePrice></QuoteResponse/>`. The Windows application then uses an XML parser to interpret the response package, and display the price on the screen.

The reason it is called a web service is that it is designed to be hosted in a web server, such as Microsoft Internet Information Server, and called over the Internet, typically via the HTTP or HTTPS protocols. This is to ensure that a web service can be called by any application, using any programming language, and under any operating system, as long as there is an active Internet connection, and of course, an open HTTP/HTTPS port, which is true for almost every computer on the Internet.

Each web service has a unique URL, and contains various methods. When calling a web service, you have to specify which method you want to call, and pass the required parameters to the web service method. Each web service method will also give a response package to tell the caller the execution results.

Besides new applications being developed specifically as web services, legacy applications can also be wrapped up and exposed as web services. So, an IBM mainframe accounting system might be able to provide external customers with a link to check the balance of an account.

Web service WSDL

In order to be called by other applications, each web service has to supply a description of itself, so that other applications will know how to call it. This description is provided in a language called a **WSDL**.

WSDL stands for Web Services Description Language. It is an XML format that defines and describes the functionalities of the web service, including the method names, parameter names, and types, and returning data types of the web service.

For a Microsoft ASMX web service, you can get the WSDL by adding `?WSDL` to the end of the web service URL, say `http://localhost/MyService/MyService.asmx?WSDL`.

Web service proxy

A client application calls a web service through a proxy. A web service proxy is a stub class between a web service and a client. It is normally auto-generated by a tool such as Visual Studio IDE, according to the WSDL of the web service. It can be re-used by any client application. The proxy contains stub methods mimicking all of methods of the web service so that a client application can call each method of the web service through these stub methods. It also contains other necessary information required by the client to call the web service such as custom exceptions, custom data and class types, and so on.

The address of the web service can be embedded within the proxy class, or it can be placed inside a configuration file.

A proxy class is always for a specific language. For each web service, there could be a proxy class for Java clients, a proxy class for C# clients, and yet another proxy class for COBOL clients.

To call a web service from a client application, the proper proxy class first has to be added to the client project. Then, with an optional configuration file, the address of the web service can be defined. Within the client application, a web service object can be instantiated, and its methods can be called just as for any other normal method.

SOAP

There are many standards for web services. **SOAP** is one of them. SOAP was originally an acronym for Simple Object Access Protocol, and was designed by Microsoft. As this protocol became popular with the spread of web services, and its original meaning was misleading, the original acronym was dropped with version 1.2 of the standard. It is now merely a protocol, maintained by W3C.

SOAP, now, is a protocol for exchanging XML-based messages over computer networks. It is widely-used by web services and has become its de-facto protocol. With SOAP, the client application can send a request in XML format to a server application, and the server application will send back a response in XML format. The transport for SOAP is normally HTTP / HTTPS, and the wide acceptance of HTTP is one of the reasons why SOAP is widely accepted today.

Web services: standards and specifications

Because SOA is an architectural style, and web service is now the de facto for building SOA applications, we need to know what standards and specifications there are for web services.

As we discussed in the previous sections, there are many standards and specifications for web services. Some have been well-developed and widely-accepted, while some are being developed, and others are just at the proposal stage. These specifications are in varying degrees of maturity, and are maintained or supported by various standards and entities. Specifications may complement, overlap, and compete with each other. As most of these standards committees and specifications are for future web services, not all of them are implemented in current web service frameworks.

Web service standards and specifications are occasionally referred to as "WS-*" although there is not a single managed set of specifications that this consistently refers to, nor a recognized owning body across all of them. The reference term "WS-*" is more of a general nod to the fact that many specifications are named with "WS-" as their prefix.

Besides XML, SOAP, and WSDL, here is a brief list of some other important standards and specifications for web services.

WS-I Profiles

The **Web Services Interoperability Organization (WS-I)** is an industry consortium chartered to promote interoperability across the stack of web services specifications. It publishes web service profiles, sample applications, and test tools to help determine profile conformance. One of the popular profiles it has published is the WS-I Basic Profile. WS-I is governed by a Board of Directors, and Microsoft is one of the board members. The web address for WS-I organization is `http://www.ws-i.org`.

WS-Addressing

WS-Addressing is a mechanism that allows web services to communicate addressing information. With traditional web services, addressing information is carried by the transport layer, and the web service message itself knows nothing about its destination. With this new standard, addressing information will be included in the XML message itself. A SOAP header can be added to the message for this purpose. The network-level transport is now responsible only for delivering that message to a dispatcher capable of reading the metadata.

WS-Security

WS-Security describes how to handle security issues within SOAP messages. It attaches signature and encryption information as well as security tokens to SOAP messages. In addition to the traditional HTTP/HTTPS authentications, it incorporates extra security features in the header of the SOAP message, working in the application layer. It ensures end-to-end security.

There are several specifications associated with WS-Security, such as WS-SecureConversation, WS-Federation, WS-Authorization, WS-Policy, WS-Trust, and WS-Privacy.

WS-ReliableMessaging

WS-ReliableMessaging describes a protocol that allows SOAP messages to be delivered reliably between distributed applications.

The WS Reliable Messaging model enforces reliability between the message source and destination. If a message cannot be delivered to the destination, the model must raise an exception, or otherwise indicate to the source that the message can't be delivered.

There are several Delivery Assurance options for WS-ReliableMessaging, including AtLeastOnce, AtMostOnce, Exactly Once, and InOrder.

WS-Coordination and WS-Transaction

WS-Coordination describes an extensible framework for providing protocols that coordinate the actions of distributed applications. The framework enables existing transaction processing, workflow, and other systems for coordination to hide their proprietary protocols and to operate in a heterogeneous environment. Additionally, this specification provides a definition for the structure of the context and the requirements for propagating context between cooperating services.

WS-Transaction describes coordination types that are used with the extensible coordination framework described in the WS-Coordination specification. It defines two coordination types: Atomic Transaction (AT) for individual operations, and Business Activity (BA) for long running transactions.

WS-AtomicTransaction provides the definition of the atomic transaction coordination type that is to be used with the extensible coordination framework described in the WS-Coordination specification. This protocol can be used to build applications that require consistent agreement on the outcome of short-lived distributed activities that have all-or-nothing semantics.

WS-BusinessActivity provides the definition of the business activity coordination type that is to be used with the extensible coordination framework described in the WS-Coordination specification. This protocol can be used to build applications that require consistent agreement on the outcome of long-running distributed activities.

Summary

In this chapter, we have learned and clarified many concepts related to SOA. The key points in this chapter are:

- SOA is an architectural design pattern
- SOA is designed for business agility
- Different users may view SOA in different ways
- Web services are the most popular and practical way of realizing SOA today
- There are many standards and specifications for web services including, but not limited to, WSDL, SOAP, WS-I Profiles, and various WS-* standards

2

WCF – Windows Communication Foundation

WCF is the latest technology from Microsoft for building services. In this chapter, we will explain what WCF is, and what it is composed of. We will also explain various .NET runtimes, .NET frameworks, Visual Studio versions, the relationships between them, and what is needed to develop or deploy WCF services. You will see some code snippets in this chapter that will help you to further understand WCF concepts, although they are not in a completed WCF project. Once we have grasped the basic concepts of WCF, we will develop a complete WCF service and create a client application to consume it in the next chapter.

For now, let us discuss the following in detail:

- What WCF is
- Use of WCF for SOA
- WCF architecture
- Basic WCF concepts

What is WCF?

WCF is the acronym for Windows Communication Foundation. It is Microsoft's latest technology that enables applications in a distributed environment to communicate with each other.

WCF is Microsoft's unified programming model for building service-oriented applications. It enables developers to build secure, reliable, transacted solutions that integrate across platforms and interoperate with existing investments. WCF is built on the Microsoft .NET Framework and simplifies the development of connected systems. It unifies a broad array of distributed systems capabilities in a composable, extensible architecture that supports multiple transports, messaging patterns, encodings, network topologies, and hosting models. It is the next version of several existing products—ASP.NET's web methods (ASMX) and Microsoft Web Services Enhancements (WSE) for Microsoft .NET, .NET Remoting, Enterprise Services, and System.Messaging.

The purpose of WCF is to provide a single programming model that can be used to create services on the .NET platform for organizations.

Why is WCF used for SOA?

As we have seen in the previous section, WCF is an umbrella technology that covers ASMX web services, .NET remoting, WSE, Enterprise Service, and System. Messaging. It is designed to offer a manageable approach to distributed computing, broad interoperability, and direct support for service orientation. WCF supports many styles of distributed application development by providing a layered architecture. At its base, the WCF channel architecture provides asynchronous, untyped message-passing primitives. Built on top of this base are protocol facilities for secure, reliable, transacted data exchange and a broad choice of transport and encoding options.

Let us take an example to see why WCF is a good approach for SOA. Suppose a company is designing a service to get loan information. This service could be used by the internal call center application, an Internet web application, and a third-party Java J2EE application such as a banking system. For interactions with the call center client application, performance is important. For communication with the J2EE-based application however, interoperability becomes the highest goal. The security requirements are also quite different between the local Windows-based application, and the J2EE-based application running on another operating system. Even transactional requirements might vary, with only the internal application being allowed to make transactional requests.

With these complex requirements, it is not easy to build the desired service with any single existing technology. For example, the ASMX technology may serve well for the interoperability, but its performance may not be ideal. The .NET remoting will be a good choice from the performance perspective, but it is not good at interoperability. Enterprise Services could be used for managing object lifetimes and defining distributed transactions, but Enterprise Services supports only a limited set of communication options.

Now with WCF, it is much easier to implement this service. As WCF has unified a broad array of distributed systems capabilities, the **get loan** service can be built with WCF for all of its application-to-application communication. The following shows how WCF addresses each of these requirements:

- Because WCF can communicate using web service standards, interoperability with other platforms that also support SOAP, such as the leading J2EE-based application servers, is straightforward.
- You can also configure and extend WCF to communicate with web services using messages not based on SOAP, for example, simple XML formats such as RSS.
- Performance is of paramount concern for most businesses. WCF was developed with the goal of being one of the fastest distributed application platforms developed by Microsoft.
- To allow for optimal performance when both parties in a communication are built on WCF, the wire encoding used in this case is an optimized binary version of an XML Information Set. Using this option makes sense for communication with the call center client application, because it is also built on WCF, and performance is an important concern.
- Managing object lifetimes, defining distributed transactions, and other aspects of Enterprise Services, are now provided by WCF. They are available to any WCF-based application, which means that the get loan service can use them with any of the other applications that it communicates with.
- Because it supports a large set of the WS-* specifications, WCF helps to provide reliability, security, and transactions when communicating with any platform that supports these specifications.
- The WCF option for queued messaging, built on **Message Queuing**, allows applications to use persistent queuing without using another set of application programming interfaces.

The result of this unification is greater functionality, and significantly reduced complexity.

WCF architecture

The following diagram illustrates the major layers of the Windows Communication Foundation (WCF) architecture. This diagram is taken from the Microsoft web site (`http://msdn.microsoft.com/en-us/library/ms733128.aspx`):

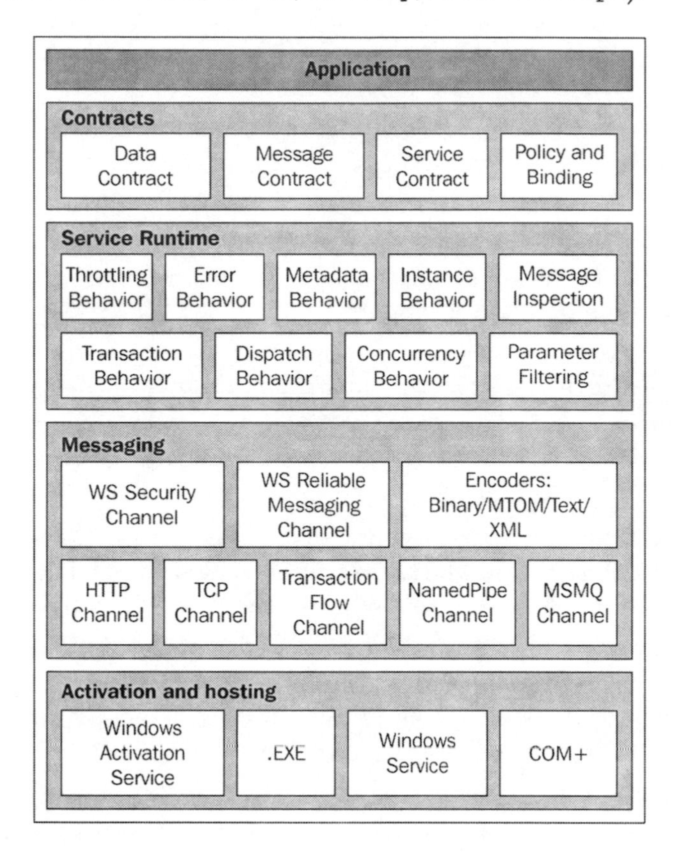

The **Contracts** layer defines various aspects of the message system. For example, the **Data Contract** describes every parameter that makes up every message that a service can create or consume.

The **Service runtime** layer contains the behaviors that occur only during the actual operation of the service, that is, the runtime behaviors of the service.

The **Messaging** layer is composed of channels. A channel is a component that processes a message in some way, for example, authenticating a message.

In its final form, a service is a program. Like other programs, a service must be run in an executable format. This is known as the **hosting** application.

In the next section, we will explain these concepts in detail.

Basic WCF concepts—WCF ABCs

There are many terms and concepts around WCF, such as address, binding, contract, endpoint, behavior, hosting, and channels. Understanding these terms is very helpful when using WCF.

Address

The WCF **Address** is a specific location for a service. It is the specific place to which a message will be sent. All WCF services are deployed at a specific address, listening at that address for incoming requests.

A WCF Address is normally specified as a URI, with the first part specifying the transport mechanism, and the hierarchical part specifying the unique location of the service. For example, `http://www.myweb.com/myWCFServices/SampleService` can be an address for a WCF service. This WCF service uses HTTP as its transport protocol, and it is located on the server `www.myweb.com`, with a unique service path of `myWCFServices/SampleService`. The following diagram illustrates the three parts of a WCF service address.

Binding

Bindings are used to specify the transport, encoding, and protocol details required for clients and services to communicate with each other. Bindings are what WCF uses to generate the underlying wire representation of the endpoint. So, most of the details of the binding must be agreed upon by the parties that are communicating. The easiest way to achieve this is for clients of a service to use the same binding that the service uses.

A binding is made up of a collection of binding elements. Each element describes some aspect of how the service communicates with clients. A binding must include at least one transport binding element, at least one message encoding binding element (which can be provided by the transport binding element by default), and any number of other protocol binding elements. The process that builds a runtime out of this description allows each binding element to contribute code to that runtime.

WCF provides bindings that contain common selections of binding elements. These can either be used with their default settings, or the default values can be modified according to user requirements. These system-provided bindings have properties that allow direct control over the binding elements and their settings.

The following are some examples of the system-provided bindings: BasicHttpBinding, WSHttpBinding, WSDualHttpBinding, WSFederationHttpBinding, NetTcpBinding, NetNamedPipeBinding, NetMsmqBinding, NetPeerTcpBinding, and MsmqIntegrationBinding. Each one of these built-in bindings has predefined required elements for a common task, and is ready to be used in your project. For instance, the BasicHttpBinding uses HTTP as the transport for sending SOAP 1.1 messages, and it has attributes and elements such as `receiveTimeout`, `sendTimeout`, `maxMessageSize`, and `maxBufferSize`. You can accept the default settings of its attributes and elements, or overwrite them as needed.

Contract

A WCF contract is a set of specifications that define the interfaces of a WCF service. A WCF service communicates with other applications according to its contracts. There are several types of WCF contracts, such as Service Contract, Operation Contract, Data Contract, Message Contract, and Fault Contract.

Service contract

A **service contract** is the interface of the WCF service. Basically, it tells others what the service can do. It may include service-level settings, such as the name of the service, the namespace of the service, and the corresponding callback contracts of the service. Inside the interface, it can define a bunch of methods, or service operations for specific tasks. Normally, a WCF service has at least one service contract.

Operation contract

An **operation contract** is defined within a service contract. It defines the parameters and return type of an operation. An operation can take data of a primitive (native) data type, such as an integer as a parameter, or it can take a message, which should be defined as a message contract type. Just as a service contract is an interface, an operation contract is a definition of an operation. It has to be implemented in order that the service functions as a WCF service. An operation contract also defines operation-level settings, such as the transaction flow of the operation, the directions of the operation (one-way, two-way, or both ways), and fault contract of the operation.

Amazon.com Returns Center
172 Trade Street
Lexington, KY 40511

Billing Address:

Robert S. Maher
52 Maple Circle
Shrewsbury, MA
01545-5342
United States of America

Shipping Address:

Robert S. Maher
52 Maple Circle
Shrewsbury, MA
01545-5342
United States of America

YOUR ORDER OF MAY 29, 2009 (ORDER ID 103-8119210-3119448)

Qty	Item
	IN THIS SHIPMENT:
1	Professional Design Patterns in VB .NET: Building Adaptable Applicati Fischer, Tom paperback 1590592743

This shipment completes your order.

DCx5dMqSR

The following is an example of an operation contract:

```
[WCF::FaultContract(typeof(MyWCF.EasyNorthwind.FaultContracts.
ProductFault))]
MyWCF.EasyNorthwind.MessageContracts.GetProductResponse
GetProduct(MyWCF.EasyNorthwind.MessageContracts.GetProductRequest
request);
```

In this example, the operation contract's name is `GetProduct`, and it takes one input parameter, which is of type `GetProductRequest` (a message contract) and has one return value, which is of type `GetProductResponse` (another message contract). It may return a fault message, which is of type `ProductFault` (a fault contract), to the client applications. We will cover **message contract** and **fault contract** in the following sections.

Message contract

If an operation contract needs to pass a message as a parameter or return a message, the type of these messages will be defined as message contracts. A message contract defines the elements of the message, as well as any message-related settings, such as the level of message security, and also whether an element should go to the header or to the body.

The following is a message contract example:

```
namespace MyWCF.EasyNorthwind.MessageContracts
{
    /// <summary>
    /// Service Contract Class - GetProductResponse
    /// </summary>
    [WCF::MessageContract(IsWrapped = false)]
    public partial class GetProductResponse
    {
            private MyWCF.EasyNorthwind.DataContracts.Product product;

            [WCF::MessageBodyMember(Name = "Product")]
            public MyWCF.EasyNorthwind.DataContracts.Product Product
            {
                    get { return product; }
                    set { product = value; }
            }
    }
}
```

In this example, the namespace of the message contract is `MyWCF.EasyNorthwind.MessageContracts`, and the message contract's name is `GetProductResponse`. This message contract has one member, which is of type `Product`.

Data contract

Data contracts are data types of the WCF service. All data types used by the WCF service must be described in metadata to enable other applications to interoperate with the service. A data contract can be used by an operation contract as a parameter or return type, or it can be used by a message contract to define elements. If a WCF service uses only primitive (native) data types, it is not necessary to define any data contract.

The following is an of example data contract:

```
namespace MyWCF.EasyNorthwind.DataContracts
{
    /// <summary>
    /// Data Contract Class - Product
    /// </summary>
    [WcfSerialization::DataContract(Namespace = "http://MyCompany.com/
                   ProductService/EasyWCF/2008/05", Name = "Product")]
    public partial class Product
    {
            private int productID;
            private string productName;

            [WcfSerialization::DataMember(Name = "ProductID",
                                IsRequired = false, Order = 0)]
            public int ProductID
            {
              get { return productID; }
              set { productID = value; }
            }

            [WcfSerialization::DataMember(Name =
                           "ProductName", IsRequired = false, Order = 1)]
            public string ProductName
            {
              get { return productName; }
              set { productName = value; }
            }
    }
}
```

In this example, the namespace of the data contract is `MyWCF.EasyNorthwind.DataContracts`, the name of the data contract is `Product`, and this data contract has two members (`ProductID` and `ProductName`).

Fault contract

In any WCF service operation contract, if an error can be returned to the caller, the caller should be warned of that error. These error types are defined as fault contracts. An operation can have zero or more fault contracts associated with it.

The following is a fault contract example:

```
namespace MyWCF.EasyNorthwind.FaultContracts
{
    /// <summary>
    /// Data Contract Class - ProductFault
    /// </summary>
    [WcfSerialization::DataContract(Namespace = "http://MyCompany.com/
              ProductService/EasyWCF/2008/05", Name = "ProductFault")]
    public partial class ProductFault
    {
            private string faultMessage;

            [WcfSerialization::DataMember(Name =
                        "FaultMessage", IsRequired = false, Order = 0)]
            public string FaultMessage
            {
              get { return faultMessage; }
              set { faultMessage = value; }
            }
    }
}
```

In this example, the namespace of the fault contract is `MyWCF.EasyNorthwind.FaultContracts`, the name of the fault contract is `ProductFault`, and the fault contract has only one member (`FaultMessage`).

Endpoint

Messages are sent between **endpoints**. Endpoints are places where messages are sent or received (or both), and they define all of the information required for the message exchange. A service exposes one or more application endpoints (as well as zero or more infrastructure endpoints). A service can expose this information as the metadata that clients can process to generate appropriate WCF clients and communication stacks. When needed, the client generates an endpoint that is compatible with one of the service's endpoints.

A WCF service endpoint has an address, a binding, and a service contract (WCF ABC).

The endpoint's address is a network address where the endpoint resides. It describes, in a standard-based way, where messages should be sent. Each endpoint normally has one unique address, but sometimes two or more endpoints can share the same address.

The endpoint's binding specifies how the endpoint communicates with the world, including things such as transport protocol (TCP, HTTP), encoding (text, binary), and security requirements (SSL, SOAP message security).

The endpoint's contract specifies what the endpoint communicates, and is essentially a collection of messages organized in the operations that have basic Message Exchange Patterns (MEPs) such as one-way, duplex, or request/reply.

The following diagram shows the components of a **WCF service endpoint.**

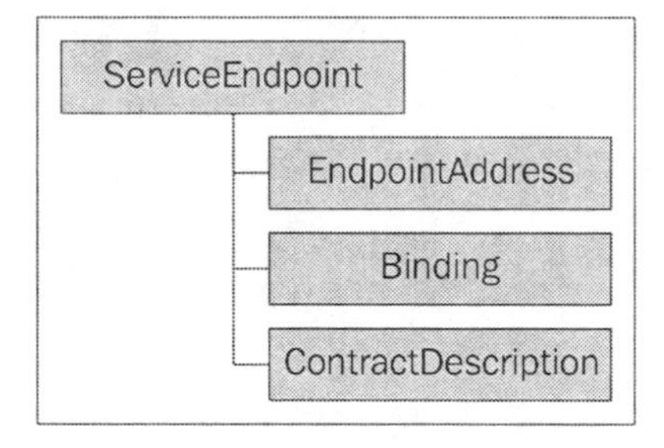

Behavior

A WCF **behavior** is a type, or settings to extend the functionality of the original type. There are many types of behaviors in WCF, such as service behavior, binding behavior, contract behavior, security behavior and channel behavior. For example, a new service behavior can be defined to specify the transaction timeout of the service, the maximum concurrent instances of the service, and whether the service publishes metadata. Behaviors are configured in the WCF service configuration file. We will configure several specific behaviors in the chapters that follow.

Hosting

A WCF service is a component that can be called by other applications. It must be hosted in an environment in order to be discovered and used by others. The WCF **host** is an application that controls the lifetime of the service. With .NET 3.0 and beyond, there are several ways to host the service.

Self hosting

A WCF service can be **self-hosted**, which means that the service runs as a standalone application and controls its own lifetime. This is the most flexible and easiest way of hosting a WCF service, but its availability and features are limited.

Windows services hosting

A WCF service can also be hosted as a Windows service. A **Windows service** is a process managed by the operating system and it is automatically started when Windows is started (if it is configured to do so). However, it lacks some critical features (such as versioning) for WCF services.

IIS hosting

A better way of hosting a WCF service is to use **IIS**. This is the traditional way of hosting a web service. IIS, by nature, has many useful features, such as process recycling, idle shutdown, process health monitoring, message-based activation, high availability, easy manageability, versioning, and deployment scenarios. All of these features are required for enterprise-level WCF services.

Windows Activation Services hosting

The IIS hosting method, however, comes with several limitations in the service-orientation world; the dependency on HTTP is the main culprit. With IIS hosting, many of WCF's flexible options can't be utilized. This is the reason why Microsoft specifically developed a new method, called **Windows Activation Services**, to host WCF services.

Windows Process Activation Service (WAS) is the new process activation mechanism for Windows Server 2008 that is also available on Windows Vista. It retains the familiar IIS 6.0 process model (application pools and message-based process activation) and hosting features (such as rapid failure protection, health monitoring, and recycling), but it removes the dependency on HTTP from the activation architecture. IIS 7.0 uses WAS to accomplish message-based activation over HTTP. Additional WCF components also plug into WAS to provide message-based activation over the other protocols that WCF supports, such as TCP, MSMQ, and named pipes. This allows applications that use the non-HTTP communication protocols to use the IIS features such as process recycling, rapid fail protection, and the common configuration systems that were only available to HTTP-based applications.

This hosting option requires that WAS be properly configured, but it does not require you to write any hosting code as part of the application. [Microsoft MSN, *Hosting Services*, retrieved on 3/6/2008 from `http://msdn2.microsoft.com/en-us/library/ms730158.aspx`]

Channels

As we have seen in the previous sections, a WCF service has to be hosted in an application on the server side. On the client side, the client applications have to specify the bindings to connect to the WCF services. The binding elements are interfaces, and they have to be implemented in concrete classes. The concrete implementation of a binding element is called a channel. The binding represents the configuration, and the channel is the implementation associated with that configuration. Therefore, there is a channel associated with each binding element. Channels stack on top of one another to create the concrete implementation of the binding—the channel stack.

The **WCF channel stack** is a layered communication stack with one or more channels that process messages. At the bottom of the stack is a transport channel that is responsible for adapting the channel stack to the underlying transport (for example, TCP, HTTP, SMTP and other types of transport). Channels provide a low-level programming model for sending and receiving messages. This programming model relies on several interfaces and other types collectively known as the WCF channel model. The following diagram shows a simple channel stack:

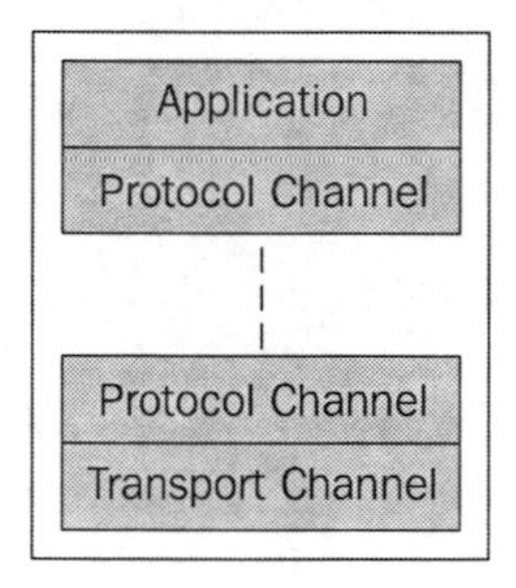

Metadata

The **metadata** of a service describes the characteristics of the service that an external entity needs to understand in order to communicate with the service. Metadata can be consumed by the ServiceModel Metadata Utility Tool (`Svcutil.exe`) to generate a WCF client and the accompanying configuration that a client application can use to interact with the service.

The metadata exposed by the service includes XML schema documents, which define the data contract of the service, and WSDL documents, which describe the methods of the service.

Though WCF services will always have metadata, it is possible to hide the metadata from outsiders. If you do so, you have to pass the metadata to the client side by other means. This practice is not common, but it gives your services an extra layer of security. When enabled via the configuration settings through metadata behavior, metadata for the service can be retrieved by inspecting the service and its endpoints. The following configuration setting in a WCF service configuration file will enable the metadata publishing for HTTP transport protocol:

```
<serviceMetadata httpGetEnabled="true" />
```

WCF production and development environments

WCF was first introduced in Microsoft's .NET Common Language Runtime (CLR) version 2.0. The corresponding framework is .NET 3.0. To develop and run WCF services, Microsoft .NET framework 3.0 or above is required.

Visual Studio is the preferred IDE for developing WCF service applications. The initial version, Visual Studio 2005, did not support WCF service application development. But with a downloadable package, "Visual Studio 2005 extensions for .NET Framework 3.0 (WCF & WPF)", Visual Studio 2005 could be used to develop WCF services. However, when Visual Studio 2008 SP1 was released, Microsoft stopped this download. So now, Visual Studio 2008 is the only Microsoft IDE available for WCF service application development. Visual Studio 2008 also supports application development for .Net framework 2.0, 3.0 and 3.5 (this is called multi-targeting).

The following table shows all of the different the versions of the .NET runtimes, .NET frameworks, and Visual Studios, along with their relationships:

<table>
<tr><th>CLR</th><th>.NET Framework</th><th colspan="7">Components</th><th>Visual Studio</th></tr>
<tr><td rowspan="4">CLR 2.0</td><td rowspan="2">.NET 3.5</td><td colspan="4">LINQ</td><td rowspan="2">ASP. NET AJAX</td><td rowspan="2">REST</td><td rowspan="2">RSS</td><td rowspan="3">VS2008</td></tr>
<tr><td>LINQ to SQL</td><td>LINQ to XML</td><td colspan="2">LINQ to Objects</td></tr>
<tr><td>.NET 3.0</td><td colspan="2">WCF</td><td colspan="2">WPF</td><td>WF</td><td colspan="2">CardSpace</td></tr>
<tr><td>.NET 2.0</td><td colspan="3">Winforms</td><td colspan="2">ASP.NET</td><td colspan="2">ADO.NET</td><td>VS2005VS2008</td></tr>
<tr><td rowspan="2">CLR 1.0</td><td>.NET 1.1</td><td colspan="3" rowspan="2">Winforms</td><td colspan="2" rowspan="2">ASP.NET</td><td colspan="2" rowspan="2">ADO.NET</td><td>VS2003</td></tr>
<tr><td>.NET 1.0</td><td>VS2002</td></tr>
</table>

Summary

In this chapter, we have learned some basic concepts of WCF. The key points in this chapter include the following:

- WCF is a better technology for developing SOA services
- A WCF service has at least one service endpoint
- A WCF service endpoint has an address, a binding, and a service contract
- A WCF service can be self-hosted, or can be hosted in a managed or an unmanaged application
- A WCF service can publish metadata, and communicates with client applications through channels
- .NET framework 3.0 or above is required to develop and run WCF service applications
- Visual Studio 2008 is the preferred IDE for WCF service application development

3

Implementing a Basic HelloWorld WCF Service

In the previous chapter, we learned many WCF concepts and saw a few code snippets.

In this chapter, we will implement a basic WCF service from scratch. We will build a `HelloWorld` WCF service by carrying out the following steps:

1. Create the solution and project
2. Create the WCF service contract interface
3. Implement the WCF service
4. Host the WCF service in the ASP.NET Development Server
5. Create a client application to consume this WCF service

Creating the HelloWorld solution and project

Before we can build the WCF service, we need to create a solution for our service projects. We also need a directory in which to save all the files. Throughout this book, we will save our project source codes in the `D:\SOAwithWCFandLINQ\Projects` directory. We will have a subfolder for each solution we create, and under this solution folder, we will have one subfolder for each project.

For this `HelloWorld` solution, the final directory structure is shown in the following image:

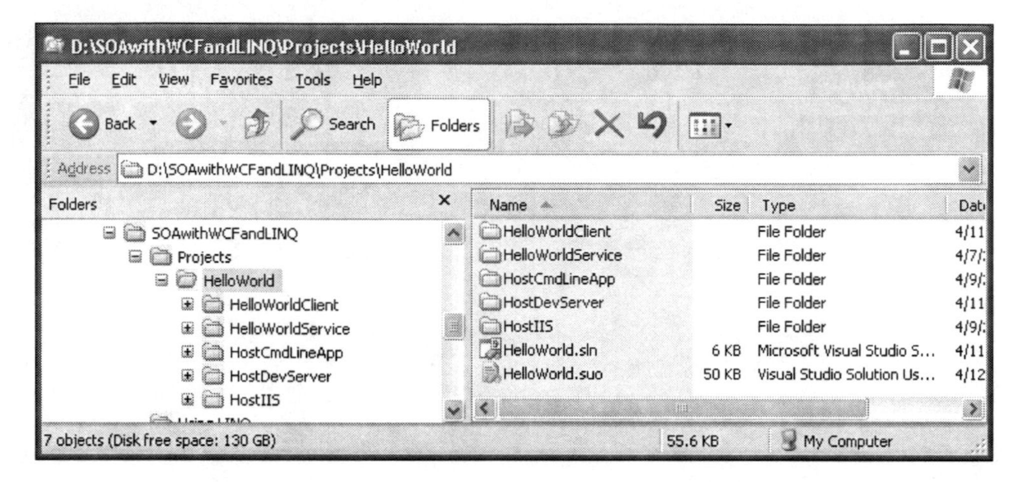

You don't need to manually create these directories via Windows Explorer; Visual Studio will create them automatically when you create the solutions and projects.

Now, follow these steps to create our first solution and the `HelloWorld` project:

1. Start Visual Studio 2008. If the **Open Project** dialog box pops up, click **Cancel** to close it.
2. Go to menu **File | New | Project**. The **New Project** dialog window will appear.

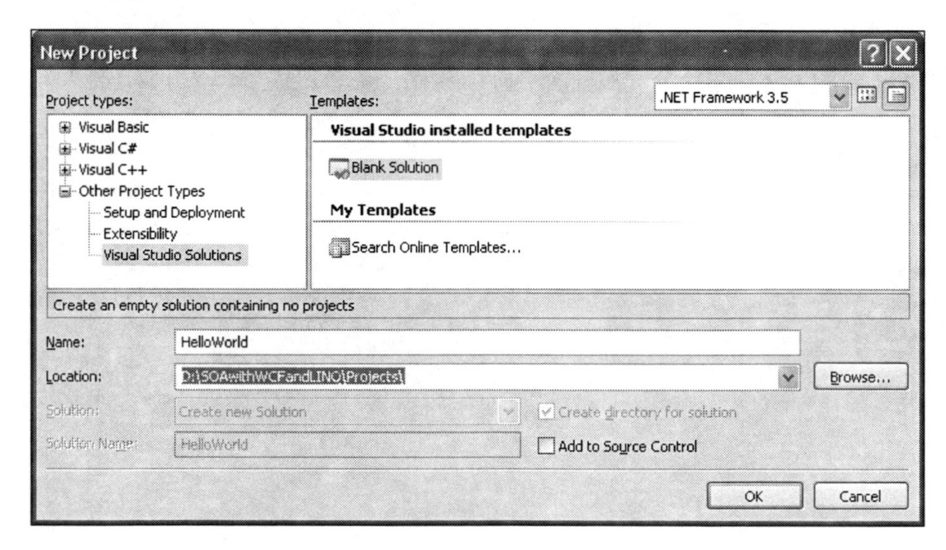

3. From the left-hand side of the window (**Project types**), expand **Other Project Types** and then select **Visual Studio Solutions** as the project type. From the right-hand side of the window (**Templates**), select **Blank Solution** as the template.
4. At the bottom of the window, type **HelloWorld** as the **Name,** and **D:\SOAwithWCFandLINQ\Projects** as the **Location**. Note that you should not enter `HelloWorld` within the location, because Visual Studio will automatically create a folder for a new solution.
5. Click the **OK** button to close this window and your screen should look like the following image, with an empty solution.

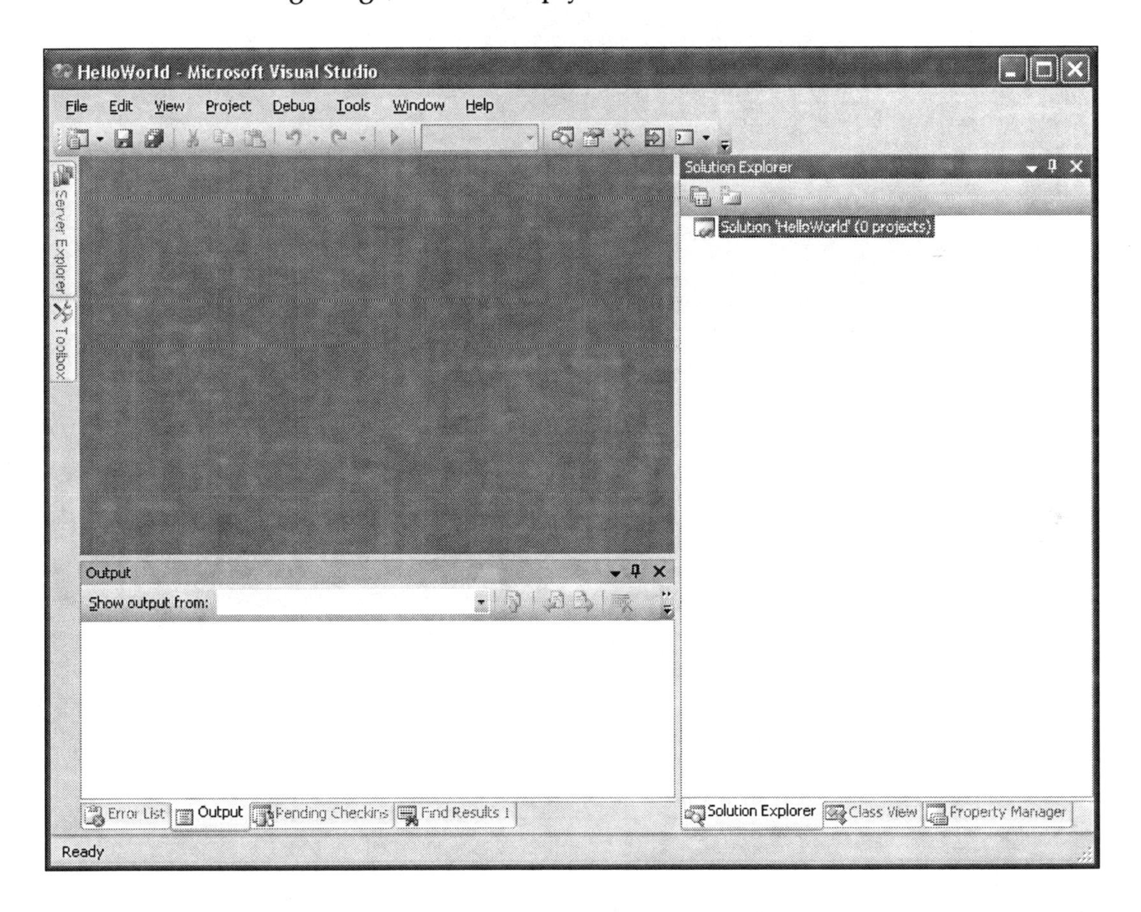

6. Depending on your settings, the layout may be different. But you should still have an empty solution in your Solution Explorer. If you don't see **Solution Explorer**, go to menu **View | Solution Explorer**, or press *Ctrl+Alt+L* to bring it up.

7. In the Solution Explorer, right-click on the solution, and select **Add | New Project...** from the context menu. You can also go to menu **File | Add | New Project...** to get the same result. The following image shows the context menu for adding a new project.

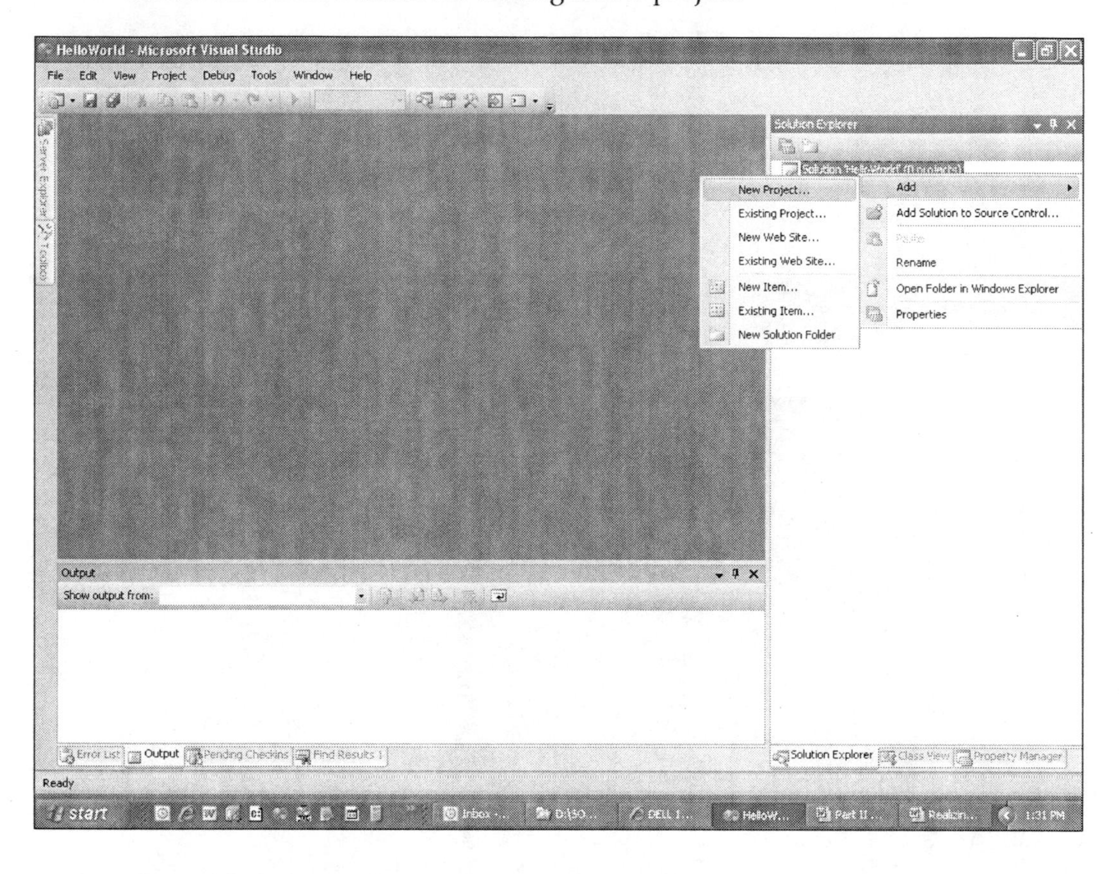

8. The **Add New Project** window should now appear on your screen. In the left-hand side of this window (**Project types**), select **Visual C#** as the project type, and on the right-hand side of the window (**Templates**), select **Class Library** as the template.

9. At the bottom of the window, type **HelloWorldService** as the **Name**. Leave **D:\SOAwithWCFandLINQ\Projects\HelloWorld** as the **Location**. Again, don't add `HelloWorldService` to the location, as Visual Studio will create a subfolder for this new project (Visual Studio will use the solution folder as the default base folder for all the new projects added to the solution).

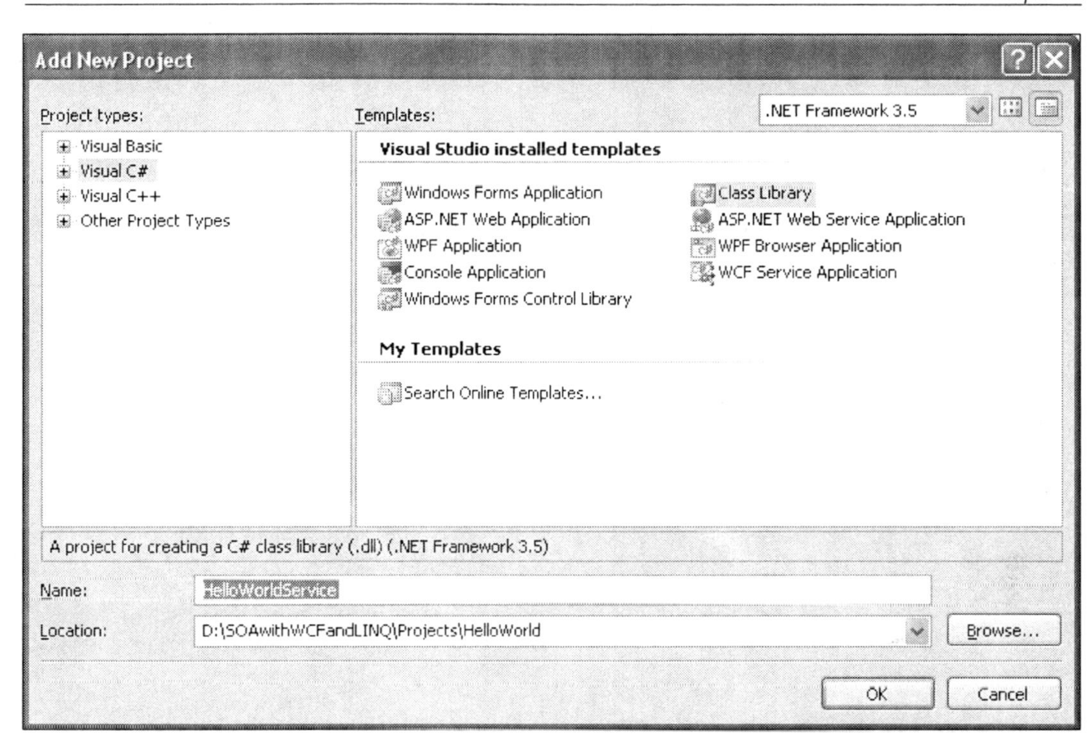

You may have noticed that there is already a template for **WCF Service Application** in Visual Studio 2008. For the very first example, we will not use this template. Instead, we will create everything by ourselves so you know what the purpose of each template is. This is an excellent way for you to understand and master this new technology. In the next chapter, we will use this template to create the project, so we don't need to manually type a lot of code. Also, later in this book, we will use the Microsoft Web Service Software Factory pattern and practice creating a 3-layer framework for our enterprise SOA solution. This way, we not only type less code, but also have lots of best practices embedded in the code automatically.

10. Now, you can click the **OK** button to close this window.

Once you click the **OK** button, Visual Studio will create several files for you. The first file is the project file. This is an XML file under the project directory, and it is called `HelloWorldService.csproj`.

Visual Studio also creates an empty class file, called `Class1.cs`. Later, we will change this default name to a more meaningful one, and change its namespace to our own one.

Three directories are created automatically under the project folder—one to hold the binary files, another to hold the object files, and a third one for the properties files of the project.

The window on your screen should now look like the following image:

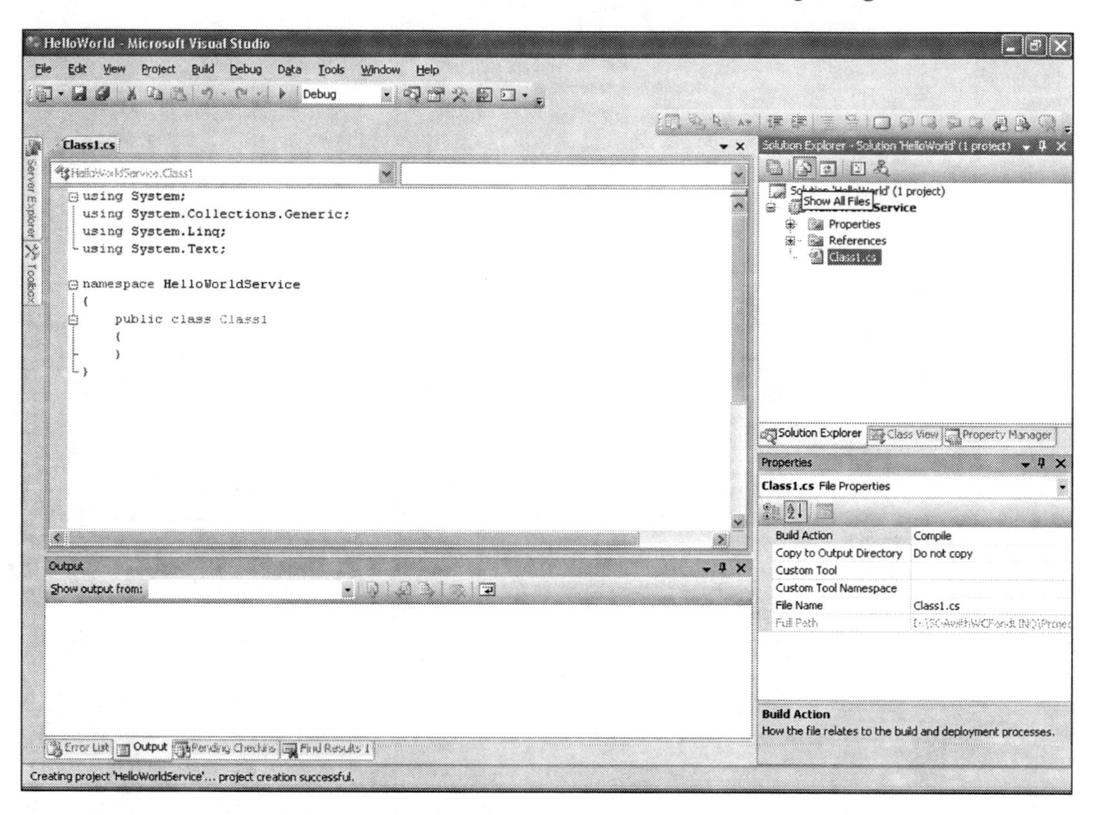

We now have a new solution and project created. Next, we will develop and build this service. But before we go any further, we need to do two things to this project:

1. Click the **Show All Files** button on the Solution Explorer toolbar. It is the second button from the left, just above the word **Solution** inside the Solution Explorer. If you allow your mouse to hover above this button, you will see the hint **Show All Files**, as shown in above diagram. Clicking this button will show all files and directories in your hard disk under the project folder-rven those items that are not included in the project. Make sure that you don't have the solution item selected. Otherwise, you can't see the **Show All Files** button.

2. Change the default namespace of the project. From the Solution Explorer, right-click on the **HelloWorldService** project, select **Properties** from the context menu, or go to menu item **Project | HelloWorldService Properties...**. You will see the project properties dialog window. On the **Application** tab, change the **Default namespace** to **MyWCFServices**.

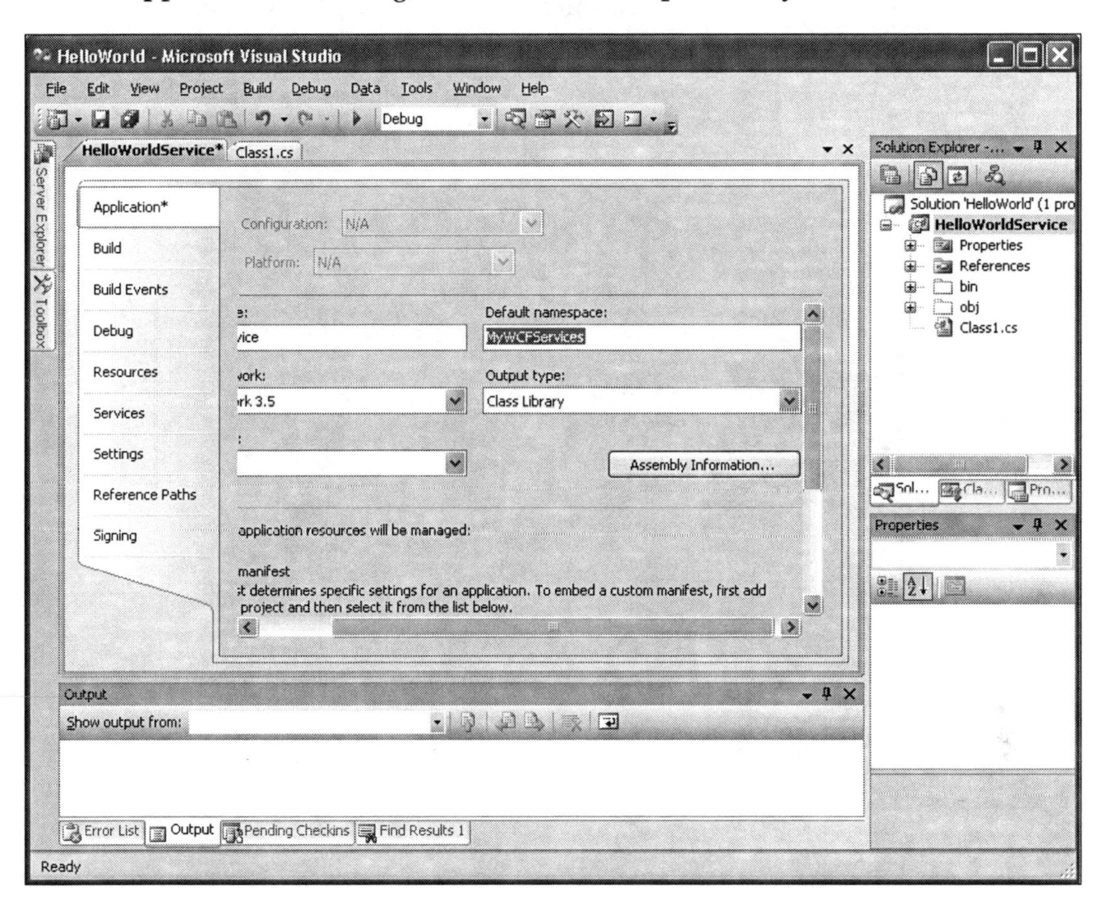

Lastly, in order to develop a WCF service, we need to add a reference to the `ServiceModel` namespace.

1. On the Solution Explorer window, right-click on the **HelloWorldService** project, and select **Add Reference...** from the context menu. You can also go to the menu item **Project | Add Reference...** to do this. The **Add Reference** dialog window should appear on your screen.

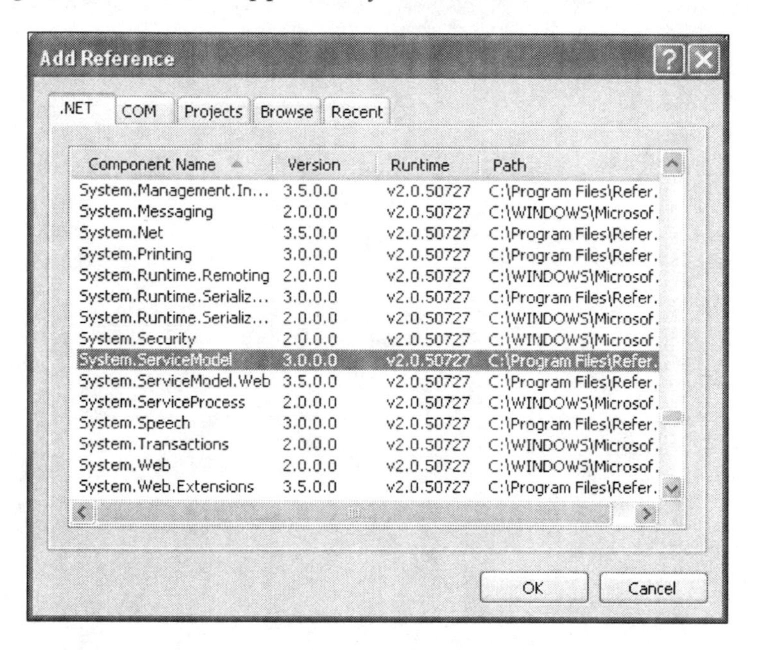

2. Select **System.ServiceModel** from the **.NET** tab, and click **OK**.

Now, on the Solution Explorer, if you expand the references of the `HelloWorldService` project, you will see that `System.ServiceModel` has been added. Also note that `System.Xml.Linq` is added by default. We will use this later when we query a database.

Creating the HelloWorldService service contract interface

In the previous section, we created the solution and the project for the `HelloWorld` WCF Service. From this section on, we will start building the `HelloWorld` WCF service. First, we need to create the service contract interface.

1. In the Solution Explorer, right-click on the `HelloWorldService` project, and select **Add | New Item....** from the context menu. The following **Add New Item - HelloWorldService** dialog window should appear on your screen.

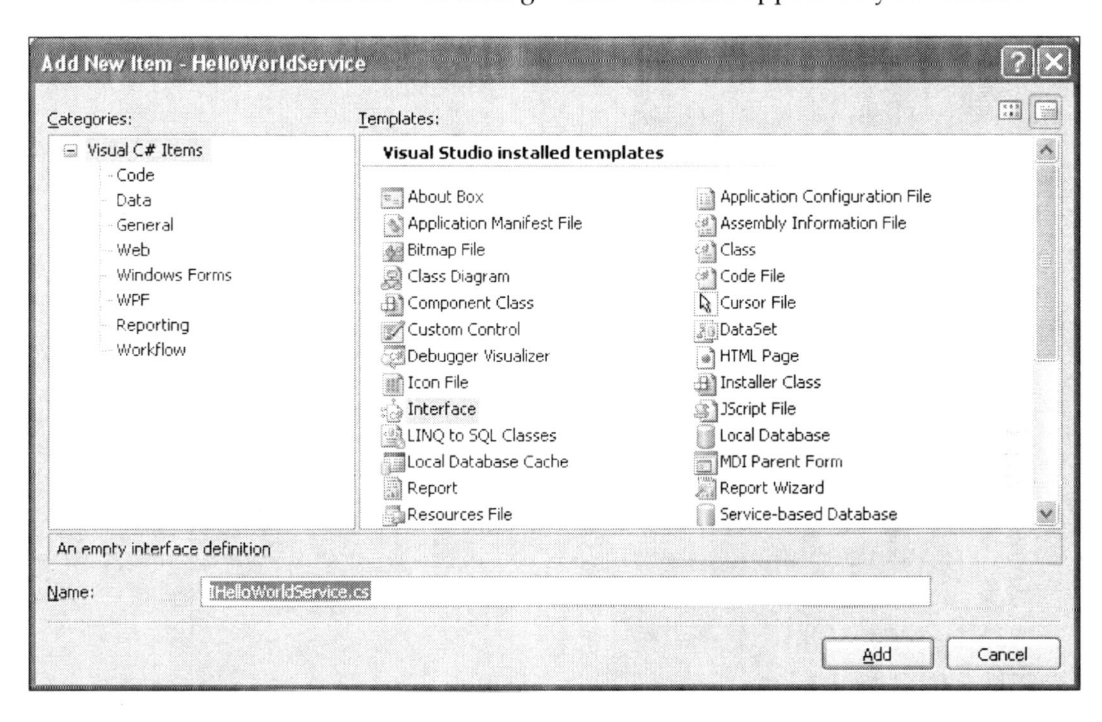

2. On the left-hand side of the window (**Categories**), select **Visual C# Items** as the category, and on the right-hand side of the window (**Templates**), select **Interface** as the template.
3. At the bottom of the window, change the **Name** from `Interface1.cs` to `IHelloWorldService.cs`.
4. Click the **Add** button.

Now, an empty service interface file has been added to the project. Follow the steps below to customize it.

1. Add a `using` statement:

```
using System.ServiceModel;
```

2. Add a `ServiceContract` attribute to the interface. This will designate the interface as a WCF service contract interface.

```
[ServiceContract]
```

3. Add a `GetMessage` method to the interface. This method will take a string as the input, and return another string as the result. It also has an attribute, `OperationContract`.

```
[OperationContract]
String GetMessage(String name);
```

4. Change the interface to public.

The final content of the file `IHelloWorldService.cs` should look like the following:

```
using System;
using System.Collections.Generic;
using System.Linq;
using System.Text;
using System.ServiceModel;
namespace MyWCFServices
{
    [ServiceContract]
    public interface IHelloWorldService
    {
        [OperationContract]
        String GetMessage(String name);
    }
}
```

Implementing the HelloWorldService service contract

Now that we have defined a service contract interface, we need to implement it. For this purpose, we will re-use the empty class file that Visual Studio created for us earlier, and modify this to make it the implementation class of our service.

Before we modify this file, we need to rename it. In the Solution Explorer window, right-click on the file **Class1.cs**, select **rename** from the context menu, and rename it to **HelloWorldService.cs.**

[Visual Studio is smart enough to change all related files, references to use this new name. You can also select the file, and change its name from the Properties window.]

Next, follow the steps below to customize this class file.

1. Change its namespace from **HelloWorldService** to `MyWCFServices`. This is because this file was added before we changed the default namespace of the project.
2. Make it inherit from the interface `IHelloWorldService`.

   ```
   public class HelloWorldService: IHelloWorldService
   ```

3. Add a `GetMessage` method to the class. This is an ordinary C# method that returns a string.

   ```
   public String GetMessage(String name)
   {
      return "Hello world from " + name + "!";
   }
   ```

The final content of the file `HelloWorldService.cs` should look like the following:

```
using System;
using System.Collections.Generic;
using System.Linq;
using System.Text;
namespace MyWCFServices
{
    public class HelloWorldService: IHelloWorldService
    {
        public String GetMessage(String name)
        {
            return "Hello world from " + name + "!";
        }
    }
}
```

Now, build the project. If there is no build error, it means that you have successfully created your first WCF service. If you see a compilation error, such as "'ServiceModel' does not exist in the namespace 'System'", this is probably because you didn't add the `ServiceModel` namespace reference correctly. Revisit the previous section to add this reference, and you are all set.

Next, we will host this WCF service in an environment and create a client application to consume it.

Hosting the WCF service in ASP.NET Development Server

The `HelloWorldService` is a class library. It has to be hosted in an environment so that client applications may access it. In this section, we will explain how to host it using the ASP.NET Development Server. Later, in the next chapter, we will discuss more hosting options for a WCF service.

Creating the host application

There are several built-in host applications for WCF services within Visual Studio 2008. However, in this section, we will manually create the host application so that you can have a better understanding of what a hosting application is really like under the hood. In subsequent chapters, we will explain and use the built-in hosting applications.

To host the library using the ASP.NET Development Server, we need to add a new web site to the solution. Follow these steps to create this web site:

1. In the Solution Explorer, right-click on the **solution** file, and select **Add | New Web Site...** from the context menu. The **Add New Web Site** dialog window should pop up.
2. Select **Empty Web Site** as the template, and leave the **Location** set as **File System**, and **language** as **Visual C#**. Change the web site name from **WebSite1** to **HostDevServer**, and click **OK**.

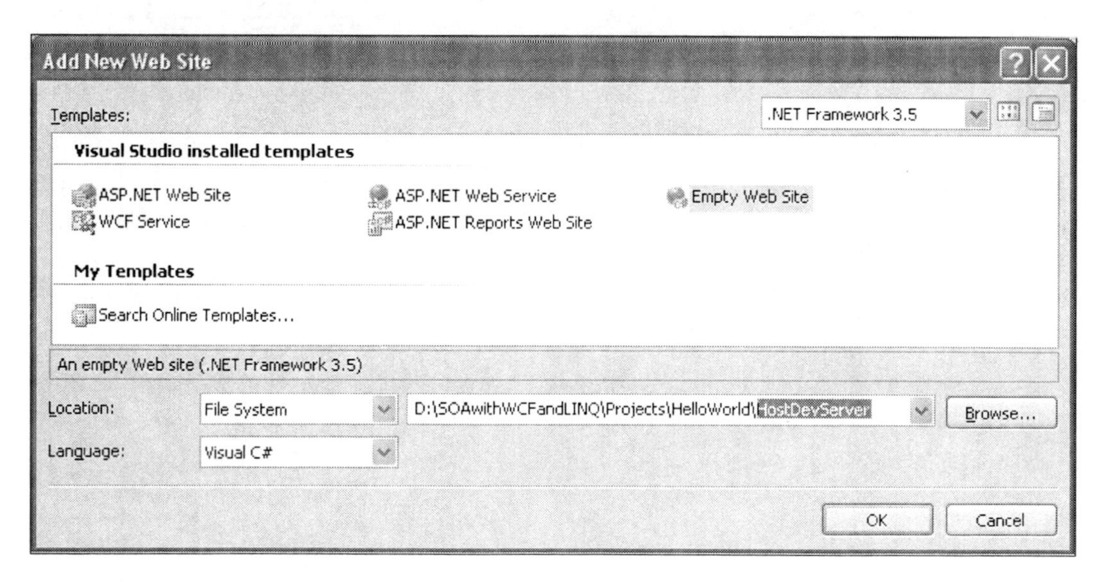

3. Now in the Solution Explorer, you have one more item (`HostDevServer`) within the solution. It will look like the following:

4. Next, we need to set the website as the startup project. In the Solution Explorer, right-click on the web site `D:\...\HostDevServer`, select **Set as StartUp Project** from the context menu (or you can first select the web site from the Solution Explorer, and then select menu item **Website | Set as StartUp Project**). The web site `D:\...\HostDevServer` should be highlighted in the Solution Explorer indicating that it is now the startup project.

5. Because we will host the `HelloWorldService` from this web site, we need to add a `HelloWorldService` reference to the web site. In the Solution Explorer, right-click on the web site `D:\...\HostDevServer`, and select **Add Reference...** from the context menu. The following **Add Reference** dialog box should appear:

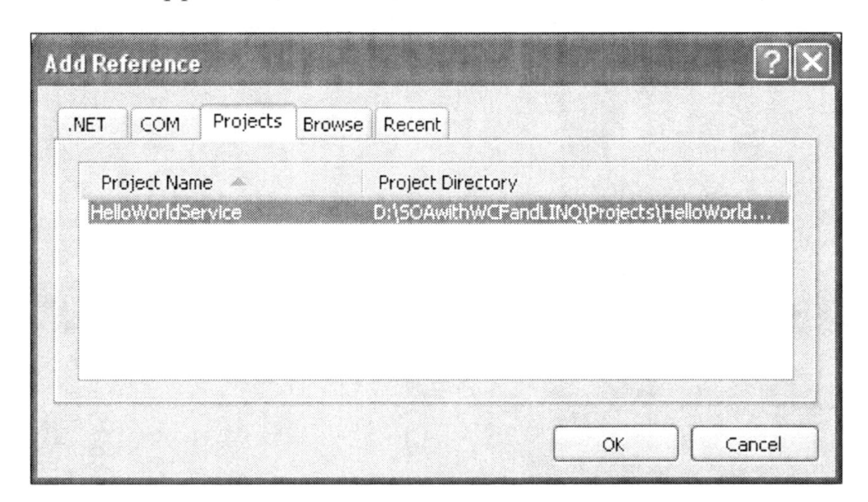

6. In the **Add Reference** dialog box, click on the **Projects** tab, select **HelloWorldService** project, and then click **OK**. You will see that a new directory (`bin`) has been created under the `HostDevServer` web site, and two files from `HelloWorldService` project have been copied to this new directory. Later on, when this web site is accessed, the web server (either ASP.NET Development Server or IIS) will look for executable code in this `bin` directory.

Testing the host application

Now we can run the website inside the ASP.NET Development Server. If you start the web site `HostDevServer`, by pressing *Ctrl+F5*, or select the **Debug | Start Without Debugging...** menu, you will see an empty web site in your browser. Because we have set this website as the startup project, but haven't set any start page, it lists all of the files and directories inside the `HostDevServer` directory (Directory Browsing is always enabled for a website within the ASP.NET Development Server).

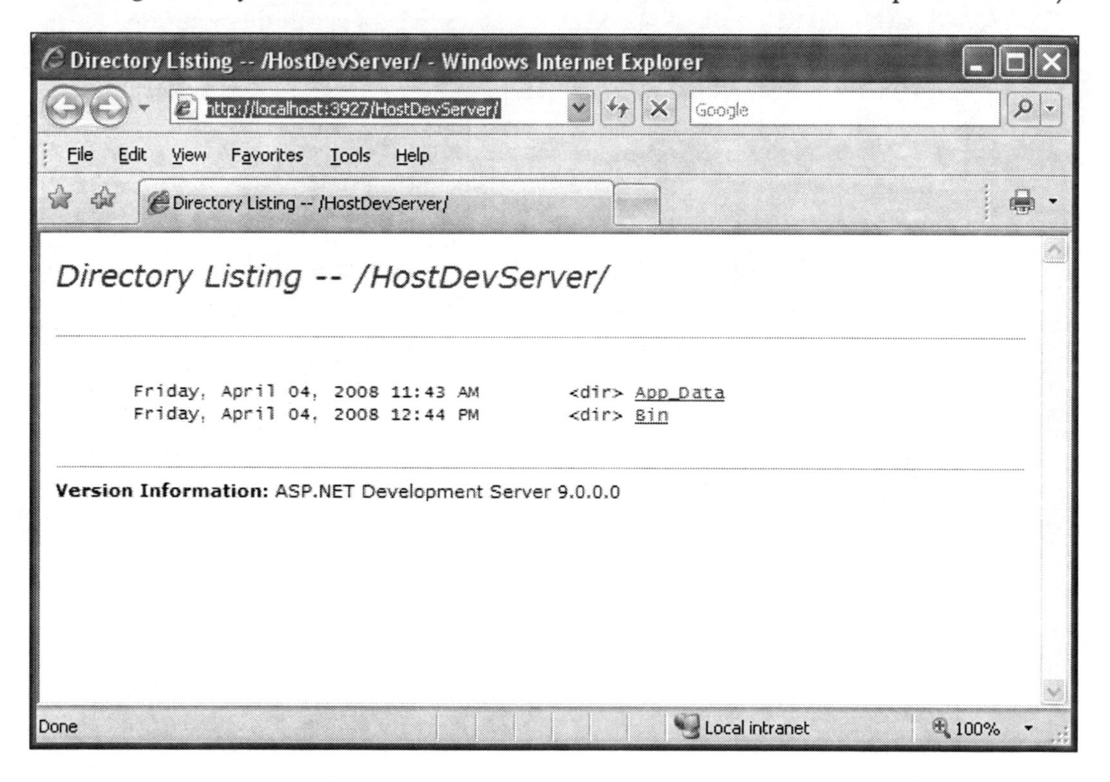

If you pressed *F5* (or selected **Debug | Start Debugging** from the menu), you may see a dialog saying **Debugging Not Enabled** (as shown below). Choose the option **Run without debugging**. (Equivalent to *Ctrl+F5*) and click the **OK** button to continue. We will explore the debugging options of a WCF service later. Until then, we will continue to use *Ctrl+F5* to start the website without debugging.

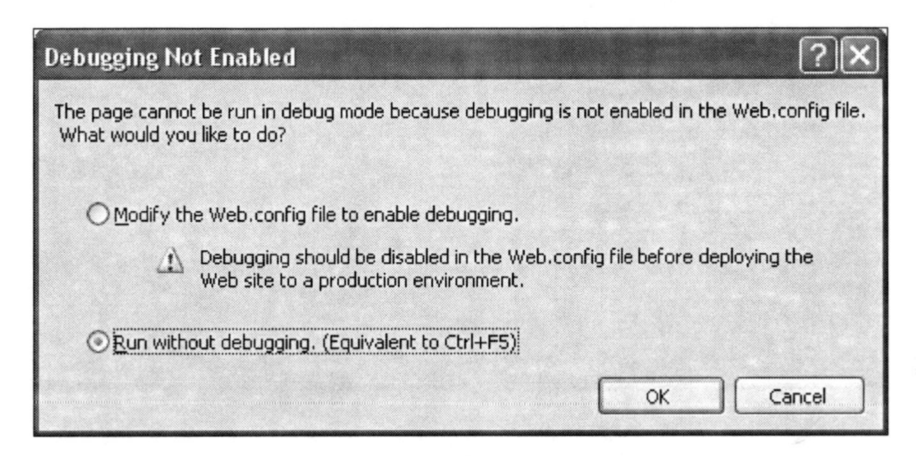

ASP.NET Development Server

At this point, you should have the `HostDevServer` site up and running. This site is actually running inside the built-in ASP.NET Development Server. It is a new feature that was introduced in Visual Studio 2005. This web server is intended to be used by developers only, and has functionality similar to that of the Internet Information Services (IIS) server. It also has some limitations; for example, you can run ASP.NET applications only locally. You can't use it as a real IIS server to publish a web site.

By default, the ASP.NET Development Server uses a dynamic port for the web server each time it is started. You can change it to use a static port via the **Properties** page of the web site. Just change the **Use dynamic ports** setting to `false`, and specify a static port, such as 8080, from the **Properties** window of the `HostDevServer` web site. You can't set the port to 80, because IIS is already using this port. However, if you stop your local IIS, you can set your ASP.NET Development Server to use port 80.

[Even you set its port to 80 it is still a local web server. It can't be accessed from outside your local PC.]

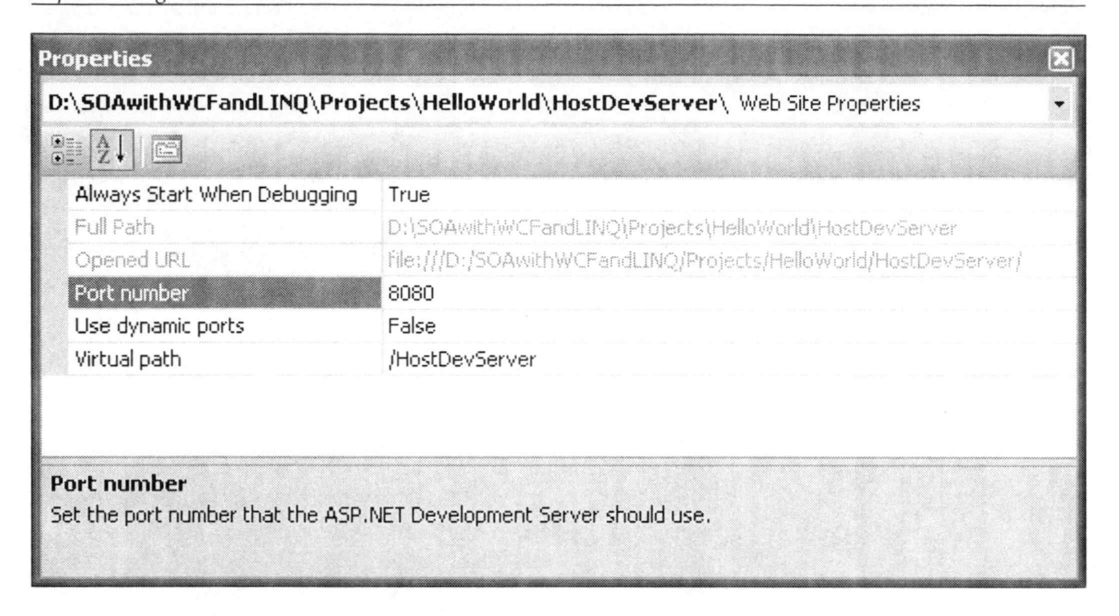

It is recommended that you use a static port so that client applications know in advance where to connect to the service. From now on, we will always use port 8080 in all of our examples.

The ASP.NET Development Server is normally started from within Visual Studio when you need to debug or unit test a web project. If you really need to start it from outside Visual Studio, you can use a command line statement in the following format:

```
start /B WebDev.WebServer [/port:<port number>] /path:<physical path>
[/vpath:<virtual path>]
```

For our web site, the statement should be like this:

```
start /B webdev.webserver.exe /port:8080 /path:"D:\SOAwithWCFandLINQ\
Projects\HelloWorld\HostDevServer" /vpath:/HostDevServer
```

The `webdev.webserver.exe` is located under your .NET framework installation directory (`C:\WINDOWS\Microsoft.NET\Framework\v2.0.50727`).

Adding an svc file to the host application

Although we can start the web site now, it is only an empty site. Currently, it does not host our `HelloWorldService`. This is because we haven't specified which service this web site should host, or an entry point for this web site. Just as an `asmx` file is the entry point for a non-WCF web service, a `.svc` file is the entry point for a WCF service, if it is hosted on a web server. We will now add such a file to our web site.

From the Solution Explorer, right-click on the web site `D:\...\HostDevServer`, and select **Add New Item...** from the context menu. The **Add New Item** dialog window should appear, as shown below. Select **Text File** as the template, and change the **Name** from **TextFile.txt** to **HelloWorldService.svc** in this dialog window.

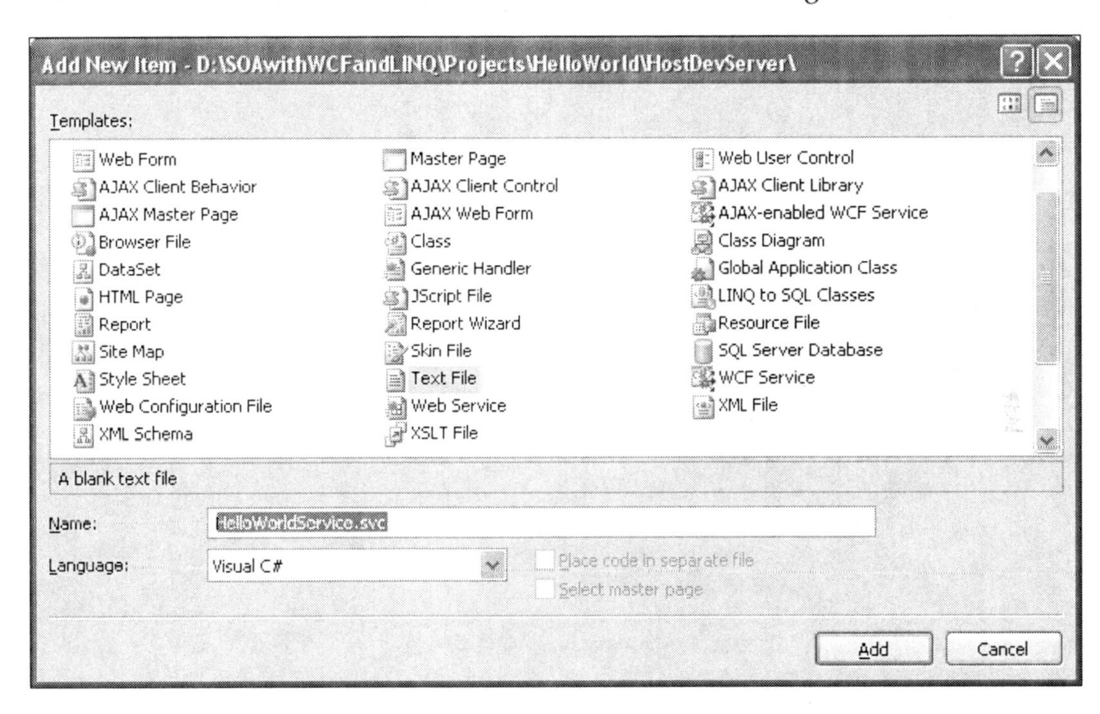

You may have noticed that there is a template, **WCF Service**, in the list. We won't use it now as it will create a new WCF service within this web site for you (we will use this template later).

After you click the **Add** button in the **Add New Item** dialog box, an empty `svc` file will be created and added to the web site. Now enter the following line in this file:

```
<%@ServiceHost Service="MyWCFServices.HelloWorldService"%>
```

Adding a web.config file to the host application

The final step is to add a `web.config` file to the web site. As in the previous step, add a text file named `web.config` to the web site and enter the following code in this file:

```
<?xml version="1.0" encoding="utf-8" ?>
<configuration>
    <appSettings>
        <add key="HTTPBaseAddress" value=""/>
    </appSettings>
    <system.serviceModel>
        <services>
            <service
                name="MyWCFServices.HelloWorldService"
                behaviorConfiguration="MyServiceTypeBehaviors">
                <endpoint
                    address=""
                    binding="wsHttpBinding"
                    contract="MyWCFServices.IHelloWorldService"/>
                <endpoint
                    contract="IMetadataExchange"
                    binding="mexHttpBinding"
                    address="mex" />
            </service>
        </services>
        <behaviors>
            <serviceBehaviors>
                <behavior name="MyServiceTypeBehaviors" >
                    <serviceMetadata httpGetEnabled="true" />
                </behavior>
            </serviceBehaviors>
        </behaviors>
    </system.serviceModel>
</configuration>
```

Within this file, we set `HTTPBaseAddress` to empty, because this WCF service is hosted inside a web server and we will use the web server default address as the service address.

The behavior `httpGetEnabled` is essential, because we want other applications to be able to locate the metadata of this service. Without the metadata, client applications can't generate the proxy and thus won't be able to use the service.

We use `wsHttpBinding` for this hosting, which means that it is secure (messages are encrypted while being transmitted), and transaction-aware (we will discuss this in a later chapter). However, because this is a WS-* standard, some existing applications (for example: a QA tool) may not be able to consume this service. In this case, you can change the service to use the `basicHttpBinding`, which uses plain unencrypted texts when transmitting messages, and is backward compatible with traditional ASP.NET web services (`asmx` web services).

The following is a brief explanation of the other elements in this configuration file:

- `Configuration` is the root node of the file.
- Within the `appSettings` node, you can add application-specific configurations. In this file, we have added one setting for the base address of the web site. In a later chapter, we will add a connection strings key to this node.
- `system.serviceModel` is the top node for all WCF service specific settings.
- Within the `services` node, you can specify WCF services that are hosted on this web site. In our example, we have only one WCF service `HelloWorldService` hosted in this web site.
- Each `service` element defines one WCF service, including its name, behavior, and endpoint.
- Two endpoints have been defined for the `HelloWorldService`, one for the service itself (an application endpoint), and another for the metadata exchange (an infrastructure endpoint).
- Within the `serviceBehaviors` node, you can define specific behaviors for a service. In our example, we have specified one behavior, which enables the service meta data exchange for the service.

Starting the host application

Now, if you start the web site by pressing *Ctrl+F5* (again, don't use *F5* or menu option **Debug | Start Debugging** until we discuss these, later), you will now find the file `HelloWorldService.svc` listed on the web page. Clicking on this file will give the description of this service, that is, how to get the `wsdl` file of this service, and how to create a client to consume this service. You should see a page similar to the following one. You can also set this file as the start page file so that every time you start this web site, you will go to this page directly. You can do this by right-clicking on this file in the Solution Explorer and selecting **Set as Start Page** from the context menu.

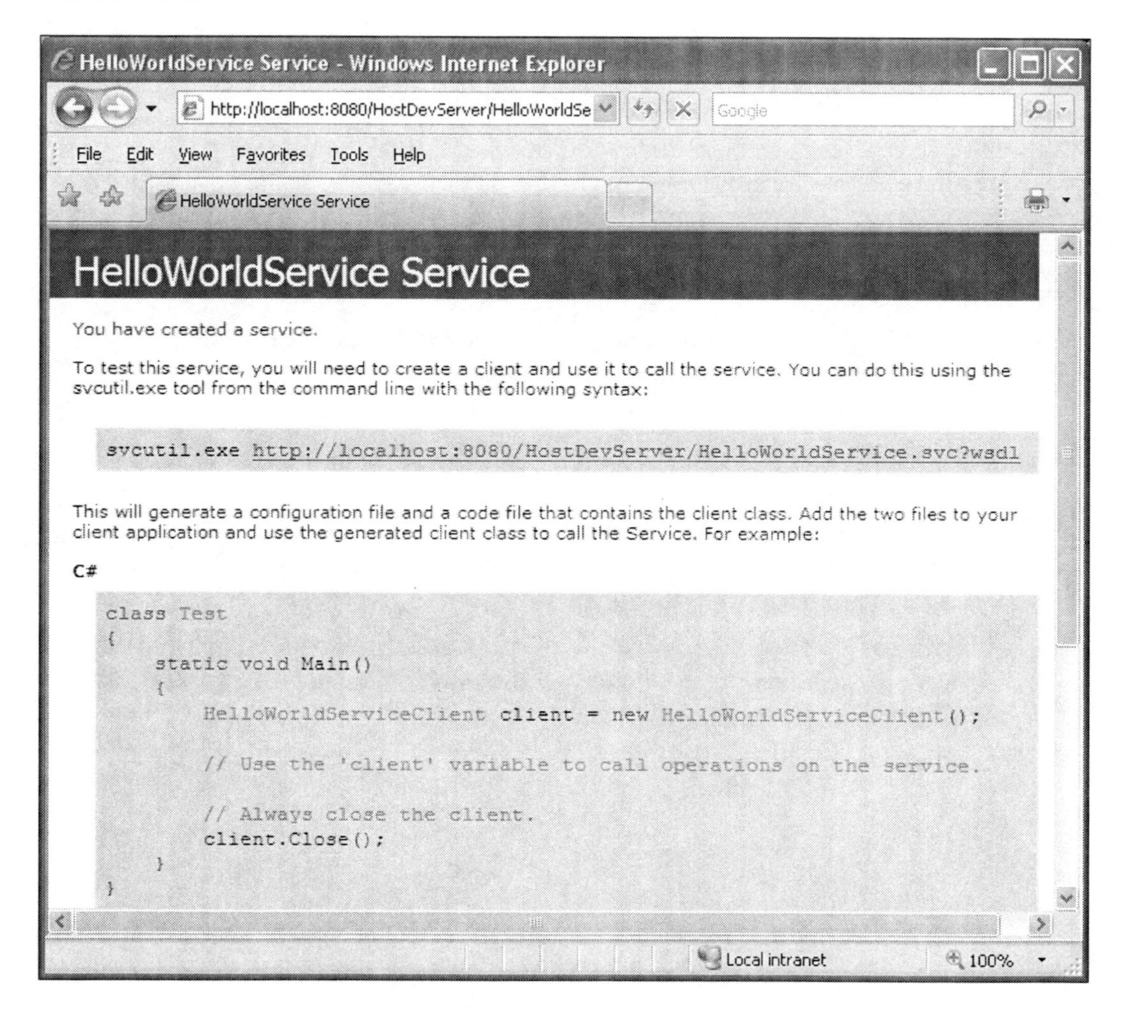

Now, click on the `wsdl` link on this page, and you will get the `wsdl xml` file for this service. The `wsdl` file gives all of the contract information for this service. In the next section, we will use this `wsdl` to generate a proxy for our client application.

Close the browser. Then, from the Windows system tray (`systray`), find the little icon labeled **ASP.NET Development Server - Port 8080** (it is on the lower-right of your screen, just next to the clock), right-click on it, and select **Stop** to stop ther service.

Creating a client to consume the WCF service

Now that we have successfully created and hosted a WCF service, we need a client to consume the service. We will create a C# client application to consume the `HelloWorldService`.

In this section, we will create a Windows console application to call the WCF service.

Creating the client application project

First, we need to create a console application project and add it to the solution. Follow these steps to create the console application:

1. In the Solution Explorer, right-click on the solution `HelloWorld`, and select **Add | New Project...** from the context menu. The **Add New Project** dialog window should appear, as shown below.

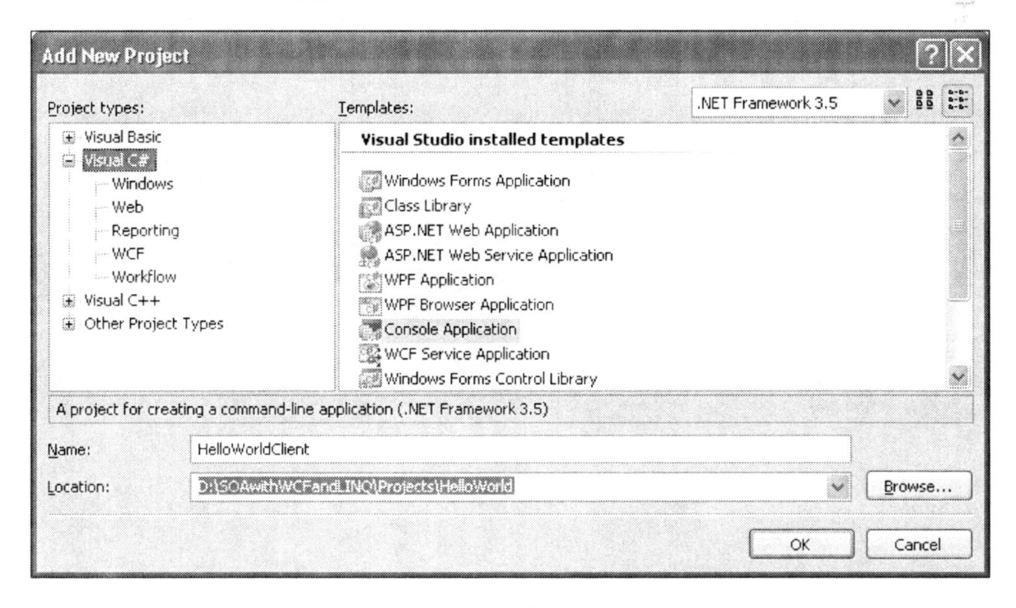

2. Select **Visual C# Windows** as the project type, and **Console Application** as the template; change the project name from the defaulted value of **ConsoleApplication1** to **HelloWorldClient**, and leave the **location** as **D:\SOAwithWCFandLINQ\Projects\HelloWorld**. Click the **OK** button. The new client project has now been created and added to the solution.

Generating the proxy and configuration files

In order to consume a WCF service, a client application must first obtain or generate a proxy class.

We also need a configuration file to specify things such as the binding of the service, the address of the service, and the contract.

To generate these two files, we can use the `svcutil.exe` tool from the command line. You can follow these steps to generate the two files:

1. Start the service by pressing *Ctrl+F5* or by selecting menu option **Debug | Start Without Debugging** (at this point your startup project should still be `HostDevServer`; if not, you need to set this to be the startup project). Now, you should see the window for the `HelloWorldService` service, as we saw in the previous section.
2. After the service has been started, run the command line `svcutil.exe` tool with the following syntax:

```
"C:\Program Files\Microsoft SDKs\Windows\v6.0\Bin\SvcUtil.exe"
http://localhost:8080/HostDevServer/HelloWorldService.svc?wsdl
/out:HelloWorldServiceRef.cs /config:app.config
```

You will see output similar to that shown in the following screenshot:

```
C:\WINDOWS\system32\cmd.exe
D:\SOAwithWCFandLINQ\Projects\HelloWorld\HelloWorldClient>"C:\Program Files\Microsoft SDKs\Windows\v6.0\Bin\SvcUtil.exe" http://localhost:8080/HostDevServer/HelloWorldService.svc?wsdl /out:HelloWorldServiceRef.cs /config:app.config
Microsoft (R) Service Model Metadata Tool
[Microsoft (R) Windows (R) Communication Foundation, Version 3.0.4506.30]
Copyright (c) Microsoft Corporation.  All rights reserved.

Attempting to download metadata from 'http://localhost:8080/HostDevServer/HelloWorldService.svc?wsdl' using WS-Metadata Exchange or DISCO.
Generating files...
D:\SOAwithWCFandLINQ\Projects\HelloWorld\HelloWorldClient\HelloWorldServiceRef.cs
D:\SOAwithWCFandLINQ\Projects\HelloWorld\HelloWorldClient\app.config

D:\SOAwithWCFandLINQ\Projects\HelloWorld\HelloWorldClient>
```

Now, two files have been generated— one for the proxy (`HelloWorldServiceRef.cs`), and the other for the configuration (`app.config`).

If you open the proxy file, you will see that the interface of the service (`IHelloWorldService`) is mimicked inside the proxy class, and a client class (`HelloWorldServiceClient`) is created to implement this interface. Inside this client class, the implementation of the service operation (`GetMessage`) is only a wrapper that delegates the call to the actual service implementation of the operation.

Inside the configuration file, you will see the definitions of the `HelloWorldService`, such as the endpoint address, binding, timeout settings, and security behaviors of the service.

Customizing the client application

Before we can run the client application, we still have some more work to do. Follow these steps to finish the customization:

1. Adding the two generated files to the project: In the Solution Explorer, click **Show All Files** to show all the files under the `HelloWorldClient` folder, and you will see these two files. However, they are not included in the project. Right-click on each of them and select **Include In Project** to include both of them in the client project. You can also use menu **Project | Add Existing Item ...** (or the context menu **Add | Existing Item ...**) to add them to the project.
2. Adding a reference to the `System.ServiceModel` namespace: Just as we did for the project `HelloWorldService`, we also need to add a reference to the WCF .NET `System.ServiceModel` assembly. From the Solution Explorer, just right-click on the **HelloWorldClient** project, select **Add Reference...** and choose **.NET System.ServiceModel**. Then, click the **OK** button to add the reference to the project.
3. Modify the `program.cs` to call the service: In `program.cs`, add the following line to initialize the service client object:

   ```
   HelloWorldServiceClient client = new HelloWorldServiceClient();
   ```

Then, we can call its method just as we would do for any other object:

```
Console.WriteLine(client.GetMessage("Mike Liu"));
```

Pass your name as the parameter to the `GetMessage` method, so that it prints out a message for you.

Running the client application

We are now ready to run this client program.

First, make sure the the `HelloWorldService` has been started. If you previously stopped it, start it now.

Then, from the Solution Explorer, right-click on the project **HelloWorldClient**, select **Set as StartUp Project**, and then press *Ctrl+F5* to run it.

You will see output as shown in the following image:

Setting the service application to AutoStart

Because we know we have to start the service before we run the client program, we can make some changes to the solution to automate this task; that is, to automatically start the service immediately before we run the client program.

To do this, in the Solution Explorer, right-click on the **Solution**, select **Properties** from the context menu, and you will see the **Solution 'HelloWorld' Property Pages** dialog box.

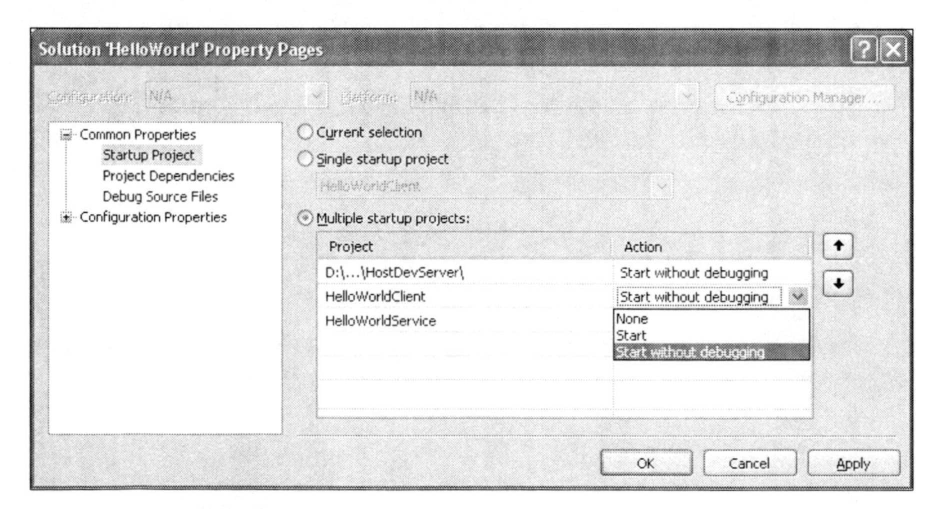

On this page, first select the option button **Multiple startup projects**. Then, change the action of `D:\...\HostDevServer\` to **Start without debugging**. Change the **HelloWorldClient** to the same action.

The **HostDevServer** must be above **HelloWorldClient.** If it is not, use the arrows to move it to the top.

To try it, first stop the service, and then press *Ctrl+F5*. You will notice that the `HostDevServer` is started first, and then the client program runs without errors.

Note that this will only work inside Visual Studio IDE. If you start the client program from Windows Explorer (`D:\SOAwithWCFandLINQ\Projects\HelloWorld\HelloWorldClient\bin\Debug\HelloWorldClient.exe`) without first starting the service, the service won't get started automatically and you will get an error message saying '**Could not connect to http://localhost:8080/HostDevServer/HelloWorldService.svc**'.

Summary

In this chapter, we have implemented a basic WCF service, hosted it within the ASP.NET Development Server, and created a command line program to reference and consume this basic WCF service. At this point, you should have a thorough understanding as to what a WCF is under the hood. You will benefit from this when you develop WCF services using Visual Studio WCF templates, or automation guidance packages. The key points covered in this chapter are:

- A WCF service is a class library, which defines one or more WCF service interface contracts
- `System.ServiceModel` assembly is referenced by all of the WCF service projects
- The implementations of a WCF service are just regular C# classes
- A WCF service must be hosted in a hosting application
- Visual Studio 2008 has a built-in hosting application for WCF services, which is called ASP.NET Development Server
- A client application uses a proxy to communicate with WCF services
- A configuration file can be used to specify settings for WCF services

4

Hosting and Debugging the HelloWorld WCF Service

In the previous chapter, we built a basic `HelloWorld` WCF service, and hosted it with the ASP.NET Development Server. In this chapter, we will explore more hosting options for WCF services, including hosting WCF services in a managed application, in a Windows Service, in IIS, and in some other advanced WCF hosting applications.

We will also explain how to debug WCF services, including debugging from the client application, debugging only the WCF service, attaching to the WCF service process, and the Just-In-Time debugger.

In this chapter, we will discuss:

- Hosting the service in a console application
- Hosting the service in a Windows Service application
- Hosting the service in IIS
- Testing the service
- Debugging the service from the client application
- Debugging only the service
- Attaching to the service process
- Just-In-Time debugger

Hosting the HelloWorld WCF service

In the previous chapter, we hosted our `HelloWorldService` in the ASP.NET Development Server. In addition to this, we have several other options for hosting a WCF service. In this section, we will explore them one by one.

Hosting the service in a managed application

We can create a .NET managed application, and host a WCF service inside the application. The hosting application can be a command line application, a Windows form application, or a web application. This hosting method gives you full control over the lifetime of the WCF service. It is very easy to debug and deploy, and supports all bindings and transports. The drawback of this hosting method is that you have to start the hosting application manually, and it has only limited support for high availability, easy manageability, robustness, recoverability, versioning, and deployment scenarios.

Hosting the service in a console application

For example, what follows are the steps to host `HelloWorldService` in a command line application. Note that these steps are very similar to the steps in the previous section where we hosted a WCF service in the ASP.NET Development Server. However, we must remember that we don't need a `.svc` file, and that the configuration file is called `app.config`, and not `web.config`. Refer to the previous section for diagrams. Also, if you want to host a WCF service in a Windows Form application, or a web application, you can follow the same steps as we have listed here simply by creating the project using an appropriate project template.

1. Add a console application project to the solution:

   In the Solution Explorer, right-click on the solution file, and select **Add | New Project...**, from the context menu. The **Add New Project** dialog box should appear. Select **Visual C#** as the project type, and **Console Application** as the template. Then, change the name from **ConsoleApplication1** to **HostCmdLineApp**, and click the **OK** button. A new project is added to the solution.

2. Set the project `HostCmdLineApp` as the startup project:

   In the Solution Explorer, right-click on the project `HostCmdLineApp`, and select **Set as StartUp Project** from the context menu. You can also select the project in the Solution Explorer, and click on menu item **Project | Set as StartUp Project** to do this.

3. Add a reference to the `HelloWorldService` project.

   In the Solution Explorer, right-click on the project `HostCmdLineApp` and select **Add Reference...**, from the shortcut menu. The **Add Reference** dialog box should appear. Click on the **Projects** tab, select the `HelloWorldService` project, and then click **OK**. Now, the `HelloWorldService` is under the **References** folder of this project. You will also notice that two files from `HelloWorldService` project have been copied to the `bin` directory under this project. If you can't see the bin directory, press *F4*, or click on the **Show All Files** icon in the Solution Explorer.

4. Add a reference to `System.ServiceModel`:

   This reference is required, as we will manually create a service host application and start and stop it in the steps that follow. In the Solution Explorer window, right click on the `HostCmdLineApp` project, and select **Add Reference...** from the context menu. You can also select menu item **Project | Add Reference...** to do this. Select `System.ServiceModel` from the .NET tab, and click **OK**.

5. Add a configuration file to define the endpoints of the service.

   The configuration file will be very similar to the configuration file we created for the `HostDevServer` project. So, in Windows Explorer, copy the `web.config` file from the project folder of `HostDevServer` to the project folder of `HostCmdLineApp`, change its name to `app.config`, then from Solution Explorer, include this file in the project `HostCmdLineApp` (if you can't see `app.config` file under this project, click the **Show All Files** button in the Solution Explorer, or click the **Refresh** button to refresh the screen).

   Open this configuration file, and change the **HTTPBaseAddress** from empty to **http://localhost:8080/HostCmdLineApp/HelloWorldService/**. This means we will host `HelloWorldService` using http, at port 8080, and under the `HostCmdLineApp` virtual directory.

The following is the full content of the `app.config` file:

```
<?xml version="1.0"?>
<configuration>
   <appSettings>
         <add key="HTTPBaseAddress" value="http://localhost:8080/
                           HostCmdLineApp/HelloWorldService/"/>
   </appSettings>
   <system.serviceModel>
         <services>
               <service name="MyWCFServices.HelloWorldService"
                     behaviorConfiguration="MyServiceTypeBehaviors">
                     <endpoint address="" binding="wsHttpBinding"
                       contract="MyWCFServices.IHelloWorldService"/>
                     <endpoint contract="IMetadataExchange"
                           binding="mexHttpBinding" address="mex"/>
               </service>
         </services>
         <behaviors>
               <serviceBehaviors>
                     <behavior name="MyServiceTypeBehaviors">
                           <serviceMetadata httpGetEnabled="true"/>
                     </behavior>
```

```
            </serviceBehaviors>
        </behaviors>
    </system.serviceModel>
    <system.web>
        <compilation debug="true"/></system.web></configuration>
```

6. Now, we need to modify the `Program.cs` file to write some code to start and stop the WCF service inside the `Program.cs`.

   First, add two `using` statements as follows:

```
using System.ServiceModel;
using System.Configuration;
```

   Then, add the following lines of codes within the static `Main` method:

```
Type serviceType=typeof(MyWCFServices.HelloWorldService);
string httpBaseAddress =
    ConfigurationSettings.AppSettings["HTTPBaseAddress"];
Uri[] baseAddress = new Uri[] {new Uri(httpBaseAddress)};
ServiceHost host = new ServiceHost(serviceType, baseAddress);
host.Open();
Console.WriteLine("HelloWorldService is now running. ");
Console.WriteLine("Press any key to stop it ...");
Console.ReadKey();
host.Close();
```

   As you can see, we just get the type of the `HelloWorldService`, construct a base address for the WCF service, create a service host passing the type and base address, and call the `Open` method of the host to start the service. To stop the service, we just call the `Close` method of the service host.

   Below is the full content of the `Program.cs` file.

```
using System;
using System.Collections.Generic;
using System.Linq;
using System.Text;
using System.ServiceModel;
using System.Configuration;

namespace HostCmdLineApp
{
    class Program
    {
        static void Main(string[] args)
        {
```

```
            Type serviceType=typeof(MyWCFServices.HelloWorldService);

            string httpBaseAddress =
                ConfigurationSettings.AppSettings["HTTPBaseAddress"];
            Uri[] baseAddress = new Uri[] {new Uri(httpBaseAddress)};

            ServiceHost host =
                           new ServiceHost(serviceType, baseAddress);
            host.Open();
            Console.WriteLine("HelloWorldService is now running. ");
            Console.WriteLine("Press any key to stop it ...");
            Console.ReadKey();
            host.Close();
        }
    }
}
```

7. After the project has been successfully built, you can press *Ctrl+F5* to start the service (if you are using Windows Server 2008 or Vista, make sure you are logged in as an Administrator). You will see a command line window indicating that the `HelloWorldService` is available and is waiting for requests.

Consuming the service hosted in a console application

To consume the service hosted in the above console application, you can follow the same steps as described in the section "Creating a Client to Consume the HelloWorld WCF Service" above, except that you pass `http://localhost:8080/HostCmdLineApp/HelloWorldService/?wsdl` and not `http://localhost:8080/HostDevServer/HelloWorldService.svc?wsdl` to the `SvcUtil.exe` when you generate the proxy class and the configuration file.

In fact, you can re-use the same client project, but inside the `app.config` file, change the following line:

```
<endpoint ddress="http://localhost:8080/HostDevServer/
HelloWorldService.svc"
```

To this line:

```
<endpoint address="http://localhost:8080/HostCmdLineApp/
HelloWorldService/"
```

Now, when you run this client program, it will use the WCF service hosted in our newly created command line application and not the previously-created `HostDevServer` application. You will get the same result as before, when the ASP.NET Development Server was used to host the WCF service.

Hosting the service in a Windows service

If you don't want to manually start the WCF service, you can host it in a Windows service. In addition to the automatic start, Windows service hosting gives you some other features such as recovery ability when failures occur, security identity under which the service is run, and some degree of manageability. Just like the self-hosting method, this hosting method also supports all bindings and transports. However, it has some limitations; for example, you have to deploy it with an installer, and it doesn't fully support high availability, easy manageability, versioning, or deployment scenarios.

The steps to create such a hosting application are very similar to what we did to host a WCF service in a command line application, except that you have to create an installer to install the Windows service in the Service Control Manager (or you can use the .NET Framework `Installutil.exe` utility).

Hosting the service in the Internet Information Server

It is a better option to host a WCF service within the Internet Information Server (IIS), because IIS provides a robust, efficient, and secure host for the WCF services. IIS also has better thread and process execution boundaries handling (in addition to many other features) compared to a regular managed application. Actually, web service development on IIS has long been the domain of ASP.NET. When ASP.NET 1.0 was released, a web service framework was part of it. Microsoft leveraged the ASP.NET HTTP pipeline to make web services a reality on the Windows platform.

The main drawback of hosting the service within the IIS prior to version 7.0 is the tight coupling between ASP.NET and Web services, which limits the transport protocol to HTTP/HTTPs.

Another thing you need to pay particular attention to when hosting WCF in the IIS is that the process and/or application domain may be recycled if certain conditions are met. By default, the WCF service session state is not saved in memory so that each recycle will lose all such information. This will be a big problem if you run a web site in a load-balanced or web-farm (web-garden) environment. In this case, you might want to turn on the ASP.NET compatibility mode (add the attribute `AspNetCompatibilityRequirements` to your WCF service) so that the session state can be persisted in an SQL Server database or in the ASP.NET State Server.

Now, we will explain how to host the `HelloWorldService` within IIS.

Preparing the folders and files

First, we need to prepare the folders and files for the host application. Follow these steps to create the folders and copy the required files:

1. Create the folders:

   In the Windows Explorer, create a new folder called `HostIIS` under `D:\SOAwithWCFandLINQ\Projects\HelloWorld`, and a new subfolder called `bin` under this `HostIIS` folder. You should now have the following new folders:

   `D:\SOAwithWCFandLINQ\Projects\HelloWorld\HostIIS`
   `D:\SOAwithWCFandLINQ\Projects\HelloWorld\HostIIS\bin`

2. Copy the files:

   Now, copy the files `HelloWorldService.dll` and `HelloWorldService.pdb` from the `HelloWorldService` project folder `D:\SOAwithWCFandLINQ\Projects\HelloWorld\HelloWorldService\bin\Debug` to the new folder we created, `D:\SOAwithWCFandLINQ\Projects\HelloWorld\HostIIS\bin`.

   Copy the files `HelloWorldService.svc` and `Web.config` from the `HostDevServer` project folder `D:\SOAwithWCFandLINQ\Projects\HelloWorld\HostDevServer` to the new folder, `D:\SOAwithWCFandLINQ\Projects\HelloWorld\HostIIS`.

   The files under the two new directories now should be like the following:

   Parent Folder: `D:\SOAwithWCFandLINQ\Projects\HelloWorld\`

Folder	HostIIS	HostIIS\bin
Files	HelloWorldService.svc	HelloWorldService.dll
	Web.config	HelloWorldService.pdb

Creating the virtual directory

Next, we need to create a virtual directory named `HelloWorldService`. Follow these steps to create this virtual directory in the IIS.

1. Open the Internet Information Services (IIS) manager via menu option **Control Panel | Administrative Tools** (or, if you prefer, from **Category View** in Control Panel, select **Performance and Maintenance**, and then **Administrative Tools**).
2. Expand the nodes of the tree in the left-hand pane until the node named **Default Web Site** becomes visible.
3. Right-click on that node, and choose **New | Virtual Directory ...** from the context menu.
4. In the **Virtual Directory Creation Wizard**, click the **Next** button, and enter **HelloWorldService** in the **Virtual Directory** alias screen.
5. Click the **Next** button, and enter **D:\SOAwithWCFandLINQ\Projects\HelloWorld\HostIIS** as the path on the **Web Site Content Directory** screen of the wizard.
6. Click the **Next** button again, and leave the options **Read** and **Run Scripts Permissions** selected on the wizard's **Virtual Directory Access Permissions** screen. Then, click on the **Next** button, and follow the instructions to exit from the wizard.
7. From the IIS window, right-click on the **HelloWorldService** virtual directory, select **Properties** from the context menu, select the **ASP.NET** tab, and modify the **ASP.NET Properties** to use the **ASP.NET 2.0.50727** version.

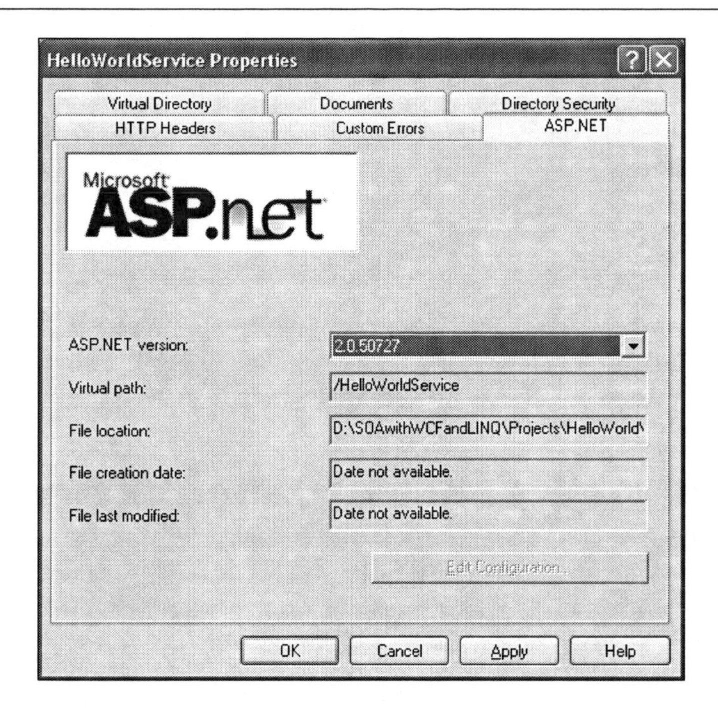

Starting the WCF service in the IIS

Once you have the files copied to the `HostIIS` folder, and have the virtual directory created, the WCF service is ready to be called by the clients. When a WCF service is hosted within IIS, we don't need to explicitly start the service. As with other normal web applications, IIS will control the lifetime of the service. As long as the IIS is started, client programs can access it.

Testing the WCF service hosted in the IIS

To test the WCF service, open an Internet browser, and enter the following URL in the address bar of the browser. You will get an almost identical screen to the one you got previously:

```
http://localhost/HelloWorldService/HelloWorldService.svc
```

You don't need to add a port after the host, because it is now hosted in the IIS with the default HTTP port 80. This also means that you can access it using your real computer (host) name, and even outside of your network if you are connected to the Internet. Two example URLs are as follows:

```
http://[your_pc_name]/HelloWorldService/HelloWorldService.svc
http://[your_pc_name].[your_company_domain].com/HelloWorldService/
HelloWorldService.svc
```

We can re-use the client program we created earlier to consume this WCF service hosted within the IIS. Just change the endpoint address line from this:

```
<endpoint address="http://localhost:8080/HostCmdLineAPP/
HelloWorldService.svc"
```

To this:

```
<endpoint address="http://localhost/HelloWorldService.svc"
```

Now, when you run this client program, it will use the WCF service hosted within the IIS, and not the previously-created `HostCmdLineApp` application. You will get the same result as before, when it was hosted in our own host application.

Advanced WCF service hosting options

The hosting methods we previously discussed were the three most popular options prior to Visual Studio 2008/Internet Information Services (IIS) 7.0 (Windows Vista / Windows 2008). In addition to these, there are some new advanced hosting methods for a WCF service in Visual Studio 2008 and IIS 7.0.

In Visual Studio 2008, there is a ready-made, general-purpose WCF Service Host (`WcfSvcHost.exe`), which makes the WCF host and development test much easier. This host will be used by default if you create a WCF service using a WCF Service Library template. We will cover this new feature in a later chapter.

Another option is to create a WCF service using a WCF Service Application template, in which case the WCF service project itself is a web site and is ready to run within its own project folder. We will also cover this new feature later.

With Internet Information Services (IIS) 7 (Windows Vista / Windows Server 2008), there is another new feature called **Windows Activation Services (WAS)**. This feature makes it possible to host a WCF service using all four WCF transport protocols (HTTP, NET.TCP, and NET.PIPE, NET.MSMQ), instead of just HTTP/HTTPS as in the case in IIS 6.0. As we will only use HTTP protocol in this book, we will not discuss this hosting method. However, in your real projects, you are recommended to explore this option and use it wherever possible.

Debugging the HelloWorld WCF service

Now that we have a fully-working WCF service, let us have a look at the debugging options of this service.

Debugging from the client application

The first and most common scenario is to debug from the client program. This means that you start a client program in debug mode, and then step into your WCF service.

Starting the debugging process

Follow these steps to start the debugging process from the client application:

1. Change the client program's web configuration file to call the `HelloWorldService` hosted within the ASP.NET Development Server. Open the file **app.config** inside the **HelloWorldClient** project, and set the address of the endpoint to this address:

   ```
   http://localhost:8080/HostDevServer/HelloWorldService.svc
   ```

2. In the Solution Explorer, right-click on the **HelloWorldClient** project, and select **Set as Startup Project** from the context menu.

3. Open the **Program.cs** file inside the `HelloWorldClient` project, and set a breakpoint at the following line:

   ```
   HelloWorldServiceClient client = new HelloWorldServiceClient();
   ```

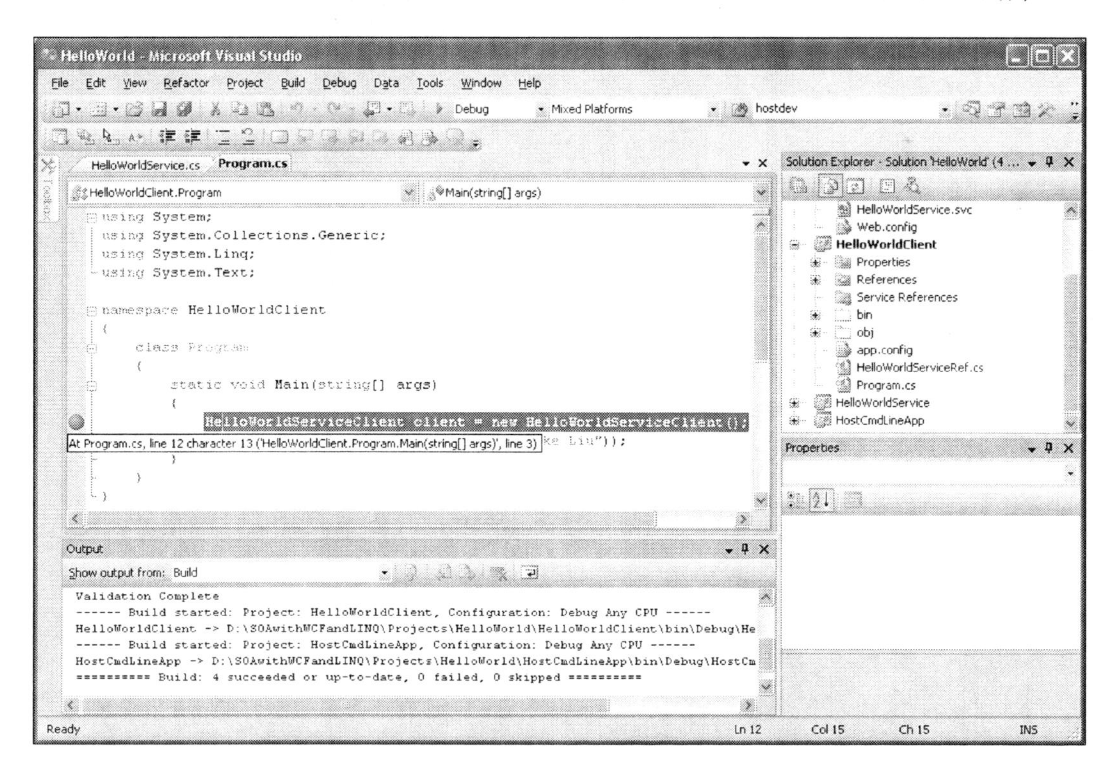

You can set a breakpoint by clicking on the gray area of the left of the line (the little ball in the diagram above), pressing *F9* while the cursor is on the line, or selecting the menu item **Debug | Toggle Breakpoint**. You should ensure that the breakpoint line is highlighted, and if you hover your mouse over the red breakpoint dot, an information line will pop up.

4. Now press *F5*, or select menu option **Debug | Start Debugging**, to start the debugging process.

As soon as you press *F5*, you will notice a little window pop up in the lower-right corner of the screen, as shown in the following image:

This is because the client program `HelloWorldClient` is referencing `HelloWorldService`, which is hosted in the ASP.NET Development Server, and you have the project property **Always Start When Debugging** set to `True`.

Note that this setting is for the WCF hosting project, not for the client or WCF service project. This is very useful when debugging, because you don't need to start it explicitly. However, sometimes, it might be annoying, especially when you have several hosting projects within the same solution. In this case, you can turn it off by setting it to `False`. However, you then have to start the Service prior to debugging the client application. Otherwise, you will get an exception. We will discuss more about this, later in this chapter.

Debugging on the client application

The cursor should have stopped on the breakpoint line, as you can see in the following **HelloWorld (Debugging)** image. The active line is highlighted, and you can examine the variables just as you do for any other C# applications.

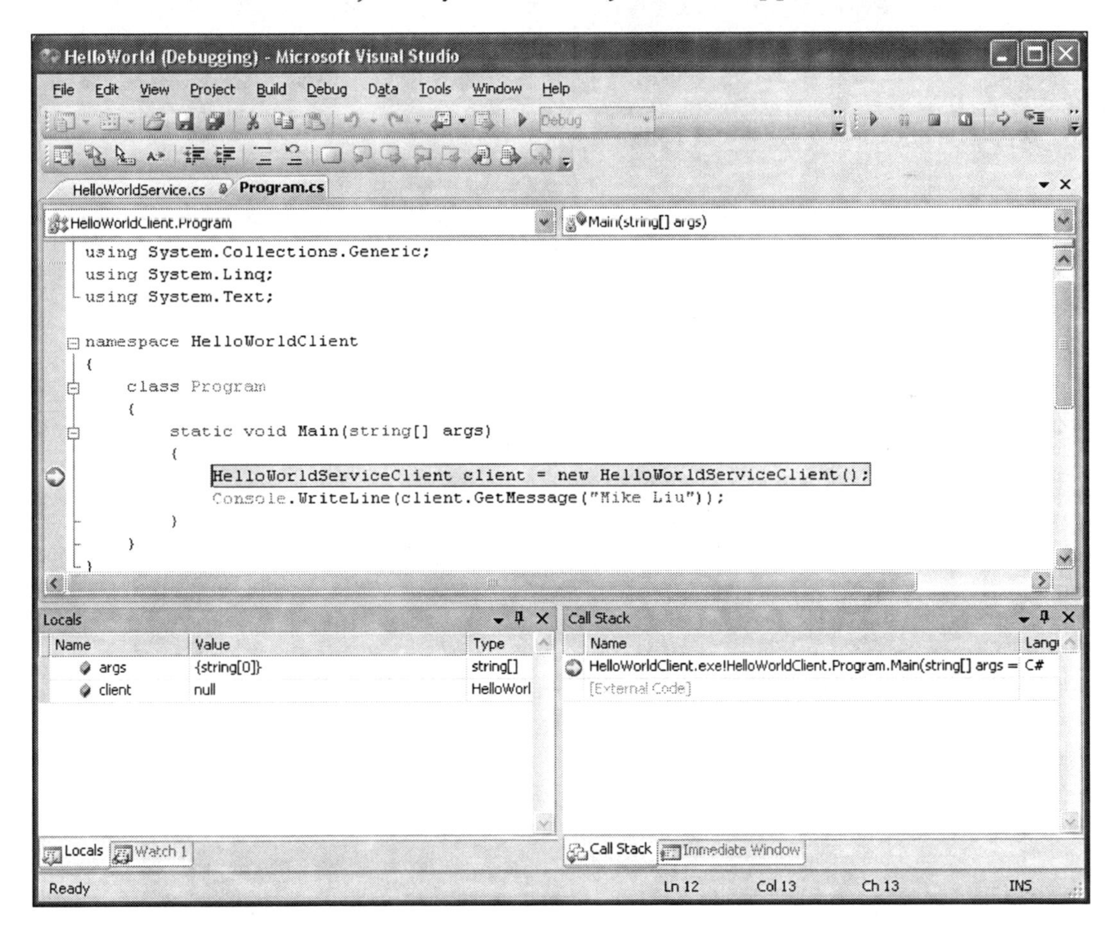

At this point, the channel between the client and the hosting server (`HostDevServer`) hasn't been created. Press *F10*, or select menu option **Debug | Step Over** to skip over this line. If you don't have the menu option **Debug | Step Over**, you may have to reset your development environment settings via menu option **Tools | Import and Export Settings...** (select **General Development Settings** from the **Import and Export Settings Wizard**, and check all of the available options).

Now, the following line of source code should be active and highlighted. At this point, we have a valid client object, which contains all of the information related to the WCF service, such as the channel, the endpoint, the members, and the security credentials. The following **Locals** image shows the details of the **Endpoint** local variable.

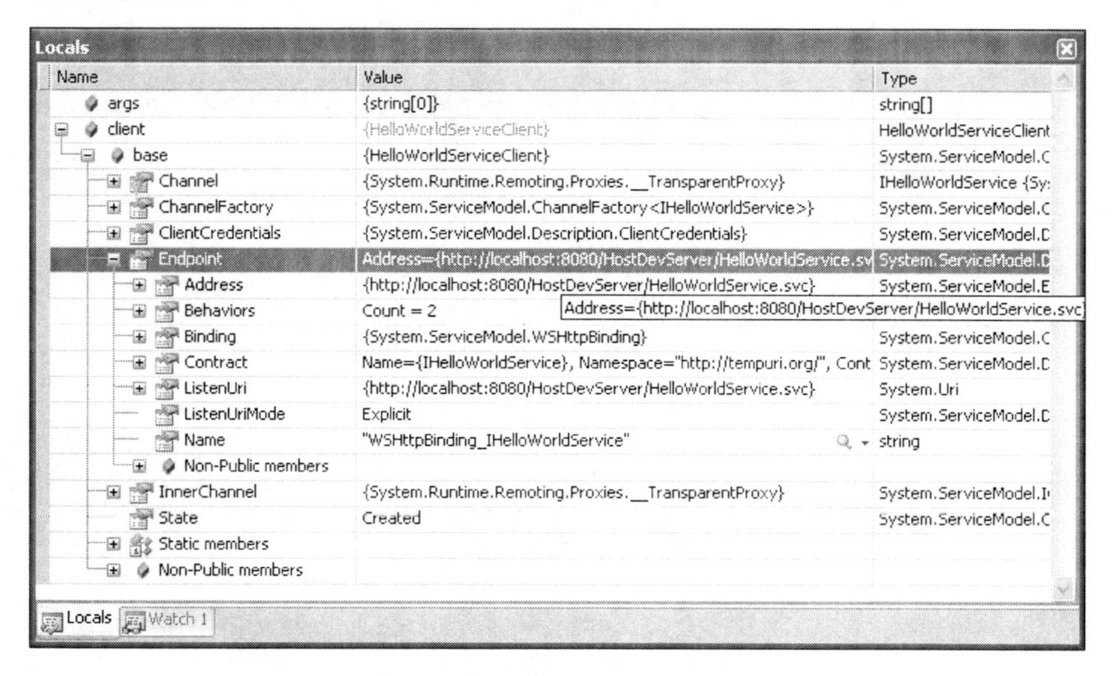

Enabling debugging of the WCF service

Let us press *F11* to step into the WCF service. But instead of stepping in, we will receive an error message, as shown in the following image stating that the service debugging is not enabled:

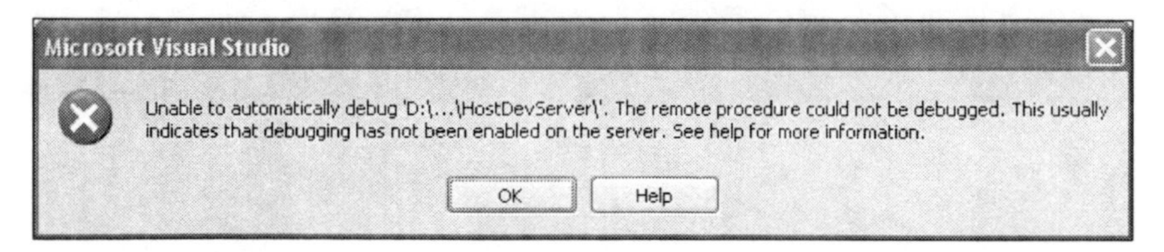

This is because we haven't enabled debugging for the `HostDevServer` application. Click the **OK** button to dismiss this dialog, and then press *Shift+F5*, or select menu option **Debug | Stop Debugging**, to return to the development mode.

To enable the debugging of `HostDevServer`, open the `web.config` file inside the `HostDevServer` project and add following nodes to this file:

```
<system.web>
    <compilation debug="true"/>
</system.web>
```

Above `system.web`, nodes should be added as child nodes of the root node `<configuration>`, and the content of the `web.config` file should now be like this:

```
<?xml version="1.0"?>
<configuration>
   <appSettings>
         <add key="HTTPBaseAddress" value=""/>
   </appSettings>
   <system.serviceModel>
         <services>
               <service name="MyWCFServices.HelloWorldService"
                    behaviorConfiguration="MyServiceTypeBehaviors">
                     <endpoint address="" binding="wsHttpBinding"
                      contract="MyWCFServices.IHelloWorldService"/>
                     <endpoint contract="IMetadataExchange"
                           binding="mexHttpBinding" address="mex"/>
               </service>
         </services>
         <behaviors>
               <serviceBehaviors>
                     <behavior name="MyServiceTypeBehaviors">
                           <serviceMetadata httpGetEnabled="true"/>
                     </behavior>
               </serviceBehaviors>
         </behaviors>
   </system.serviceModel>
   <system.web>
    <compilation debug="true"/>
  </system.web>
</configuration>
```

Stepping into the WCF service

Now, press *F5* to start debugging again. Press *F10* to skip the first line, and then press *F11* to step into the service code. The cursor now resides on the opening bracket of the `GetMessage` method of the `HelloWorldService`. You can now examine the variables inside `HelloWorldService`, just as you would for any other programs. Keep pressing *F10*, and you should eventually come back to the client program.

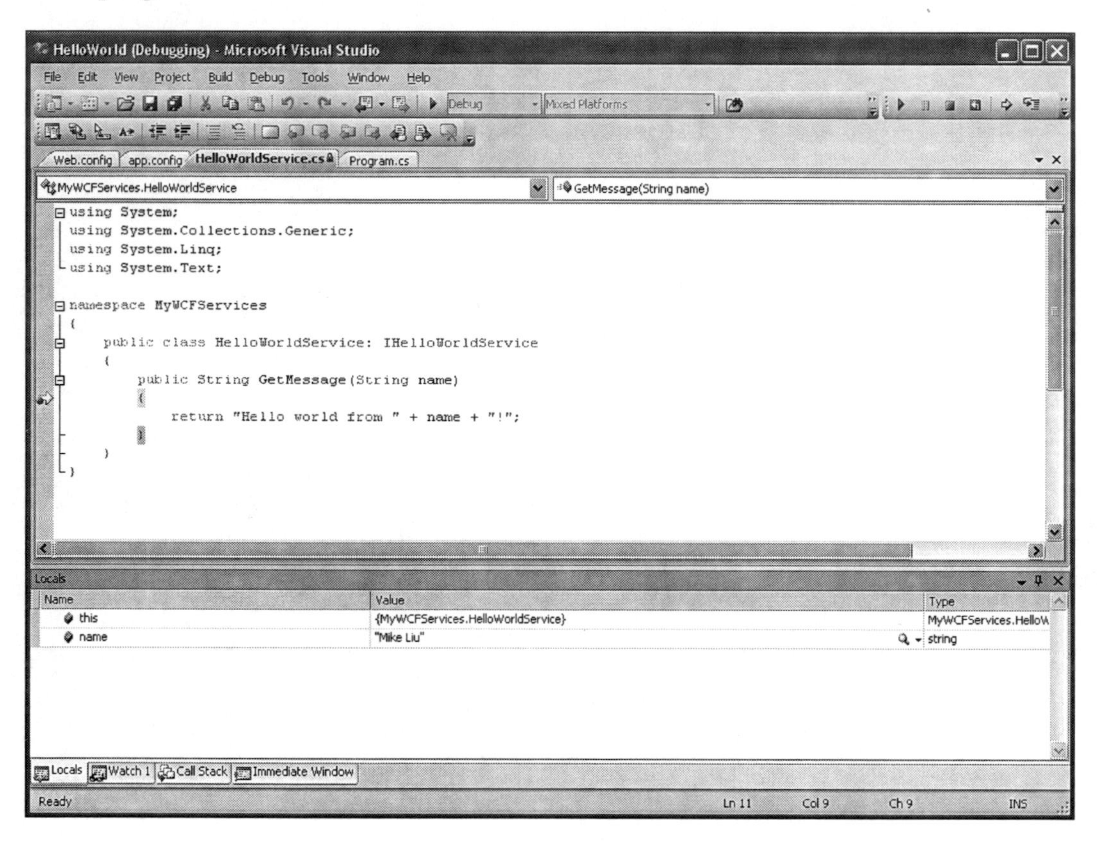

However, if you stay inside the `HelloWorldService` for too long, when you come back to `HelloWorldClient`, you will get an exception window saying that it has timed out. This is because, by default, the `HelloWorldClient` will call `HelloWorldService`, and wait for a response for a maximum time of one minute. You can change this to a longer value in the configuration file `web.config`, depending on your own needs.

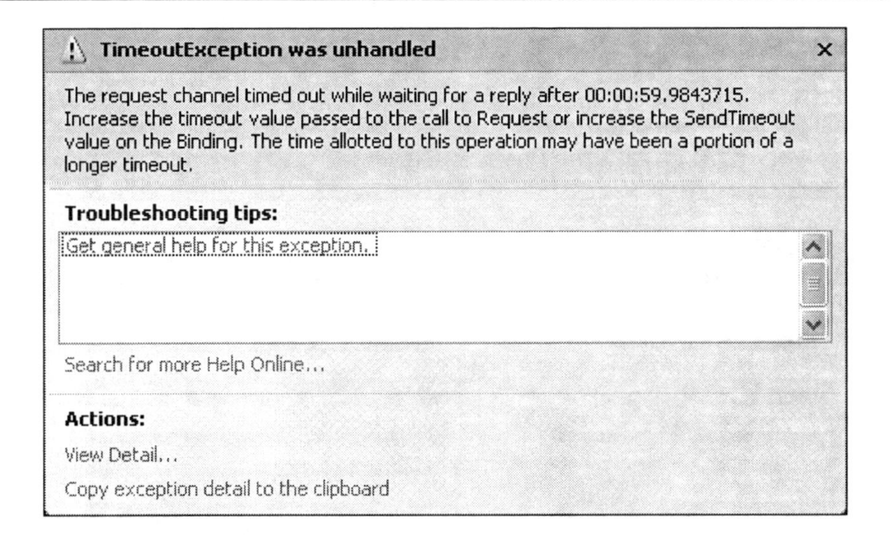

You may also have noticed that you don't see the output window of the `HelloWorldClient`. This is because, in debug mode, once a console application finishes, the console window is closed. You can add one line to the end of `Program.cs` to wait for a keystroke so that you can look at the output before it closes. You can do this by adding the following line of code:

```
Console.ReadKey();
```

Debugging only the WCF service

In the previous section, we started debugging from the client program, and then stepped into the service program. Sometimes, we may not want to run the client application in debug mode. For example, if the client application is a third-party product we won't have the source code, or the client application may be a BPM product that runs on a different machine. In this case, if we need to, we can run the service in debugging mode and debug only the service.

Starting the WCF Service in debugging mode

To start `HelloWorldService` in the debug mode, first set `HostDevServer` as the startup project. Then open **HelloWorldService.cs** from the **HelloWorldService** project and set a breakpoint at the line inside the `GetMessage` method, as shown below.

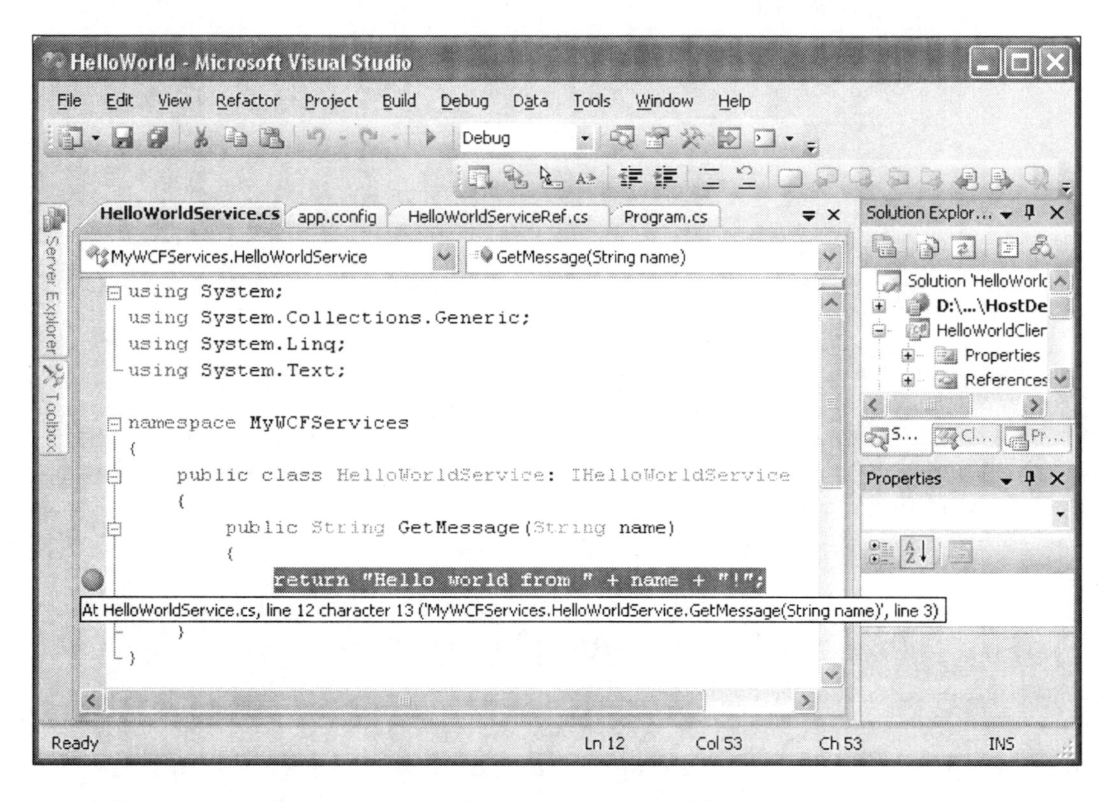

Now press *F5* to start the service in debugging mode.

Once you press *F5*, the WCF service will be running in debugging mode, waiting for requests. A browser will open displaying all of the files under the `HostDevServer` folder. If you go back to Visual Studio IDE, you may find that a new solution folder, **Script Documents,** has been added to the solution. This folder is the actual content of the web page being displayed in the browser. Because its content is dynamically generated, this folder will only be included in the solution when the `HostDevServer` is being debugged. Whenever you stop the debugging session, this folder will go away automatically.

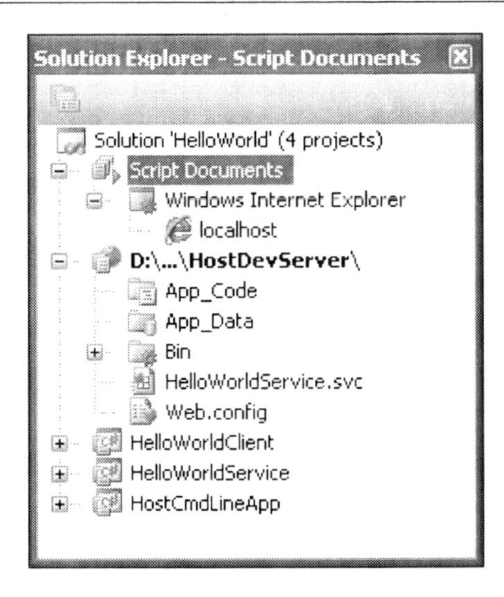

After you press *F5* to start a WCF service in debugging mode, you might see an error message warning you that script debugging is disabled, as shown the following **Script Debugging Disabled** image:

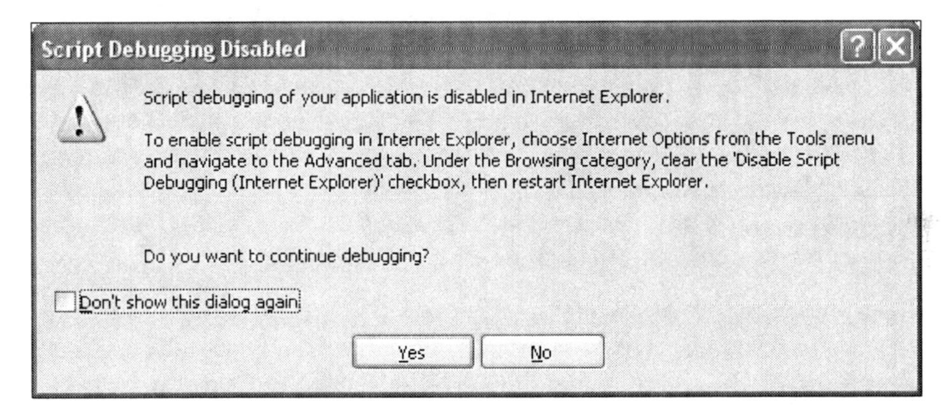

For this dialog box, you can do as instructed (clear the checkbox from the Internet Explorer under **Tools | Advanced | Browsing | Disable Script Debugging**), or you can just click the **Yes** button to continue debugging without enabling script debugging for Internet Explorer, because we will not debug any script from Internet Explorer (our application is not a web application).

Once you clicked the **Yes** button (or you may never see this message box because you have the correct settings), the service will be started in debugging mode.

Starting the client application in non-debugging mode

Now that we have the WCF service running in debugging mode, we need to start the client application in non-debugging mode so that the debugging process can start from the WCF service side, and not from the client side.

For this example, you can't start the `HelloWorldClient` program from the same Visual Studio IDE instance. The reason for this is that, once you have started the `HelloWorldService` in debugging mode, the solution is in running status. You can't start another project from the same solution inside the same Visual Studio instance while the `HelloWorldService` project is running. Actually, the **Set as Startup Project** menu option is disabled, making it impossible to set any other project as the startup project. Also, a bunch of other menu options are disabled, meaning that you can't change them while in debugging mode.

There are two ways to start the `HelloWorldClient` program in non-debugging mode. The first one is to start it in another instance of Visual Studio. While leaving the previous instance of Visual Studio running for the `HelloWorldService` in debugging mode, start a new Visual Studio instance, and open the `HelloWorld` solution. Set `HelloWorldClient` as the startup project, and then press *Ctrl+F5* to start it in non-debugging mode. As soon as you press *Ctrl+F5*, you will see that the previous Visual Studio is active and the cursor has stopped on the breakpoint line. You can now examine all of the variables inside `HelloWorldService`, as you would do for any other program. Press *F10* once and you will be taken to the end of the `GetMessage` method; press *F10* again and you will be taken outside of the `HelloWorldService` project. Because the `HelloWorldClient` is now not running in debugging mode, you will see the output window immediately.

Another way to start `HelloWorldClient` is to start it from Windows Explorer. Go to the `D:\SOAwithWCFandLINQ\Projects\HelloWorld\HelloWorldClient\bin\Debug` directory and double click **HelloWorldClient.exe** file. You will then get the same result as you did when you started it from inside a new Visual Studio instance.

Starting the WCF service and client applications in debugging mode

What if you start `HelloWorldClient` in debugging mode, while `HelloWorldService` is also running in the debugging mode? Suppose you have started `HelloWorldService` in debugging mode, have set a breakpoint inside the `GetMessage` method, and have attached a debugger to the `HelloWorldService`. Now, if you start another Visual Studio instance, open the solution, set `HelloWorldClient` as the startup project, and press *F5* to start `HelloWorldClient` also in debugging mode, you will get an exception, as shown in the following image indicating that you attach to the server process:

The main reason for this is that, by default, `HostDevServer` has the setting **Always Start When Debugging** set to True. Because of this setting, when `HelloWorldClient` is started in debugging mode, it also tries to start the service. However, as we have started it in another Visual Studio instance, it will not start a new one. Instead, it will just re-use the existing one. Now, when the breakpoint inside the `HelloWorldService` is hit, the second Visual Studio instance will try to attach to the `HelloWorldService` process, which fails because the first Visual Studio instance has already attached a debugger to it.

To overcome this, just change the setting **Always Start When Debugging** to **False**, and control the startup of each project manually, or when you start debugging from the client program, don't start the service in advance. The following **Properties** image shows the setting of this property:

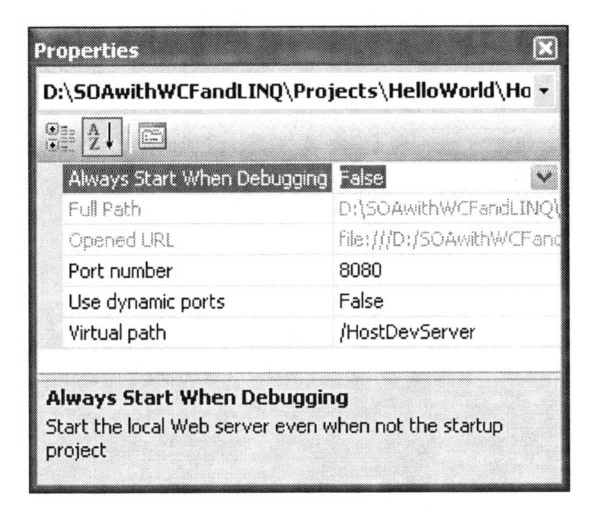

Attaching to a WCF service process

The third common scenario for debugging is when attaching to a running WCF service. Suppose that `HelloWorldService` is hosted and running outside Visual Studio, either in IIS or a managed application such as `HostCmdLineApp`. The client application is also running outside of Visual Studio. At a certain point, you may want to start debugging the running WCF service. In this case, we can attach to the WCF service process, and start debugging from the middle of a process.

Running the WCF service and client applications in non-debugging mode

To try this scenario, change the `app.config file` to use the IIS hosting `HelloWorldService`. This means that we use the following address for the endpoint in the `app.config` file for the `HelloWorldClient` project:

```
http://localhost/HelloWorldService/HelloWorldService.svc
```

Build the solution, and set a breakpoint inside the `GetMessage` method of the `HelloWorldService` project. Then, run the `HelloWorldClient` in non-debugging mode by pressing *Ctrl+F5*. You will see there is no way to hit the breakpoint we had previously set inside `HelloWorldService`. This is because the service is now hosted by the IIS, and it is not under debugging by any debugger.

Debugging the WCF service hosted in IIS

To debug the service hosted by the IIS, we can attach it to the IIS process. Start Visual Studio, select menu option **Debug | Attach to Process...**. The **Attach to Process** window should now appear. If you can't see the **Debug** menu from Visual Studio, just open any project or, create an empty new project.

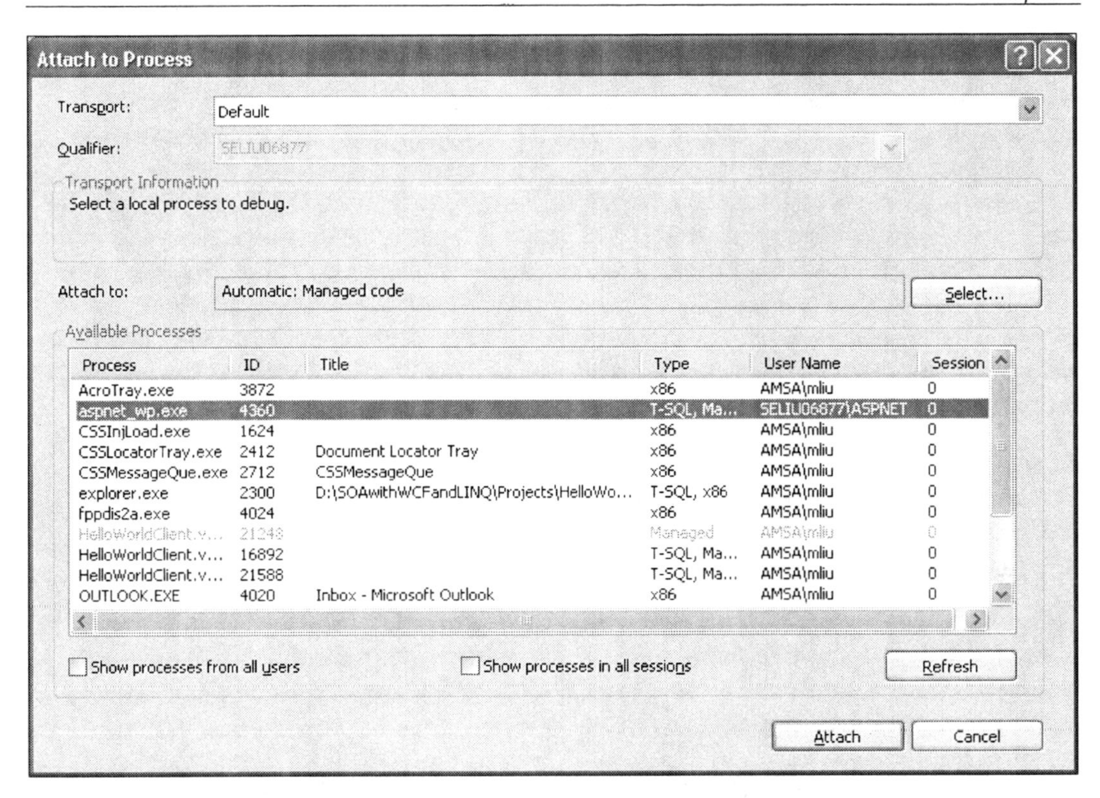

Select process `aspnet_wp.exe` from the list of available processes, and click the **Attach** button. You will find this process attached to the debugger. Open the `HelloWorldService.cs` file and set a breakpoint if you haven't done so already. Now run the `HelloWorldClient` program in non-debugging mode (use *Ctrl+F5*) from another Visual Studio instance or from Windows Explorer, and you will see that the breakpoint is now hit.

When you have finished debugging `HelloWorldService` using this method, you can select menu option **Debug | Detach All** or **Debug | Stop Debugging** to exit debugging mode.

You may also have noticed that when you attach to `aspnet_wp.exe`, the ASP.NET Development Server is also started. We will not use it at all at this time. This is again because the **Always Start When Debugging** property of `HostDevServer` is set to True, and as we did earlier, you can turn it off if you feel it is annoying.

Just-In-Time debugger

As you can see, we have to start the `HelloWorldService` before we can run the client program. The actual step to start the `HelloWorldService` varies depending on the hosting method that you are using. For example, if you are hosting `HelloWorldService` in a managed application as we did for `HostCmdLineApp`, you have to start the application manually. If you are hosting `HelloWorldService` in the ASP.NET Development Server, you can manually start it from Visual Studio, or set **Always Start When Debugging** to True. If you are hosting `HelloWorldService` in IIS, you don't need to do anything (except to make sure that the IIS service has been started). Lastly, if you host `HelloWorldService` in a Windows service, you should set its startup type to automatic, or you will have to manually start it.

What happens when you run the client program, the service is not started, and it is not set to automatically start when being referenced? For example, if you have hosted `HelloWorldService` in IIS, and for some reason IIS has been stopped, then what will happen to the client program?

To try this, we need to first stop IIS. There are several ways to stop IIS, and one of them is to open a command line window (via menu option **Start | All Programs | Accessories | Command Prompt**) and run the following command: `Net Stop W3SVC`, as shown in following image:

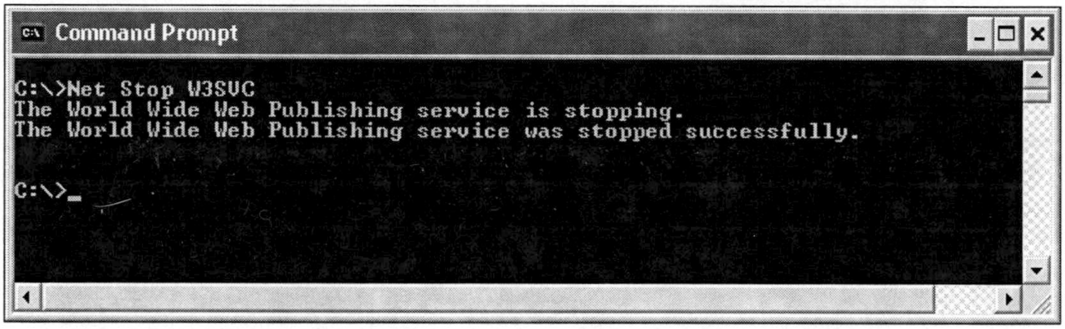

```
Command Prompt

C:\>Net Stop W3SVC
The World Wide Web Publishing service is stopping.
The World Wide Web Publishing service was stopped successfully.

C:\>_
```

Once IIS has been stopped, `HelloWorldService` is no longer accessible. If you start the `HelloWorldClient` program now, you will get an error. Depending on the mode in which you are running `HelloWorldClient`, you will get two different errors.

First, if you start `HelloWorldClient` in debugging mode (by pressing *F5*) from Visual Studio, it will stop on the line to call the `GetMessage` method, showing you an exception. This is because the client program can't connect to the server (the server has actively refused it). As we haven't added any code to handle exceptions, .NET runtime throws an unhandled exception. We will discuss exceptions (WCF Fault Contracts) in one of the following chapters. For now, you have to select menu option **Debug | Stop Debugging** to stop the client program.

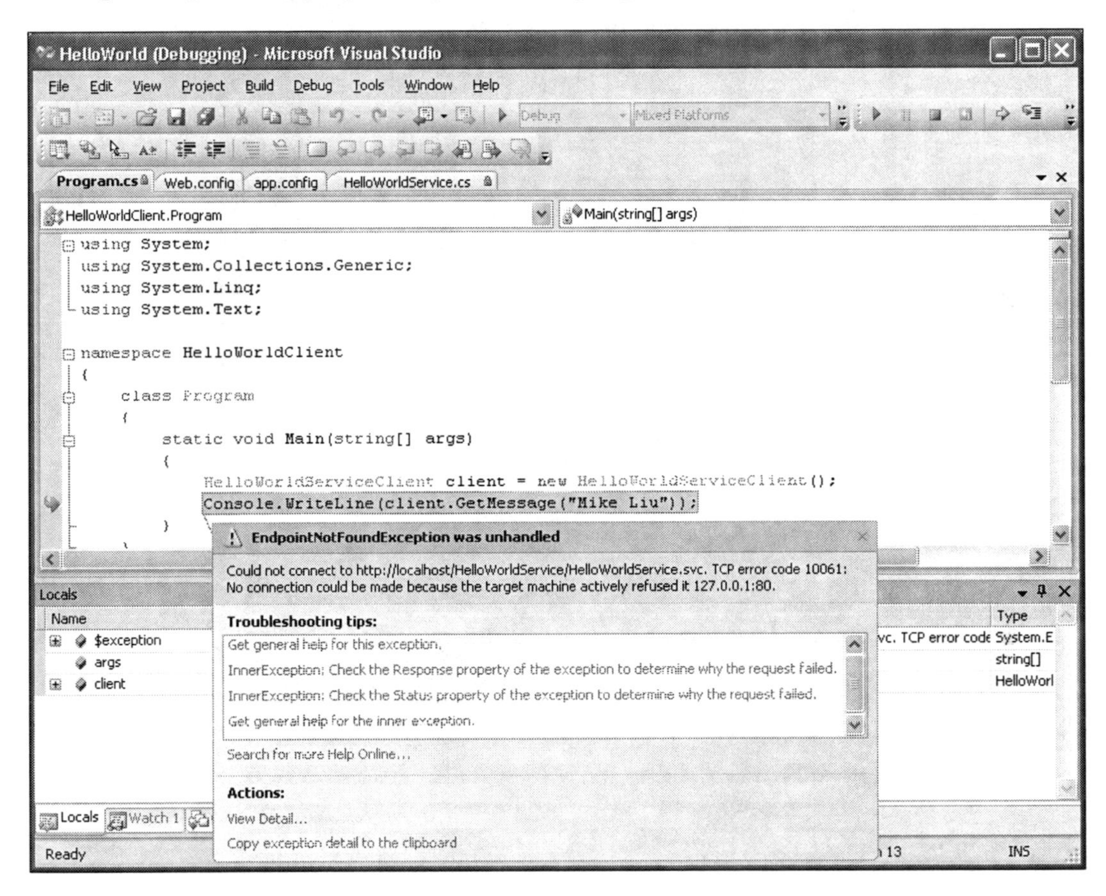

If you start `HelloWorldClient` in non-debugging mode (by pressing *Ctrl+F5*, or by double-clicking the `HelloWorldClient.exe` file from Windows Explorer `D:\SOAwithWCFandLINQ\Projects\HelloWorld\HelloWorldClient\bin\Debug\`), you will see the **Visual Studio Just-In-Time Debugger** screen.

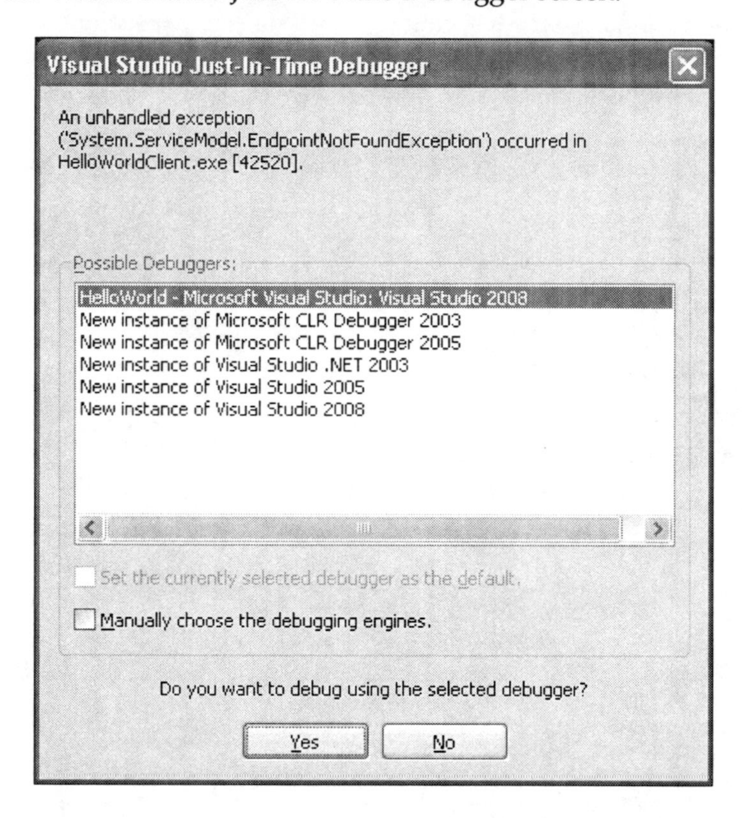

This is a nice feature of the .NET framework, because even though we have started the program in non-debugging mode, we can still step into the codesif something unexpected happens (however, the executable must be built with debugging information, that is, not a release one). In this case, if you click the **Yes** button, the Visual Studio window with the `HelloWorld` solution will be active, and you will see the same image as when you started the debugging process from Visual Studio. So, you know it is due to `HelloWorldService`. This will be very helpful when you are testing a big application, as you don't need to restart your program in debugging mode and repeat what you've done to reach the same problem spot. Instead, you can start the debugging process right on the spot, and then fix it quickly if it is only a configuration problem.

In the above example, if the client program is started from Windows Explorer, and the `HelloWorld` solution is not open in any Visual Studio IDE, it may even offer to start a new instance of Visual Studio for debugging. If you have multiple versions of Visual Studio .NET IDEs installed, it will list all of them for you to pick one. It is better to choose Visual Studio 2008 because, if you choose others, you may run into some unexpected problems.

Summary

In this chapter, we have hosted the `HelloWorld` WCF service in several different ways and explained the different scenarios of debugging a WCF service. The key points in this chapter include:

- A WCF Service can be hosted in the ASP.NET Development Server, in a managed application, a Windows Service, IIS, in Visual Studio 2008 WCF Service Host, or in WAS
- IIS is a better WCF hosting option for interacting with legacy applications, and WAS is even better when interoperability is not the highest priority
- You can start the debugging process for a WCF service from the client application, from the service application, or by attaching to the service process
- The Just-In-Debugger is helpful for determining the reason of the exception when the application is running outside of Visual Studio

5

Implementing a WCF Service in the Real World

In the previous chapter, we created a basic WCF service. The WCF service we created, `HelloWorldService`, has only one method, called `GetMessage`. Because this is just an example, we implemented this WCF service in one layer only. Both the service interface and implementation are all within one deployable component.

In this chapter and the next one, we will implement a WCF Service, which will be called `RealNorthwindService`, to reflect a real world solution. In this chapter we will separate the service interface layer from the business logic layer, and in the next chapter we will add a data access layer to the service.

In this chapter, we will create and test the WCF service by following these steps:

- Create the project using a WCF Service Library template
- Create the project using a WCF Service Application template
- Create the Service Operation Contracts
- Create the Data Contracts
- Add a Product Entity project
- Add a business logic layer project
- Call the business logic layer from the service interface layer
- Test the service

Why layering a service?

An important aspect of SOA design is that service boundaries should be explicit, which means hiding all the details of the implementation behind the service boundary. This includes revealing or dictating what particular technology was used.

Further more, inside the implementation of a service, the code responsible for the data manipulation should be separated from the code responsible for the business logic. So in the real world it is always a good practice to implement a WCF service in three or more layers. The three layers are the service interface layer, the business logic layer, and the data access layer.

- **Service interface layer**: This layer will include the service contracts and operation contracts that are used to define the service interfaces that will be exposed at the service boundary. Data contracts are also defined to pass in to and out of the service. If any exception is expected to be thrown outside of the service, then Fault contracts will also be defined at this layer.
- **Business logic layer**: This layer will apply the actual business logic to the service operations. It will check the preconditions of each operation, perform business activities, and return any necessary results to the caller of the service.
- **Data access layer**: This layer will take care of all of the tasks needed to access the underlying databases. It will use a specific data adapter to query and update the databases. This layer will handle connections to databases, transaction processing, and concurrency controlling. Neither the service interface layer nor the business logic layer needs to worry about these things.

Layering provides separation of concerns and better factoring of code, which gives you better maintainability and the ability to split layers out into separate physical tiers, for scalability. The data access code should be separated out into its own layer that focuses on performing translation services between the databases and the application domain. Services should be placed in a separate service layer that focuses on performing translation services between the service-oriented external world and the application domain.

The service interface layer will be compiled into a separate class assembly, and hosted in a service host environment. The outside world will only know about and have access to this layer. Whenever a request is received by the service interface layer, the request will be dispatched to the business logic layer, and the business logic layer will get the actual work done. If any database support is needed by the business logic layer, it will always go through the data access layer.

Creating a new solution and project using WCF templates

We need to create a new solution for this example, and add a new WCF project to this solution. This time we will use the built-in Visual Studio WCF templates for the new project.

Using the C# WCF service library template

There are two built-in WCF service templates within Visual Studio 2008: Visual Studio WCF Service Library and Visual Studio Service Application. In this section, we will use the service library template, and in the next section, we will use the service application template. Later, we will explain the differences between these two templates and choose the template that we are going to use for this chapter.

Follow these steps to create the `RealNorthwind` solution and the project using service library template:

1. Start Visual Studio 2008, select menu option **File | New | Project...,** and you will see the **New Project** dialog box. Do not open the `HelloWorld` solution from the previous chapter, as from this point onwards, we will create a completely new solution and save it in a different location.
2. In the **New Project** window, specify **Visual C# | WCF** as the project type, **WCF Service Library** as the project template, **RealNorthwindService** as the (project) name, and **RealNorthwind** as the solution name. Make sure that the checkbox **Create directory for solution** checkbox is selected.

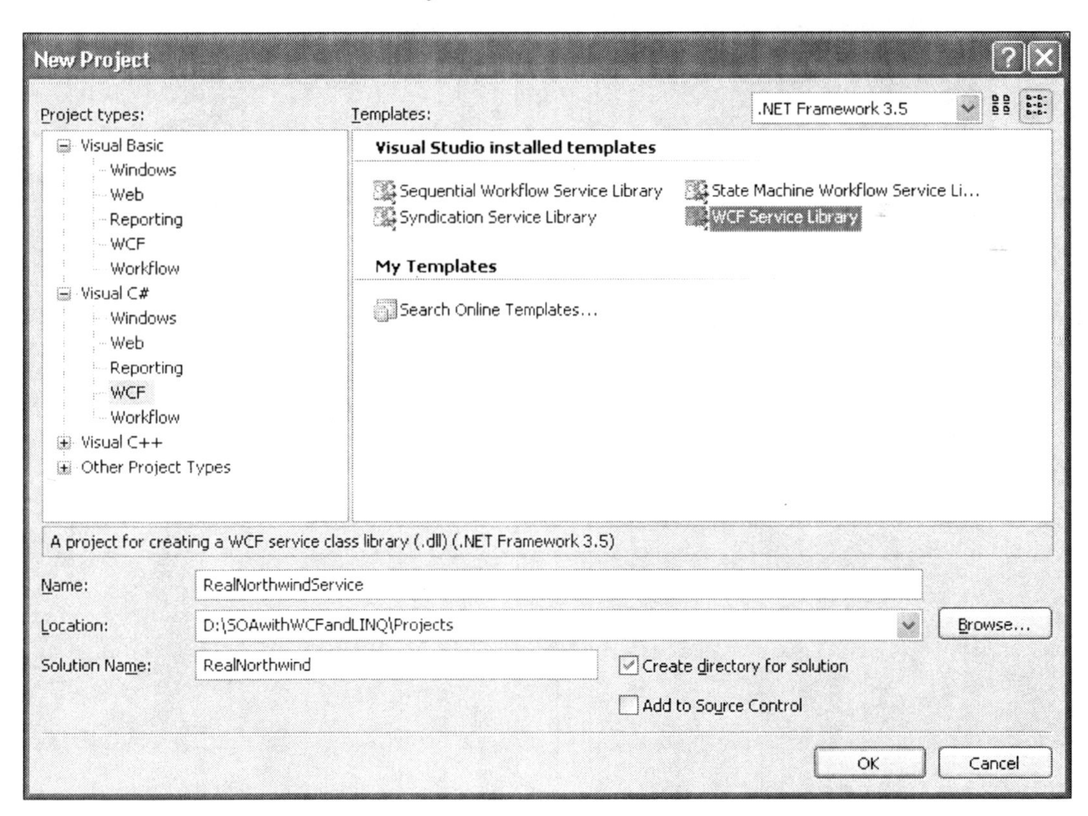

3. Click the **OK** button, and the solution is created with a WCF project inside it. The project already has a `IService1.cs` file to define an service interface and `Service1.cs` to implement the service. It also has an `app.config` file, which we will cover shortly.

Using the C# WCF service application template

Instead of using the Visual Studio WCF Service Library template to create our new WCF project, we can also use the Visual Studio Service Application template to create the new WCF project.

Because we have created the solution, we will add a new project using the Visual Studio WCF Service Application template.

1. Right-click on the solution item in the Solution Explorer, select menu option **Add | New Project...** from the context menu, and you will see the **Add New Project** dialog box.
2. In the **Add New Project** window, specify **Visual C#** as the project type, **WCF Service Application** as the project template, **RealNorthwindService2** as the (project) name, and leave the default location of **D:\SOAwithWCFandLINQ\Projects\RealNorthwind** unchanged.

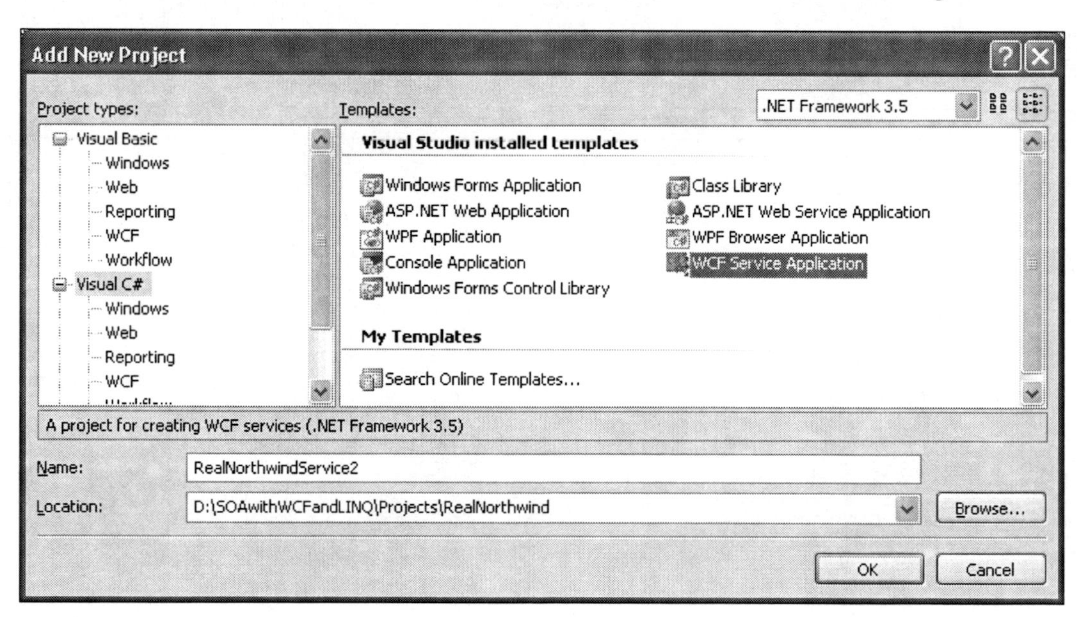

3. Click the **OK** button and the new project will be added to the solution. The project already has an `IService1.cs` file to define a service interface, and `Service1.svc.cs` to implement the service. It also has a `Service1.svc` file, and a `web.config` file, which are used to host the new WCF service. It has also had the necessary references added to the project such as `System.ServiceModel`.

You can follow these steps to test this service:

- Change this new project `RealNorthwindService2` to be the startup project (right-click on it from the Solution Explorer, and select **Set as Startup Project**). Then, run it (*Ctrl+F5* or *F5*). You will see that it can now run. You will see that an ASP.NET Development Server has been started, and a browser is open listing all of the files under the `RealNorthwindService2` project folder. Clicking on the **Service1.svc** file will open the Metadata page of the WCF service in this project. This is the same as we had discussed in the previous chapter for the `HostDevServer` project.
- If you have pressed *F5* in the previous step to run this project, you will see a warning message box asking you if you want to enable debugging for the WCF service. As we said earlier, you can choose enable debugging or just run in non-debugging mode.

You may also have noticed that the WCF Service Host is started together with the ASP.NET Development Server. This is actually another way of hosting a WCF service in Visual Studio 2008. It has been started at this point because, within the same solution, there is a WCF service project (`RealNorthwindService`) created using the WCF Service Library template. We will cover more of this host in a later section.

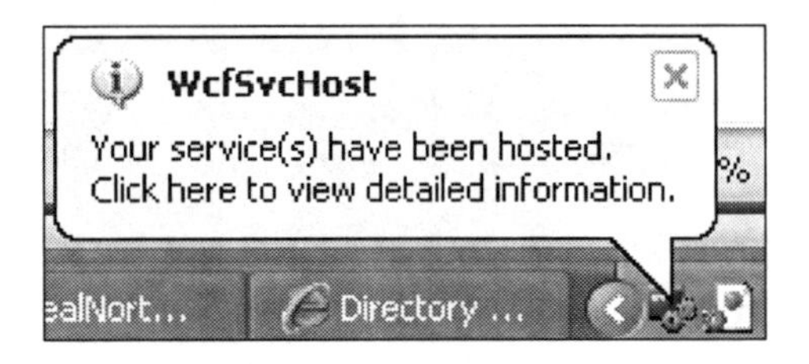

So far, we have used two different Visual Studio WCF templates to create two projects. The first project, using C# WCF Service Library template, is a more sophisticated one because this project is actually an application containing a WCF service, a hosting application (`WcfSvcHost`), and a WCF Test Client. This means that we don't need to write any other code to host it, and as soon as we have implemented a service, we can use the built-in WCF Test Client to invoke it. This makes it very convenient for WCF development.

The second project, using C# WCF Service Application template, is actually a website. This is the hosting application of the WCF service, so you don't have to create a separate hosting application for the WCF service. This is like a combination of the `HelloWorldService` and the `HostDevServer` applications we created in the previous chapter. As we have already covered them and you now have had a solid understanding of these styles, we will not discuss them any more. But keep in mind that you have this option, although in most cases it is better to keep the WCF service as clean as possible, without any hosting functionalities attached to it.

To focus on the WCF service using the WCF Service Library template, we now need to remove the project `RealNorthwindService2` from the solution.

In the Solution Explorer, right-click on the **RealNorthwindService2** project item, and select **Remove** from the context menu. Then, you will see a warning message box. Click the **OK** button in this message box, and the `RealNorthwindService2` project will be removed from the solution. Note that all the files of this project are still on your hard drive. You will need to delete them using Windows Explorer.

Creating the service interface layer

In the previous section, we created a WCF project using the WCF Service Library template. In this section, we will create the service interface layer contracts.

Because two sample files have already been created for us, we will try to re-use them as much as possible. Then, we will start customizing these two files to create the service contracts.

Creating the service interfaces

To create the service interfaces, we need to open the `IService1.cs` file, and do the following:

1. Change its namespace from `RealNorthwindService` to:

   `MyWCFServices.RealNorthwindService`

2. Change the interface name from **IService1** to **IProductService**. Don't be worried if you see the warning message before the interface definition line, as we will change the `web.config` file in one of the following steps.
3. Change the first operation contract definition from this line:

   ```
   string GetData(int value);
   ```

   To this line:

   ```
   Product GetProduct(int id);
   ```

4. Change the second operation contract definition from this line:

   ```
   CompositeType GetDataUsingDataContract(CompositeType composite);
   ```

   To this line:

   ```
   bool UpdateProduct(Product product);
   ```

5. Change the file's name from **IService1.cs** to **IProductService.cs**.

With these changes, we have defined two service contracts. The first one can be used to get the product details for a specific product ID, while the second one can be used to update a specific product. The product type, which we used to define these service contracts, is still not defined. We will define it right after this section.

The content of the service interface for `RealNorthwindService.ProductService` should look like this now:

```
using System;
using System.Collections.Generic;
using System.Linq;
using System.Runtime.Serialization;
using System.ServiceModel;
using System.Text;

namespace MyWCFServices.RealNorthwindService
{
    // NOTE: If you change the interface name "IService1" here, you
must also update the reference to "IService1" in App.config.
    [ServiceContract]
    public interface IProductService
    {
        [OperationContract]
        Product GetProduct(int id);

        [OperationContract]
        bool UpdateProduct(Product product);

        // TODO: Add your service operations here
    }
}
```

This is not the whole content of the `IProductService.cs` file. The bottom part of this file now should still have the class `CompositeType`, which we will change to our `Product` type in the next section.

Creating the data contracts

Another important aspect of SOA design is that you shouldn't assume that the consuming application supports a complex object model. A part of the service boundary definition is the data contract definition for the complex types that will be passed as operation parameters or return values.

For maximum interoperability and alignment with SOA principles, you should not pass any .NET specific types such as `DataSet` or `Exceptions` across the service boundary. You should stick to fairly simple data structure objects such as classes with properties, and backing member fields. You can pass objects that have nested complex types such as 'Customer with an Order collection'. However, you shouldn't make any assumption about the consumer being able to support object-oriented constructs such as inheritance, or base-classes for interoperable web services.

In our example, we will create a complex data type to represent a product object. This data contract will have five properties: `ProductID`, `ProductName`, `QuantityPerUnit`, `UnitPrice`, and `Discontinued`. These will be used to communicate with client applications. For example, a supplier may call the web service to update the price of a particular product, or to mark a product for discontinuation.

It is preferable to put data contracts in separate files within a separate assembly, but to simplify our example, we will put the `DataContract` within the same file as the service contract. So, we will modify the file `IProductService.cs` as follows:

1. Change the `DataContract` name from `CompositeType` to `Product`.
2. Change the fields from the following lines:

   ```
   bool boolValue = true;
   string stringValue = "Hello ";
   ```

   To these 7 lines:

   ```
   int productID;
   string productName;
   string quantityPerUnit;
   decimal unitPrice;
   bool discontinued;
   ```

3. Delete the old `BoolValue`, and `StringValue` `DataMember` properties. Then, for each of the above fields, add a `DataMember` property. For example, for `productID`, we will have this `DataMember` property:

   ```
   [DataMember]
   public int ProductID
   {
      get { return productID; }
      set { productID = value; }
   }
   ```

A better way is to take advantage of the automatic property feature of C#, and add the following `ProductID` `DataMember` without defining the `productID` field:

```
[DataMember]
public int ProductID { get; set; }
```

To save some space, we will use the latter format. So, we need to delete all of those field definitions, and add an automatic property for each field, with the first letter capitalized.

The data contract part of the finished service contract file `IProductService.cs` should now look like this:

```
[DataContract]
public class Product
{
        [DataMember]
        public int ProductID { get; set; }
        [DataMember]
        public string ProductName { get; set; }
        [DataMember]
        public string QuantityPerUnit { get; set; }
        [DataMember]
        public decimal UnitPrice { get; set; }
        [DataMember]
        public bool Discontinued { get; set; }
}
```

Implementing the service contracts

To implement the two service interfaces that we defined in the previous section, open the `Service1.cs` file and do the following:

1. Change its namespace from `RealNorthwindService` to `MyWCFServices.RealNorthwindService`.
2. Change the class name from `Service1` to `ProductService`. Make it inherit from the `IProductService` interface, instead of `IService1`. The class definition line should be like this:

   ```
   public class ProductService : IProductService
   ```

3. Delete the `GetData` and `GetDataUsingDataContract` methods
4. Add the following method, to get a product:

   ```
   public Product GetProduct(int id)
   {
       // TODO: call business logic layer to retrieve product
       Product product = new Product();
       product.ProductID = id;
       product.ProductName = "fake product name from service layer";
       product.UnitPrice = (decimal)10.0;
       return product;
   }
   ```

In this method, we created a fake product and returned it to the client. Later, we will remove the hard-coded product from this method, and call the business logic to get the real product.

5. Add the following method to update a product:

   ```
   public bool UpdateProduct(Product product)
   {
       // TODO: call business logic layer to update product
       if (product.UnitPrice <= 0)
           return false;
       else
           return true;
   }
   ```

   Also, in this method, we don't update anything. Instead, we always return `true` if a valid price is passed in. In one of the following sections, we will implement the business logic to update the product and apply some business logics to the update.

6. Change the file's name from `Service1.cs` to `ProductService.cs`. The content of the `ProductService.cs` file should be like this:

```
using System;
using System.Collections.Generic;
using System.Linq;
using System.Runtime.Serialization;
using System.ServiceModel;
using System.Text;
namespace MyWCFServices.RealNorthwindService
{
    // NOTE: If you change the class name "Service1" here,
    you must also update the reference to "Service1" in App.config.
    public class ProductService : IProductService
    {
        public Product GetProduct(int id)
        {
            // TODO: call business logic layer to retrieve product
            Product product = new Product();
            product.ProductID = id;
            product.ProductName = "fake product name
            from service layer";
            product.UnitPrice = (decimal)10;
            return product;
        }
        public bool UpdateProduct(Product product)
        {
            // TODO: call business logic layer to update product
            if (product.UnitPrice <= 0)
                return false;
            else
                return true;
        }
    }
}
```

Modifying the app.config file

Because we have changed the service name, we have to make the appropriate changes to the configuration file.

Follow these steps to change the configuration file:

1. Open `app.config` file from the Solution Explorer.
2. Change the `RealNorthwindService` string to `MyWCFServices.RealNorthwindService`. This is for the namespace change.
3. Change the `Service1` string to `ProductService`. This is for the actual service name change.
4. Change the service address port from `8731` to `8080`. This is to prepare for the client application.
5. You can also change the `Design_Time_Addresses` to whatever address you want, or delete this part from the service, `baseAddress`. This can be used to test your service locally.

The content of the `app.config` file should now look like this:

```
<?xml version="1.0" encoding="utf-8" ?>
<configuration>
  <system.web>
    <compilation debug="true" />
  </system.web>
  <!-- When deploying the service library project, the content of
       the config file must be added to the host's app.config file.
       System.Configuration does not support config files for
       libraries. -->
  <system.serviceModel>
    <services>
      <service name="MyWCFServices.RealNorthwindService.
               ProductService" behaviorConfiguration="MyWCFServices.
               RealNorthwindService.ProductServiceBehavior">
        <host>
          <baseAddresses>
            <add baseAddress = "http://localhost:8080/Design_Time_
             Addresses/MyWCFServices/RealNorthwindService/
             ProductService/" />
          </baseAddresses>
        </host>
        <!-- Service Endpoints -->
        <!-- Unless fully qualified, address is relative to base
                                     address supplied above -->
        <endpoint address ="" binding="wsHttpBinding"
        contract="MyWCFServices.RealNorthwindService.IProductService">
          <!-- Upon deployment, the following identity element should
           be removed or replaced to reflect the identity under which
           the deployed service runs.  If removed, WCF will infer an
           appropriate identity automatically. -->
```

```
        <identity>
          <dns value="localhost"/>
        </identity>
      </endpoint>
      <!-- Metadata Endpoints -->
      <!-- The Metadata Exchange endpoint is used by the service
       to describe itself to clients. -->
      <!-- This endpoint does not use a secure binding and should be
       secured or removed before deployment -->
      <endpoint address="mex" binding="mexHttpBinding" contract=
       "IMetadataExchange"/>
    </service>
  </services>
  <behaviors>
    <serviceBehaviors>
      <behavior name="MyWCFServices.RealNorthwindService.
       ProductServiceBehavior">
        <!-- To avoid disclosing metadata information,
        set the value below to false and remove the metadata
        endpoint above before deployment -->
        <serviceMetadata httpGetEnabled="True"/>
        <!-- To receive exception details in faults for debugging
         purposes, set the value below to true.  Set to false before
         deployment to avoid disclosing exception information -->
        <serviceDebug includeExceptionDetailInFaults="False" />
      </behavior>
    </serviceBehaviors>
  </behaviors>
 </system.serviceModel>
</configuration>
```

Testing the service using WCF Test Client

Because we are using the WCF Service Library template in this example, we are now ready to test this web service. As we pointed out when creating this project, this service will be hosted in the Visual Studio 2008 WCF Service Host environment.

This is a new feature of Visual Studio 2008; if you are using Visual Studio 2005, you won't have this built-in functionality.

To start the service, press *F5* or *Ctrl+F5*. The `WcfSvcHost` will be started and the WCF Test Client is also started. This is a Visual Studio 2008 built-in test client for WCF Service Library projects.

In order to run the WCF Test Client, you have to log in to your machine as a local administrator.

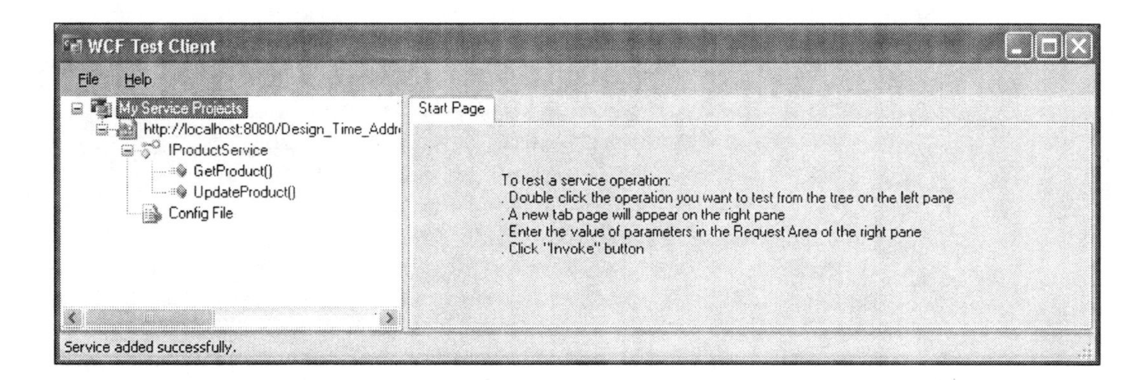

From this WCF Test Client, we can double-click on an operation to test it. First, let us test the `GetProduct` operation.

1. In the left panel of the client, double-click on the `GetProduct` operation; the `GetProduct` **Request** will be shown on the right-side panel.
2. In this **Request** panel, specify an integer for the product ID, and click the **Invoke** button to let the client call the service. You may get a dialog box to warn you about the security of sending information over the network. Click the **OK** button to acknowledge this warning (you can check the **'In the future, do not show this message'** option, so that it won't be displayed again).

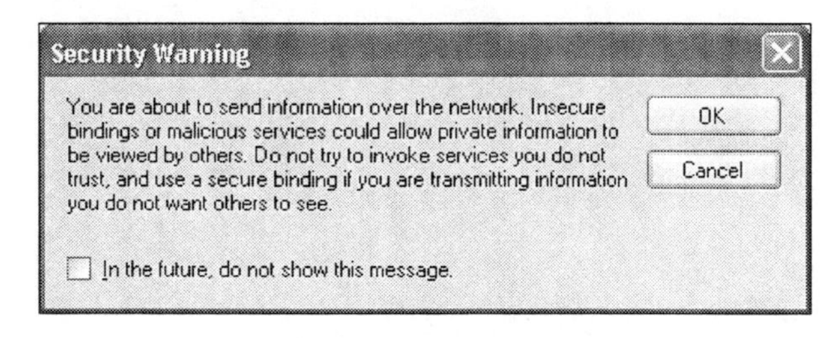

Now the message **Invoking Service...** will be displayed in the status bar, as the client is trying to connect to the server. It may take a while for this initial connection to be made, as several things need to be done in the background. Once the connection has been established, a channel will be created and the client will call the service to perform the requested operation. Once the operation has completed on the server side, the response package will be sent back to the client, and the WCF Test Client will display this response in the bottom panel.

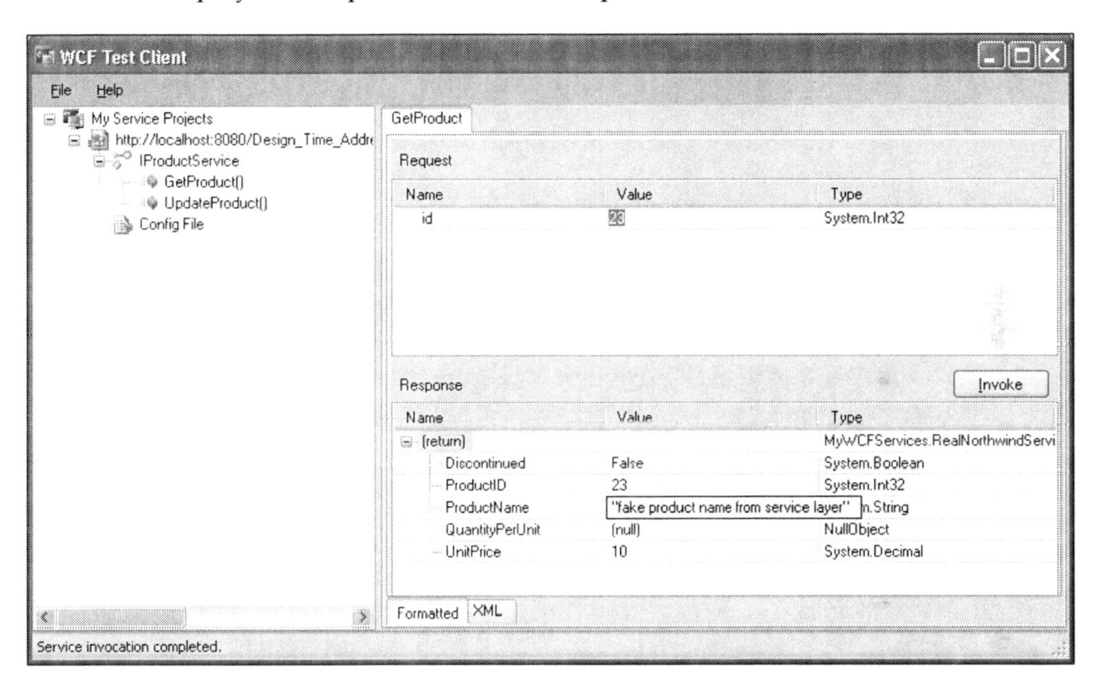

If you have started the test client in the debugging mode (by pressing *F5*), you can set a breakpoint at a line inside the `GetProduct` method in the `RealNorthwindService.cs` file, and when the **Invoke** button is clicked, the breakpoint will be hit so that you can debug the service as we explained earlier.

Note that the response is always the same, no matter what product ID you use to retrieve the product. Specifically, the product name is hard-coded, as shown in the diagram. Moreover, from the client response panel, we can see that several properties of the `Product` object have been assigned default values.

Also, because the product ID is an integer value from the WCF Test Client, you can only enter an integer for it. If a non-integer value is entered, when you click the **Invoke** button, you will get an error message box to warn you that you have entered the wrong type.

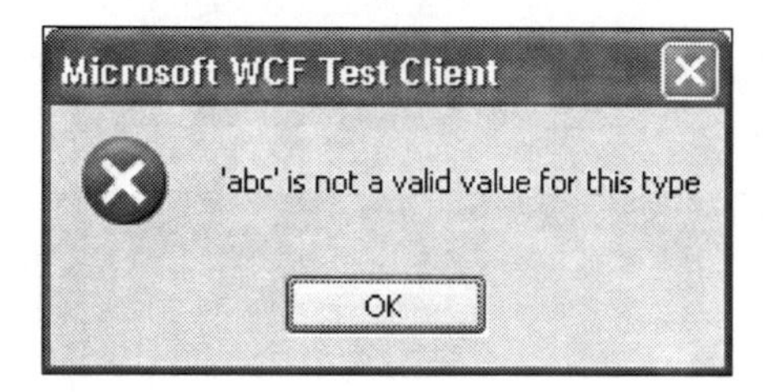

Now let's test the operation, `UpdateProduct`.

- Double-click the `UpdateProduct` operation in the left panel, and `UpdateProduct` will be shown in the right-side panel, in a new tab.
- Enter a decimal value for the `UnitPrice` parameter, then click the **Invoke** button to test it. Depending on the value you entered in the `UnitPrice` column, you will get a `True` or `False` response package back.

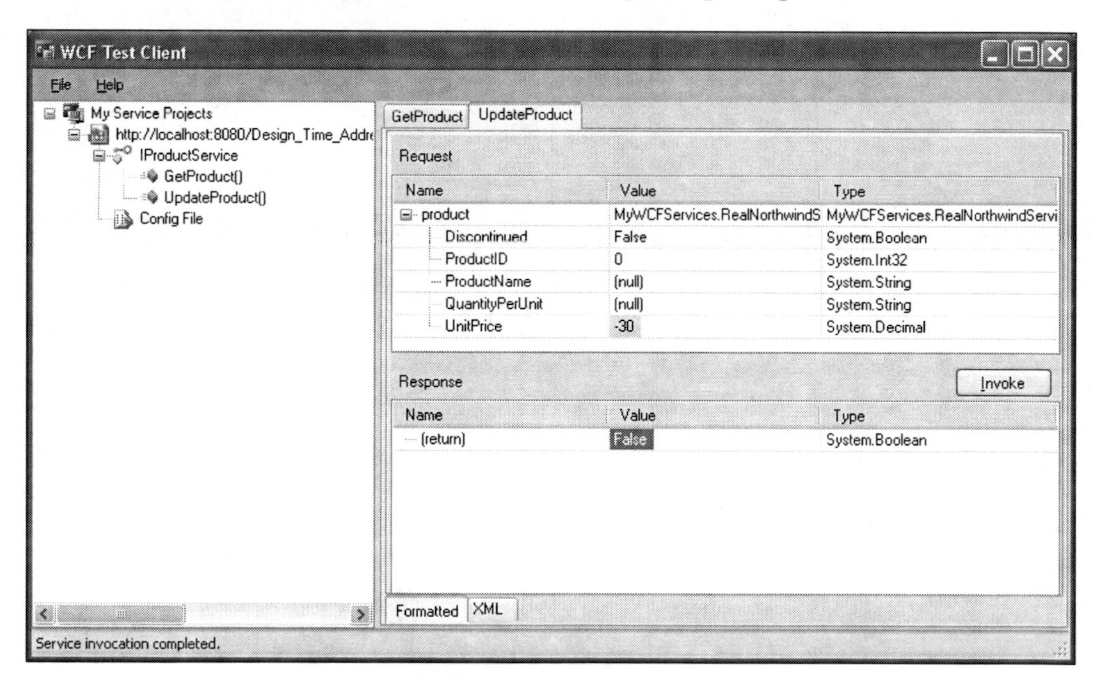

The Request/Response packages are displayed in grids by default, but you have the option of displaying them in the XML format. Just select the **XML** tab from the bottom of the right-hand side panel, and you will see the XML formatted **Request/ Response** packages. From these XML strings, you will discover that they are SOAP messages.

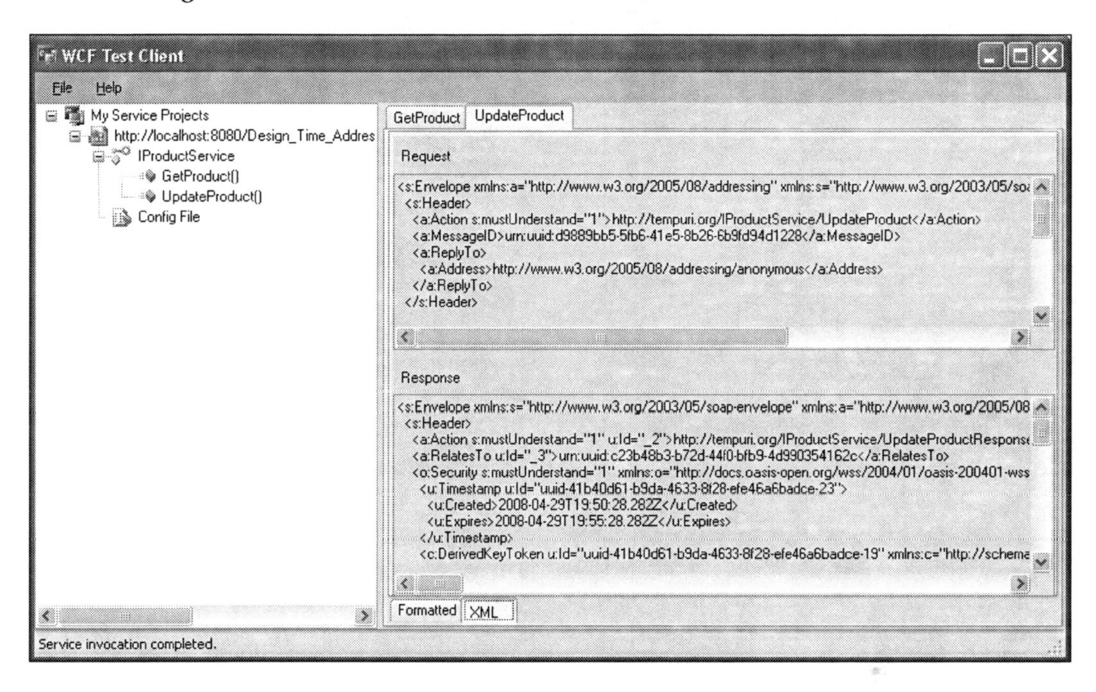

Besides testing operations, you can also look at the configuration settings of the web service. Just double-click on **Config File** from the left-side panel and the configuration file will be displayed in the right-side panel. This will show you the bindings for the service, the addresses of the service, and the contract for the service.

What you see here for the configuration file is not an exact image of the actual configuration file. It hides some information, such as debugging mode and service behavior, and includes some additional information on reliable sessions and compression mode.

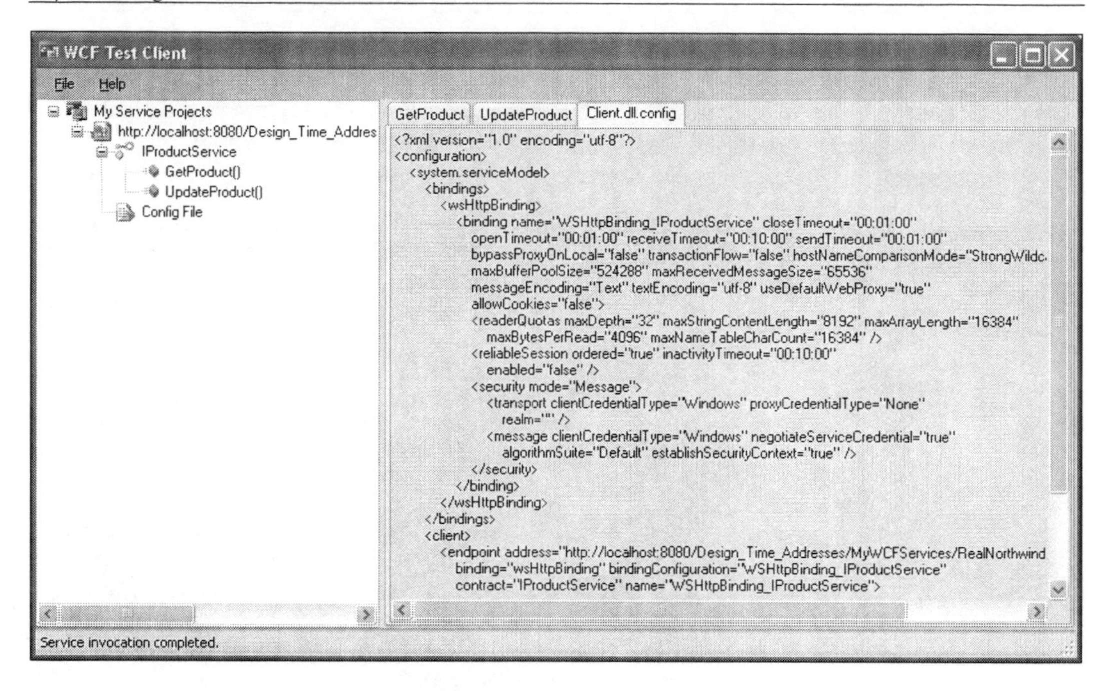

If you are satisfied with the test results, just close the WCF Test Client, and you will go back to Visual Studio IDE. Note that as soon as you close the client, the WCF Service Host is stopped. This is different from hosting a service inside the ASP.NET Development Server, where after you close the client, the ASP.NET Development Server still does not stop.

Testing the service using our own client

It is very convenient to test a WCF service using the built-in WCF Test Client, but sometimes, it is desirable to test a WCF service using your own test client. The built-in WCF Test Client is limited to only simple WCF services. So for complex WCF services, we have to create our own test client. For this purpose, we can use the methods we learned earlier, to host the WCF service in IIS, the ASP.NET Development Server, or a managed .NET application, and create a test client to test the service.

In addition to the previous methods we learned, we can also use the built-in WCF Service Host to host the WCF service. So we don't need to create a host application, but just need to create a client. In this section, we will use this hosting method, to save us some time.

First, let us find a way to get the Metadata for the service. From the Visual Studio 2008 built-in WCF Test Client, you can't examine the WSDL of the service, although the client itself must have used the WSDL to communicate with the service. To see the WSDL outside of the WCF Service Test Client, just copy the address of the service from the configuration file and paste it into a web browser. In our example, the address of the service is: `http://localhost:8080/Design_Time_Addresses/MyWCFServices/RealNorthwindService/ProductService/`. So, copy and paste this address to a web browser, and we will see the WSDL languages of the service, just as we have seen many times before.

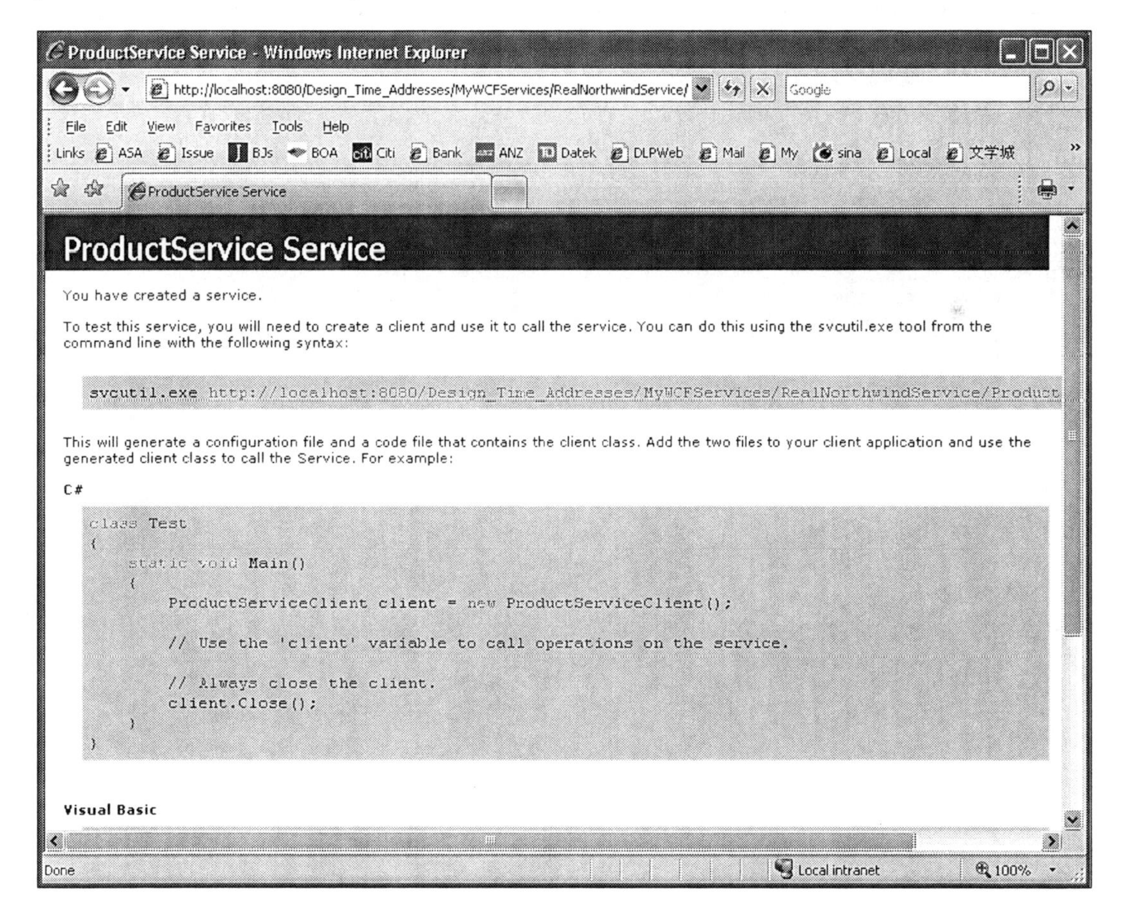

To get the Metadata for the service, the service host application must run. The easiest way to start the `RealNorthwindService` in the WCF Service Host is to start the WCF Test Client and leave it running.

Now that we know how to get the Metadata for our service, we can start building the test client. We can leave the host application running, and manually generate the proxy classes using the same method that we used earlier. But this time we will let Visual Studio do it for us. So you can close the WCF Test Client for now.

Follow these steps to build your own client to test the WCF service:

1. Add a new **Console Application** project to the `RealNorthwind` solution. Let's call it `RealNorthwindClient`.
2. Add a reference to the WCF service. In the Visual Studio Solution Explorer, right-click on the **RealNorthwindClient** project, select **Add Service Reference ...** from the context menu, and you will see the **Add Service Reference** dialog box.

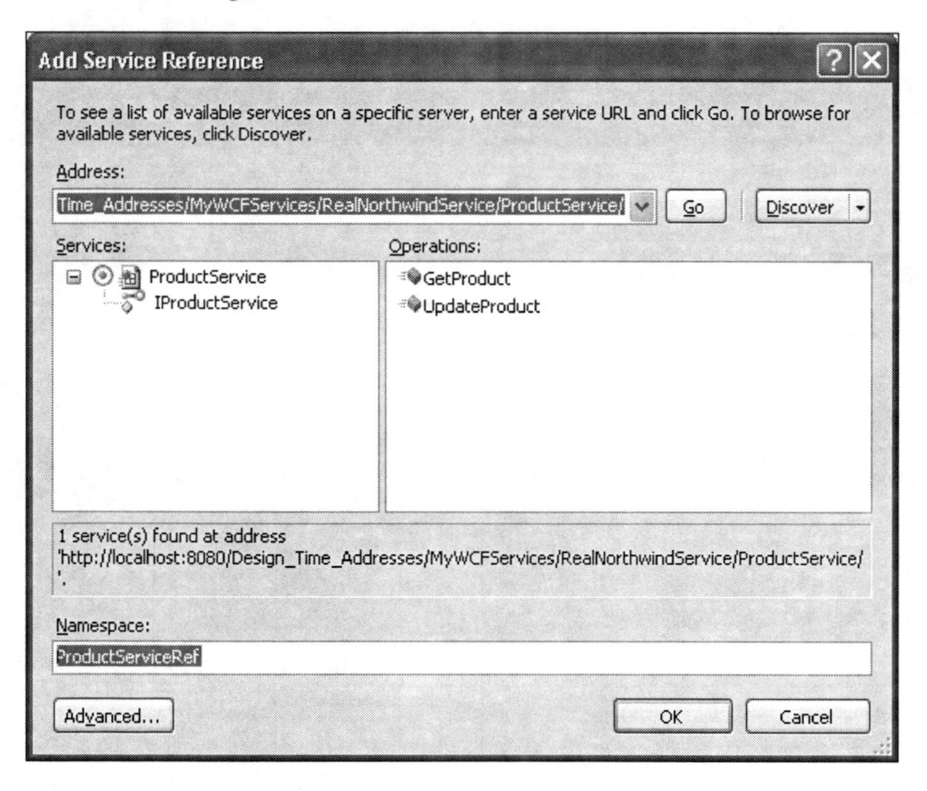

3. In the **Add Service Reference** dialog box, type the following address into the **Address** box, and then click the **Go** button to connect to the service:

   `http://localhost:8080/Design_Time_Addresses/MyWCFServices/RealNorthwindService/ProductService/`

   Also, you can simply click the **Discover** button (or click on the little arrow next to the **Discover** button, and select **Services in Solution**) to find this service.

In order to connect to or discover a service in the same solution, you don't have to start the host application for the service. The WCF Service Host will be automatically started for this purpose. However, if it is not started in advance, it may take a while for the **Add Service Reference** window to download the required Metadata information for the service.

The `ProductService` should now be listed on the left-hand side of the window. You can expand it and select the service contract to view its details.

4. Next, let's change the namespace of this service from `ServiceReference1` to `ProductServiceRef`. This will make the reference meaningful in the code.
5. If you want to make this client run under .NET 2.0, click the **Advanced** button in the **Add Service Reference** window, and in the **Service Reference Settings** pop-up dialog box, click the **Add Web Reference** button. This will cause the proxy code will be generated based on the .NET 2.0 web services.

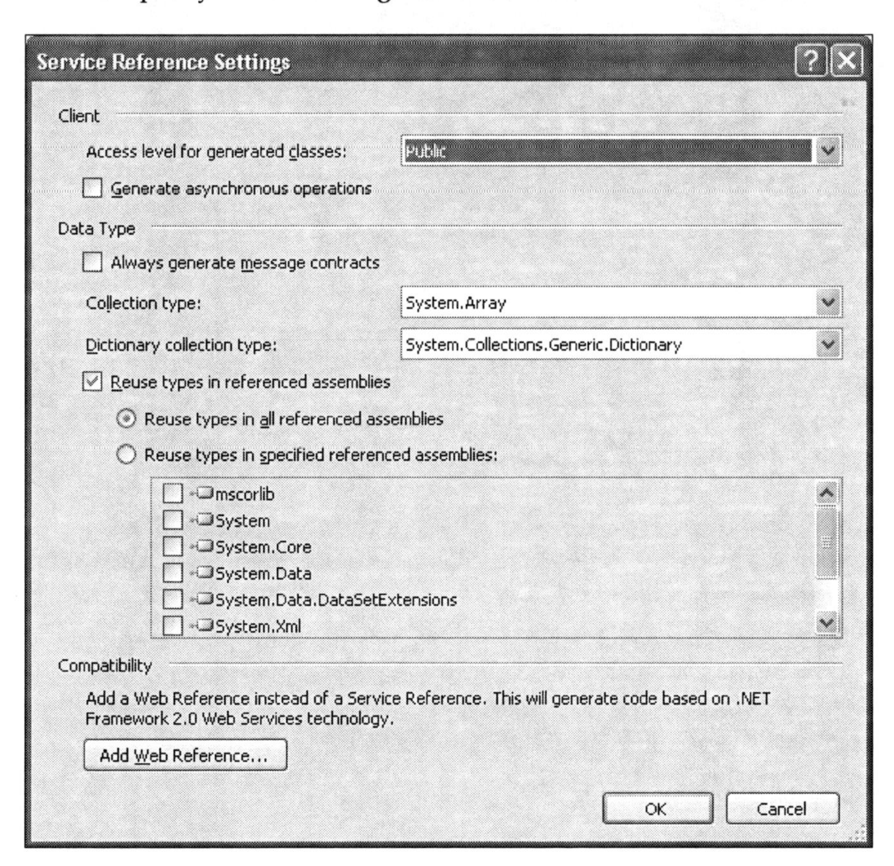

In this example, we won't do this. So, click the **Cancel** button to discard these changes.

6. Now click the **OK** button in the **Add Service Reference** dialog box to add the service reference. You will see that a new folder, named **ProductServiceRef**, is created under **Service References** in the Solution Explorer for the **RealNorthwindClient** project. This folder contains lots of files, including the WSDL file, the service map, and the actual proxy code. If you can't see them, click **Show All Files** in the Solution Explorer.

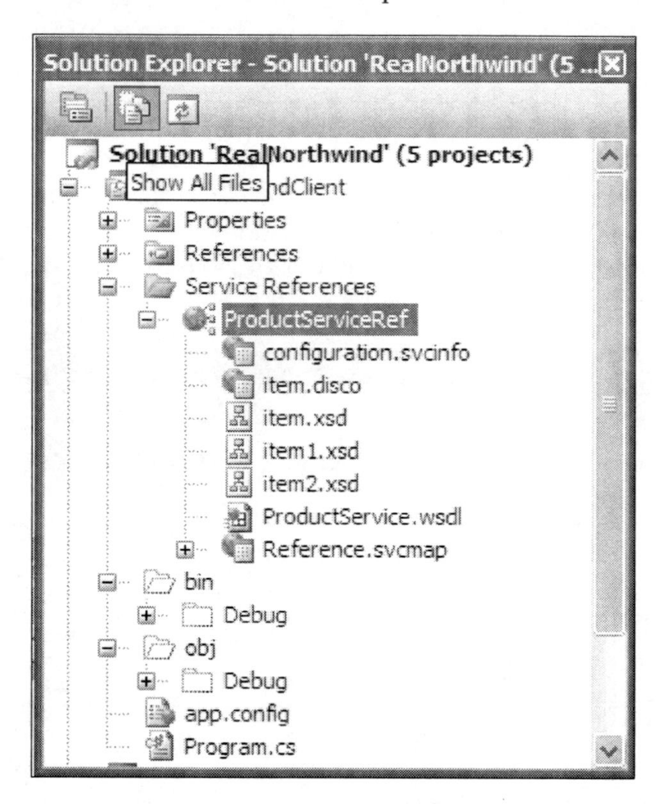

A new file, `App.config`, is also added to the project, as well as several WCF-related references such as `System.ServiceModel` and `System.Runtime.Serialization`.

At this point, the proxy code to connect to the WCF service and the required configuration file have both been created and added to the project for us, without us having to enter a single line of code. What we need to do next is to write just a few lines of code to call this service.

Just as we did earlier, we will modify `Program.cs` to call the WCF service.

1. First, open `Program.cs` file, and add the following `using` line to the file:

   ```
   using RealNorthwindClient.ProductServiceRef;
   ```

2. Then, inside the `Main` method, add the following line of code to create a client object:

   ```
   ProductServiceClient client = new ProductServiceClient();
   ```

3. Finally, add the following lines to the file, to call the WCF service to get and update a product:

   ```
   Product product = client.GetProduct(23);
   product.UnitPrice = (decimal)20.0;
   bool result = client.UpdateProduct(product);
   ```

The content of the `Program.cs` file is:

```
using System;
using System.Collections.Generic;
using System.Linq;
using System.Text;
using RealNorthwindClient.ProductServiceRef;

namespace RealNorthwindClient
{
    class Program
    {
        static void Main(string[] args)
        {
            ProductServiceClient client = new ProductServiceClient();

            Product product = client.GetProduct(23);
            Console.WriteLine("product name is " +
                              product.ProductName);
            Console.WriteLine("product price is " +
                      product.UnitPrice.ToString());

            product.UnitPrice = (decimal)20.0;
            bool result = client.UpdateProduct(product);
            Console.WriteLine("Update result is " +
                                 result.ToString());
        }
    }
}
```

Now you can run the client application to test the service. Remember that you need to set `RealNorthwindClient` to be the startup project before pressing *F5* or *Ctrl+F5*.

If you want to start it in debugging mode (*F5*), you need to add a `Console.ReadLine();` statement to the end of the program, so that you can see the output of the program. The WCF Service Host application will be started automatically before the client is started (but the WCF Test Client won't be started).

If you want to start the client application in non-debugging mode (*Ctrl+F5*), you need to start the WCF Service Host application (and the WCF Test Client application) in advance. You can start it from another Visual Studio IDE instance, or you can set the `RealNorthwindService` as the startup project, start it in the non-debugging mode (*Ctrl+F5*), leave it running, and then change `RealNorthwindClient` to be the startup project, and start it in non-debugging mode. Also, you can set the solution to start with multiple projects with the `RealNorthwindService` as the first project to be run, and `RealNorthwindClient` as the second project to be run.

The output of this client program is as shown in the following figure:

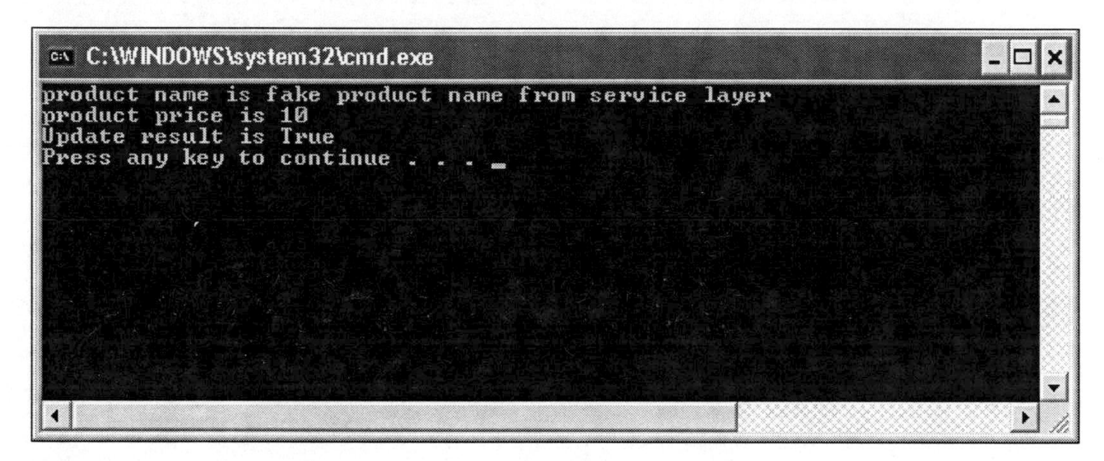

Adding a business logic layer

Until now, the web service has contained only one layer. In this section, we will add a business logic layer, and define some business rules in this layer.

Adding the product entity project

Before we add the business logic layer, we need to add a project for business entities. The business entities project will hold of all business entity object definitions such as products, customers, and orders. These entities will be used across the business logic layer, the data access layer and the service layer. They will be very similar to the data contracts we defined in the previous section, but will not be seen outside of the service. The Product entity will have the same properties as the product contract data, plus some extra properties such as `UnitsInStock` and `ReorderLevel`. These properties will be used internally, and shared by all layers of the service. For example, when an order is placed, the `UnitsInStock` should be updated as well. Also, if the updated `UnitsInStock` is less than the `ReorderLevel`, an event should be raised to trigger the re-ordering process.

The business entities by themselves do not act as a layer. They are just pure C# classes representing internal data within the service implementations. There is no logic inside these entities. Also, in our example these entities are very similar to the data contracts (with only two extra fields in the entity class), but in reality the entity classes could be very different from the data contracts, from property names and property types, to data structures.

As with the data contracts, the business entities' classes should be in their own assembly. So, we first need to create a project for them. Just add a new C# class library, `RealNorthwindEntities`, to the Solution. Then, rename the `Class1.cs` to `ProductEntity.cs`, and modify it as follows:

1. Change its namespace from `RealNorthwindEntities` to `MyWCFServices.RealNorthwindEntities`
2. Change the class name from `Class1` to `ProductEntity`, if it hasn't been changed already
3. Add the following properties to this class:

   `ProductID, ProductName, QuantityPerUnit, UnitPrice, Discontinued, UnitsInStock, UnitsOnOrder, ReorderLevel`

Five of the above properties are also in the `Product` service data contract. The last three properties are for use inside the service implementations. Actually, we will use `UnitsOnOrder` to trigger business logic when updating a product, and update `UnitsInStock` and `ReorderLevel` to trigger business logic when saving an order (inside this book, we will not create a service for saving an order, but we assume that this is a required operation and will be implemented later).

The following is the code list of the `ProductEntity` class:

```
using System;
using System.Collections.Generic;
using System.Linq;
using System.Text;
namespace MyWCFServices.RealNorthwindEntities
{
    public class ProductEntity
    {
            public int ProductID { get; set; }
            public string ProductName { get; set; }
            public string QuantityPerUnit { get; set; }
            public decimal UnitPrice { get; set; }
            public int UnitsInStock { get; set; }
            public int ReorderLevel { get; set; }
            public int UnitsOnOrder { get; set; }
            public bool Discontinued { get; set; }
    }
}
```

Adding the business logic project

Next, let us create the business logic layer project. Again, we just need to add a new C# class library project, `RealNorthwindLogic`, to the solution. So, rename the `Class1.cs` to `ProductLogic.cs`, and then modify it as follows:

1. Change its namespace from `RealNorthwindLogic` to `MyWCFServices.RealNorthwindLogic`
2. Change the class name from `Class1` to `ProductLogic`, if it hasn't been changed
3. Add a reference to the project `RealNorthwindEntities`, as shown in the following **Add Reference** image:

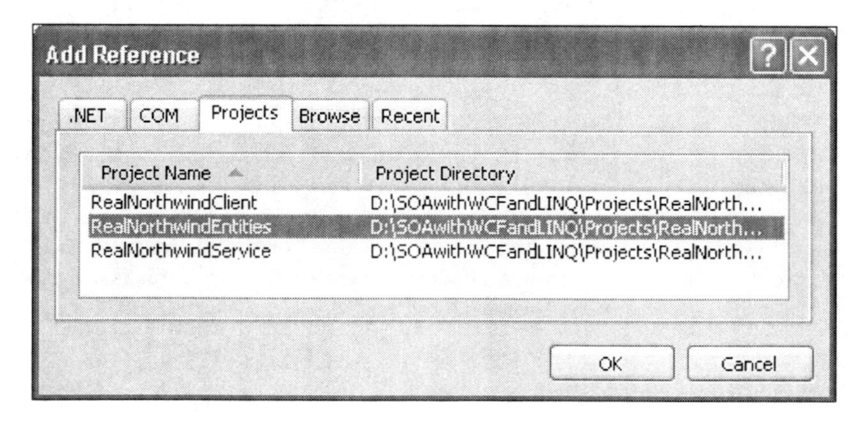

Now, we need to add some code to the `ProductLogic` class.

1. Add the following `using` line:

   ```
   using MyWCFServices.RealNorthwindEntities;
   ```

2. Add the method `GetProduct`. It should look like this:

   ```
   public ProductEntity GetProduct(int id)
   {
       // TODO: call data access layer to retrieve product
       ProductEntity p = new ProductEntity();
       p.ProductID = id;
       p.ProductName = "fake product name from business logic layer";
       p.UnitPrice = (decimal)20.00;
       return p;
   }
   ```

   In this method, we create a `ProductEntity` object, assign values to some of its properties, and return it to the caller. Everything is still hard-coded so far.

We hard code the product name as "fake product name from business logic layer", so that we know this is a different product from the one returned directly from the service layer.

3. Add the method `UpdateProduct`, as follows:

   ```
   public bool UpdateProduct(ProductEntity product)
   {
       // TODO: call data access layer to update product
       // first check to see if it is a valid price
       if (product.UnitPrice <= 0)
           return false;
       // ProductName can't be empty
       else if (product.ProductName == null || product.ProductName.
                                                       Length == 0)
           return false;
       // QuantityPerUnit can't be empty
       else if (product.QuantityPerUnit == null || product.
                               QuantityPerUnit.Length == 0)
           return false;
       // then validate other properties
       else
       {
   ```

```
            ProductEntity productInDB = GetProduct(product.ProductID);
            // invalid product to update
            if (productInDB == null)
                return false;
            // a product can't be discontinued if there are
                  non-fulfilled orders
            if (product.Discontinued == true && productInDB.
                  UnitsOnOrder > 0)
                return false;
            else
                return true;
        }
    }
```

4. Add test logic to the `GetProduct` method

   We still haven't updated anything in a database, but this time, we have added several pieces of logic to the `UpdateProduct` method. First, we check the validity of the `UnitPrice` property, and return `false` if it is not a valid one. We then check the product name and quantity per unit properties, to make sure they are not empty. We then try to retrieve the product, to see if it is a valid product to update. We also added a check to make sure that a supplier can't discontinue a product if there are unfulfilled orders for this product. However, at this stage, we can't truly enforce this logic, because when we check the `UnitsOnOrder` property of a product, it is always 0 as we didn't assign a value to it in the `GetProduct` method. For test purposes, we can change the `GetProduct` method to include the following line of code:

   ```
   if(id > 50) p.UnitsOnOrder = 30;
   ```

   Now, when we test the service, we can select a product with an ID that is greater than 50, and try to update its `Discontinued` property to see what result we will get.

After you put all of this together, the content of the `ProductLogic.cs` file should be as follows:

```
using System;
using System.Collections.Generic;
using System.Linq;
using System.Text;
using MyWCFServices.RealNorthwindEntities;
using MyWCFServices.RealNorthwindDAL;

namespace MyWCFServices.RealNorthwindLogic
{
    public class ProductLogic
    {
```

```
        public ProductEntity GetProduct(int id)
        {
            // TODO: call data access layer to retrieve product
            ProductEntity p = new ProductEntity();
            p.ProductID = id;
            p.ProductName =
                        "fake product name from business logic layer";
            //p.UnitPrice = (decimal)20.0;
            if(id > 50) p.UnitsOnOrder = 30;
            return p;
        }
        public bool UpdateProduct(ProductEntity product)
        {
            // TODO: call data access layer to update product
            // first check to see if it is a valid price
            if (product.UnitPrice <= 0)
                return false;
            // ProductName can't be empty
            else if (product.ProductName == null || product.
                                       ProductName.Length == 0)
                return false;
            // QuantityPerUnit can't be empty
            else if (product.QuantityPerUnit == null || product.
                                        QuantityPerUnit.Length == 0)
                return false;
            // then validate other properties
            else
            {
                ProductEntity productInDB =
                                        GetProduct(product.ProductID);
                // invalid product to update
                if (productInDB == null)
                    return false;
                // a product can't be discontinued if there are
                   non-fulfilled orders
                else if (product.Discontinued == true && productInDB.
                   UnitsOnOrder > 0)
                    return false;
                else
                    return true;
            }
        }
    }
}
```

Calling the business logic layer from the service interface layer

We now have the business logic layer ready, and can modify the service contracts to call this layer, so that we can enforce some business logic.

First, we want to make it very clear that we are going to change the service implementations, and not the interfaces. So we will only change the `ProductService.cs` file.

We will not touch the file `IProductService.cs`. All of the existing clients (if there are any) that are referencing our service will not notice that we are changing the implementation.

Follow these steps to customize the service interface layer:

1. Add a reference to the business logic layer.

   In order to call a method inside the business logic layer, we need to add a reference to the assembly that the business logic is included in. We will also use the `ProductEntity` class. So we need a reference to the `RealNorthwind-Entities` as well.

   To add a reference, from the Solution Explorer, right-click on the project **RealNorthwindService**, select **Add Reference ...** from the context menu, and select **RealNorthwindLogic** from the **Projects** tab. Also, select `RealNorth-windEntities` as we will need a reference to the `ProductEntity` inside it. Just hold down the *Ctrl* key while you are selecting multiple projects. Click the **OK** button to add references to the selected projects.

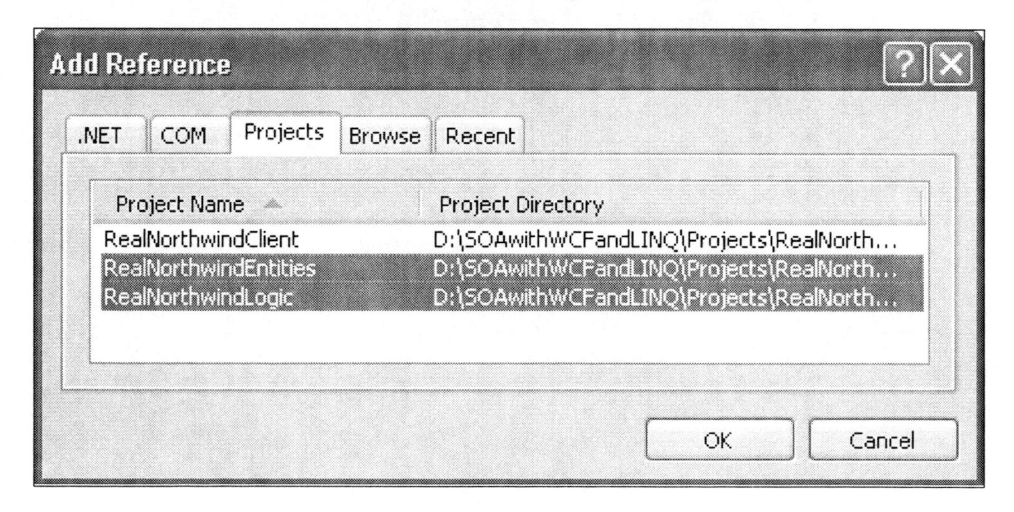

2. Now we have added two references. We can add the following two `using` statements to the `ProductService.cs` file so that we don't need to type the full names for their classes.

```
using MyWCFServices.RealNorthwindEntities;
using MyWCFServices.RealNorthwindLogic;
```

3. Now, inside the `GetProduct` method, we can use the following statements to get the product from our business logic layer:

```
ProductLogic productLogic = new ProductLogic();
ProductEntity product = productLogic.GetProduct(id);
```

4. However, we cannot return this product back to the caller, because this product is of the type `ProductEntity`, which is not the type that the caller is expecting. The caller is expecting a return value of the type `Product`, which is a data contract defined within the service interface. We need to translate this `ProductEntity` object to a `Product` object. To do this, we add the following new method to the `ProductService` class:

```
    private void TranslateProductEntityToProductContractData(
        ProductEntity productEntity,
        Product product)
    {
        product.ProductID = productEntity.ProductID;
        product.ProductName = productEntity.ProductName;
        product.QuantityPerUnit = productEntity.QuantityPerUnit;
        product.UnitPrice = productEntity.UnitPrice;
        product.Discontinued = productEntity.Discontinued;
    }
```

Inside this translation method, we copy all of the properties from the `ProductEntity` object to the service contract data object, but not the last three properties—`UnitsInStock`, `UnitsOnOrder`, and `ReorderLevel`. These three properties are used only inside the service implementations. Outside callers cannot see them at all.

The `GetProduct` method should now look like this:

```
public Product GetProduct(int id)
{
    ProductLogic productLogic = new ProductLogic();
    ProductEntity productEntity = productLogic.GetProduct(id);
    Product product = new Product();
    TranslateProductEntityToProductContractData
                        (productEntity, product);
    return product;
}
```

We can modify the `UpdateProduct` method in the same way, making it like this:

```
public bool UpdateProduct(Product product)
{
    ProductLogic productLogic = new ProductLogic();
    ProductEntity productEntity = new ProductEntity();
    TranslateProductContractDataToProductEntity(
                         product, productEntity);

    return productLogic.UpdateProduct(productEntity);
}
```

5. Note that we have to create a new method to translate a product contract data object to a `ProductEntity` object. In translation, we leave the three extra properties unassigned in the `ProductEntity` object, because we know a supplier won't update these properties. Also, we have to create a `ProductLogic` variable in both the methods, so that we can make it a class member:

   ```
   ProductLogic productLogic = new ProductLogic();
   ```

The final content of the `ProductService.cs` file is as follows:

```
using System;
using System.Collections.Generic;
using System.Linq;
using System.Runtime.Serialization;
using System.ServiceModel;
using System.Text;
using MyWCFServices.RealNorthwindEntities;
using MyWCFServices.RealNorthwindLogic;

namespace MyWCFServices.RealNorthwindService
{
    // NOTE: If you change the class name "Service1" here, you must
       also update the reference to "Service1" in App.config.
    public class ProductService : IProductService
    {
        ProductLogic productLogic = new ProductLogic();

        public Product GetProduct(int id)
        {
            /*
            // TODO: call business logic layer to retrieve product
            Product product = new Product();
            product.ProductID = id;
```

```
            product.ProductName =
                            "fake product name from service layer";
            product.UnitPrice = (decimal)10.0;
            */
            ProductEntity productEntity = productLogic.GetProduct(id);
            Product product = new Product();
            TranslateProductEntityToProductContractData(
                            productEntity, product);
            return product;
        }
        public bool UpdateProduct(Product product)
        {
            /*
            // TODO: call business logic layer to update product
            if (product.UnitPrice <= 0)
                return false;
            else
                return true;
            */
            ProductEntity productEntity = new ProductEntity();
            TranslateProductContractDataToProductEntity(
                            product, productEntity);
            return productLogic.UpdateProduct(productEntity);
        }
        private void TranslateProductEntityToProductContractData(
            ProductEntity productEntity,
            Product product)
        {
            product.ProductID = productEntity.ProductID;
            product.ProductName = productEntity.ProductName;
            product.QuantityPerUnit = productEntity.QuantityPerUnit;
            product.UnitPrice = productEntity.UnitPrice;
            product.Discontinued = productEntity.Discontinued;
        }
        private void TranslateProductContractDataToProductEntity(
            Product product,
            ProductEntity productEntity)
        {
            productEntity.ProductID = product.ProductID;
            productEntity.ProductName = product.ProductName;
            productEntity.QuantityPerUnit = product.QuantityPerUnit;
            productEntity.UnitPrice = product.UnitPrice;
            productEntity.Discontinued = product.Discontinued;
        }
    }
}
```

Testing the WCF service with a business logic layer

We can now compile and test the new service with a business logic layer. We will use the WCF Test Client to simplify the process.

1. Make the project `RealNorthwindService` the startup project
2. Start the WCF Service Host application and WCF Service Test Client, by pressing *F5* or *Ctrl+F5*
3. In the WCF Service Test Client, double-click on the `GetProduct` operation, to bring up the `GetProduct` test screen
4. Enter a value of 56 for the ID field and then click the **Invoke** button

   You will see that this time the product is returned from the business logic layer, instead of the service layer. Also, note that the `UnitsOnOrder` property is not displayed as it is not part of the service contract data type. However, we know that a product has a property `UnitsOnOrder`, and we will actually use this for our next test.

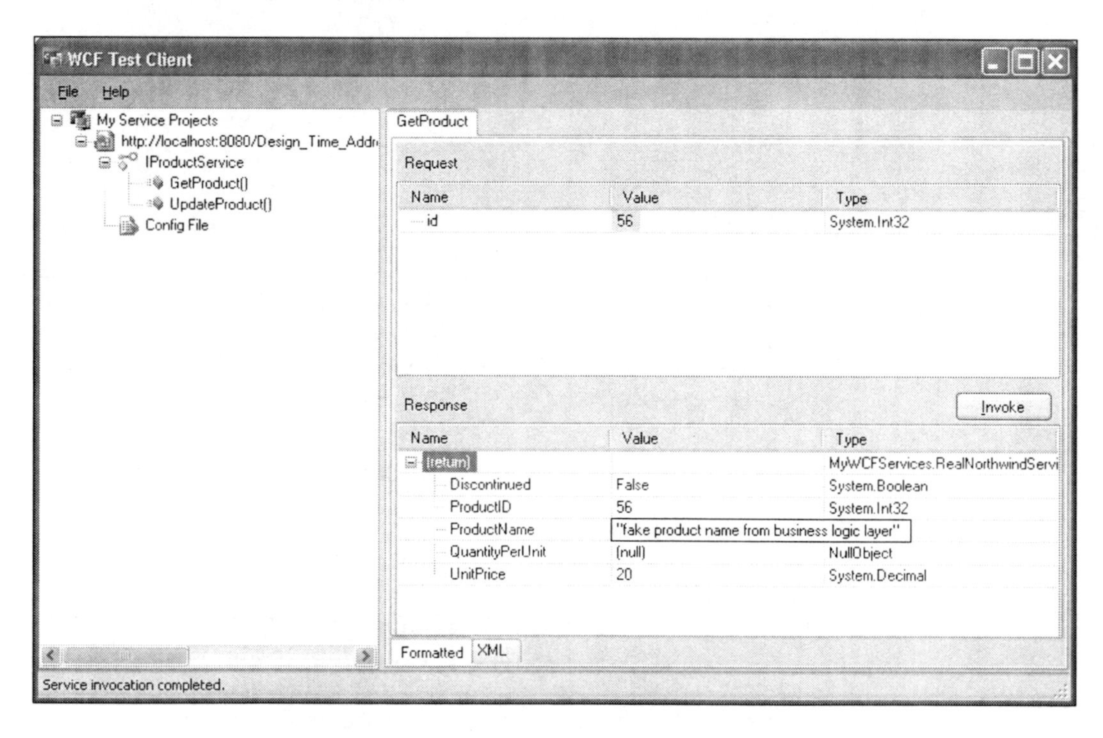

Now, let us try to update a product.

1. In the WCF Service Test Client, double-click on the `UpdateProduct` operation to bring up the `UpdateProduct` test screen.
2. Enter **-10** as the price, and click the **Invoke** button. You will see that the **Response** result is **False**.
3. Enter a valid price, say **25.60**, a name, and a quantity per unit, leave the **Discontinued** property set to `False`, and then click the **Invoke** button. You will see that the **Response** result is now **True**.
4. Change the **Discontinued** value from `False` to `True`, and click the **Invoke** button again. The **Response** result is still **True**. This is because we didn't change the product ID, and it has defaulted to 0.
5. Change the product ID to **51**, leave the **Discontinued** value as **True** and product price as **25.60**, and click the **Invoke** button again. This time, you will see that the **Response** result is **False**. This is because the business logic layer has checked the `UnitsOnOrder` and `Discontinued` properties, and didn't allow us to make the update.

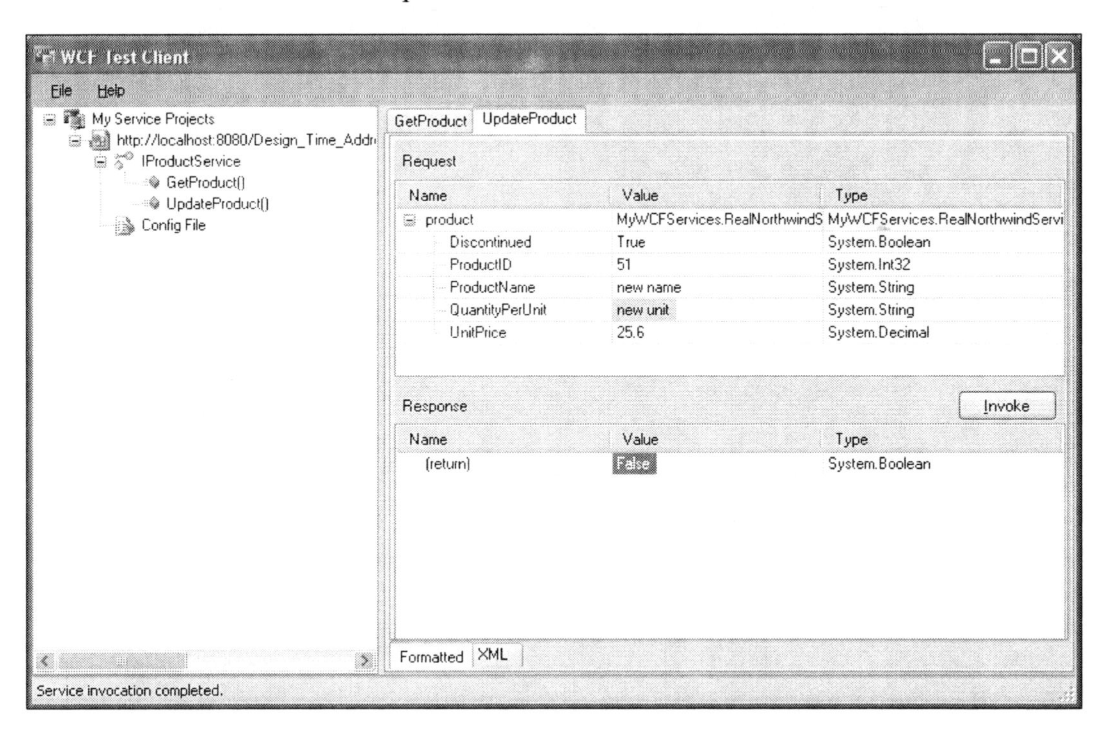

Summary

In this chapter, we have created a real world WCF service that has a service contract layer, and a business logic layer. The key points in this chapter include:

- WCF Services should have explicit boundaries
- The WCF Service Application template can be used to create WCF services with a hosting web site created within the project
- The WCF Service Library template can be used to create WCF services that will be hosted by the WCF Service Host, and these can be tested using the WCF service Test Client
- The service interface layer should contain only the service contracts, such as the operation contracts, and data contracts
- The business logic layer should contain the implementation of the service
- The business entities represent the internal data of the service shared by all of the layers of the service, and they should not be exposed to the clients

6

Adding Database Support and Exception Handling to the RealNorthwind WCF Service

In the previous chapter, we created a WCF service with two layers. We didn't add the third layer, that is, the data access layer. Therefore, all of the service operations just returned a fake result from the business logic layer.

In this chapter, we will add the third layer to the WCF service. We will also introduce message contracts for service message exchange and fault contracts for service error handling.

We will accomplish the following tasks in this chapter:

- Create the data access layer project
- Modify the business logic layer to call the data access layer
- Prepare the Northwind database for the service
- Connect the WCF service to the Northwind database
- Test the service with the data access layer
- Add a fault contract to the service
- Throw a fault contract exception to the client
- Catch the fault contract in the client program
- Test the service fault contract

Adding a data access layer

Now, we have two layers in our solution. We need to add one more layer—the data access layer. We need to query a real database to get the product information, and update the database for a given product.

Creating the data access layer project

First, we will create the project for the data access layer. As we did for the business logic layer, what we need to do is add a C# class library project, named `RealNorthwindDAL`, where DAL stands for Data Access Layer, to the solution. Then, rename the `Class1.cs` to `ProductDAL.cs`, and modify it as follows:

1. Change its namespace from `RealNorthwindDAL` to `MyWCFServices.RealNorthwindDAL`.
2. Change the class name from `Class1` to `ProductDAL`, if it hasn't been changed already.
3. Add a reference to project `RealNorthwindEntities`.

Now, let's modify `ProductDAL.cs` for our product service:

1. Add the following `using` statement:

   ```
   using MyWCFServices.RealNorthwindEntities;
   ```

2. Add two new methods to the `ProductDAL` class. The first method is `GetProduct`, which will be as follows:

   ```
   public ProductEntity GetProduct(int id)
   {
       // TODO: connect to DB to retrieve product
       ProductEntity p = new ProductEntity();
       p.ProductID = id;
       p.ProductName = "fake product name from data access layer";
       p.UnitPrice = (decimal)30.00;
       return p;
   }
   ```

   In this method, all the product information is still hard coded, though we have changed the product name to be specific to the data access layer. We will soon modify this method to retrieve the actual product information from a real Northwind database.

3. The second method is `UpdateProduct`, which will be as follows:

   ```
   public bool UpdateProduct(ProductEntity product)
   {
       // TODO: connect to DB to update product
       return true;
   }
   ```

Again, we didn't update any database in this method. We will also modify this method soon to update to the real Northwind database.

The content of the `ProductDAL.cs` file should now be as follows:

```
using System;
using System.Collections.Generic;
using System.Linq;
using System.Text;
using MyWCFServices.RealNorthwindEntities;
namespace MyWCFServices.RealNorthwindDAL
{
    public class ProductDAL
    {
        public ProductEntity GetProduct(int id)
        {
            // TODO: connect to DB to retrieve product
            ProductEntity p = new ProductEntity();
            p.ProductID = id;
            p.ProductName = "fake product name from data access layer";
            p.UnitPrice = (decimal)30.00;
            if (id > 50) p.UnitsOnOrder = 30;
            return p;
        }
        public bool UpdateProduct(ProductEntity product)
        {
            // TODO: connect to DB to update product
            return true;
        }
    }
}
```

Calling the data access layer from the business logic layer

Before we modify these two methods to interact with a real database, we will first modify the business logic layer to call them, so that we know that the three-layer framework is working.

1. Add a reference of this new layer to the business logic layer project. From the Solution Explorer, just right-click on the **RealNorthwindLogic** project item, select **Add Reference ...** from the context menu, select **RealNorthwindDAL** from the **Projects** tab, and then click the **OK** button.
2. Open the `ProductLogic.cs` file under the `RealNorthwindLogic` project, and add a `using` statement:
   ```
   using MyWCFServices.RealNorthwindDAL;
   ```
3. Add a new class member:
   ```
   ProductDAL productDAL = new ProductDAL();
   ```
4. Modify the method `GetProduct` to contain only this line:
   ```
   return productDAL.GetProduct(id);
   ```
   We will use the data access layer to retrieve the product information. At this point, we will not add any business logic to this method.
5. Modify the method `UpdateProduct` to look like this:
   ```
   public bool UpdateProduct(ProductEntity product)
   {
       // TODO: call data access layer to update product
       // first check to see if it is a valid price
       if (product.UnitPrice <= 0)
           return false;
       // ProductName can't be empty
       else if (product.ProductName.Length == 0)
           return false;
       // QuantityPerUnit can't be empty
       else if (product.QuantityPerUnit.Length == 0)
           return false;
       // then validate other properties
       else
       {
           ProductEntity productInDB = GetProduct(product.ProductID);
           // invalid product to update
           if (productInDB == null)
               return false;
   ```

```
            // a product can't be discontinued if there are non-
                                                fulfilled orders
            if (product.Discontinued == true && productInDB.
                                         UnitsOnOrder > 0)
                return false;
            else
                return productDAL.UpdateProduct(product);
        }
    }
```

In this method, we have replaced the last `return` statement to call the data access layer method `UpdateProduct`. This means that all of the business logic is still enclosed in the business logic layer, and the data access layer should be used only to update the product in the database.

Here is the full content of the `ProductLogic.cs` file:

```
using System;
using System.Collections.Generic;
using System.Linq;
using System.Text;
using MyWCFServices.RealNorthwindEntities;
using MyWCFServices.RealNorthwindDAL;
namespace MyWCFServices.RealNorthwindLogic
{
    public class ProductLogic
    {
        ProductDAL productDAL = new ProductDAL();
        public ProductEntity GetProduct(int id)
        {
            /*
            // TODO: call data access layer to retrieve product
            ProductEntity p = new ProductEntity();
            p.ProductID = id;
            p.ProductName =
                        "fake product name from business logic layer";
            //p.UnitPrice = (decimal)20.0;
            if(id > 50) p.UnitsOnOrder = 30;
            return p;
            */
            return productDAL.GetProduct(id);
        }
        public bool UpdateProduct(ProductEntity product)
        {
            // TODO: call data access layer to update product
            // first check to see if it is a valid price
            if (product.UnitPrice <= 0)
                return false;
            // ProductName can't be empty
```

```
            else if (product.ProductName == null || product.
                                    ProductName.Length == 0)
                return false;
            // QuantityPerUnit can't be empty
            else if (product.QuantityPerUnit == null || product.
                                    QuantityPerUnit.Length == 0)
                return false;
            // then validate other properties
            else
            {
                ProductEntity productInDB =
                   GetProduct(product.ProductID);
                // invalid product to update
                if (productInDB == null)
                    return false;
                // a product can't be discontinued if there
                                  are non-fulfilled orders
                else if (product.Discontinued ==
                                 true && productInDB.UnitsOnOrder > 0)
                    return false;
                else
                    return productDAL.UpdateProduct(product);
            }
        }
    }
}
```

If you run the program and test it using the WCF Test Client, you will get exactly the same result as before, although now it is a three layer application, and you will see a different, although obviously still fake product name.

Preparing the database

As we have had the three-layer framework ready, we will now implement the data access layer to actually communicate with a real database.

In this book, we will use the Microsoft sample database, **Northwind**. This database is not installed by default in SQL Server 2005 or SQL Server 2008.

1. Download the database package. Just search for "Northwind Sample Databases" on the Internet, or go to this page:

   `http://www.microsoft.com/downloads/details.aspx?FamilyId=06616212-0356-46A0-8DA2-EEBC53A68034&displaylang=en`

   and download file `SQL2000SampleDb.msi`.

2. Install (extract) it to: `C:\SQL Server 2000 Sample Databases`.
3. Open SQL Server 2005/2008 Management Studio.
4. Connect to your database engine.
5. Right click on the **Databases** node, and select **Attach...** from the context menu, as shown in the SQL Server Management Studio diagram below:

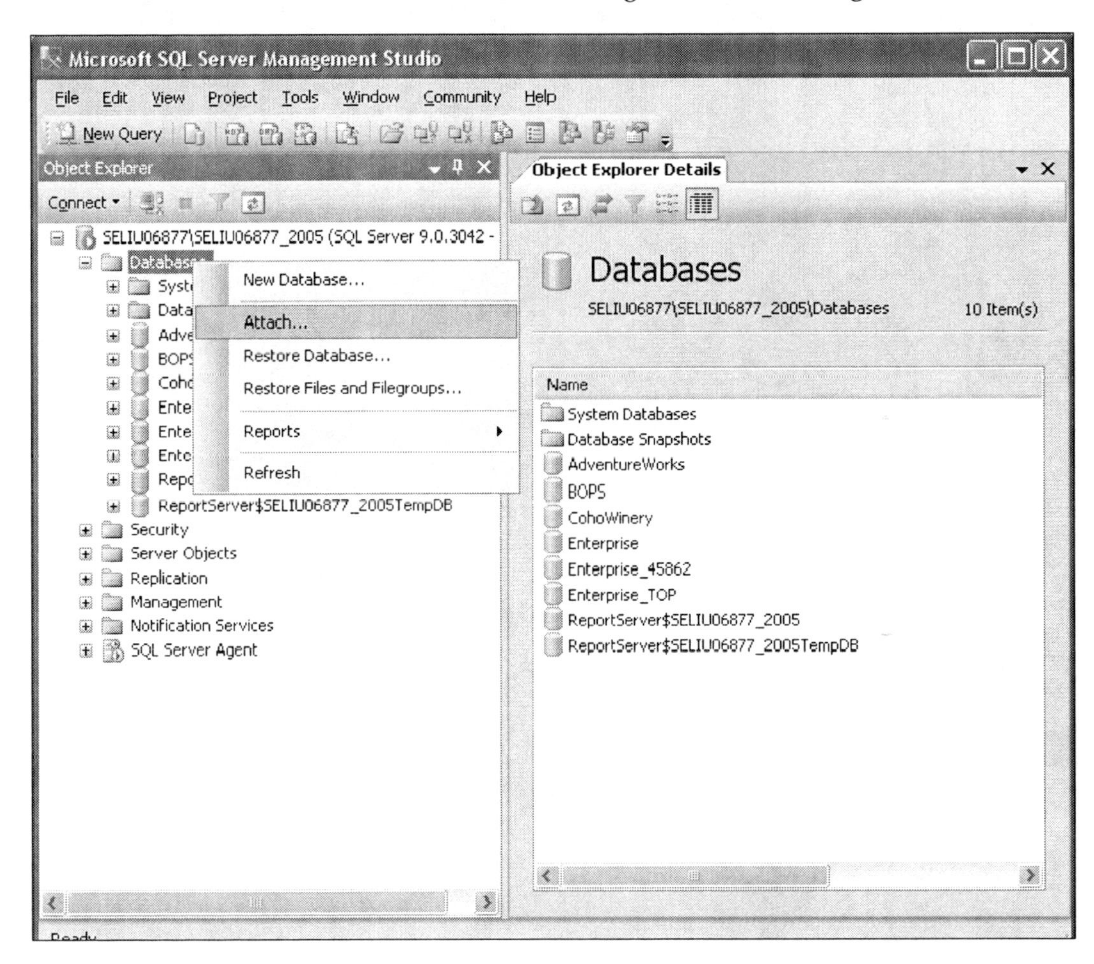

6. In the pop-up **Attach Databases** dialog box, click **Add**, browse to the file **C:\SQL Server 2000 Sample Databases\NORTHWND.MDF**, click **OK**, and you now have the Northwind database attached to your SQL Server 2005 or 2008 engine.

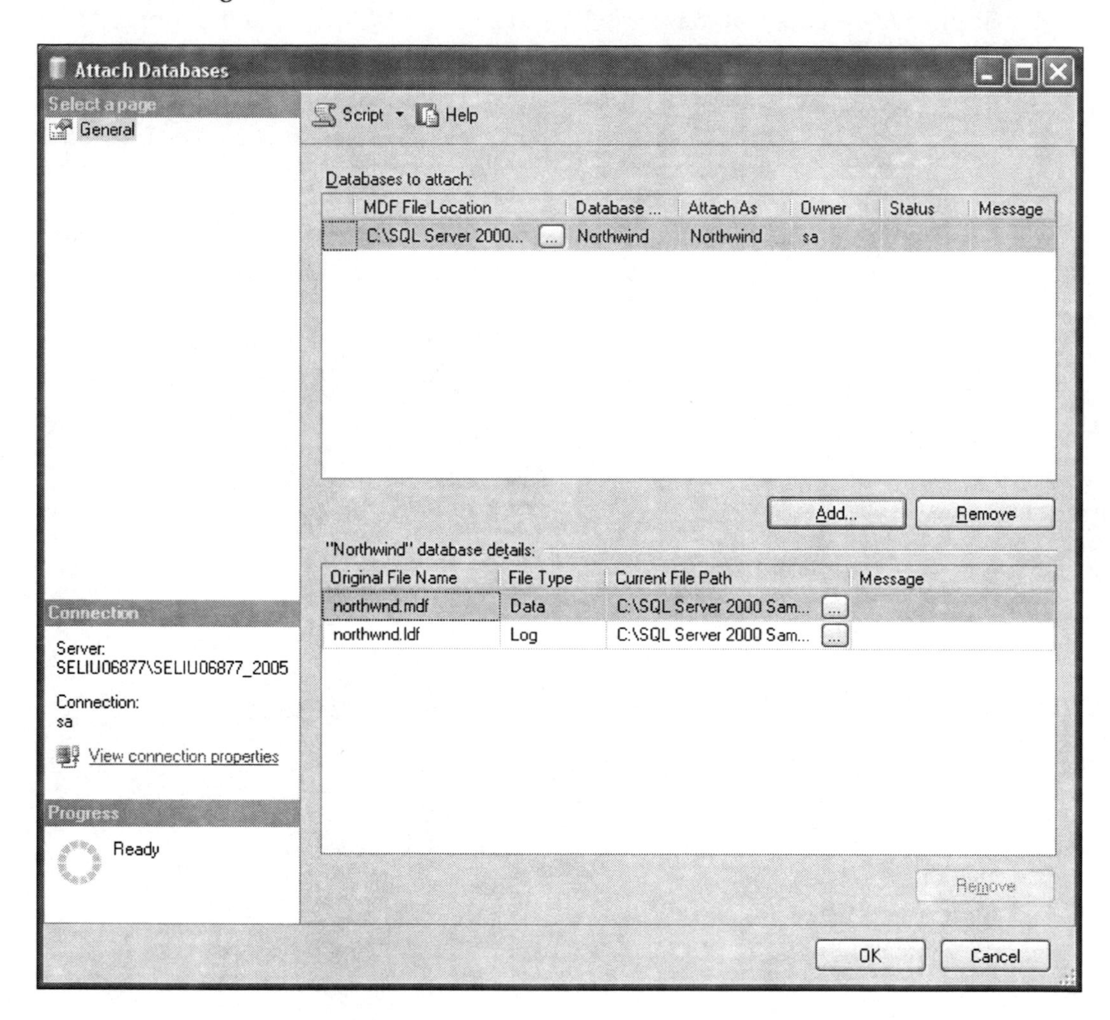

Adding the connection string to the configuration file

Now that we have the Northwind database attached, we will modify our data access layer to use this actual database. At this point, we will use a raw `SqlClient` adapter to do the database work. We will replace this layer with LINQ to SQL in a later chapter.

Before we start coding, we need to finish the following tasks, to add a connection string to the configuration file. We don't want to hard-code the connection string in our project. Instead, we will set it in the `App.config` file, so that it can be changed on the fly.

1. Add a reference to `System.Configuration` to the `RealNorthwindDAL` project. We will store connection string in the configuration file, and we need this assembly to read it.
2. Add the following configuration settings to the `App.config` file under the `RealNorthwindService` project.

```
<appSettings>
  <add key="NorthwindConnectionString"
       value="server=your_db_server\your_db_instance;
       uid=your_user_name; pwd=your_password;
       database=Northwind"/>
</appSettings>
```

   There are a couple of things to note for this new key in the configuration file.

   - It should be added to the `App.config` file in the `RealNorthwindService` project, not to the `RealNorthwindDAL` project. Actually, there is no file called `App.config` in the `RealNorthwindDAL` project.
   - The node `appSettings` should be a child node of the root `configuration` node, that is, the highlighted lines should be placed immediately after the line `<configuration>`. So, the first few lines of the `App.config` file should be as follows (highlighted lines are new lines to add):

```
<?xml version="1.0" encoding="utf-8" ?>
<configuration>
<appSettings>
  <add key="NorthwindConnectionString"
       value="server=your_db_server\your_db_instance;
       uid=your_user_name; pwd=your_password;
       database=Northwind"/>
</appSettings>
  <system.web>
    <compilation debug="true" />
  </system.web>
```

3. Replace `your_db_server` with your actual database server name. If the database is located on your own machine, you can use `local` as the db server name.

4. Replace `your_db_instance` with your database's instance name. If you have installed your SQL server with the default instance, don't put anything here.
5. Replace `your_user_name` and `your_password` with your actual logon and password to the SQL server database. This user must have write access to the Northwind database.
6. If you use `sa` to log in to your database, make sure that in your database, the user `sa` is enabled for login. Some installation may have automatically disabled `sa` from logging on to the database (use **SQL Server Management Studio | Login Properties - sa | status | Permission** to connect to database engine and login).
7. If you don't have an SQL Server logon, or you just want to use Windows authentication, you can use trusted connection, or SSPI integrated security connection. The key for the trusted connection will be:

    ```
    <add key="NorthwindConnectionString" value="server= your_db_
    server\your_db_instance;database=Northwind;
    Trusted_Connection=yes" />
    ```

    The key for the integrated security connection will be:

    ```
    <add key="NorthwindConnectionString" value="server= your_
    db_server\your_db_instance;database=Northwind;Integrated
    Security=SSPI" />
    ```

Querying the database (GetProduct)

Because we have added the connection string as a new key to the configuration file, we need to retrieve this key in the DAL class, so that we can use it when we want to connect to the database. Follow these steps to get and use this new key from within the DAL class:

1. Open the file `ProductDAL.cs` in the `RealNorthwindDAL` project, and first add two `using` statements:

    ```
    using System.Data.SqlClient;
    using System.Configuration;
    ```

2. Add a new class member to the `ProductDAL` class:

    ```
    string connectionString = ConfigurationManager.AppSettings["Northw
    indConnectionString"];
    ```

    We will use this connection string to connect to the Northwind database, for both the `GetProduct` and `UpdateProduct` methods.

3. Modify the `GetProduct` method to get the product from the database, as follows:

```
public ProductEntity GetProduct(int id)
{
    /*
    // TODO: connect to DB to retrieve product
    ProductEntity p = new ProductEntity();
    p.ProductID = id;
    p.ProductName = "fake product name from data access layer";
    p.UnitPrice = (decimal)30.00;
    if (id > 50) p.UnitsOnOrder = 30;
    return p;
    */

    ProductEntity p = null;
    using (SqlConnection conn =
                            new SqlConnection(connectionString))
    {
        SqlCommand comm = new SqlCommand();
        comm.CommandText =
                "select * from Products where ProductID=" + id;
        comm.Connection = conn;
        conn.Open();
        SqlDataReader reader = comm.ExecuteReader();
        if (reader.HasRows)
        {
            reader.Read();
            p = new ProductEntity();
            p.ProductID = id;
            p.ProductName =
                (string)reader["ProductName"];
            p.QuantityPerUnit =
                (string)reader["QuantityPerUnit"];
            p.UnitPrice =
                (decimal)reader["UnitPrice"];
            p.UnitsInStock =
                (short)reader["UnitsInStock"];
            p.UnitsOnOrder =
                (short)reader["UnitsOnOrder"];
            p.ReorderLevel =
                (short)reader["ReorderLevel"];
            p.Discontinued =
                (bool)reader["Discontinued"];
        }
    }
    return p;
}
```

In this method, we first create an `SqlConnection` to the Northwind database, and then issue an SQL query to get product details for the ID.

The following statement is a new feature of C# 3.0, and equivalent to the traditional `try...catch...finally...` mechanism to deal with `SqlConnection` matters:

```
using (SqlConnection conn = new SqlConnection(connectionString))
```

Testing the GetProduct method

If you now set the `RealNorthwindService` as the startup project and run the application, you can get the actual product information from the database, as seen in the following screenshot:

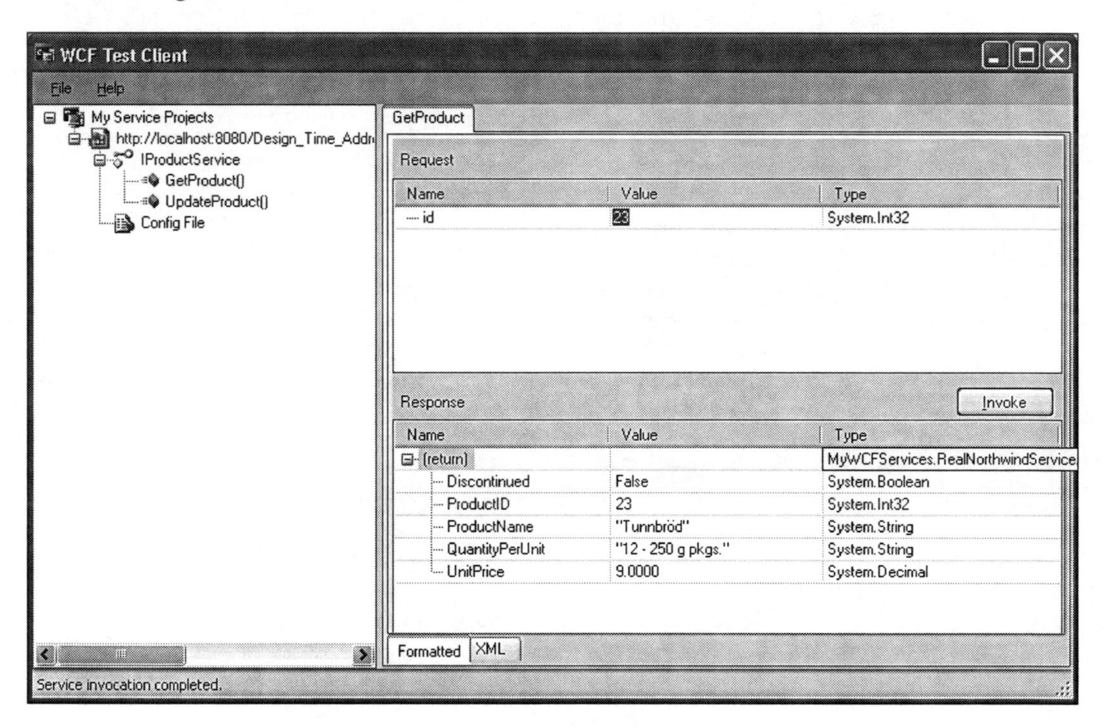

If you get an error screen, it is probably because you have set your connection string incorrectly. Double-check the new `appSettings` key in your `App.config` file, and try again until you can connect to your database.

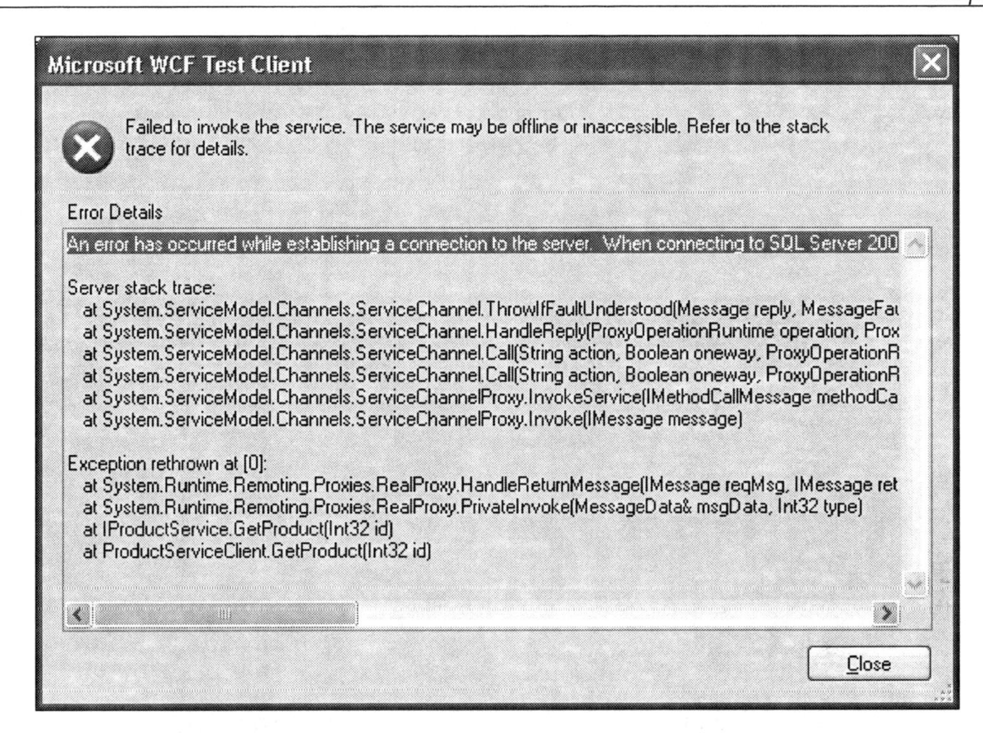

Instead of the connection error message, you might see the following error message:

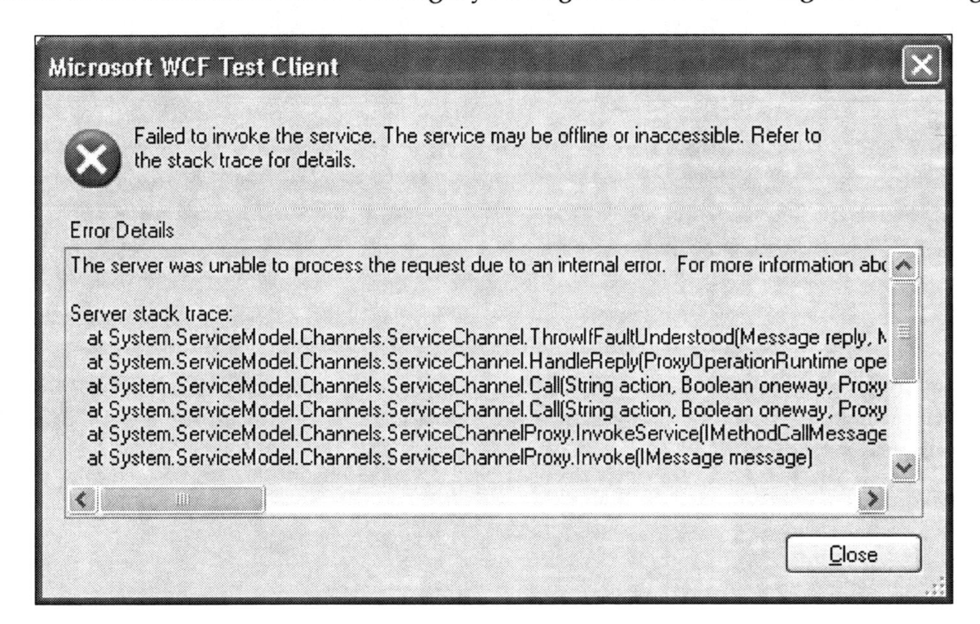

This error will happen when you try to get the product information for a product with a product ID of 0. The error message doesn't give much detail about what went wrong here, because we didn't let the server reveal the details of any error. Let's follow the instructions in the error message to change the setting `IncludeExceptionDetailInFaults` to `True` in the `App.config` file, and run it again. Now you will see that the error detail has changed to "**Object reference not set to an instance of an object**."

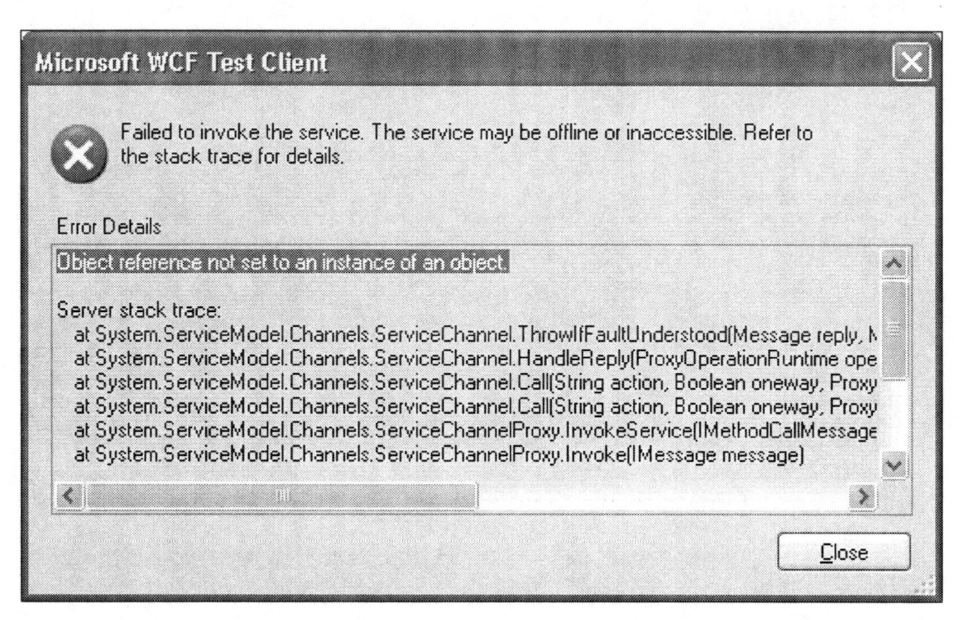

A little investigation will tell us that this is a bug in our `ProductService` class. Inside the `ProductService GetProduct` method, after we call business logic layer to get the product detail for an ID, we will get a null product if the ID is not in the database. When we pass this null object to the next method (`TranslateProductEntityToProductContractData`), we get the above error message. Actually, this will happen whenever you enter a product ID outside of the range 1-77. This is because, in the sample Northwind database, there are only 77 products, with product IDs ranging from 1 to 77. To fix this problem, we can add the following statement inside the `GetProduct` method right, immediately after the call to the business logic layer:

```
if (productEntity == null)
    throw new Exception("No product found with id " + id);
```

So in the `ProductService.cs` file, the `GetProduct` method will now be:

```
public Product GetProduct(int id)
{
    ProductLogic productLogic = new ProductLogic();
    ProductEntity productEntity = productLogic.GetProduct(id);
    if (productEntity == null)
     throw new Exception("No product found with id " + id);
    Product product = new Product();
    TranslateProductEntityToProductContractData(productEntity,
product);
    return product;
}
```

For now, we will raise an exception if an invalid product ID is entered. Later, we will convert this exception to a `FaultContract`, so that the caller will know in advance that an error has occurred.

Now run the application again, and if you enter an invalid product ID, say 0, you will get an error message, "**No product found with id 0**". This is a much clearer than the previous "**Object reference not set to an instance of an object**" error message.

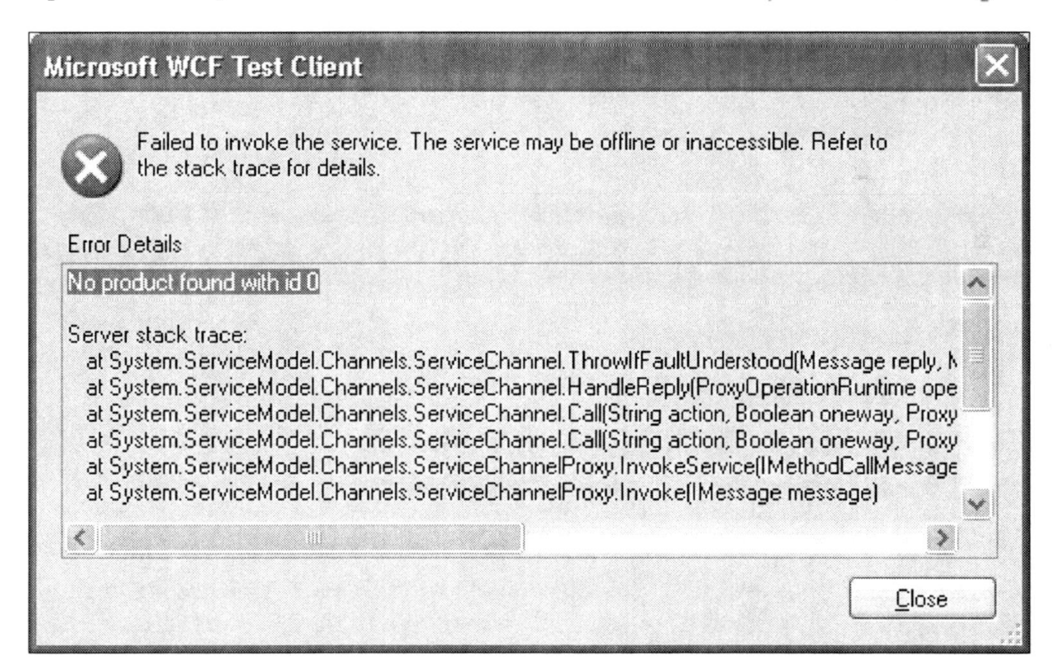

Updating the database (UpdateProduct)

Next, we will modify the `UpdateProduct` method to update the product record in the database. The `UpdateProduct` in the `RealNorthwindDAL` project should be modified as follows:

```
public bool UpdateProduct(ProductEntity product)
{
    using (SqlConnection conn = new SqlConnection(connectionString))
    {
        SqlCommand cmd = new SqlCommand("UPDATE products
          SET ProductName=@name,QuantityPerUnit=@unit,UnitPrice=@
          price,Discontinued=@discontinued WHERE ProductID=@id",conn);
        cmd.Parameters.AddWithValue("@name", product.ProductName);
        cmd.Parameters.AddWithValue("@unit", product.QuantityPerUnit);
        cmd.Parameters.AddWithValue("@price", product.UnitPrice);
        cmd.Parameters.AddWithValue("@discontinued", product.
                                                Discontinued);
        cmd.Parameters.AddWithValue("@id", product.ProductID);
        conn.Open();
        int numRows = comm.ExecuteNonQuery();
        if (numRows != 1)
            return false;
    }
    return true;
}
```

Inside this method, we have used parameters to specify arguments to the update command. This is a good practice because it will prevent SQL Injection attacks as the SQL statement is precompiled instead of being dynamically built.

We can follow these steps to test it:

1. Start the WCF Test Client
2. Double-click on the `UpdateProduct()` operation
3. Enter a valid product id, name, price and quantity per unit
4. Click on **Invoke**

You should get a `True` response. To prove it, just go to the `GetProduct`() page, enter the same product ID, click on **Invoke**, and you will see that all of your updates have been saved to the database.

The content of the `ProductDAL.cs` file is now:

```
using System;
using System.Collections.Generic;
using System.Linq;
using System.Text;
using MyWCFServices.RealNorthwindEntities;
using System.Data.SqlClient;
using System.Configuration;

namespace MyWCFServices.RealNorthwindDAL
{
    public class ProductDAL
    {
        string connectionString =
        ConfigurationManager.AppSettings["NorthwindConnectionString"];

        public ProductEntity GetProduct(int id)
        {
            /*
            // TODO: connect to DB to retrieve product
            ProductEntity p = new ProductEntity();
            p.ProductID = id;
            p.ProductName = "fake product name from data access layer";
            p.UnitPrice = (decimal)30.00;
            if (id > 50) p.UnitsOnOrder = 30;
            return p;
            */

            ProductEntity p = null;
            using (SqlConnection conn =
                    new SqlConnection(connectionString))
            {
                SqlCommand comm = new SqlCommand();
                comm.CommandText =
                        "select * from Products where ProductID=" + id;
                comm.Connection = conn;
                conn.Open();
                SqlDataReader reader = comm.ExecuteReader();
                if (reader.HasRows)
                {
                    reader.Read();
                    p = new ProductEntity();
                    p.ProductID = id;
                    p.ProductName =
                        (string)reader["ProductName"];
```

```
                    p.QuantityPerUnit =
                        (string)reader["QuantityPerUnit"];
                    p.UnitPrice =
                        (decimal)reader["UnitPrice"];
                    p.UnitsInStock =
                        (short)reader["UnitsInStock"];
                    p.UnitsOnOrder =
                        (short)reader["UnitsOnOrder"];
                    p.ReorderLevel =
                        (short)reader["ReorderLevel"];
                    p.Discontinued =
                        (bool)reader["Discontinued"];
                }
            }
            return p;
        }

        public bool UpdateProduct(ProductEntity product)
        {
            using (SqlConnection conn =
                    new SqlConnection(connectionString))
            {
                SqlCommand cmd = new SqlCommand("UPDATE products
                SET ProductName=@name,QuantityPerUnit=@
                unit,UnitPrice=@price,Discontinued=@discontinued WHERE
                ProductID=@id", conn);
                cmd.Parameters.AddWithValue("@name", product.
                                                ProductName);
                cmd.Parameters.AddWithValue("@unit", product.
                                            QuantityPerUnit);
                cmd.Parameters.AddWithValue(
                "@price", product.UnitPrice);
                cmd.Parameters.AddWithValue("@discontinued",
                                    product.Discontinued);
                cmd.Parameters.AddWithValue("@id", product.ProductID);
                conn.Open();
                int numRows = cmd.ExecuteNonQuery();
                if (numRows != 1)
                    return false;
            }
            return true;
        }
    }
}
```

Adding error handling to the service

In the previous sections, when we were trying to retrieve a product but the product ID passed in was not a valid one, we just threw an exception. Exceptions are technology-specific and, therefore, are not suitable for crossing the service boundary of SOA compliant services. All exceptions generate a fault on the communication channel, resulting in unhappy proxies, as a recover and retry is not possible. Thus, for WCF services, we should not throw normal exceptions.

What we need are SOAP faults that meet industry standards for seamless interoperability.

In the service interface layer, operations that may throw a `FaultExceptions` must be decorated with one or more `FaultContract` attributes, defining the exact `FaultException`.

On the other hand, the service consumer should catch specific `FaultExceptions` to be in a position to handle the specified exceptions.

Adding a fault contract

We will now change the exception in the `GetProduct` operation to a `FaultContract`.

But before we implement our first `FaultContract`, we need to modify the `App.config` file in the `RealNorthwindService` project. We will change the setting `includeExceptionDetailInFaults` back to `False`, so that every unhandled, non-Fault exception will be a violation. Client applications won't know the details of those exceptions.

You can definitely set `includeExceptionDetailInFaults` to `True` when debugging, as this will be very helpful in diagnosing problems during the development stage. But in production, it should always be set to `False`.

So, open the `App.config` file in the `RealNorthwindService` project, change `includeExceptionDetailInFaults` from `True` to `False`, and save it.

Next, we will define the `FaultContract`. For simplicity, we will define only one `FaultContract`, and leave it inside the file `IProductService.cs`, although in a real system you can have as many `Fault Contracts` as you want, and they should also normally be in their own files.

The `FaultContract` will be as follows:

```
[DataContract]
public class ProductFault
{
    public ProductFault(string msg)
    {
        FaultMessage = msg;
    }
    [DataMember]
    public string FaultMessage;
}
```

We then decorate the service operation `GetProduct` with the following attribute:

```
[FaultContract(typeof(ProductFault))]
```

This is to tell the service consumers that this operation may throw a fault of the type `ProductFault`.

The content of `IProductService.cs` should now be:

```
using System;
using System.Collections.Generic;
using System.Linq;
using System.Runtime.Serialization;
using System.ServiceModel;
using System.Text;
namespace MyWCFServices.RealNorthwindService
{
    // NOTE: If you change the interface name "IService1" here, you
       must also update the reference to "IService1" in App.config.
    [ServiceContract]
    public interface IProductService
    {
        [OperationContract]
        [FaultContract(typeof(ProductFault))]
        Product GetProduct(int id);
        [OperationContract]
        bool UpdateProduct(Product product);
        // TODO: Add your service operations here
    }
    [DataContract]
    public class Product
    {
        [DataMember]
        public int ProductID;
        [DataMember]
        public string ProductName;
```

```
            [DataMember]
            public string QuantityPerUnit;
            [DataMember]
            public decimal UnitPrice;
            [DataMember]
            public bool Discontinued;
        }
        [DataContract]
        public class ProductFault
        {
            public ProductFault(string msg)
            {
                FaultMessage = msg;
            }
            [DataMember]
            public string FaultMessage;
        }
    }
```

Throwing a fault exception

Once we have modified the interface, we need to modify the implementation. Open the `ProductService.cs` file, and change the following lines:

```
        if (productEntity == null)
            throw new Exception("No product found with id " + id);
```

to these lines:

```
        if (productEntity == null)
        {
            //throw new Exception("No product found with id " + id);
            if (id != 999)
                throw new FaultException<ProductFault>(new ProductFault(
                   "No product found with id " + id), "Product Fault");
            else
                throw new Exception("Test Exception");
        }
```

This will throw a `ProductFault` exception if an invalid ID is passed to the `GetProduct` operation. However, we will throw a normal C# exception if the passed ID is 999. Later, we will use this special ID to do an extra test.

Now, build the `RealNorthwindService` project. After has been successfully built, we will use the client that we built earlier to test this service. We will examine the channel status after an exception has been thrown. We can't do this with the WCF Service Test Client, because in WCF Test Client, each request will create a new channel, and we don't have a way to examine the channel state after the service call.

Updating client program to catch the fault exception

Now, let's update the client program, so that the fault exception is handled.

1. First, we need to update the service reference, because we have changed the contracts for the service. From the `RealNorthwindClient` project, expand the **Service References** node and right-click on **ProductServiceRef**. Select **Update Service Reference** from the context menu, and the **Updating Service Reference** dialog box will pop up. The WCF Service Host will be started automatically, and the updated metadata information will be downloaded to the client side. Proxy code will be updated with modified and new service contracts.

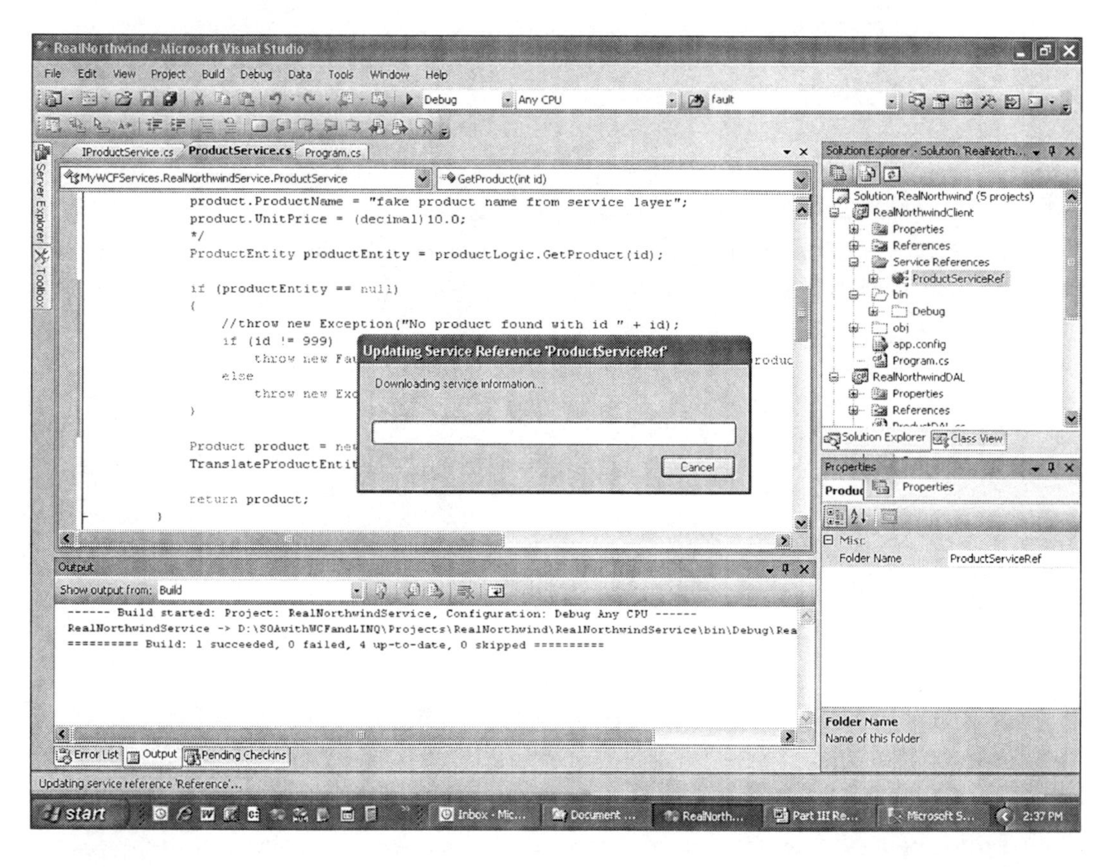

2. Then, open Program.cs under RealNorthwindClient project, and add the following method to the class Program:

```
static void TestException(ProductServiceClient client, int id)
{
    Console.WriteLine("\n\nTest {0} Fault Exception for product id
                {1}...", (id != 999)?"handled":"unhandled", id);

    try
    {
        Product product = client.GetProduct(id);
    }
    catch (TimeoutException ex)
    {
        Console.WriteLine("The service operation timed out. " +
                                                    ex.Message);
    }
    catch (FaultException<ProductFault> ex)
    {
        Console.WriteLine("ProductFault: " + ex.ToString());
    }
    catch (FaultException ex)
    {
        Console.WriteLine("Unknown Fault: " + ex.ToString());
    }
    catch (CommunicationException ex)
    {
        Console.WriteLine("There was a communication problem. " +
                                   ex.Message + ex.StackTrace);
    }
    Console.WriteLine("\n\nChannel Status after the exception: " +
                           client.InnerChannel.State.ToString());
    Console.WriteLine("Press any key to continue ...");
    Console.ReadKey();
}
```

Inside this method, we first call GetProduct with a passed-in ID. If the ID is an invalid product ID, the service will throw a ProductFault exception. So we have to add the catch statement to catch the ProductFault exception. We examine the channel status after the fault exception. We have also added several other exceptions, such as timeout exception, communication exception, and general fault exception, so that we can handle every situation. Note that the order of the catch statements are very important and shouldn't be changed.

If 999 is passed to this method as the ID, the service will throw an exception, instead of a fault exception. We will also examine the channel status of this unhandled exception.

3. Now, add the following statements to the end of the function `Main` in this class:

```
TestException(client, 0); // channel is still open after a
                                          FaultException
TestException(client, 999); // channel is Faulted after a non
                                    handled fault exception
Console.WriteLine("\n\nTest Faulted client ...");
product = client.GetProduct(20); // can't use a client with a
                                            Faulted channel
Console.WriteLine("Press any key to continue ...");
Console.ReadLine();
```

So we will first test the `ProductFault` exception, followed by the regular C# exception, and finally we will try to use the faulted channel.

The full content of the `Program.cs` is now as follows:

```
using System;
using System.Collections.Generic;
using System.Linq;
using System.Text;
using RealNorthwindClient.ProductServiceRef;
using System.ServiceModel;

namespace RealNorthwindClient
{
    class Program
    {
        static void Main(string[] args)
        {
            ProductServiceClient client = new ProductServiceClient();

            Product product = client.GetProduct(23);
            Console.WriteLine("product name is " + product.
                                              ProductName);
            Console.WriteLine("product price is " + product.UnitPrice.
                                                      ToString());

            product.UnitPrice = (decimal)20.0;
            bool result = client.UpdateProduct(product);
            Console.WriteLine("Update result is " + result.
                                              ToString());

            TestException(client, 0); // channel is still open after
                                                 a FaultException
```

```
            TestException(client, 999); // channel is Faulted after a
                                           non handled fault exception
            Console.WriteLine("\n\nTest Faulted client ...");
            product = client.GetProduct(20); // can't use a client
                                             with a Faulted channel
            Console.WriteLine("Press any key to continue ...");
            Console.ReadLine();
        }
        static void TestException(ProductServiceClient client, int id)
        {
            Console.WriteLine("\n\nTest {0} Fault Exception for
            product id {1}...", (id != 999)?"handled":"unhandled", id);
            try
            {
                Product product = client.GetProduct(id);
            }
            catch (TimeoutException ex)
            {
                Console.WriteLine("The service operation timed out. "
                                                      + ex.Message);
            }
            catch (FaultException<ProductFault> ex)
            {
                Console.WriteLine("ProductFault: " + ex.ToString());
            }
            catch (FaultException ex)
            {
                Console.WriteLine("Unknown Fault: " + ex.ToString());
            }
            catch (CommunicationException ex)
            {
                Console.WriteLine("There was a communication problem.
                                  " + ex.Message + ex.StackTrace);
            }
            Console.WriteLine("\n\nChannel Status after the exception:
                          " + client.InnerChannel.State.ToString());
            Console.WriteLine("Press any key to continue ...");
            Console.ReadKey();
        }
    }
}
```

Disabling the Just My Code debugging option

Before we run the program, we need to change a debugging setting. Select menu option **Tools | Options**, go to the **Debugging | General** tab, deselect the **Enable Just My Code(Managed only)** checkbox, as shown in the **Options** image below:

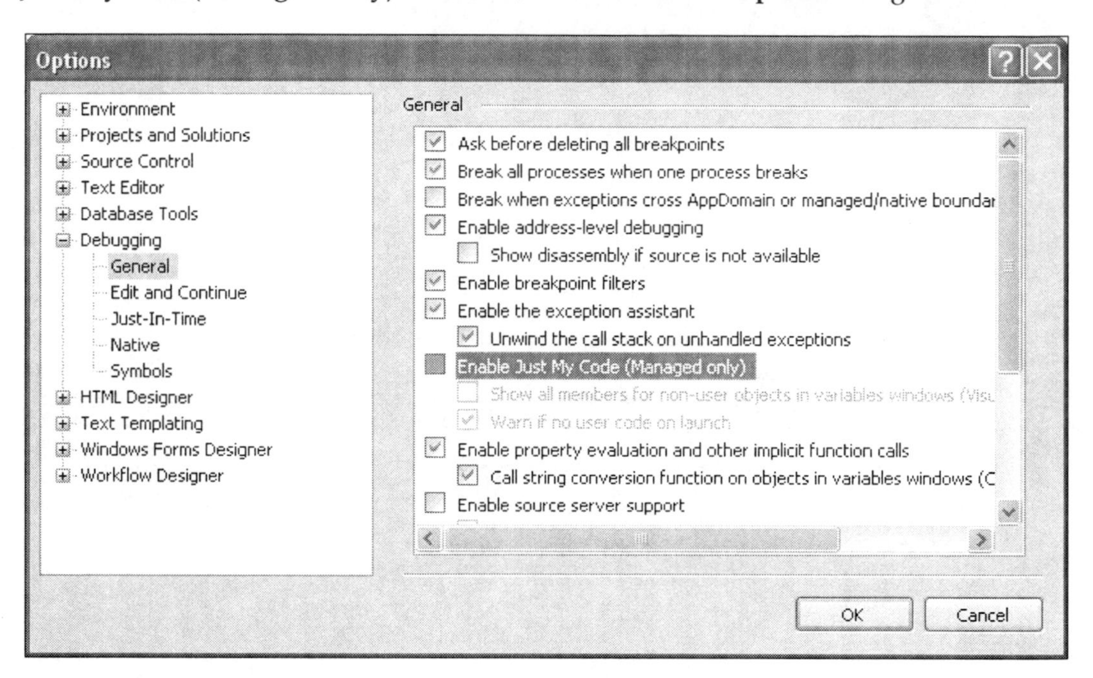

Enable Just My Code means that while debugging, you look at only the code you have written, and ignore the third-party code that is inside your application (such as the framework and libraries). **Just My Code** hides non-user code so that it does not appear in the debugger windows. When you step through the code, the debugger steps through any non-user code but does not stop in it. For example, if you call a .NET Framework API that throws an exception, you're going to break in your code that called the API, rather than farther down in the framework. This becomes particularly useful when user and non-user code call back and forth between each other. You can set the **My Code** status on a per-function level, to specify whether you want certain code debugged.

In our example, if you don't deselect **Enable Just My Code**, that is, if **Just Debug My Code** is selected, what happens is that when you debug the client program, you will get an exception popped up in Visual Studio after:

```
throw new FaultException<ProductFault>(new ProductFault("No product
found with id " + id), "Product Fault");
```

It complains that the exception is not being handled by the user, as seen in the **RealNorthwind (Debugging) - Microsoft Visual Studio** image below:

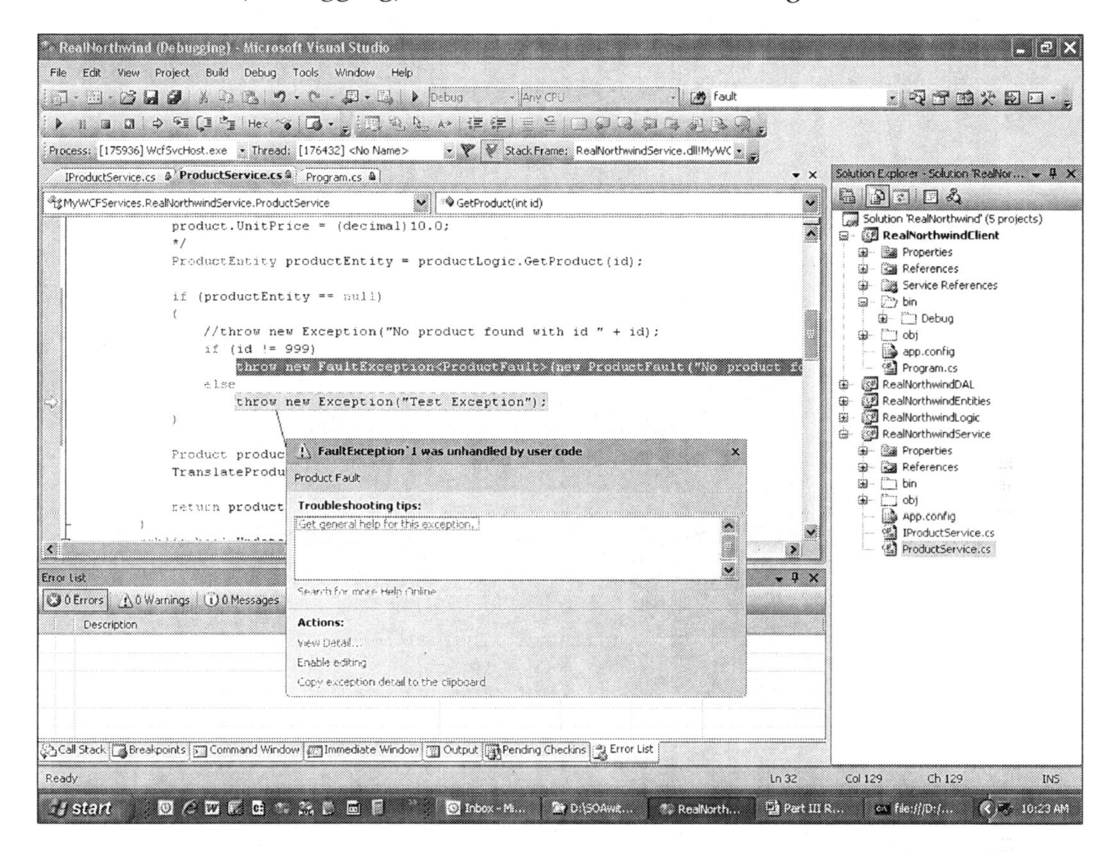

Note that this exception window is pointing to the following statement in Visual Studio:

```
throw new Exception("Test Exception");
```

But it is not because this line raised an exception. It is because this line is the line after the one that raised the exception, which is the **throw new FaultException** line. Actually, if you press *F5* to continue, the next time the "`throw new Exception`" line raises an exception, the popped up window will point to:

```
Product product = new Product();
```

We know that the `ProductFault` exception will be handled by our client program, but now, Visual Studio thinks that it is not. To avoid this annoyance, you can disable the **Just My Code** option. However, you should be aware that disabling this option might have some side effects. For example, Visual Studio will not complain if there is a real unhandled exception. You may want to enable it after you have completed your testing.

Testing the fault exception

Once you have changed the **Just My Code** option, you can press *F5* to run the client program (remember to set the `RealNorthwindClient` to be the startup project). You will get the output shown in the following screenshot:

```
file:///D:/SOAwithWCFandLINQ/Projects/RealNorthwind/RealNorthwindClient/bin/Debug/Re...
product name is Tunnbröd
product price is 20.0000
Update result is True


Test handled Fault Exception for product id 0...
ProductFault: System.ServiceModel.FaultException`1[RealNorthwindClient.ProductSe
rviceRef.ProductFault]: Product Fault (Fault Detail is equal to RealNorthwindCli
ent.ProductServiceRef.ProductFault).


Channel Status after the exception: Opened
Press any key to continue ...
```

As you can see from the output, the client channel to the service is still open, after the `ProductFault` is handled in the client program. Next, we will use the same client to get the product details for ID 999.

Press *Enter*, and more output will be shown, with a fault exception as shown in the image here:

```
file:///D:/SOAwithWCFandLINQ/Projects/RealNorthwind/RealNorthwindClient/bin/Debug/Re...
Test unhandled Fault Exception for product id 999...
Unknown Fault: System.ServiceModel.FaultException`1[System.ServiceModel.Exceptio
nDetail]: Test Exception (Fault Detail is equal to An ExceptionDetail, likely cr
eated by IncludeExceptionDetailInFaults=true, whose value is:
System.Exception: Test Exception
   at MyWCFServices.RealNorthwindService.ProductService.GetProduct(Int32 id) in
D:\SOAwithWCFandLINQ\Projects\RealNorthwind\RealNorthwindService\ProductService.
cs:line 34
   at SyncInvokeGetProduct(Object , Object[] , Object[] )
   at System.ServiceModel.Dispatcher.SyncMethodInvoker.Invoke(Object instance, O
bject[] inputs, Object[]& outputs)
   at System.ServiceModel.Dispatcher.DispatchOperationRuntime.InvokeBegin(Messag
eRpc& rpc)
   at System.ServiceModel.Dispatcher.ImmutableDispatchRuntime.ProcessMessage5(Me
ssageRpc& rpc)
   at System.ServiceModel.Dispatcher.ImmutableDispatchRuntime.ProcessMessage4(Me
ssageRpc& rpc)
   at System.ServiceModel.Dispatcher.ImmutableDispatchRuntime.ProcessMessage3(Me
ssageRpc& rpc)
   at System.ServiceModel.Dispatcher.ImmutableDispatchRuntime.ProcessMessage2(Me
ssageRpc& rpc)
   at System.ServiceModel.Dispatcher.ImmutableDispatchRuntime.ProcessMessa...).


Channel Status after the exception: Faulted
Press any key to continue ...
```

From the output, we know that the channel has now faulted. This means that now the client does not have a valid way to communicate with the service. To prove it, press *Enter* to try to connect to the service using the same client object, and you will get an unhandled exception "**The communication object, System.ServiceModel. Channels.ServiceChannel", cannot be used for communication because it is in the Faulted state**", as shown in the **RealNorthwind (Debugging)** image, below. The program will not continue, so you have to stop it.

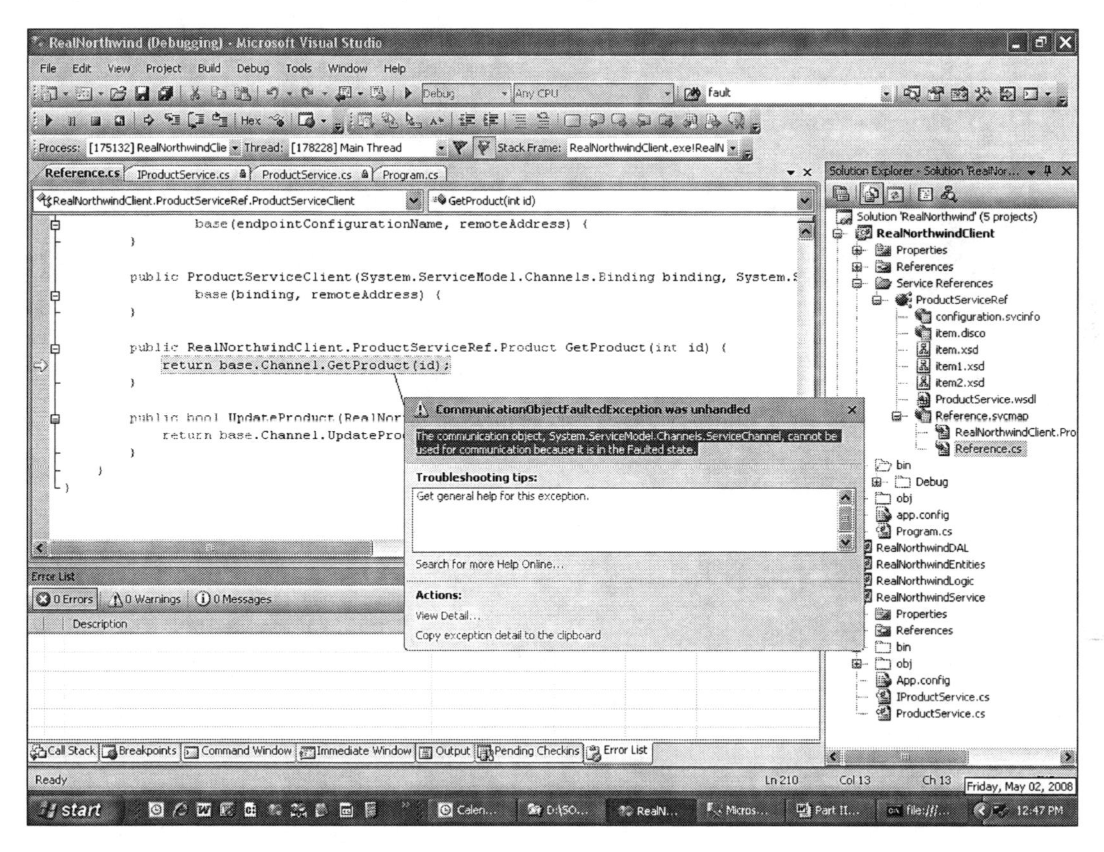

In the source code, if we have to call the service again, we have to abort this client, and create a new one for the communication.

Summary

In this chapter, we have added the third layer—the data access layer—to the `RealNorthwindService`. We have also added exception handling to the service. The key points covered in this chapter include:

- Database connection strings should be stored in configuration files, not in C# code
- The data access layer should contain the code to access the underlying databases; it should not contain business logic
- If service contracts have been changed, the client has to update the reference to the service
- You should throw fault contracts instead of exceptions to the client from WCF services
- A handled fault exception won't make a communication channel invalid but an exception will

7

Modeling a WCF Service with Service Factory

In the previous two chapters, we created a real-world WCF service with three layers. We created these three layers manually with Visual Studio, and added the required code, configuration settings, and other files. In this chapter and the next one, we will establish the same framework with one of Microsoft's Patterns and Practices, Microsoft Web Service Software Factory. In this chapter, we will use the Service Factory to create models for all of the contracts, specify implementation technologies for the models, and generate the source code from those models. In the next chapter, we will finish the service by adding the necessary code to it and testing it using a generated Windows client.

In this chapter, we will follow these steps to model the WCF service:

- Explain guidance packages and the Service Factory
- Download and install the required software
- Model the data contracts
- Model the service contracts
- Specify the implementation technology for the models
- Create the service projects
- Generate source code from the models

What is the Service Factory?

The **Web Service Software Factory** (also known as the **Service Factory**) is an integrated collection of tools, patterns, source code, and prescriptive guidance. It is designed to help you quickly and consistently construct WCF and ASMX Web services that adhere to well-known architecture and design patterns.

The Service Factory contains automation and guidance integrated into Visual Studio for building services. The core of the automation components is a Web services domain model. This domain model contains elements such as service contracts, operations, messages, and data contracts. This domain model manifests itself in the form of three integrated **domain-specific languages** (DSLs) that are used to model services: the Service Contract Model, the Data Contract Model, and the Host Model.

According to the Microsoft Service Factory team (Microsoft, *Web Service Software Factory: Modeling Edition*, retrieved on 5/2/2008 from `http://msdn.microsoft.com/en-us/library/bb931187.aspx`), the design goals of Service Factory are:

- The Service Factory will provide higher productivity because it raises the abstraction level for building services.
- Applications built using the Service Factory will have a higher quality because the generated code encapsulates best practices.
- The Service Factory will be designed to be extensible so that it can adapt to the needs of a particular team's development processes and organizational environment.
- When using the Service Factory, implementation technology related decisions should be delayed until as late as possible. These decisions include which messaging platform (WCF and ASMX) to use, and which Visual Studio projects to use in making up the solution for the service.
- Changes to the service and its design should require as little rework as possible.

What are Guidance Packages?

One of the key requirements of the Service Factory is **Guidance Automation Extensions**. So, to fully understand the Service Factory, we also need to know what Guidance Automation Extensions are.

There are two packages related to guidance automation. One is **Guidance Automation Extension** (GAX), and the other is **Guidance Automation Toolkit** (GAT).

The Guidance Automation Extension (GAX) expands the capabilities of Visual Studio by allowing architects and developers to run guidance packages, such as those included in Software Factories, which automate key development tasks from within the Visual Studio environment.

The Guidance Automation Toolkit (GAT) is an extension to Visual Studio that allows architects to author-rich, integrated user experiences for re-usable assets including frameworks, components, and patterns. The resulting Guidance Packages are composed of templates, wizards, and recipes, which help developers build solutions in a manner consistent with the architecture guidelines.

For our purposes, we don't need to create our own guidance packages, so we will neither need to download nor install the Guidance Automation Toolkit. We do need to download and install the Guidance Automation Extensions, because GAX is a required component for the Service Factory.

Preparing environments

To use the Service Factory, you have to download and install both the Guidance Automation Extensions and the Service Factory. You need to first install the Guidance Automation package, and then install the Service Factory.

Installing Guidance Automation packages

Based on the above information, we will only need to download and install Guidance Automation Extensions for Visual Studio 2008. You can go to `download.microsoft.com`, search for "Guidance Automation Extensions", and you will find the link for the guidance automation package. You need to sign in to download this package. After downloading the package, install it on your PC.

Installing Microsoft Service Software Factory

Next, we need to download and install the Service Factory. Go to `download.microsoft.com`, search for "web service software factory", and you will find the link for the Service Factory. Again, you need to sign in to download this package. There are two versions of the download: one for the binary package, and one for the source code. We only need the binary one. After downloading the package, install it on your PC, and we are ready to use it.

Differences between the December 2006 version and the February 2008 version

If you have used the Service Factory December 2006 version, you will notice that there are several differences between that one and the 2008 one. Among these changes, probably the most significant one is that with the 2006 version, you need to have a database first, and create the Data Contract, Business Entities, and so on, based on that database, whereas with the 2008 version, you create Data Contracts, and Service Interfaces before you even decide which language to use. The services are now designed in a technology-independent manner. The new Service Factory is more like a modeling tool at the beginning, and a code generation tool at the end. This is why it is now called "Service Factory: Modeling Edition".

Modeling the data contracts

Now let's start using the Service Factory to build a WCF service. We will build a three-layer WCF service, similar to what we did in the previous chapters.

We will model the data contracts, then the service contracts, and finally, link the data contracts to the service contracts. Once we have all of the contracts ready, we will customize the data access and business logic layers, and host the service in IIS. We will also create a test client to test the service.

In this section, we will model the data contracts.

Creating the solution

First, we need to create a solution using the Service Factory. Follow these steps to create the solution:

1. Start Visual Studio 2008
2. Select menu item **File | New | Project...**.
3. Select **Guidance Packages | Service Factory: Modeling Edition** as the project type, and **Model Project** as the template
4. Enter **EasyNorthwind** as the **Name**, and leave the **Location** as the default value (**D:\SOAwithWCFandLINQ\Projects**)
5. When you click the **OK** button, the **New Project** dialog box should pop up on your screen.

The Guidance Packages project type will be shown only after you have installed the Guidance packages.

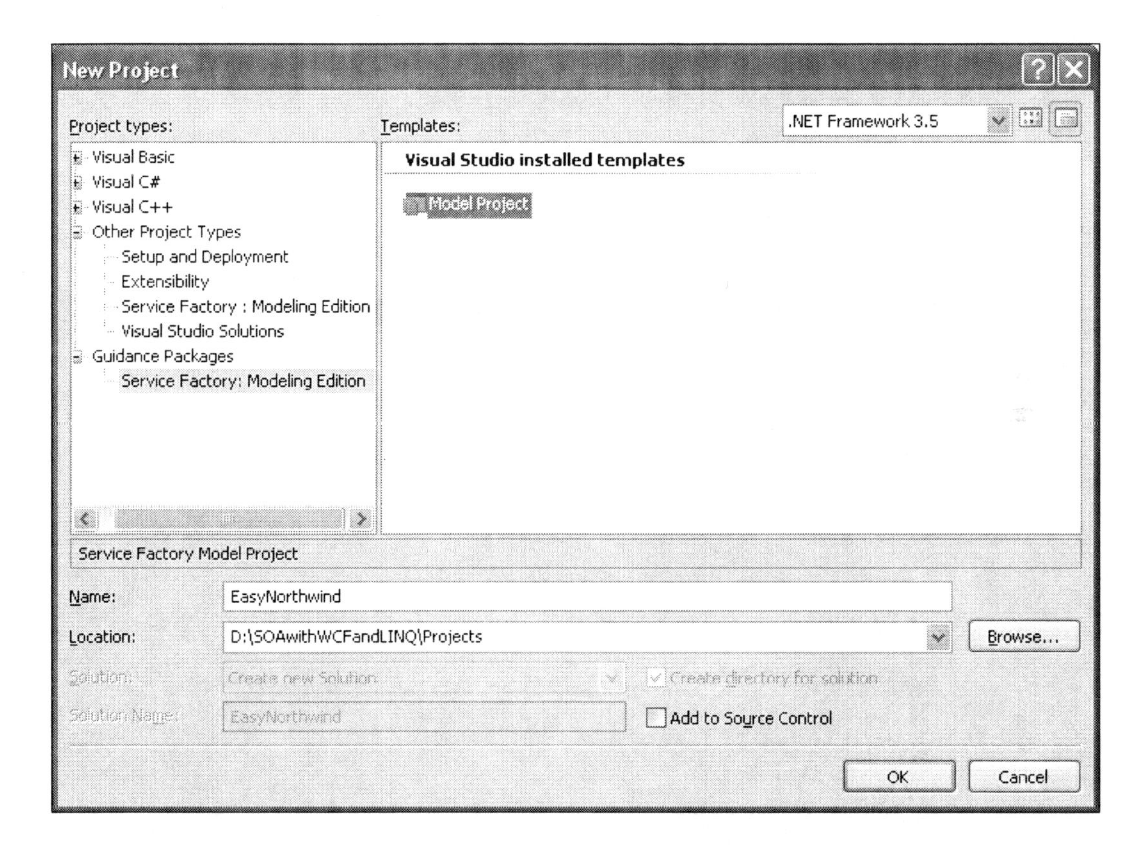

6. Next, let's rename the model project. In the Solution Explorer, right-click the bottom node **EasyNorthwind**, and rename it to **EasyNorthwind Models**. This is the folder where we will store all of the models for this solution.

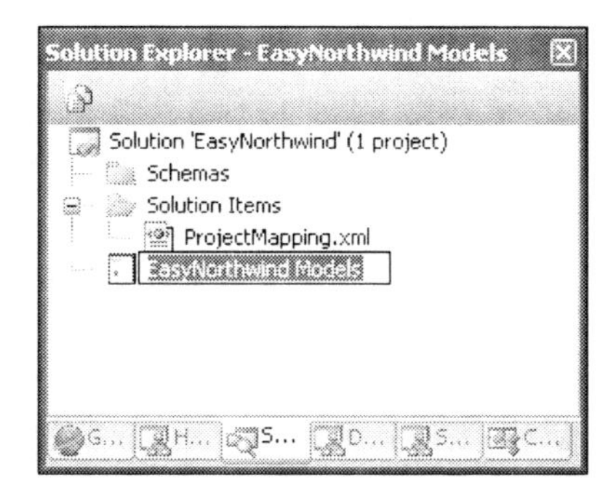

Adding the data contract model

Now, the solution has only one empty models folder. Let's add our data contract model using the following steps:

1. In the Solution Explorer, right-click the **EasyNorthwind Models**.
2. Select **Add | New Model...** to add a new model.
3. In the pop-up **Service Factory | Specify model options** dialog box, select **Data Contract Model** type, enter **ProductService** as the model name, and `http://MyCompany.com/ProductService/EasyWCF/2008/05` as the XML namespace.
4. Click the **Finish** button.

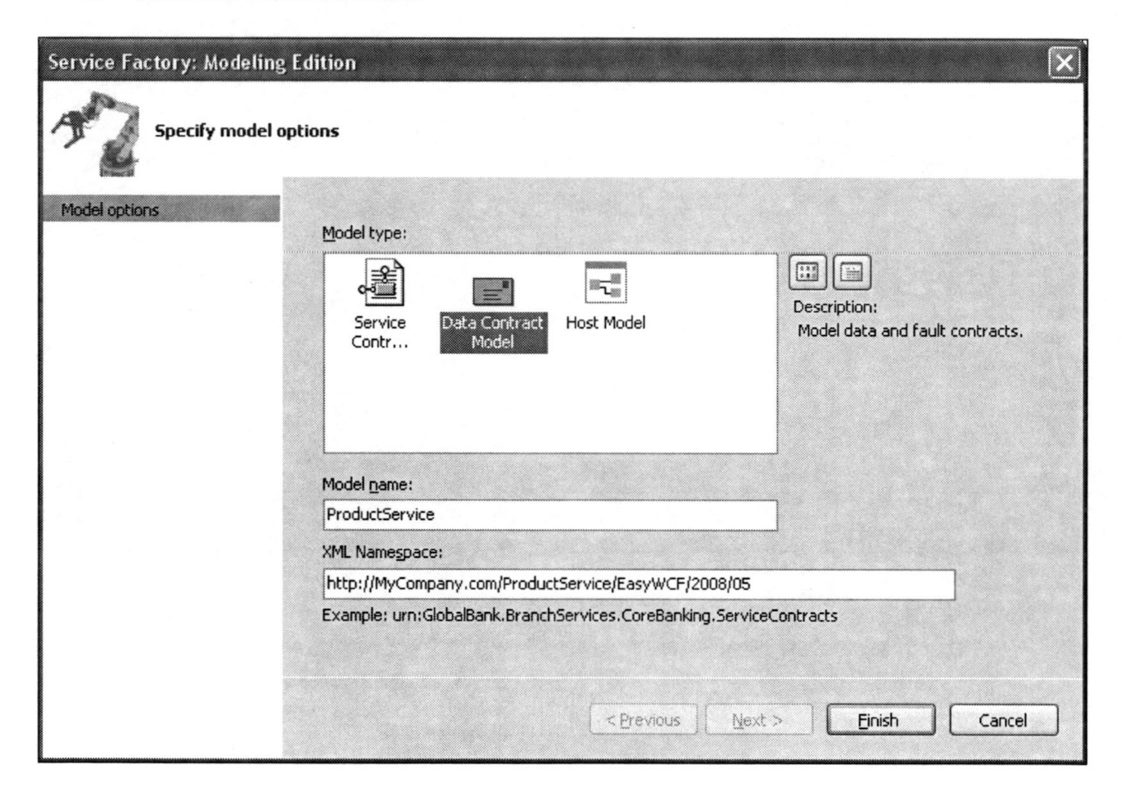

Adding the product data contract

Now that the **ProductService** data contract has been added to the solution models, we can model the data contracts.

1. Open the **Toolbox** window. If you can't find **Toolbox** in your left side of Visual Studio, press *Ctrl+Alt+X*, or select menu item **View | Toolbox,** to open it. The **EasyNorthwind - Microsoft Visual Studio** image below shows the toolbox for **Data Contract** Tools.
2. Drag a **Data Contract** (Data Contract) into the data contract design pane.

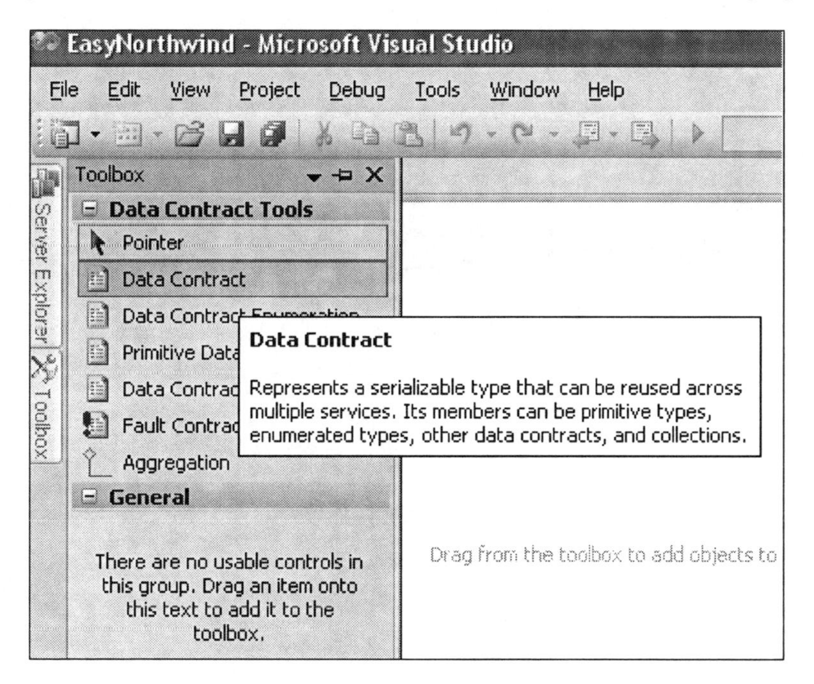

3. Click on the new data contract shape, and change its name from **DataContract1** to **Product**.

4. Right-click on this **Product data contract** and add a **Primitive Data Member** to it:

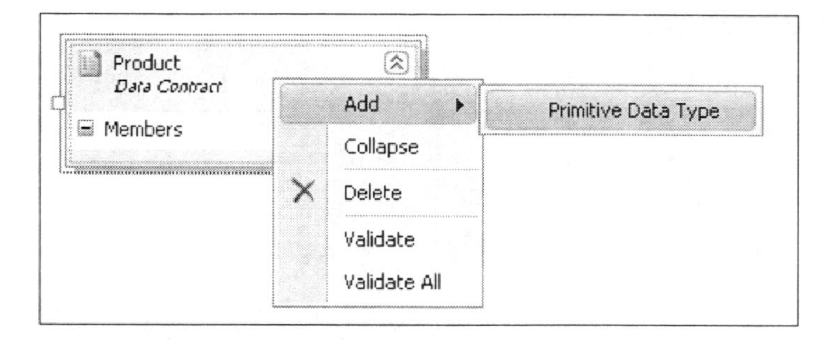

5. Rename this data member from **PrimitiveDataType1** to **ProductID**, and, while the **ProductID** is still selected, click on the **ellipsis** button for its type in the **Properties** window, and change the primitive's type to be **System.Int32**.

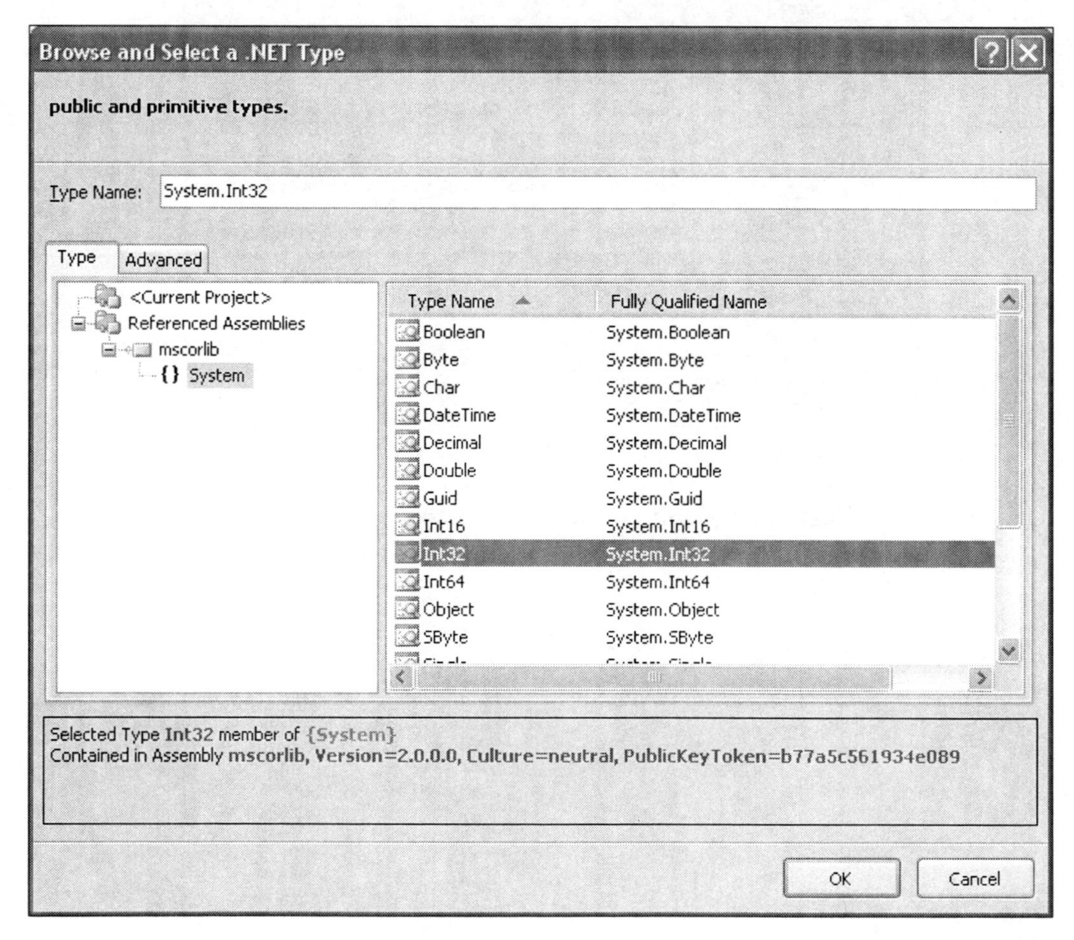

6. Use the same method to add the following primitive data members, with the corresponding types shown here:

Member Name	Member Data Type
ProductID	System.Int32
ProductName	System.String
QuantityPerUnit	System.String
UnitPrice	System.Decimal
Discontinued	System.Boolean

Adding the product fault contract

Next, we will add a product fault contract to the product service's data contract model. Follow these steps to add this fault contract:

1. From the Toolbox, drag a **Fault Contract** shape (Fault Contract) into the **ProductService** data contract design pane.
2. Rename it to **ProductFault**.
3. Right-click on it, and add a new primitive data member **FaultMessage** to this fault contract, with the type **System.String**.

The final diagram of the **ProductService** Data Contract Model should look like the following **ProductService.datacontract*** image below:

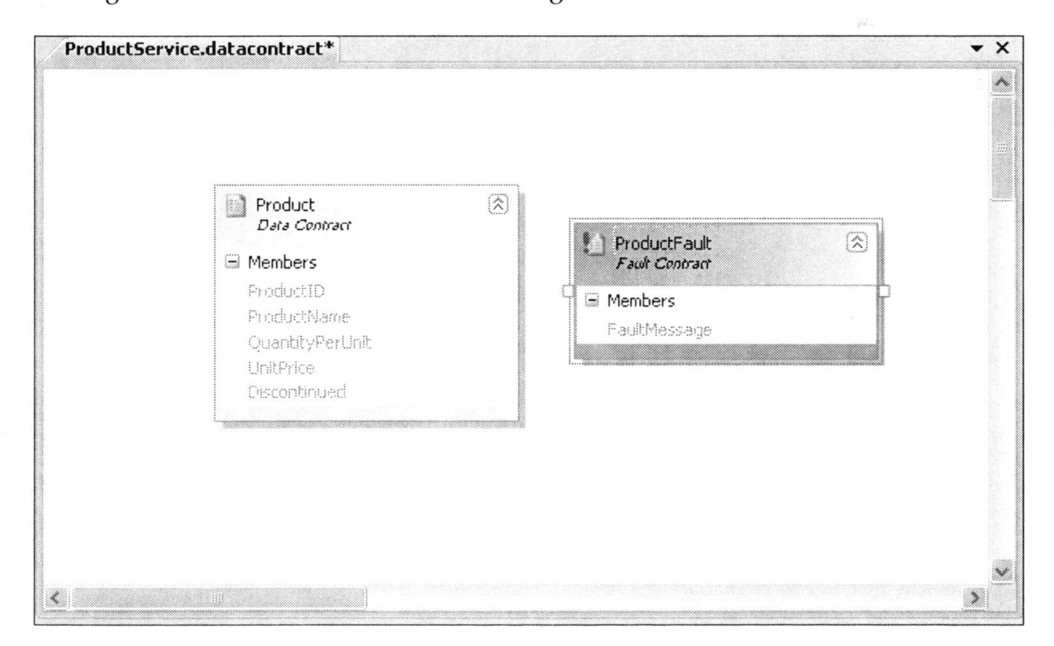

The **Data Contract Explorer**, which is a window next to the Solution Explorer, also provides all of the information about the Data Contracts:

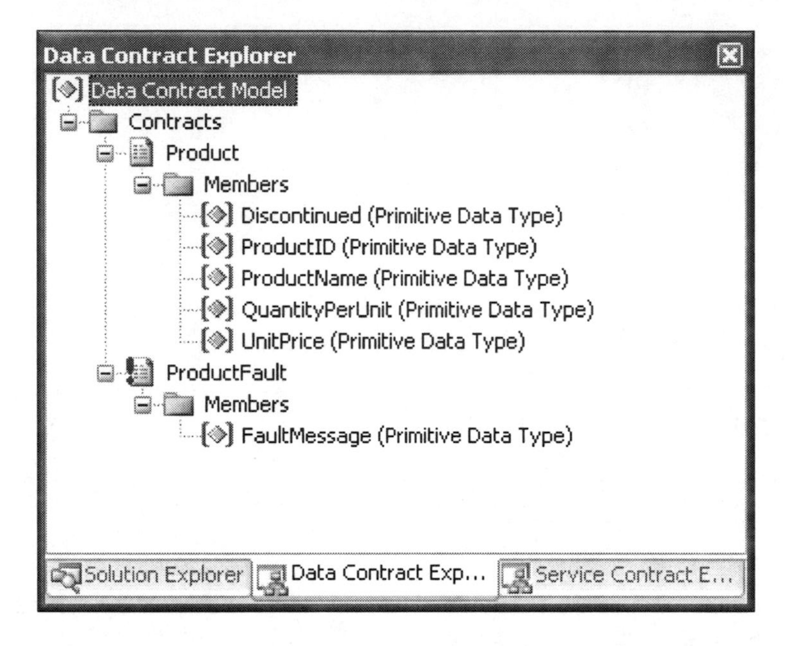

Modeling the service contracts

In the previous sections, we modeled the data contract, and the Fault contract. In this section, we will model the service contracts, including the service operations, service contracts, and message contracts. We have to model the data contract and fault contract first because we will use them when modeling the service contracts.

Adding the ProductService contract model

As for to the Data Contract Model, we now need to add a Service Contract Model. Follow these steps to add the service contract model:

1. From the Solution Explorer, right-click on **EasyNorthwind Models**.
2. Select **Add | New Model ...** to add a new model.
3. In the pop-up **Service Factory | Specify model options** dialog box, select **Service Contract** model type, enter **ProductService** as the model name, and `http://MyCompany.com/ProductService/EasyWCF/2008/05` as the XML namespace.
4. Click **Finish** to add this model.

Adding the GetProduct operation

Next, we will add an operation, a request, and response message, a product service contract, and finally the product service itself.

Let's follow these steps to add the `GetProduct` operation first:

1. Open the **Service Contract Toolbox** window.
2. Drag an **Operation** shape (Operation) onto the service contract design pane.
3. Click on the new operation shape, and rename it from **Operation1** to **GetProduct**.
4. Right-click on this **GetProduct** operation and add a **Data Contract Fault** member to it.
5. Change the name of this fault contract member from **DataContractFault1** to **ProductFault**.

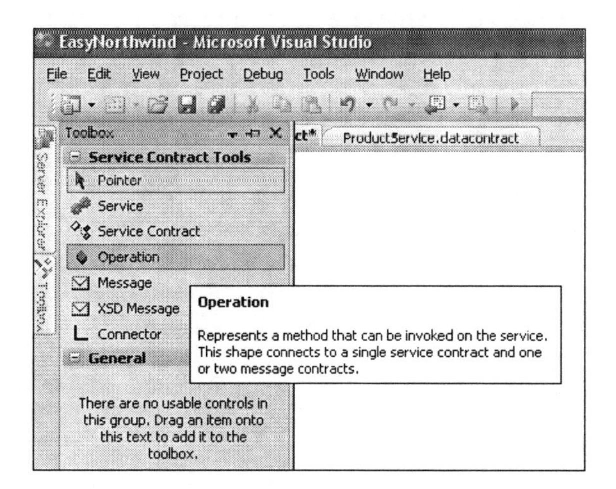

6. With the **ProductFault** member still selected, click on the ellipsis button for its type on its **Properties** window.

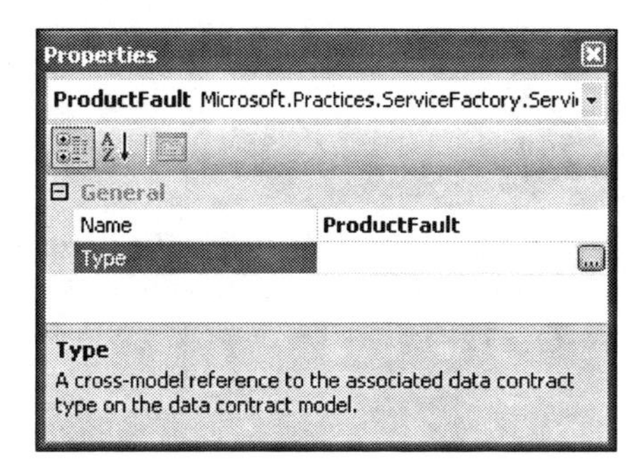

7. In the pop-up **DSL Model Element Selector** dialog box, select **ProductFault** and click the **OK** button. This fault member is now linked to the data contract **ProductFault**.

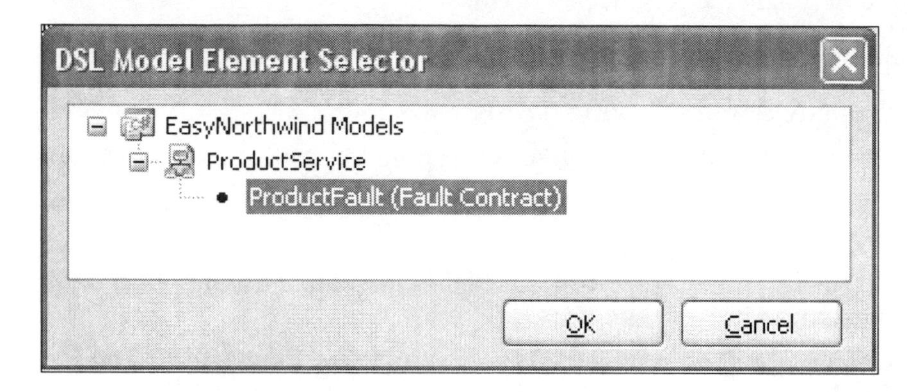

If you have a blank **DSL Model Element Selector** screen, it means you haven't saved your **Data Contract Model**. You need to click the **Save All** button from the menu tools bar, and try again to populate this window.

Adding the message contracts

In the previous section, we have added the `GetProduct` operation, but we only defined the fault contract of this operation. We didn't specify its request and response messages. In this section, we will define the request and response messages of this operation, and later we will connect these messages to the operation.

Follow these steps to define the request and response messages:

1. Open the **Toolbox** window.
2. Drag a **Message** shape (Message) onto the service contract design pane.
3. Click on the new message shape, and rename it from **Message1** to **GetProductRequest**.
4. Right-click on this **GetProductRequest** message and add a primitive message part to it.
5. Change the name of this part from **PrimitiveMessagePart1** to **ProductID,** and change its type to be **System.Int32**.
6. Add another message item, rename it to **GetProductResponse**, and add a Data **Contract Message Part** named **Product** and change its type to **EasyNorthwind Models\ProductService\product**.

[ You can also put the **GetProduct** response message into an XML schema file and load it into the model using XSD message shape.]

Adding the service contracts

Before we connect the messages to the operation, we need to add the top level service contracts. This will include the service contract, and the service itself.

1. Open the **Toolbox** window.
2. Drag a **Service Contract** shape (Service Contract) onto the service contract design pane.
3. Click on the new service contract shape, and rename it from **ServiceContract1** to **ProductServiceContract**.
4. Drag a **Service** shape onto the service contract design pane.
5. Click on the new service shape, and rename it from **Service1** to **ProductService**.

Adding the connectors

We have now created all of the required items for the service contracts. Next, we need to connect them together to form the message flow. Follow these steps:

1. Open the **Toolbox** window.
2. Click on the **Connector** shape (Connector).
3. Drag it from the **GetProductRequest** message to the **GetProduct** operation.
4. Click on the **Connector** again and drag it from the **GetProduct** operation to the **GetProductResponse.**

[ The direction of the arrow is important, as this indicates the message flow. That is, it decides which is the request message and which is the response message.]

5. Connect the **ProductServiceContract** service contract to the **GetProduct** operation, and the **ProductService** service to the **ProductServiceContract** service contact.

6. We also need to change the serializer type for this **Service Contract Model**. Click on any empty space in the **Service Contract Model** design pane and change its **Serializer Type** from **XmlSerializer** to **DataContractSerializer.**

   A **serializer** is used to convert the members of the service objects into XML for communication between the service and the client applications. By definition, a `DataContractSerializer` can serialize and de-serialize data contracts and message contracts, whereas an **XmlSerializer** can only serialize and de-serialize data types that are defined using programming constructors such as properties and fields. Because we have defined data contracts and message contracts in our service interfaces, we have to change the serializer type to **DataContractSerializer**.

The final Service Contract Model for **ProductService** is shown in the following **ProductService.servicecontract** screenshot:

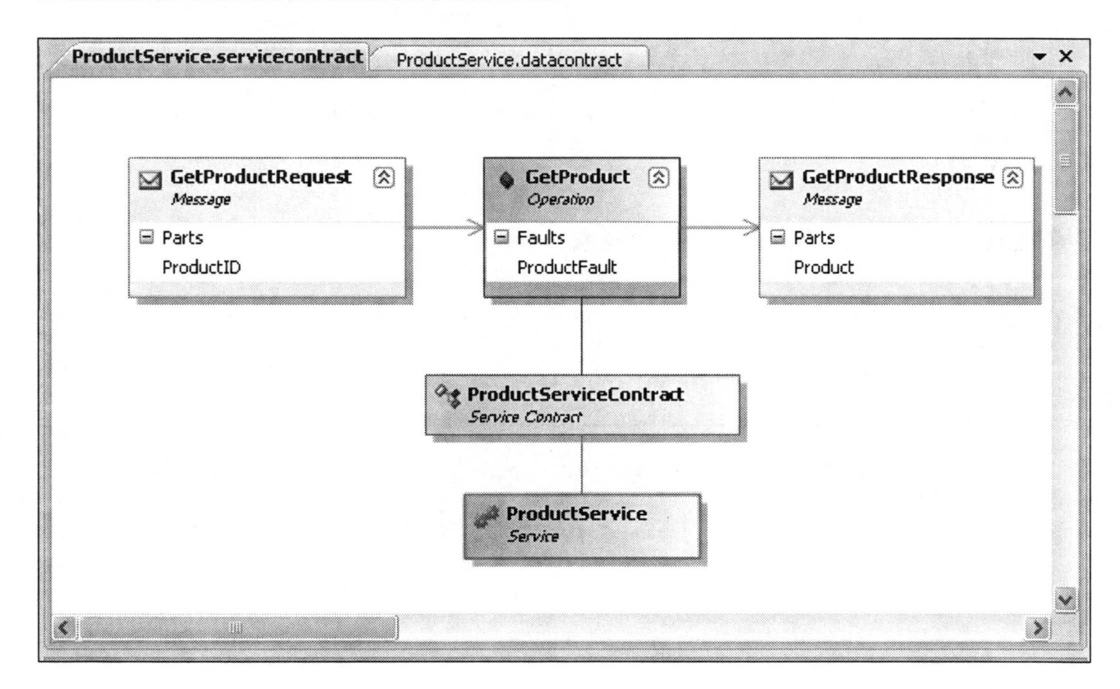

The same model appears in the Service Contract Explorer as follows:

Specifying the implementation technology for the models

We have modeled all of the contracts, and are ready to generate code. But before we ask the code generator to generate the code, we need to specify which technology we are going to use, so that the code generator will know what kind of code it needs to generate for us.

Choosing the implementation technology for service contract model

First, we need to specify which technology we will use to implement the service contracts. Follow these steps to specify the technology:

1. Open the **Service Contract Model**.
2. Click on any empty space in the design pane.

3. In the **Properties** window, click on the drop-down arrow for **Implementation Technology**, and choose **WCF Extension**. You will have the following properties window displayed on your screen:

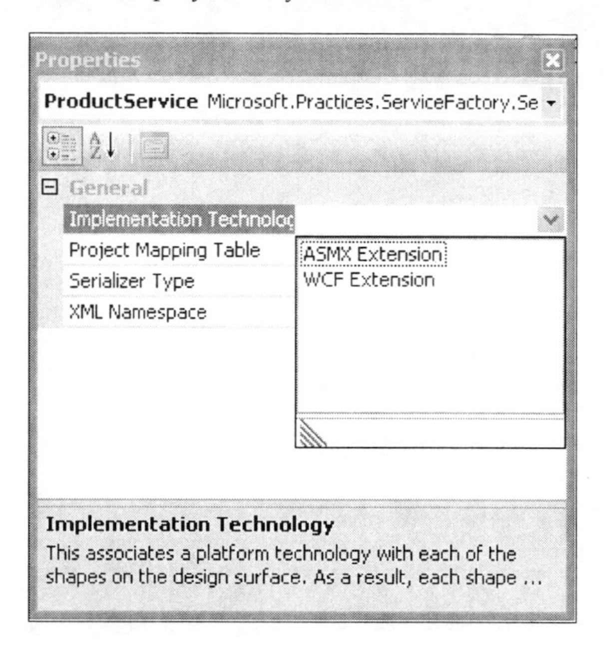

Changing the property values for service contracts

You have now selected the implementation technology for the service contracts. Click on a shape on the **Service Contract Model**, such as the **GetProduct** operation, and you will see that several WCF-specific settings have been added to its **Properties** window. Next, we need to change some of these settings.

1. Select the **GetProduct** operation.
2. Copy its **Action** property from the **Properties** window.
3. Paste the value into the **Reply Action** property. Now the **Reply Action** property has the same value as the **Action** property.
4. Select the **GetProductRequest** shape.
5. Change its **Is Wrapped** property to **True**.

Choosing the implementation technology for the data contract model

In the previous section, we set the implementation technology for the service contracts as WCF Extension. In this section, we will set the implementation technology for the data contracts.

1. Open the **Data Contract** model.
2. Click on an empty space in the design pane.
3. In the **Properties** window, change the model's **Implementation Technology** to **WCF Extension**. The **Properties** screen is identical to the diagram you saw in the previous section.

Changing the order property for data members

Once the implementation technology has been chosen for the **Data Contract Model**, we need to change some WCF-specific settings for the data members, as follows:

1. While the **Data Contract Model** diagram is still open, first select **Product Data Contract**.
2. Click on the **ProductName** member.
3. Change its **Order** property to 1.
4. Change the order property of **QuantityPerUnit**, **UnitPrice**, and **Discontinued** to 2, 3, and 4 respectively.

You can also do this by right-clicking on an empty space in the data contract model pane, and selecting **Order All Data Members** from the context menu, as shown below. The Service Factory will assign an order to each data member according to the position in its corresponding data contract.

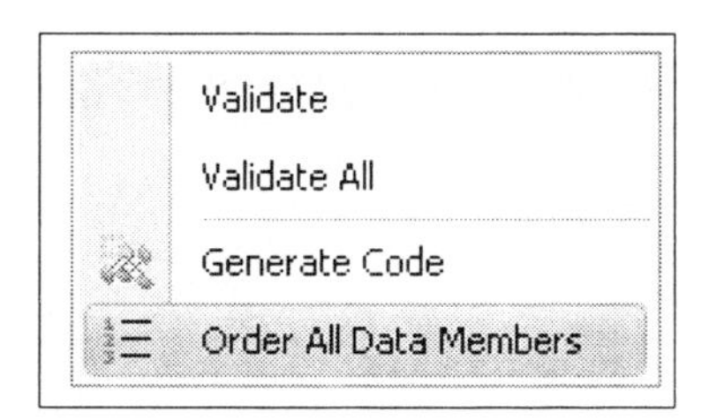

Generating source code

At this point, we have specified WCF as the technology for the service implementation, but we still haven't generated any code. The Solution Explorer only has few nodes, as shown in the following image:

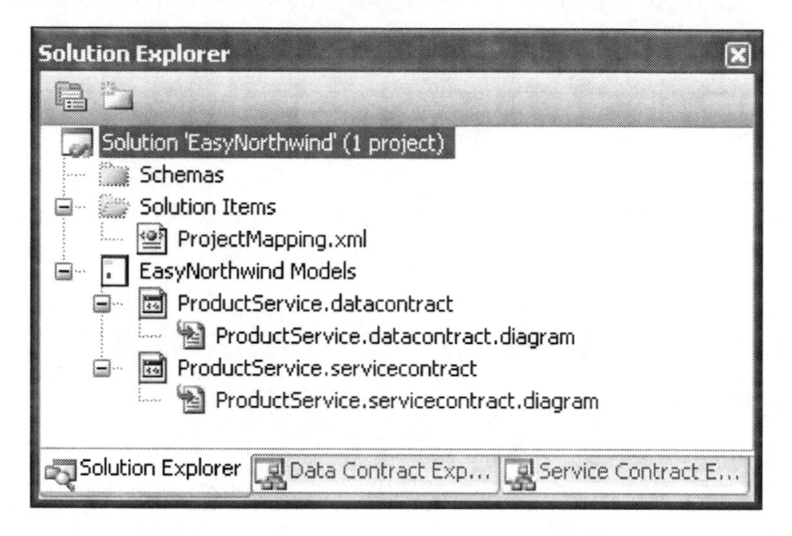

The solution item **ProjectMapping.xml** is an empty file, with no project included. Next, we will create the framework projects for the service, and generate lots of source code from the models.

Creating the service projects

Before we can generate the source code from the models, we need to create a few projects, and add them to the solution. Follow these steps to create all of the required projects:

1. From the Solution Explorer, right-click on the top node **EasyNorthwind** solution item.
2. Select **Add | New Project...** from the context menu.

3. On the pop-up **Add New Project** window, select **Guidance Packages | Service Factory: Modeling Edition** as the project type, and **WCF Implementation Projects** as the template.
4. Enter **MyWCF.EasyNorthwind** as the **Name**, and leave the **Location** as the default directory **D:\SOAwithWCFandLINQ\Projects\EasyNorthwind**. The **Add New Project** dialog box should pop up on your screen:

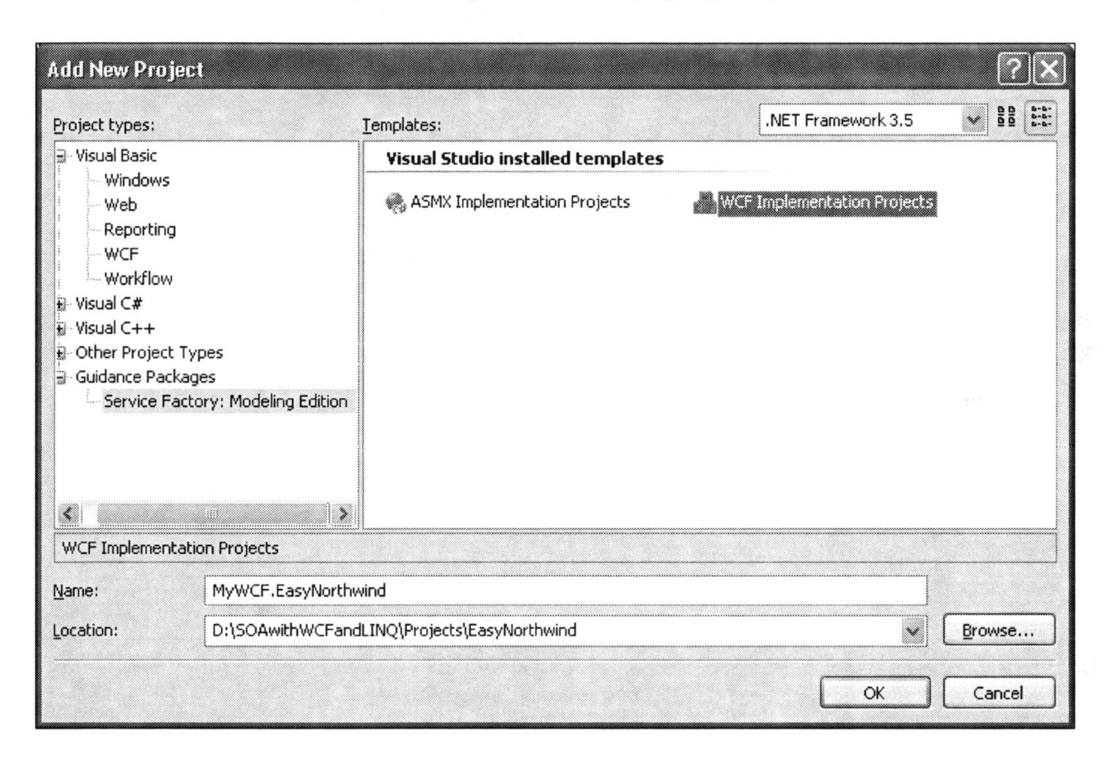

5. Click **OK**.

   Service Factory will generate ten projects according to the Service Contract and Data Contract Models, including the Business Entities projects, Business Logic projects, Data Access Layer projects, Data Contracts projects, Fault Contracts projects, Message Contract projects, Service Contracts projects, and Service Implementation projects. The Solution Explorer is now full of projects, as shown in the following image:

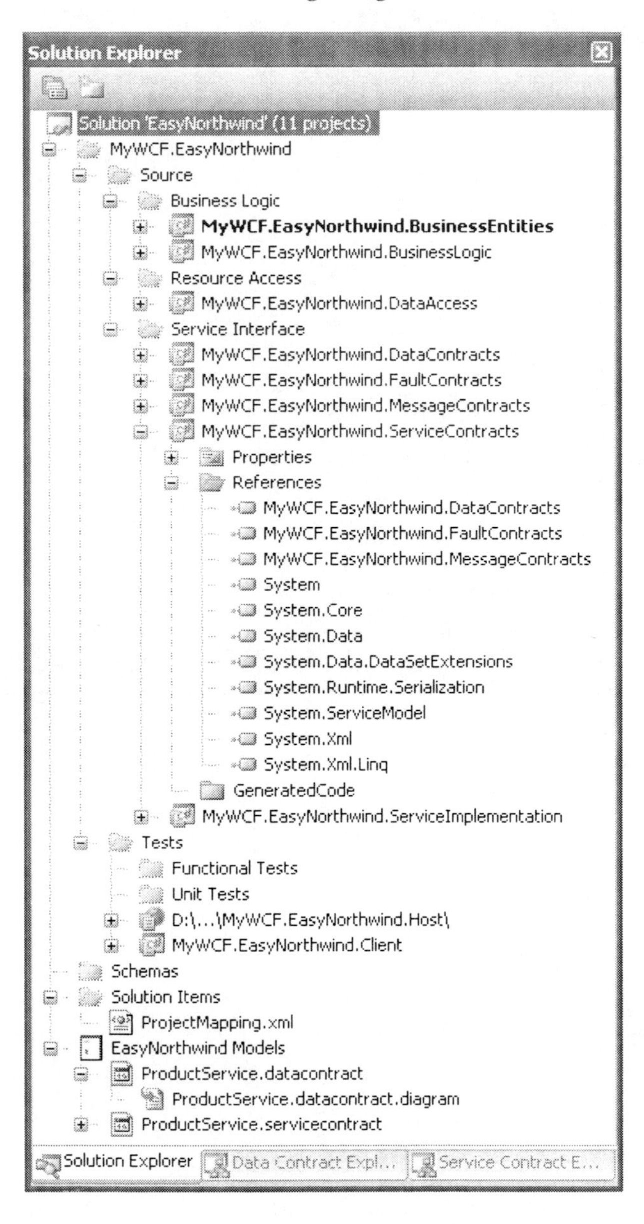

Inside each project, the Service Factory has added the required references, and some configuration files. For example, the **ServiceContracts** project has references to **MyWCF.EasyNorthwind . DataContracts**, **MyWCF.EasyNorthwind.FaultContracts**, and **MyWCF.EasyNorthwind.MessageContracts**, as well as **System.Runtime. Serialization**, and **System.ServiceModel**.

It has also generated a hosting application and a testing client for the service, which we will customize later.

Linking contract models to projects

Now that we have all of the projects generated, we can tell the Service and Data Contract Models which project they should link to.

- Open the **Service Contract Model** diagram, click on an empty space in the design pane, and from the **Properties** window, change the property **Project Mapping Table** to **MyWCF.EasyNorthwind**.

  The project mapping table, **MyWCF.EasyNorthwind,** is an element within the **ProjectMapping.xml** file. This element was added to the project mapping XML file when we created the projects in the previous section. It maps from solution projects to a set of predefined roles. So, after we specify the **Project Mapping Table** of the service contract model to this element, and later generate the code, the Service Factory will know which project the generated artifacts should go to.

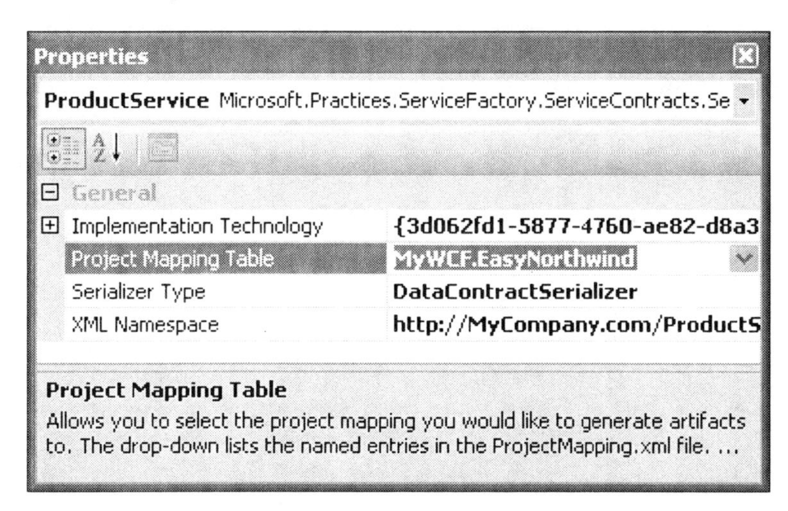

- Open the **Data Contract Model** diagram, click on an empty space in the design pane, and from the **Properties** window, change the property **Project Mapping Table** to **MyWCF.EasyNorthwind**.

Validating the contract models

At this point, we have finished modeling our service contracts, and have also specified technologies for the service implementation. Both models should now be valid.

To see the validation results, right-click on an empty space in the design pane for either of the contract models, select **Validate All** from the context menu, and you will see the following messages in the output window:

------ Validation started: Model elements validated: 17 ------

======== Validation complete: 0 errors, 0 warnings, 0 information messages =======

If you have tried to validate any model prior to this point, you may have seen a few validation errors, such as "**Project Mapping Table property is empty**".

You can compile and build the solution successfully now, though it is not yet complete (actually, there is no source code to build in the solution at this point).

Generating the source code

The Service Factory has now generated ten projects, but it hasn't generated any source code from the Service and Data Contract Models. You can build and run it now, but it won't be functioning as a WCF service. In this section, we will ask Service Factory to generate all of the necessary source code for the service.

1. Open the Data Contract Model.
2. Right-click on the design pane.
3. Select **Generate Code** from the context menu.

   The Factory will generate source code for all of the defined Data contracts and Fault contracts in the model.

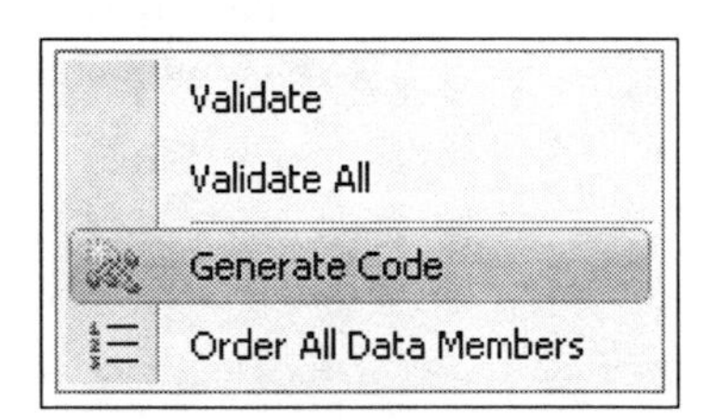

4. Open the Service Contract Model.
5. Right-click on the design pane.
6. Select **Generate Code** from the context menu.

   The Factory will generate source code for all of the service interfaces, service implementations, operations, messages, and any other necessary files.

You may see a warning message saying that a custom tool failed. Do not worry about this warning. It's ok for us to move on.

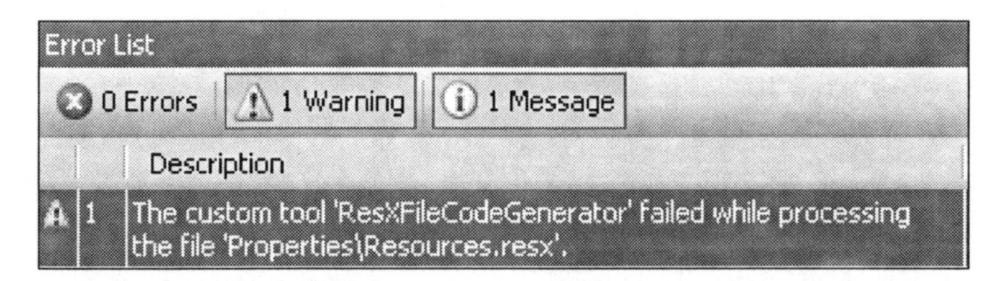

You can also right-click on any shape in the Contract Model diagrams, and select **Generate Code** for that shape only. This feature is helpful if, later on, you need to change some of the models.

Now, open a project under the Service Interface folder, such as **MyWCF.EasyNorthwind.DataContracts**. You will see the generated files under the **GeneratedCode** folder.

This will generate the source code for all of the service interface projects, including the Data Contracts project, Fault Contracts project, Message Contracts project, Service Contracts project, and Service Implementation projects. If you check the business entities project, the business logic project, or the data access project, you will find that no source code has been generated yet. There is no code generated for the test client, or the host application either. So the **EasyNorthwind** solution is still not a complete WCF service. In the next chapter, we will complete it by generating and customizing all of the other projects.

Build the solution again. There should be no errors.

Summary

In this chapter, we have used Service Factory to create the framework of a three-layer WCF service. We used Service Factory to model the data contracts, service contracts, and we then generated code from these models. We are not only writing less source code manually, but we are also incorporating lots of best practices into our service. This version's service is in much better shape than the previous one.

The key points covered in this chapter include:

- Guidance Packages and Service Factory are required to model the contracts
- Data contracts, including fault contracts, are modeled before service contracts and data contract models will be used by the service contract models
- Connectors are used to connect the service contracts with the operation contracts, and the message contracts
- Implementation technologies are not specified for the contracts in the models, until the source code is about to be generated
- Service Factory will only generate source code for the service interface projects, and not for the business logic project, the business entities project, or the data access project

8

Implementing the WCF Service with Service Factory

In the previous chapter, we modeled and generated the source code for a WCF service using Service Factory. Although the service interface code is generated based on the Contract Models, no business entity, or data access layer, or business logic layer code has been generated at all. The Modeling Edition of the Service Factory doesn't give any tool to automatically generate code for them. You may recall that with the previous version's Service Factory, you could generate business entities from a database, but this is not the case for this version.

In this chapter, we will manually add code for these projects, so that we have a completed WCF service. We will also generate the host application and test client using Service Factory, and then test the WCF service.

We will follow these steps to complete the `EasyNorthwind` service in this chapter:

- Adding the business entities
- Adding the data access class
- Adding the business logic class
- Translating the messages
- Customizing the Fault contract class
- Modifying the service interface layer to call the business logic layer
- Modeling the host application and generating source code for the host application
- Creating the test client
- Testing the WCF service using the test client

Creating the business entities

First, we will create our business entities for the service. Follow these steps to add the product entity to the project:

1. In the Solution Explorer, right-click on the **MyWCF.EasyNorthwind.BusinessEntities** project.
2. Select **Add | Class...** from the context menu.
3. In the popped up **Add New Item** window, enter **ProductEntity.cs** as the name.
4. Click **Add**.

Now, customize the `ProductEntity.cs` file:

- Change it to be a public class
- Add new members for the product entity

The final `ProductEntity` class file should look like this:

```
using System;
using System.Collections.Generic;
using System.Linq;
using System.Text;
namespace MyWCF.EasyNorthwind.BusinessEntities
{
    public class ProductEntity
    {
        public int ProductID {get; set;}
        public string ProductName {get; set;}
        public string QuantityPerUnit {get; set;}
        public decimal UnitPrice {get; set;}
        public int UnitsInStock {get; set;}
        public int ReorderLevel {get; set;}
        public int UnitsOnOrder {get; set;}
        public bool Discontinued { get; set; }
    }
}
```

Build the business entities project, to make sure that there is no build error.

Customizing the data access layer

We have to do the same thing to the data access layer, that is, manually add the code to access the databases. In addition, we have to add the connection strings to the configuration file, and add references to the business entities project.

Adding the connection strings

For this service, we will still use the Northwind sample database. So, we first need to specify the connection strings to this database.

With Service Factory, the host application is under the `MyWCF.EasyNorthwind\Tests\MyWCF.EasyNorthwind.Host` folder. It will use the ASP.NET Development Server to host the WCF services, and the configuration file is called `web.config`. We need to modify this file to specify the connection string.

- Open the `web.config` file in the host folder, and find the following node:

  ```
  <connectionStrings/>
  ```

- Change it to:

  ```
  <connectionStrings configSource="connections.config"/>
  ```

This means that we will have a separate file to hold all of the connection strings, and this file is called `connections.config`.

The content of the file `connections.config` is:

```
<?xml version="1.0" encoding="utf-8" ?>
<connectionStrings>
  <add name="NorthwindConnectionString"
   providerName="System.Data.SqlProvider"
          connectionString="server=your_db_server\your_db_instance;
  uid=your_user_name; pwd=your_password;
       database=Northwind;" />
</connectionStrings>
```

Just add a new item (XML file) to the host application project, name it `connections.config`, and put the above content inside the file and save it.

Or you can just replace the line `<connectionStrings/>` with the following lines in the `web.config` file, and not create a new file for this example:

```
<connectionStrings>
  <add name="NorthwindConnectionString"
   providerName="System.Data.SqlProvider"
connectionString="server=your_db_server\your_db_instance;
 uid=your_user_name; pwd=your_password;
      database=Northwind;" />
</connectionStrings>
```

But remember to replace the database server name, db instance name, your user name, and your password, according to your database setup.

You can also use the following `connectionString` if you are using windows authentication:

```
connectionString="server=your_db_server\your_db_instance; database=Nor
thwind;Trusted_Connection=yes"
```

And use the following `connectionString` if you are using an integrated security connection:

```
connectionString="server=your_db_server\your_db_instance; database=Nor
thwind;Integrated Security=SSPI"
```

Adding a reference to the BusinessEntities project

Next, add a reference to the `MyWCF.EasyNorthwind.BusinessEntities` project in the data access project.

The data access layer needs to reference the `BusinessEntities` project, because this layer communicates with the business logic layer through business entities. It will retrieve information from the database, store the information in business entities, and pass the business entities back to the business logic layer. When saving the data back to the database, it will get the business entities from the business logic layer, connect to the database, and commit the changes back to the database.

Adding the data access class

Now, add a new class file to the data access project, name it `ProductDAL.cs`, and customize it as follows:

1. Add three `using` statements for the `BusinessEntities`, `SqlClient` and `Configuration` namespaces.
2. Change the file to be a public class.
3. Add a new method, `GetProduct`, to retrieve a product from the database.

The final `ProductDAL` class file should look like this:

```
using System;
using System.Collections.Generic;
using System.Linq;
using System.Text;
using MyWCF.EasyNorthwind.BusinessEntities;
using System.Data.SqlClient;
using System.Configuration;

namespace MyWCF.EasyNorthwind.DataAccess
{
    public class ProductDAL
    {
        string connectionString = ConfigurationManager.ConnectionStrin
                    gs["NorthwindConnectionString"].ConnectionString;

        public ProductEntity GetProduct(int id)
        {
            ProductEntity p = null;
            using (SqlConnection conn =
                                new SqlConnection(connectionString))
            {
                SqlCommand comm = new SqlCommand();
                comm.CommandText =
                       "select * from Products where ProductID=" + id;
                comm.Connection = conn;
                conn.Open();
                SqlDataReader reader = comm.ExecuteReader();
                if (reader.HasRows)
                {
                    reader.Read();
                    p = new ProductEntity();
                    p.ProductID = id;
                    p.ProductName =
```

```
                        (string)reader["ProductName"];
                    p.QuantityPerUnit =
                        (string)reader["QuantityPerUnit"];
                    p.UnitPrice =
                        (decimal)reader["UnitPrice"];
                    p.UnitsInStock =
                        (short)reader["UnitsInStock"];
                    p.UnitsOnOrder =
                        (short)reader["UnitsOnOrder"];
                    p.ReorderLevel =
                        (short)reader["ReorderLevel"];
                    p.Discontinued =
                        (bool)reader["Discontinued"];
                }
            }
            return p;
        }
    }
}
```

Again, build the data access project, to make sure that there is no build error.

Customizing the business logic

For the business logic project, we need to add a class file, `ProductLogic.cs`, and customize it as follows:

1. Add two `using` statements for the `BusinessEntities`, and `DataAccess` namespaces.
2. Change it to be a public class.
3. Add a new method, `GetProduct`, to call the data access layer to retrieve a product from database.

The final `ProductLogic` class file should look like this:

```
using System;
using System.Collections.Generic;
using System.Linq;
using System.Text;
using MyWCF.EasyNorthwind.BusinessEntities;
using MyWCF.EasyNorthwind.DataAccess;

namespace MyWCF.EasyNorthwind.BusinessLogic
{
    public class ProductLogic
    {
        ProductDAL productDAL = new ProductDAL();

        public ProductEntity GetProduct(int id)
        {
            return productDAL.GetProduct(id);
        }
    }
}
```

Build the business logic project, to make sure that there is no build error.

Translating the messages

We have now customized the data access and business logic layers, and connected them together. Now, we will connect the service interface layer to the business logic layer, and customize the service contracts.

First, we will build a translator to translate data between the business entities, and the data contracts.

1. From the Solution Explorer, right-click on the project item, **MyWCF.EasyNorthwind.ServiceImplementation**.
2. Select **Create Translator** from the context menu. Note that the **Create Translator** context menu item is available only for the service implementation project. You won't see it if you right-click on any other project. This is because Service Factory expects you to create translator classes only for the service implementation project, and it knows which project is the service implementation project by its role, which is defined in the `ProjectMapping.xml` file.

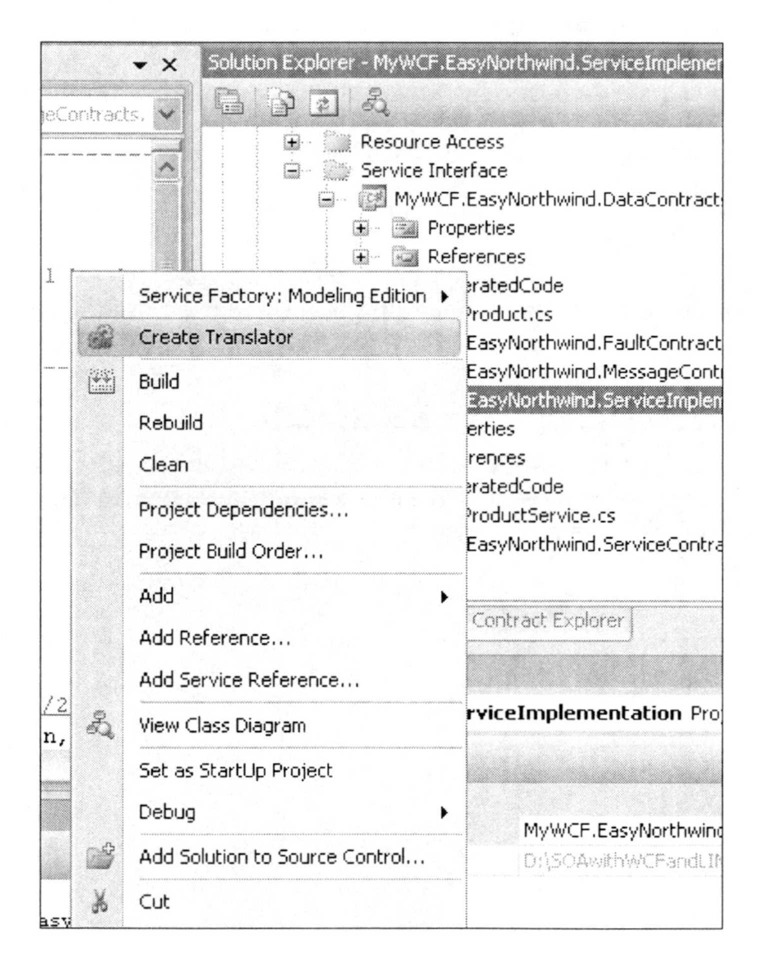

You will see that the **Service Factory: Modeling Edition | Contract Type Mapper Generator** window has popped up. In this window, we will select two classes from the solution, and create a map between the fields of those two classes. First, we will select these two classes.

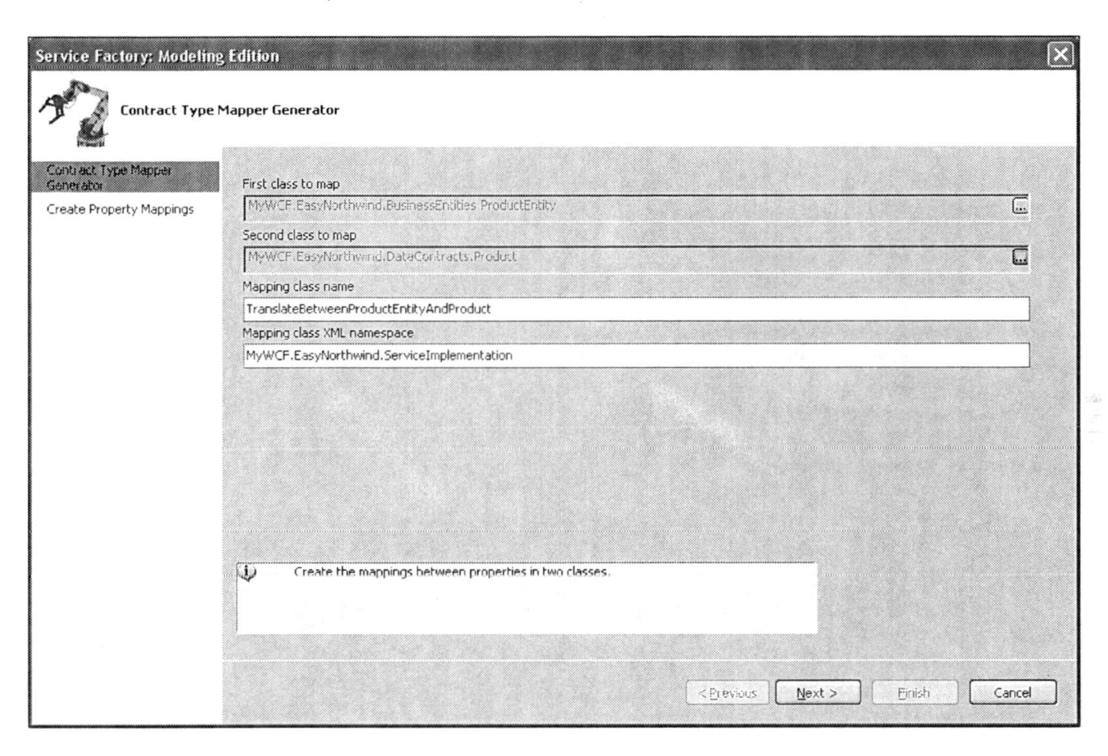

3. Click on the ellipsis button for the **First class to map**. The **Browse and Select a .NET Type** window pops up.

All of the referenced assemblies in the current service implementation project are listed in the leftmost pane, including our own MyWCF * assemblies, alongwith some system assemblies. You can choose any of them as the first class to translate from.

4. In our example, select **MyWCF.EasyNorthwind.BusinessEntities** in the left pane, and **ProductEntity** in the right pane. The selected type name now should be **MyWCF.EasyNorthwind.BusinessEntities.ProductEntity**.

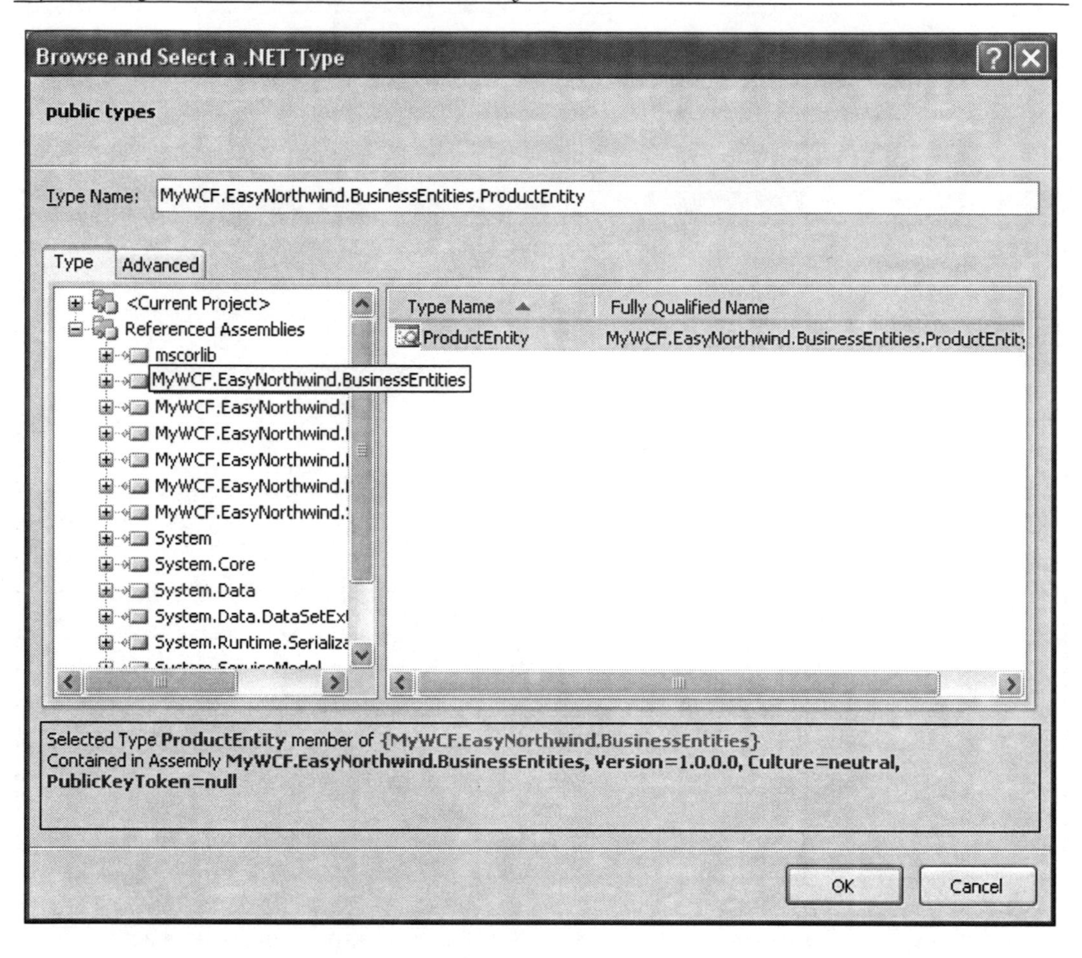

5. Click **OK** to close this window.
6. Select **MyWCF.EasyNorthwind.DataContracts.Product** as the second class to map.
7. Leave the **Mapping class name** to the defaulted **TranslateBetweenProductEntityAndProduct**, and the **Mapping class XML namespace** to **MyWCF.EasyNorthwind.ServiceImplementation**.
8. Click **Next**.
9. The **Create Property Mappings** window should pop up. In this window, select **ProductID(Int32)** from the leftmost pane, and **ProductID(Int32)** from the rightmost pane, and then click **Map** to map them.

10. Follow the same steps to map the other four properties (**ProductName**, **QuantityPerUnit**, **UnitPrice** and **Discontinued**). Leave three of the **ProductEntity** properties unmapped (**UnitsInStock**, **ReorderLevel** and **UnitsOnOrder**).
11. Finally, click **Finish** to generate the mapping class code. You will notice a new file has been added to the project, under the **GeneratedCode** folder, with all of the property mapping information for the two mapped classes.

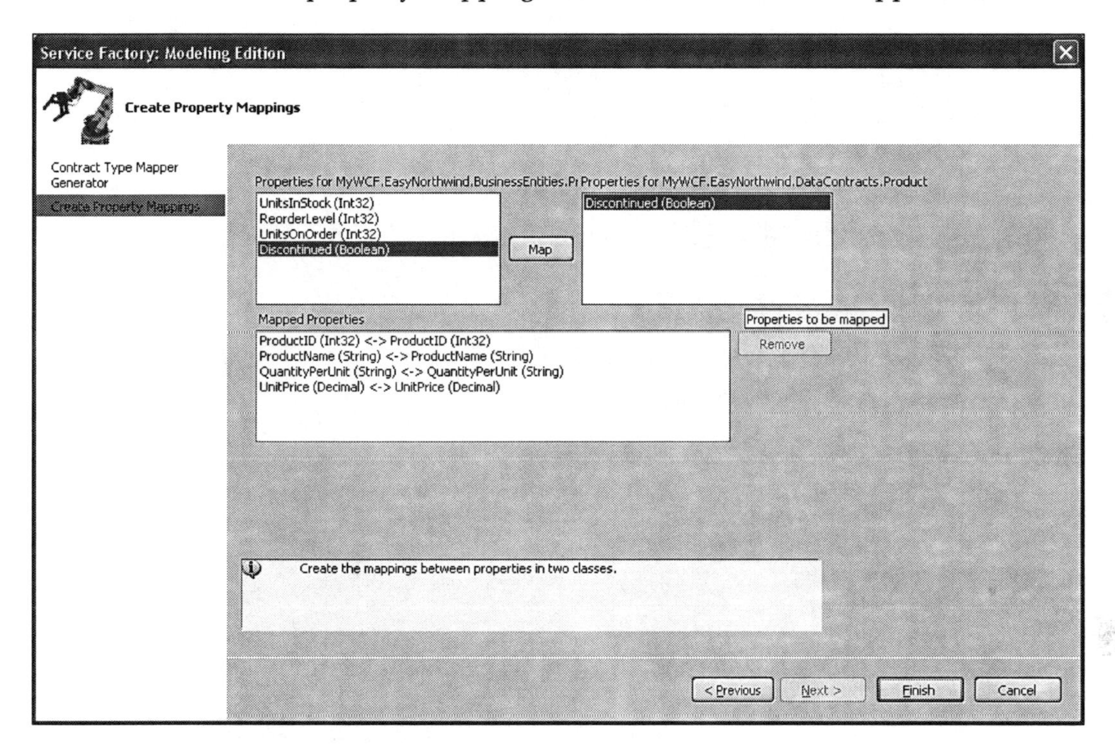

You can now build the service implementation project, to make sure that there is no build error.

Customizing the Fault contract

If you open the `ProductFault.cs` file in the `FaultContracts` project under the `GeneratedCode` folder, you will see that the `ProductFault` class doesn't have a constructor. To make it easier to throw a `ProductFault` exception in the product service, we will customize it to include a constructor with a string parameter as the fault message.

We can open the `ProductFault.cs` file and modify it directly, adding the constructor as needed. However, because this class is generated by Service Factory, any change to it will be lost if we ever need to regenerate it. For example, we may want to add a new member to the fault in the future, such as the feedback method for a specific fault, at which point we will have to regenerate it.

So we will add another file, called `ProductFault.cs`, but make it a partial class, to extend the generated `ProductFault` class.

Follow these steps to add the partial class:

1. In the Solution Explorer, right-click on the project, **MyWCF.EasyNorthwind.FaultContracts**.
2. Select **Add | Class...** from the context menu.
3. Add a new class file, named **ProductFault.cs**.

Then, customize the file as follows:

- Change it to be a public partial class
- Add a constructor with one string parameter

The content of this file should look like this:

```
using System;
using System.Collections.Generic;
using System.Linq;
using System.Text;

namespace MyWCF.EasyNorthwind.FaultContracts
{
    public partial class ProductFault
    {
        public ProductFault(string message)
        {
            this.faultMessage = message;
        }
    }
}
```

Again, build the `FaultContracts` project to make sure that there is no build error.

Customizing the product service

Now that we have finished customizing the data access layer and business logic layer, the last step of the service implementation is to customize the `ProductService.cs` file. If you open it now, you will find that it contains an empty method, `GetProduct`. We will customize it to call the business logic layer to retrieve a product, and throw a `FaultException` if no product is found.

We can also open the `ProductService.cs` file and modify it directly, adding the required functionality for the method `GetProduct`. However, because this class is generated by Service Factory, any change to it will be lost if we ever need to regenerate it. For example, we may want to add a new operation to the service in the future, which would necessitate it.

Just as we did for the `ProductFault` class, we will add another file, called `ProductService.cs`, but we will make it a partial class, to extend the generated `ProductService` class.

Follow these steps to add the partial class:

1. In the Solution Explorer, right-click on the project **MyWCF.EasyNorthwind.ServiceImplementation**.
2. Select **Add | Class...** from the context menu.
3. Add a new class file named `ProductService.cs`.

Then, customize this file as follows:

1. Change it to make it a public partial class.
2. Add six `using` statements for the `BusinessEntities`, `DataContracts`, `MessageContracts`, `BusinessLogic`, `FaultContracts`, and `ServiceModel` namespaces.
3. Add a method, `GetProduct`, to call the business logic layer to retrieve details for a product, convert the product entity to a product contract, and then return it as a message.

The content of `ProductService.cs` should look like this:

```
using System;
using System.Collections.Generic;
using System.Linq;
using System.Text;
using MyWCF.EasyNorthwind.BusinessEntities;
using MyWCF.EasyNorthwind.DataContracts;
using MyWCF.EasyNorthwind.MessageContracts;
```

```
using MyWCF.EasyNorthwind.BusinessLogic;
using MyWCF.EasyNorthwind.FaultContracts;
using System.ServiceModel;

namespace MyWCF.EasyNorthwind.ServiceImplementation
{
    public partial class ProductService
    {
        ProductLogic productLogic = new ProductLogic();

        public override GetProductResponse GetProduct(
                            GetProductRequest request)
        {
            // call business entity layer to retrieve a product
            ProductEntity productEntity =
                            productLogic.GetProduct(request.ProductID);

            // throw a Fault if no product found
            if (productEntity == null)
                throw new FaultException<ProductFault>(new
                     ProductFault("No product found with id " +
                     request.ProductID), "Product Fault");

            // translate it to a Product Data Contract object
            Product product;
            product = TranslateBetweenProductEntityAndProduct.
                      TranslateProductEntityToProduct(productEntity);

            // create a response message
            GetProductResponse response = new GetProductResponse();
            response.Product = product;

            // return the response message
            return response;
        }
    }
}
```

If you have used the previous version's Service Factory, you may recall that some of the tasks we put in the service implementation class were handled by a service adapter. This version's Service Factory doesn't create an adaptor by default. Instead, it puts all of them in the service implementation class. You can always create your own adaptor to provide an extra level of decoupling between the business logic and the service interface.

You can now build the `ServiceImplementation` project, to make sure that there is no build error.

Modeling the host application and the test client

Now that we have the service ready, we need a host application to host it, and a client application to test it. But if you open the `Host` or `Client` folders in the solution, you will see that they are not completed. We have to do some extra work to make them work.

Service Factory does not use WCF Service Host to host the service. Instead, it chooses to use the ASP.NET Development Server to host the service. It also creates a separate host application, so that the service projects and the host application are stored in separate folders.

The test client Service Factory created for us is a Windows application, with a text box and a **Execute** button in it.

Service Factory also supplies a host model that we can use to model the host and client applications. Next, we will use this model to generate the basic host and client applications. We will host the **EasyNorthwind** WCF service in this new host application, and test it with the new test client.

Modeling the host application

Follow these steps to model the host application:

1. In the Solution Explorer, right-click on the **EasyNorthwind Models** item.
2. Select **Add | New Model** from the context menu
3. On the pop-up dialog window, choose **Host Model** as the **Model Type**, enter **EasyNorthwind** as the model name, and enter `http://EasyNorthwind.MyWCF.MyCompany.com` as the XML namespace

4. Click **Finish**

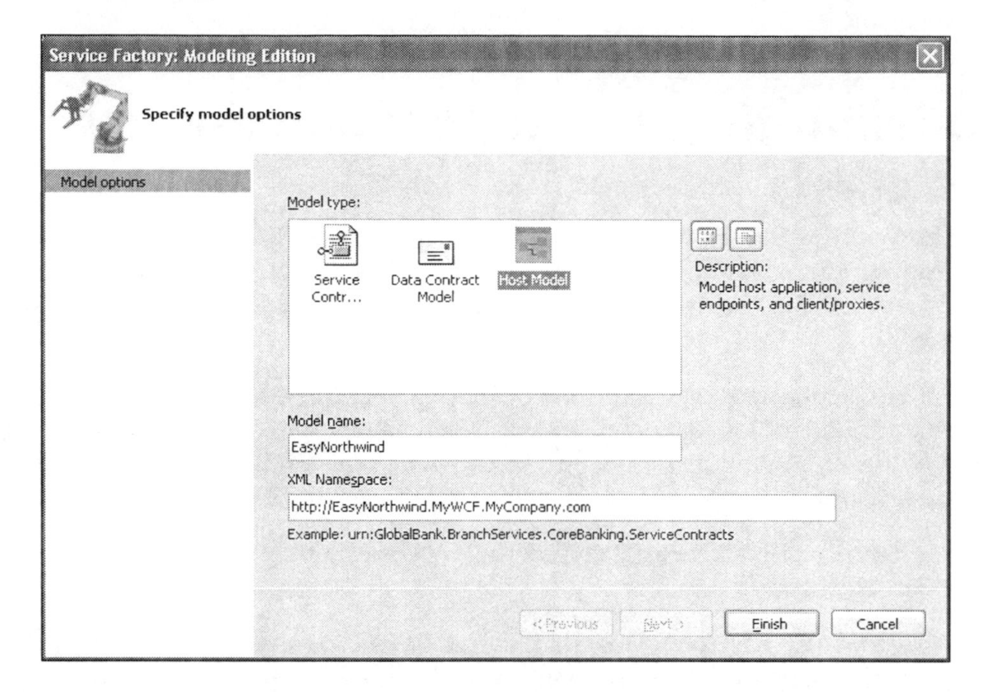

Now, the Host Model diagram should open up on your screen. As this model is empty, we can't do anything with this diagram. We first have to add a host application to the model to enable it.

Follow these steps to add a host application to this host model:

1. The **Host Explorer** should have opened now on the right-hand side (if not, or you just closed it, select menu item **View | Other Windows | Host Explorer** to open it now). From the explorer, right-click on the **Host Model** item, and select **Add New Host Application** from the context menu.

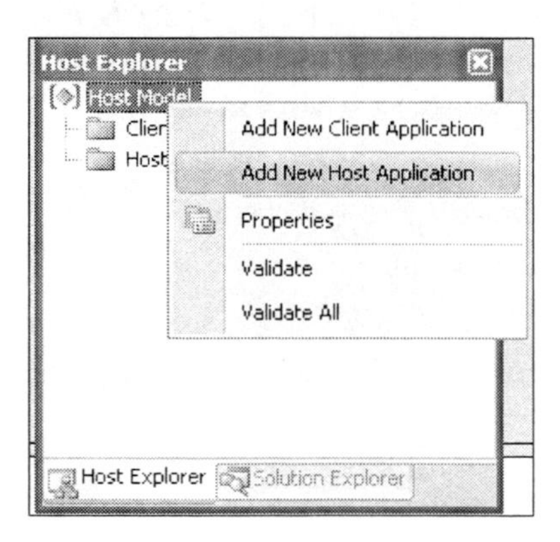

2. Now, in the **Properties** window, change the name of the new host application from **HostApplication1** to **EasyNorthwindHost**, select **WCF Extensions** as the **Implementation Technology**, and select **MyWCF.EasyNorthwind.Host** as the **Implementation Project**.

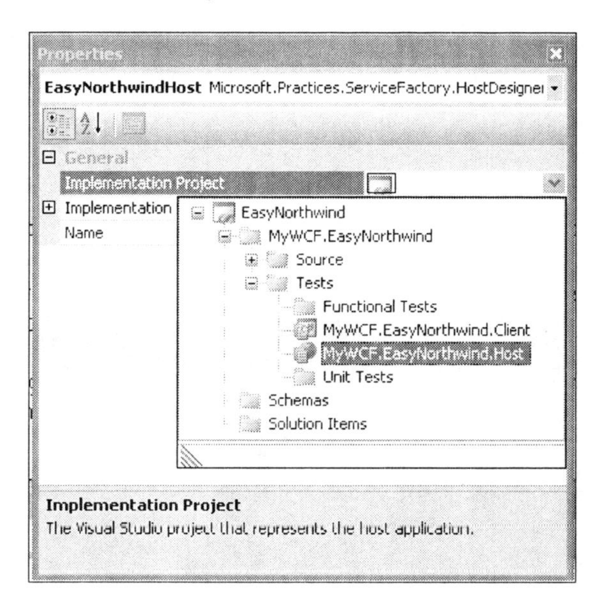

3. In the **Host Explorer**, right-click on the **EasyNorthwinHost** item, and select **Add New Service Reference** from the context menu.

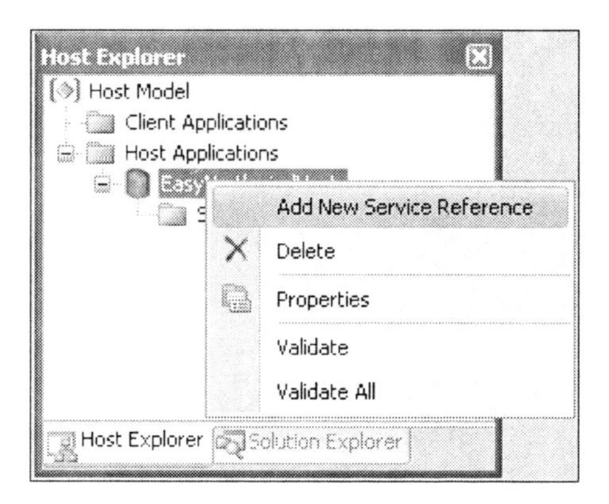

4. From the **Properties** window, change the name of the new service reference from **ServiceReference1** to **ProductServiceRef**. Change **Enable Metadata Publishing** to **True**, and select **EasyNorthwind Models\productService\productService** as the **Service Implementation Type**.

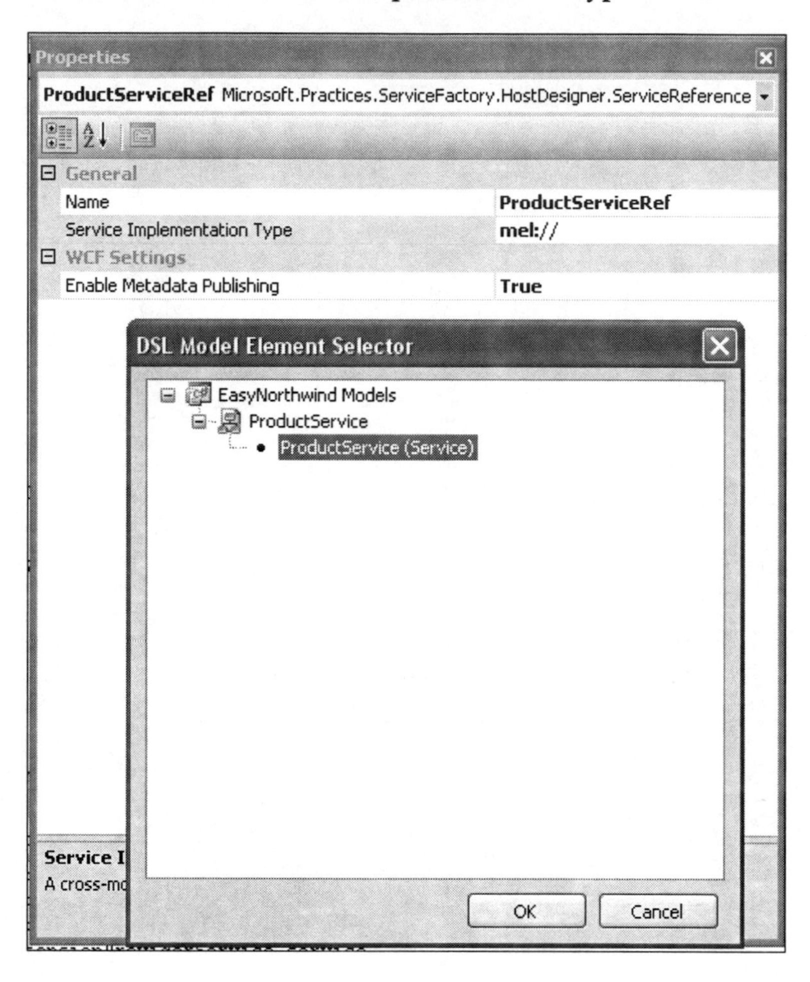

Now that we have the host application created, and the service reference added, we need to define an endpoint for it. Later, in this chapter, the test client will communicate with this endpoint to test the service.

1. In the **Host Explorer**, right-click on the **ProductServiceRef**, and select **Add New Endpoint** from the context menu.

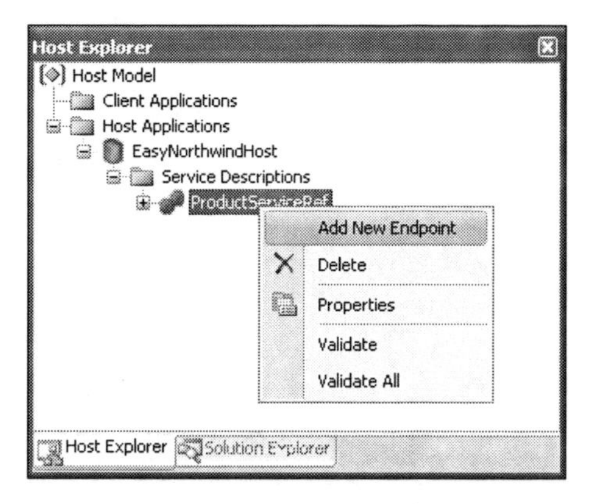

2. In the **Properties** window, rename the new endpoint from **Endpoint1** to **ProductEndpoint**.

Generating the host application

Now that we have finished modeling the host application, we will generate the source code for the host application from this host model.

But before we can generate the source code for the host application, we need to validate this host model. You can do this from the **Host Explorer**, or from within the **Host Model** diagram.

1. From the **Host Explorer**, you can right-click on the **ProductServiceRef**, and select **Validate All** from the context menu.
2. You can also validate the model from the **Host Model** diagram by clicking on the link, **Validate Model** (the **ProductServiceRef** must be selected in the Host Explorer in order to see this link).

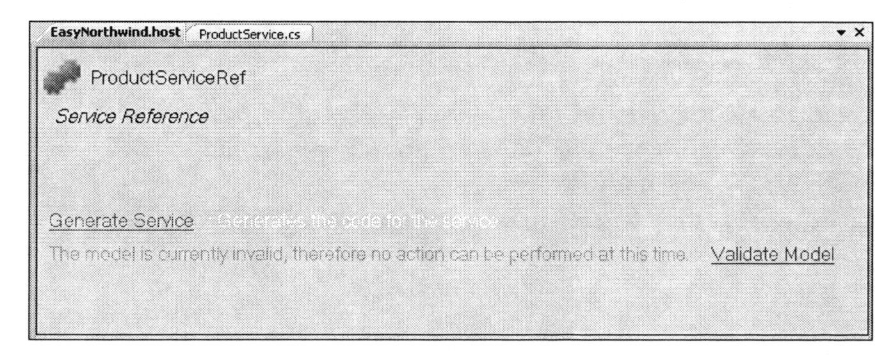

Once the model has been validated, the **Validate Model** link will disappear, and a new link will appear as **Generate Service**.

3. Now, click on the link **Generate Service**. This will generate the service reference file `ProductServiceRef.svc`, populate the configuration file `web.config`, and copy all of the service related assemblies to the `bin` directory. All of these files are under the folder `D:\SOAwithWCFandLINQ\Projects\EasyNorthwind\MyWCF.EasyNorthwind\Tests\MyWCF.EasyNorthwind.Host`.
4. Before we go onto model the client application, we need to change one property for the host application. In the **Solution Explorer**, select **D:\...\MyWCF.EasyNorthwind.Host** project, change its **use dynamic ports** setting to **False**, and enter **8080** as the **port number**.

Adding the test client to the host model

The host application has now been generated. Next, we will create the test client application. We will use this test client to test the service.

As with the host application, Service Factory also allows us to create a test client from the host model. First, we need to follow these steps to add a client application to the host model.

1. Open the **Host Explorer.** If it is blank, just double-click on the **EasyNorthwind.host** item in the **Solution Explorer** under the **EasyNorthwind Models** folder.
2. Right-click on **Host Model** and select **Add New Client Application** from the context menu.

3. In the **Properties** window, change the name of the new client application from **ClientApplication1** to **EasyNorthwindClient**, select **WCF Extensions** as the **Implementation Technology**, and select **MyWCF.EasyNorthwind. Client** as the **Implementation Project**.
4. Right-click on the **EasyNorthwindClient** item, and select **Add New Proxy** from the context menu.
5. Select the new proxy, and change its name from **Proxy1** to **EasyNorthwindProxy**. Then right-click on it, and select **ProductEndpoint** for its **Endpoint** property.

The final **Host Explorer** looks like this:

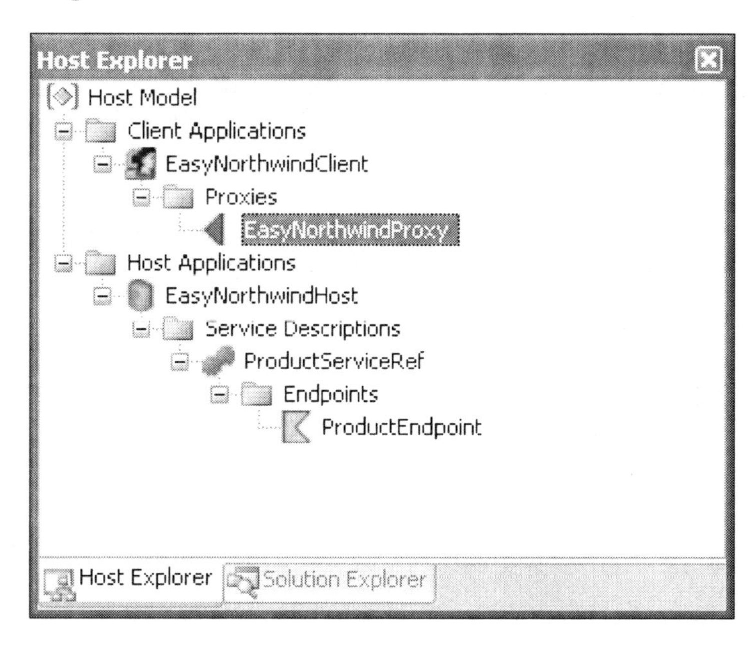

Generating the client proxy

We have added the test client to the host model and added a reference to the endpoint of the service. Next, we will generate the source code for the test client from this model.

In this section, we will use Service Factory to generate the proxy classes of the WCF service for the client application. In one of the previous chapters, we used the tool `SvcUtil.exe` to generate the proxy files manually. Here, Service Factory will do this job for us. After we have generated the proxy files, we will customize the test client to call the service in the next section.

Follow the steps below to generate the proxy files:

1. First, we need to start the host application. Open the **Solution Explorer**, right-click on **D:\...\MyWCF.EasyNorthwind.Host** under the **MyWCF.EasyNorthwind\Tests** folder, and select **Build Web Site** from the context menu. Right-click on it again, and select **View in Browser**. The ASP.NET Development Server will be started, and a browser will open to show all of the files under the virtual folder **MyWCF.EasyNorthwind.Host.**
2. Now, open the **Host Explorer**, and click on the **EasyNorthwindProxy** item under the **EasyNorthwindClient\Proxies** folder. Then, in the Host Model diagram, click on the **Generate Proxy** link. The **Add WCF Service Reference** dialog box will pop up.
3. In the **Add WCF Service Reference** dialog box, accept all of the default settings, and click **Next**. Service Factory will now download the metadata of the service, and list all of the endpoints for the service. Accept **ProductEndpoint**, click **Next**, and then click **Finish** to close the window.

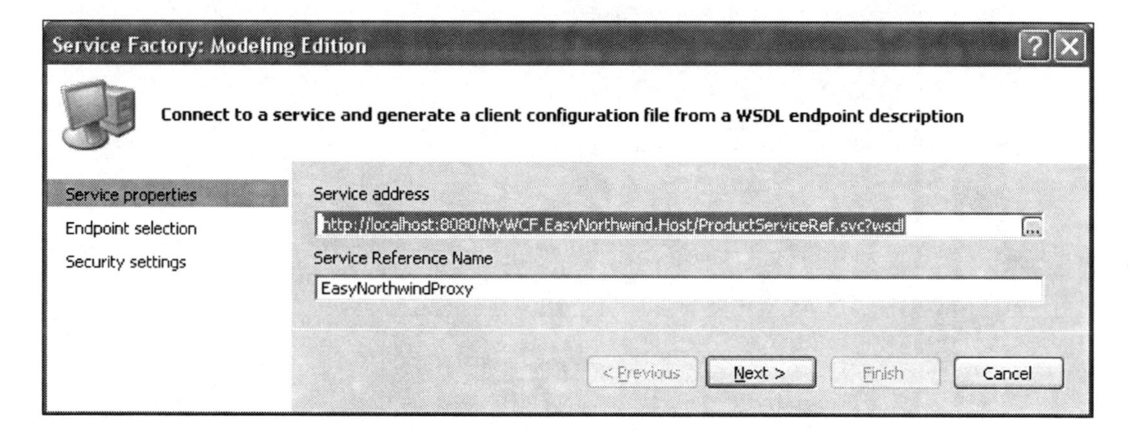

This will generate the service reference file, `EasyNorthwindProxy.cs`, and populate the configuration file, `app.config`. These two files are under the folder: `D:\SOAwithWCFandLINQ\Projects\EasyNorthwind\MyWCF.EasyNorthwind\Tests\MyWCF.EasyNorthwind.Client`.

If you haven't started the host application, when you click **Next**, you will get an error saying "can't download metadata".

You can now build the client project, to make sure there is no build error.

Customizing the client

In the previous sections, we added the test client to the host model, and generated the proxy files for the client application from the host model. However, the test client currently contains only an empty Windows Form, one proxy file, and one configuration file.

So, the last step is to customize the client application. Service Factory has added the service reference, and populated the configuration file for us. What is left for us to do is to add code to call the service, and display the result.

First, we will customize the `MainForm` of this client application:

1. Open the `MainForm.cs` file, change the **Search label** text to **Product ID**.
2. Add a label below the product ID textbox, with the text, **Product Details**.
3. Add a textbox control below the product details label, and name it **txtResult**.

The form should look like this:

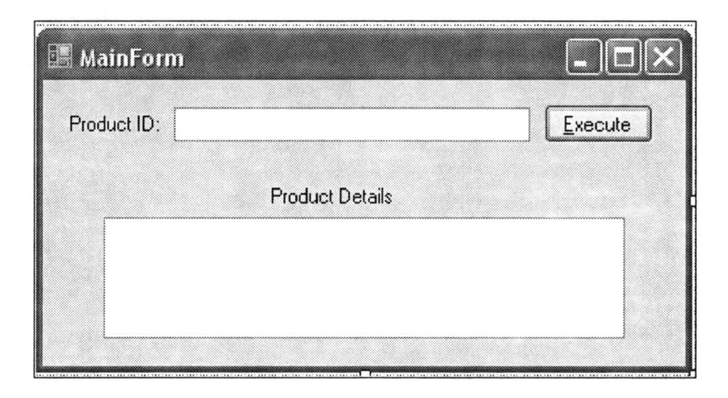

Now, we need to follow the steps below to add the code in the Form.

1. Double-click on the **Execute** button to add an event handler. This will also bring the code for the `MainForm` to the front.
2. First, add two `using` statements for the `EasyNorthwindProxy` and `ServiceModel` namespaces, like this:

   ```
   using MyWCF.EasyNorthwind.Client.EasyNorthwindProxy;
   using System.ServiceModel;
   ```

3. Then, modify the `ExecuteButton_Click` method to call the service to retrieve the product details, and display the result.

The content of the `MainForm.cs` file is like this:

```
using System;
using System.Collections.Generic;
using System.ComponentModel;
using System.Data;
using System.Drawing;
using System.Text;
using System.Windows.Forms;
using MyWCF.EasyNorthwind.Client.EasyNorthwindProxy;
using System.ServiceModel;

namespace MyWCF.EasyNorthwind.Client
{
    public partial class MainForm : Form
    {
        public MainForm()
        {
            InitializeComponent();
        }

        private void ExecuteButton_Click(object sender, EventArgs e)
        {
            ProductServiceContractClient client =
              new ProductServiceContractClient();
            GetProductRequest request = new GetProductRequest();

            string result = "";
            try
            {
                request.ProductID = Int32.Parse(SearchText.Text.
                                                    ToString());
                Product product = client.GetProduct(request);

                StringBuilder sb = new StringBuilder();
```

```
                sb.Append("ProductID:" + product.ProductID.ToString()
                                                            + "\r\n");
                sb.Append("ProductName:" + product.ProductName +
                                                           "\r\n");
                sb.Append("QuantityPerUnit:" + product.QuantityPerUnit
                                                               + "\r\n");
                sb.Append("UnitPrice:" + product.UnitPrice.
                                   ToString("C") + "\r\n");
                sb.Append("Discontinued:" + product.Discontinued.
                                                    ToString());
                result = sb.ToString();
            }
            catch (TimeoutException ex)
            {
                result = "The service operation timed out. " +
                                                   ex.Message;
            }
            catch (FaultException<ProductFault> ex)
            {
                result = "ProductFault returned: " +
                             ex.Detail.FaultMessage;
            }
            catch (FaultException ex)
            {
                result = "Unknown Fault: " + ex.ToString();
            }
            catch (CommunicationException ex)
            {
                result = "There was a communication problem. " +
                                 ex.Message + ex.StackTrace;
            }
            catch (Exception ex)
            {
                result = "Other excpetion: " + ex.Message +
                                             ex.StackTrace;
            }
            txtResult.Text = result;
        }
    }
}
```

Testing the service

Now, set the `MyWCF.EasyNorthwind.Client` project as the startup project, and press *F5* to start it. Note that if you start it in non-debugging mode by pressing *Ctrl+F5*, you will have to start the host application first, or set the solution to start with multiple projects, as we did in one of the previous chapters.

You will see the main window for the test client. Enter a valid product ID and click **Execute** to get the product details.

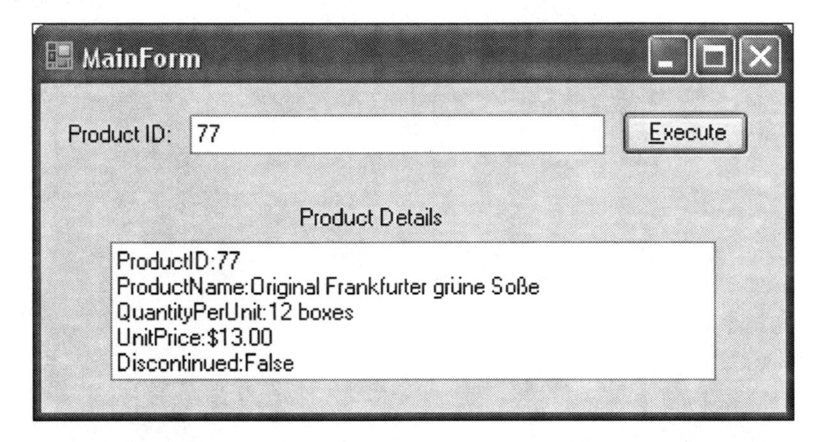

You will also notice that another dialog box has popped up, warning that we can't debug the host.

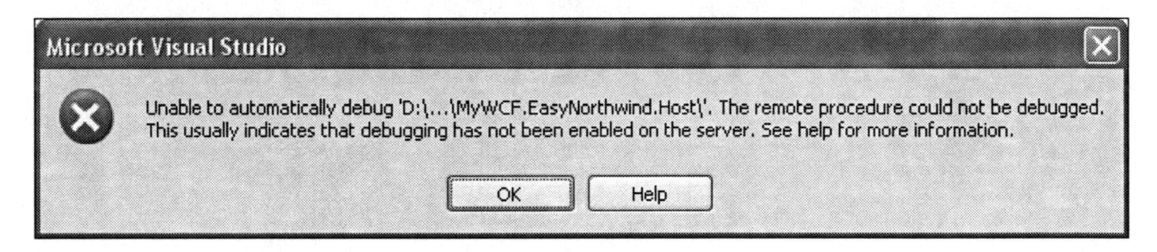

This is because we haven't enabled the debugging setting for the host application. Just click **OK** to close this dialog box, or you can modify the debugging setting to `true` in the `web.config` file, under the `MyWCF.EasyNorthwind.Host` project:

```
<compilation debug="true">
```

Note that after you change the above line in the `web.config` file in the host application, and when you rebuild the solution, you will get two messages in the **Error List** window.

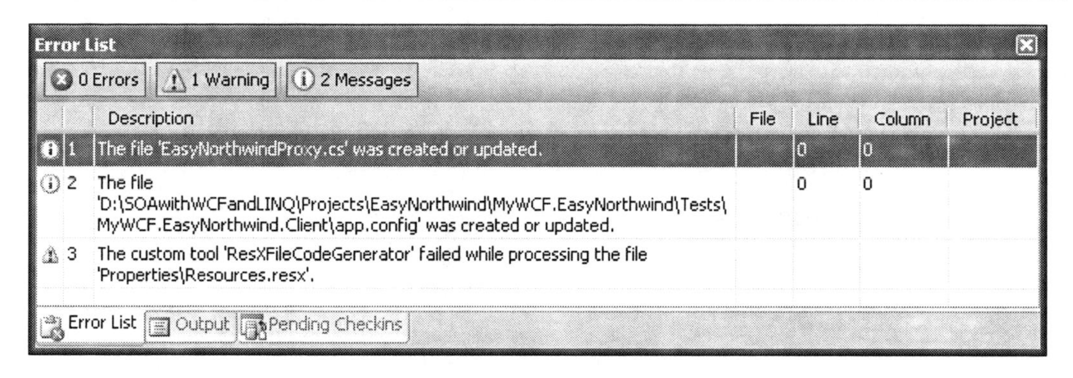

This is because the client application configuration file is referencing the host application project, so after the host application is updated, the client configuration file will be updated automatically. However, the client application project does not depend on any other project. So, if you rebuild any other project, Visual Studio won't rebuild the client application. The client is independent of the server projects. Visual Studio keeps all project dependencies in the solution's, **Property Pages**. You can open this window via menu option **View | Property Pages** or **Project | Properties**, while the solution item is selected in the Solution Explorer.

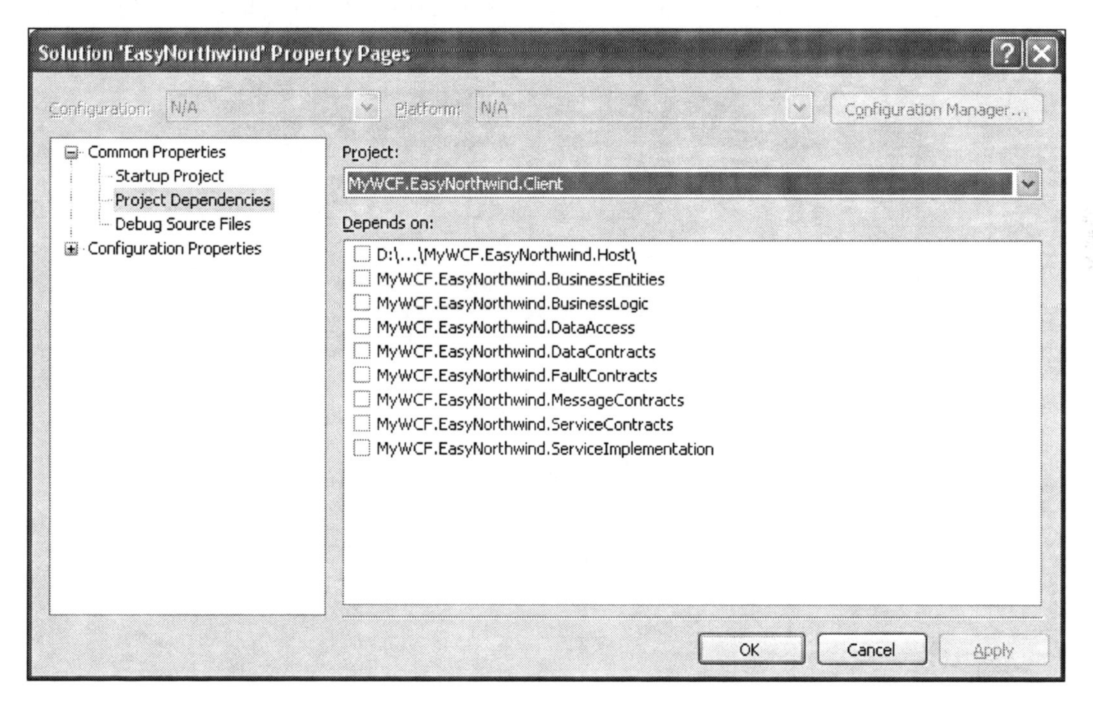

At the beginning of this section, we tested this service with a valid product ID. Now, follow these steps to test the service with an invalid product ID:

1. Enter an invalid product ID. You will get a **No product found** fault exception.

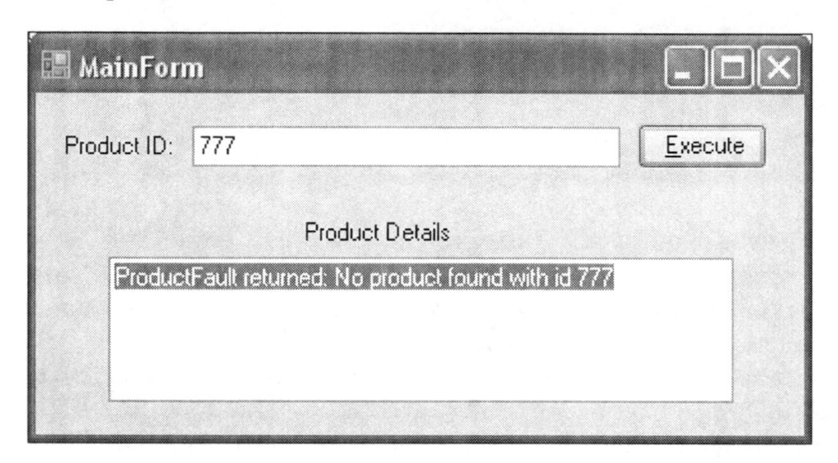

2. Enter a string as the product ID. When you click the **Execute** button, you will get an invalid format exception.

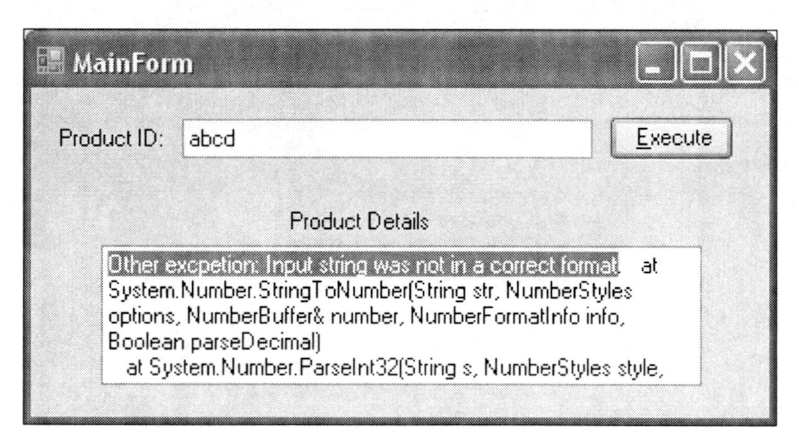

3. And finally, if you shut down the host server (right-click on the little ASP.NET Development Server icon on your task bar, and select **Stop**), or if you start the client without starting the host server, you will get a communication exception.

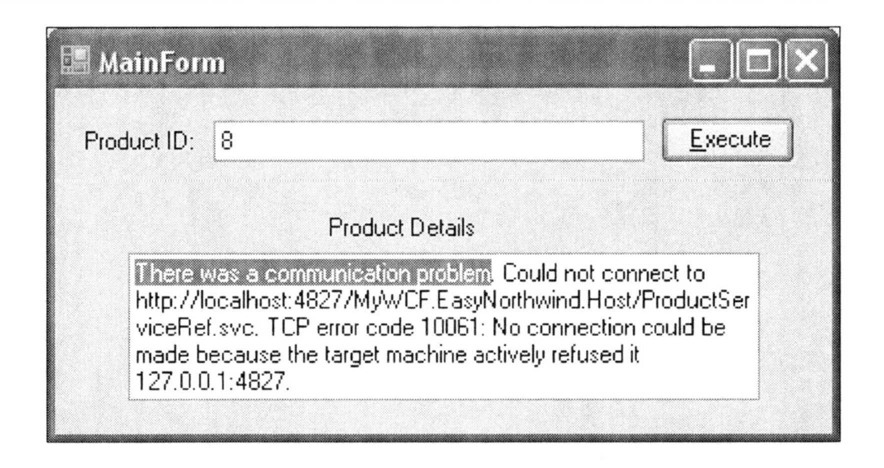

Summary

In this chapter, we completed the `EasyNorthwind` WCF service. We added the business entities, the business logic layer, and the data access layer. We modeled the host application, created the test client, and tested the WCF service. The key points in this chapter include:

- For business entities, the business logic layer, and the data access layer, Service Factory creates the projects for you, but does not generate the source code
- Service Factory generates translators between business entities and data contracts
- Business entities, the business logic layer, and data access layer objects are just Plain Old C# Objects (POCO) with no WCF attribute added to them and there is no need to add a reference to the `ServiceModel` namespace
- When customizing a generated class, you should add a new partial class instead of modifying the generated class directly
- Connection strings can be included in a separate XML file rather than the main configuration file
- In addition to the Service Contract Model, and the Data Contract Model, there is a Host Model in the Service Factory that allows you to model a host application and generate source code for the host application
- The Host Model can also generate proxy files for a client application

9
Introducing Language-Integrated Query (LINQ)

In the previous two chapters of this book, we used Service Factory to create the WCF service. In the data access layer, we used the raw ADO.NET SQL adapters to communicate with the Northwind database. In one of the following chapters, we will explain how to use LINQ to SQL in our data access layer.

But before using LINQ to SQL in our data access layer, we need to understand what it actually means by saying LINQ, or LINQ to SQL. Before understanding LINQ, we first need to understand some new C# features related to LINQ. In this chapter, we will first explore these new C# features related to LINQ, and then we will explore LINQ.

In this chapter, we will cover:

- What LINQ is
- New data type `var`
- Automatic properties
- Object initializer and Collection initializer
- Anonymous types
- Extension methods
- Lambda expressions
- Built-in LINQ extension methods and method syntax
- LINQ query syntax and query expression
- Built-in LINQ operators

What is LINQ

Language-Integrated Query (LINQ) is a set of features in Visual Studio 2008 that extends powerful query capabilities to the language syntax of C# and Visual Basic.

Let us see an example first. Suppose there is a list of integers like this:

```
List<int> list = new List<int>() { 1, 2, 3, 4, 5, 6, 100 };
```

To find all the even numbers in this list, you might write some code like this:

```
List<int> list1 = new List<int>();
foreach (var num in list)
{
    if (num % 2 == 0)
        list1.Add(num);
}
```

Now with LINQ, you can select all of the even numbers from this list, and assign the query result to a variable,in just one sentence, like this:

```
var list2 = from number in list
            where number % 2 == 0
            select number;
```

In this example, `list2` and `list1` are equivalent. `list2` contains the same numbers as `list1` does. As you can see, you don't write a `foreach` loop. Instead, you write an SQL statement.

But what do `from`, `where` and `select` mean here? Where are they defined? How and when can I use them? Let us start the exploration now.

Creating the test solution and project

To show these LINQ-related new features, we will need a test project to demonstrate what they are, and how to use them. So we first need to create the test solution, and the project.

Follow these steps to create the solution, and the project.

1. Start Visual Studio 2008.
2. Select menu option **File | New | Project...** to create a new solution.
3. In the **New Project** window, select **Visual C# | Console Application** as the **Project type** and **Template**.

4. Enter **TestLINQ** as the **Solution Name**, and **TestNewFeaturesApp** as the (project) **Name**.
5. Click **OK** to create the solution and the project.

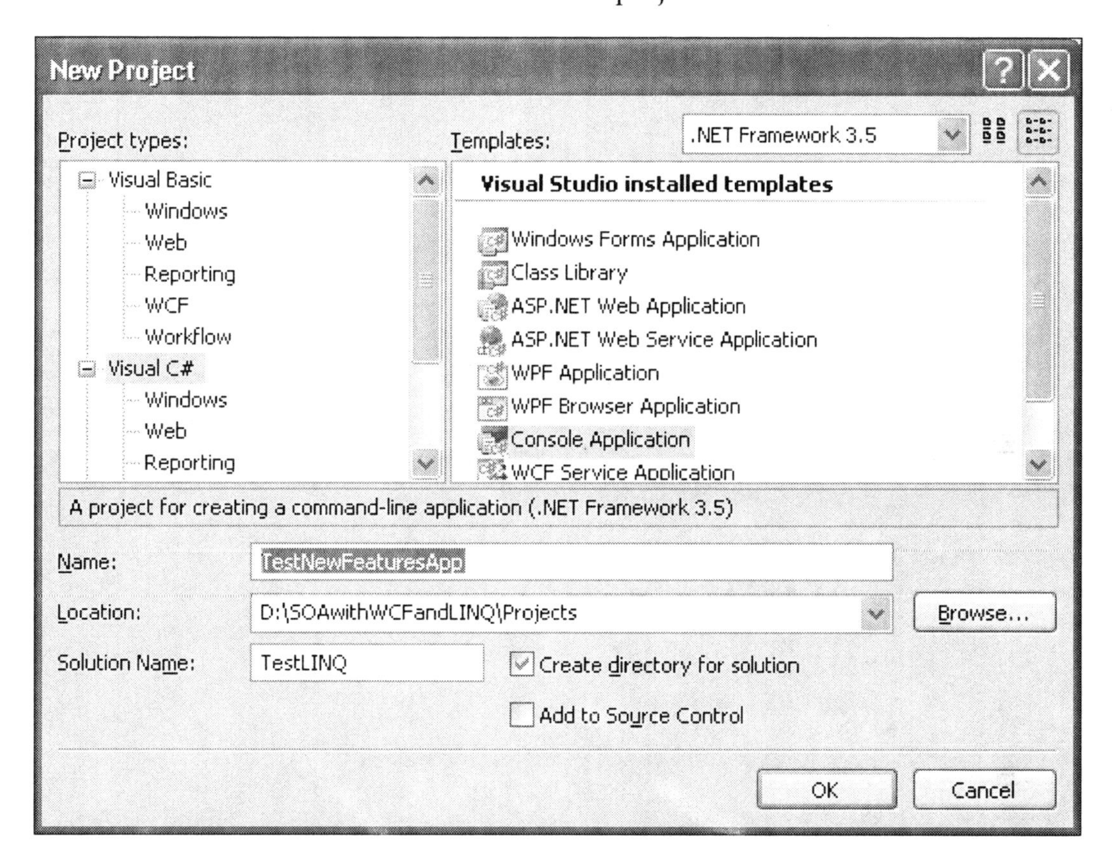

New data type var

The first new feature that is very important for LINQ is the new data type, `var`. This is a new keyword that can be used to declare a variable, and this variable can be initialized to any valid C# data.

In the C# 3.0 specification, such variables are called implicitly-typed local variables.

A `var` variable must be initialized when it is declared. The compile-time type of the initializer expression must not be of `null` type, but the real time expression can be `null`. Once it is initialized, its data type is fixed to the type of the initial data.

The following statements are valid uses of the `var` keyword:

```
// valid var statements
var x = "1";
var n = 0;
string s = "string";
var s2 = s;
s2 = null;
string s3 = null;
var s4 = s3;
```

At compile time, the above `var` statements are compiled to IL like this:

```
string x = "1";
int n = 0;
string s2 = s;
```

The `var` keyword is only meaningful to the Visual Studio 2008 compiler. The compiled assembly is actually a valid .NET 2.0 assembly. It doesn't need any special instructions or libraries to support this feature.

The following statements are invalid usages of the `var` keyword:

```
// invalid var statements
var v;
var nu = null;
var v2 = "12"; v2 = 3;
```

The first one is illegal because it doesn't have an initializer.

The second one initializes variable `nu` to `null` which is not allowed, although once defined, a `var` type variable can be assigned `null`. If you think that at compile time, the compiler needs to create a variable using this type of initializer, then you understand why the initializer can't be `null` at compile time.

The third one is illegal because once defined, an integer can't be converted to a string implicitly (`v2` is a type of string).

Automatic properties

In the past, for a class member, if we wanted to define it as a property member, we had to define a private member variable first. For example, for the `Product` class, we can define a property, `ProductName` as follows:

```
private string productName;
public string ProductName
{
    get { return productName; }
    set { productName = value; }
}
```

This may be useful if we need to add some logic inside the `get/set` methods. But if we don't need to, the above format gets tedious, especially if there are many members.

Now, with the new version of C#, the above property can be simplified into one statement:

```
public string ProductName { get; set; }
```

When Visual Studio compiles this statement, it will automatically create a private member variable `productName`, and use the old style's `get/set` methods to define the property. This could save on lots of typing.

Just as with the new type `var`, the automatic properties are only meaningful to the Visual Studio 2008 compiler. The compiled assembly is actually a valid .NET 2.0 assembly.

Interestingly, later on, if you find you need to add logic to the `get/set` methods, you can still convert this automatic property to the old style's property.

Now, let us create this class in the test project:

```
public class Product
{
    public int ProductID { get; set; }
    public string ProductName { get; set; }
    public decimal UnitPrice { get; set; }
}
```

We can put this class inside the `Program.cs` file, within the namespace, `TestNewFeaturesApp`. We will use this class throughout this chapter.

Object initializer

In the past, we couldn't initialize an object without using a constructor. For example, we could create and initialize a `Product` object like this:

```
Product p = new product(1, "first candy", 100.0);
```

Or, we could create the object, and then initialize it later, like this:

```
Product p = new Product();
p.ProductID = 1;
p.ProductName = "first candy";
p.UnitPrice=(decimal)100.0;
```

Now with the new **object initializer** feature, we can do it as follows:

```
Product product = new Product
{
    ProductID = 1,
    ProductName = "first candy",
    UnitPrice = (decimal)100.0
};
```

At compile time, the compiler will automatically insert the necessary property setter code. So, again this new feature is a Visual Studio 2008 compiler feature. The compiled assembly is actually a valid .NET 2.0 assembly.

We can also define and initialize a variable with an array like this:

```
var arr = new[] { 1, 10, 20, 30 };
```

This array is called an **implicitly typed array**.

Collection initializer

Similar to the object initializer, we can also initialize a collection when we declare it, like this:

```
List<Product> products = new List<Product> {
    new Product {
        ProductID = 1,
        ProductName = "first candy",
        UnitPrice = (decimal)10.0 },
    new Product {
        ProductID = 2,
        ProductName = "second candy",
        UnitPrice = (decimal)35.0 },
    new Product {
        ProductID = 3,
        ProductName = "first vegetable",
        UnitPrice = (decimal)6.0 },
    new Product {
        ProductID = 4,
```

```
                    ProductName = "second vegetable",
                    UnitPrice = (decimal)15.0 },
                new Product {
                    ProductID = 5,
                    ProductName = "third product",
                    UnitPrice = (decimal)55.0 }
            };
```

Here, we created a list and initialized it with five new products. For each new product, we used the object initializer to initialize its value.

Just as with the object initializer, this new feature **collection initializer** is also a Visual Studio 2008 compiler feature, and compiled assembly is valid .NET 2.0 assembly.

Anonymous types

With the new feature of the object initializer, and the new `var` data type, we can create anonymous data types easily in C# 3.0.

For example, if we define a variable like this:

```
var a = new { Name = "name1", Address = "address1" };
```

At compile time, the compiler will actually create an anonymous type as follows:

```
class __Anonymous1
{
    private string name;
    private string address;
    public string Name {
        get{
            return name;
        }
        set {
            name=value
        }
    }
    public string Address {
        get{
            return address;
        }
        set{
            address=value;
        }
    }
}
```

The name of the anonymous type is automatically generated by the compiler, and cannot be referenced in the program text.

If two anonymous types have the same members with the same data types in their initializers, then these two variables have the same types. For example, if there is another variable defined like this:

```
var b = new { Name = "name2", Address = "address2" };
```

Then we can assign `a` to `b` like this:

```
b = a;
```

The anonymous type is particularly useful for LINQ when the result of LINQ can be shaped to be whatever you like. We will give more examples of this when we discuss LINQ.

As mentioned earlier, this new feature is again a Visual Studio 2008 compiler feature, and compiled assembly is a valid .NET 2.0 assembly.

Extension methods

Extension methods are static methods that can be invoked using the instance method syntax. In effect, extension methods make it possible for us to extend existing types and constructed types with additional methods.

For example, we can define an extension method as follows:

```
public static class MyExtensions
{
    public static bool IsCandy(this Product p)
    {
        if (p.ProductName.IndexOf("candy") >= 0)
            return true;
        else
            return false;
    }
}
```

In this example, the static method `IsCandy` takes a `this` parameter of `Product` type, and searches for the word `candy` inside the product name. If it finds a match, it assumes this is a `candy` product and returns `true`. Otherwise, it returns `false`, meaning this is not a `candy` product.

To simplify the example, we put this class inside the same namespace as our main test application, `TestNewFeaturesApp`. Now, in the program, we can call this extension method like this:

```
if (product.IsCandy())
    Console.WriteLine("yes, it is a candy");
else
    Console.WriteLine("no, it is not a candy");
```

It looks as if `IsCandy` is a real instance method of the `Product` class. Actually, it is a real method of the `Product` class, but it is not defined inside the `Product` class. Instead, it is defined in another static class.

Not only does it look like a real instance method, but this new extension method actually pops up when a dot is typed following the `product` variable. The following image shows the intellisense of the `product` variable within Visual Studio 2008.

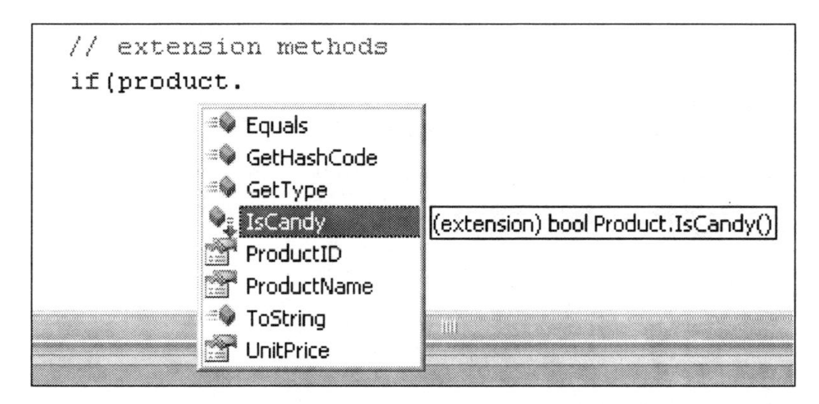

Under the hood in Visual Studio 2008, when a method call on an instance is being compiled, the compiler first checks to see if there is an instance method in the class for this method. If there is no matching instance method, it looks for an imported static class, or any static class within the same namespace. It also searches for an extension method with the first parameter that is the same as the instance type (or is a super type of the instance type). If it finds a match, the compiler will call that extension method. This means that instance methods take precedence over extension methods, and extension methods that are imported in inner namespace declarations take precedence over extension methods that are imported in outer namespaces.

In our example, when `product.IsCandy()` is being compiled, the compiler first checks the `Product` class and doesn't find a method named `IsCandy`. It then searches the static class, `MyExtensions`, and finds an extension method with the name `IsCandy`, and with a first parameter of the type, `Product`.

At compile time, the compiler actually changes `product.IsCandy()` to this call:

```
MyExtensions.IsCandy(product)
```

However, in the source code, this method is the same as another method defined inside the `Product` class, and that is why it is called an extension method.

Surprisingly, extension methods can be defined for sealed classes. In our example, you can change the `Product` class to be sealed, and it still runs without any problem. This gives us great flexibility to extend system types, because many of the system types are sealed.

On the other hand, extension methods are less discoverable, and are harder to maintain, so they should be used with great caution. If your requirements can be achieved with an instance method, one should never define an extension method to do the same work.

Not surprisingly, this new feature is again a Visual Studio 2008 compiler feature, and compiled assembly is a valid .NET 2.0 assembly.

Extension methods are the base of LINQ. We will discuss the various extension methods defined by .NET 3. in the namespace `System.Linq`, later.

Now, the `Program.cs` file should like this:

```
using System;
using System.Collections.Generic;
using System.Linq;
using System.Text;
namespace TestNewFeaturesApp
{
    class Program
    {
        static void Main(string[] args)
        {
            // valid var statements
            var x = "1";
            var n = 0;
            string s = "string";
            var s2 = s;
            s2 = null;
            string s3 = null;
            var s4 = s3;
            /*
            string x = "1";
            int n = 0;
            string s2 = s;
            */
            // invalid var statements
            /*
```

```
var v;
var nu = null;
var v2 = "12"; v2 = 3;
*/

//object initializer
/*
Product p = new product(1, "first candy", 100.0);
Product p = new Product();
p.ProductID = 1;
p.ProductName = "first candy";
p.UnitPrice=(decimal)100.0;
*/

Product product = new Product
{
    ProductID = 1,
    ProductName = "first candy",
    UnitPrice = (decimal)100.0
};
var arr = new[] { 1, 10, 20, 30 };

// collection initializer
List<Product> products = new List<Product> {
    new Product {
        ProductID = 1,
        ProductName = "first candy",
        UnitPrice = (decimal)10.0 },
    new Product {
        ProductID = 2,
        ProductName = "second candy",
        UnitPrice = (decimal)35.0 },
    new Product {
        ProductID = 3,
        ProductName = "first vegetable",
        UnitPrice = (decimal)6.0 },
    new Product {
        ProductID = 4,
        ProductName = "second vegetable",
        UnitPrice = (decimal)15.0 },
    new Product {
        ProductID = 5,
        ProductName = "third product",
        UnitPrice = (decimal)55.0 }
};
```

```
            // anonymous types
            var a = new { Name = "name1", Address = "address1" };
            var b = new { Name = "name2", Address = "address2" };
            b = a;
            /*
            class __Anonymous1
            {
                private string name;
                private string address;
                public string Name {
                    get{
                        return name;
                    }
                    set {
                        name=value
                    }
                }
                public string Address {
                    get{
                        return address;
                    }
                    set{
                        address=value;
                    }
                }
            }
            */
            // extension methods
            if (product.IsCandy()) //if(MyExtensions.IsCandy(product))
                Console.WriteLine("yes, it is a candy");
            else
                Console.WriteLine("no, it is not a candy");
        }
    }

    public sealed class Product
    {
        public int ProductID { get; set; }
        public string ProductName { get; set; }
        public decimal UnitPrice { get; set; }
    }
    public static class MyExtensions
    {
```

```
            public static bool IsCandy(this Product p)
            {
                if (p.ProductName.IndexOf("candy") >= 0)
                    return true;
                else
                    return false;
            }
        }
    }
```

In this example, we have

- Defined several `var` type variables
- Defined a sealed class `Product`
- Created a product list
- Created a product with the name of "first candy"
- Defined a static class, and added a static method `IsCandy` with a `this` parameter of the type `Product`, to it making this method an extension method
- Called the extension method on the `candy` product, and printed out a message according to its name

If you run the program, the output will look like this:

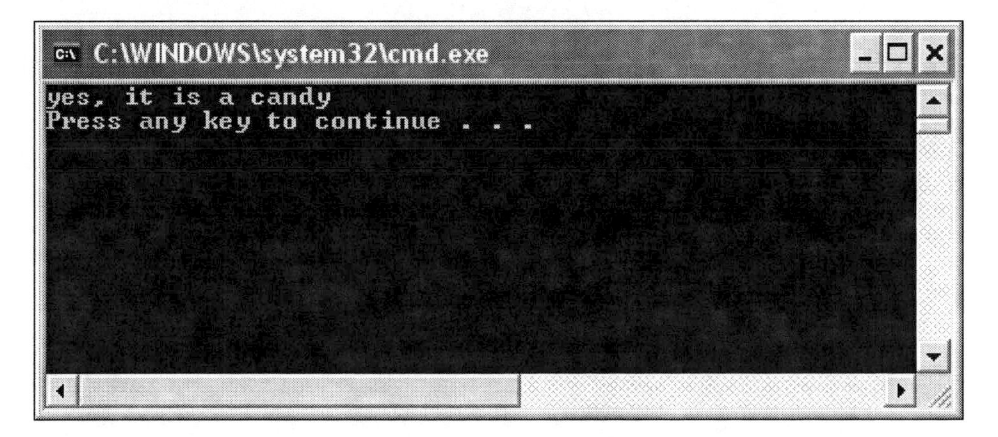

Lambda expressions

With the C# 3.0 new feature extension method, and the C# 2.0 new feature anonymous method (or inline method), Visual Studio 2008 introduces a new expression called **lambda expression**.

Lambda expression is actually a syntax change for anonymous methods. It is just a new way of writing anonymous methods.

Firstly, in C# 3.0, there is a new generic delegate type, `Func<A,R>`, which presents a function taking an argument of type `A`, and returns a value of type `R`:

```
delegate R Func<A,R> (A Arg);
```

In fact, there are several overloaded versions of `Func`, of which `Func<A,R>` is one.

Now, we will use this new generic delegate type to define an extension:

```
public static IEnumerable<T> Get<T>(this IEnumerable<T> source,
Func<T, bool> predicate)
{
    foreach (T item in source)
    {
       if (predicate(item))
           yield return item;
    }
}
```

This extension method will apply to an object that extends the `IEnumerable` interface, and has one parameter of type `Func`, which you can think of as a pointer to a function. This parameter function is the predicate to specify the criteria for the selection. This method will return a list of objects that match the predicate criteria.

Now we can create a new function as the predicate:

```
public static bool IsVege(Product p)
{
    return p.ProductName.Contains("vegetable");
}
```

Then we can use the extension method `Get` to retrieve all of the vegetable products, like this:

```
var veges1 = products.Get(IsVege);
```

We have now created the products list, with five products, of which two are vegetables. So `veges1` is actually of the `IEnumerable<Product>` type, and should contain two products. We can write the following test statements to print out the results:

```
Console.WriteLine("\nThere are {0} vegetables:", veges1.Count());
foreach (Product p in veges1)
{
    Console.WriteLine("Product ID: {0}  Product name: {1}",
                      p.ProductID, p.ProductName);
}
```

The output will be:

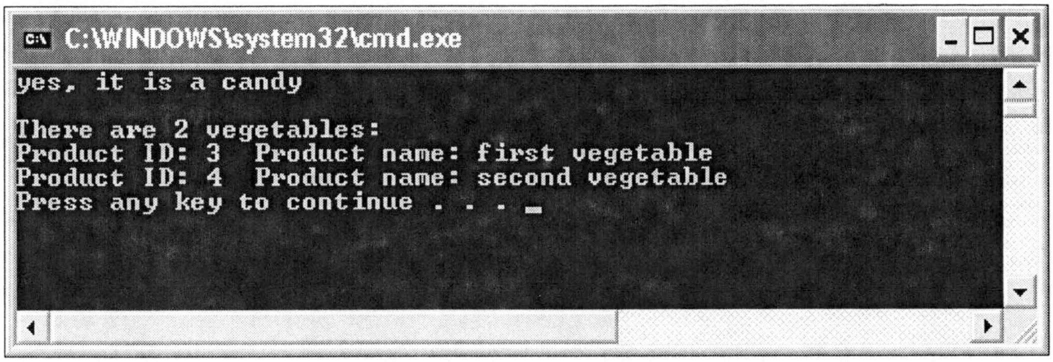

```
C:\WINDOWS\system32\cmd.exe
yes, it is a candy

There are 2 vegetables:
Product ID: 3  Product name: first vegetable
Product ID: 4  Product name: second vegetable
Press any key to continue . . .
```

Or we can first create a new variable of type `Func`, assign the function pointer of `IsVege` to this new variable, and then pass this new variable to the `Get` method like this:

```
Func<Product, bool> predicate = IsVege;
var veges2 = products.Get(predicate);
```

Variable `veges2` will contain the same products as `veges1`.

Now, let us use the C# 2.0 anonymous method to rewrite the above statement, which will now become:

```
var veges3 = products.Get(
    delegate (Product p)
    {
        return p.ProductName.Contains("vegetable");
    }
);
```

At this time, we put the body of the predicate method `IsVege` inside the extension method call, with the keyword `delegate`. So, in order to get the vegetables from the products list, we don't have to define a specific predicate method. We can specify the criteria on the spot, when we need it.

The lambda expression comes into play right after the above step. In C# 3.0, with lambda expression, we can actually write the following one line statement to retrieve all of the vegetables from the `products` list:

```
var veges4 = products.Get(p => p.ProductName.Contains("vegetable"));
```

In the above statement, the parameter of the method `Get` is a lambda expression. The first `p` is the parameter of the lambda expression, just like the parameter `p` in the anonymous method when we get `veges3`. This parameter is implicitly typed and, in this case, is of the type `Product`, because this expression is applied to a `Products` object, which contains a list of `Product` objects. This parameter can also be explicitly typed, like this:

```
var veges5 = products.Get((Product p) => p.ProductName.
Contains("vegetable"));
```

The parameter is followed by the `=>` token, and then followed by an expression or a statement block, which will be the predicate.

So, now we can easily write the following statement to get all of the `candy` products:

```
var candies = products.Get(p => p.ProductName.Contains("candy"));
```

At compile time, all lambda expressions are translated into anonymous methods according to the lambda expression conversion rules. So, again this feature is only a Visual Studio 2008 feature. We don't need any special .NET runtime library or instructions to run an assembly containing lambda expressions.

In short, lambda expressions are just another way of writing anonymous methods in a more concise, functional syntax.

Built-in LINQ extension methods and method syntax

With Visual Studio 2008, .NET framework 3.5 defines lots of extension methods in the namespace `System.Linq`, including `Where`, `Select`, `SelectMany`, `OrderBy`, `OrderByDescending`, `ThenBy`, `ThenByDescending`, `GroupBy`, `Join` and `GroupJoin`.

We can use these extension methods just as we would use our own extension methods. For example, we can use the `Where` extension method to get all vegetables from the `Products` list, like this:

```
var veges6 = products.Where(p => p.ProductName.Contains("vegetable"));
```

This will give us the same result as `veges1` through `veges5`.

As a matter of fact, the definition of the built-in LINQ extension method `Where` is just like our extension method `Get`, but in a different namespace:

```
namespace System.Linq
{
    public static class Enumerable
    {
        public static IEnumerable<T> Where<T>(this IEnumerable<T>
                                 source, Func<T, bool> predicate)
        {
            foreach (T item in source)
            {
                if (predicate(item))
                    yield return item;
            }
        }
    }
}
```

The statements that use LINQ extension methods are called using the LINQ method syntax.

Unlike the other C# 3.0 new features that we have talked about in previous sections, these LINQ specific extension methods are defined in .NET framework 3.5. So, to run an assembly containing any of these methods, you need .NET framework 3.5 installed.

LINQ query syntax and query expression

With built-in LINQ extension methods, and lambda expressions, Visual Studio 2008 allows us to write SQL-like statements in C# when invoking these methods. The syntax of these statements is called **LINQ query syntax**, and the expression in query syntax is called a **query expression**.

For example, we can change this statement:

```
var veges6 = products.Where(p => p.ProductName.Contains("vegetable"));
```

To the following query statement, by using the new LINQ query syntax:

```
var veges7 = from p in products
             where p.ProductName.Contains("vegetable")
             select p;
```

In the above C# statement, we can directly use the SQL keywords `select`, `from`, and `where` to "query" an in-memory collection list. In addition to the in-memory collection lists, we can use the same syntax to manipulate data in XML files, in the dataset, and in the database. In the following sections, we will see how to query a database using LINQ to SQL.

Combined with the anonymous data type, we can shape the result of the query in the following statement:

```
var candyOrVeges = from p in products
                   where p.ProductName.Contains("candy")
                         || p.ProductName.Contains("vegetable")
                   orderby p.UnitPrice descending, p.ProductID
                   select new { p.ProductName, p.UnitPrice };
```

As you have seen, query syntax is a very convenient, declarative shorthand for expressing queries using the standard LINQ query operators. It offers a syntax that increases the readability and clarity of expressing queries in code, and can be easy to read and write correctly.

Not only is query syntax easy to read and write, Visual Studio actually provides complete intellisense and compile-time checking support for query syntax. For example, when typing in `p` and the following dot, we get all of the `Product` members listed in the intellisense list, as shown in the following image:

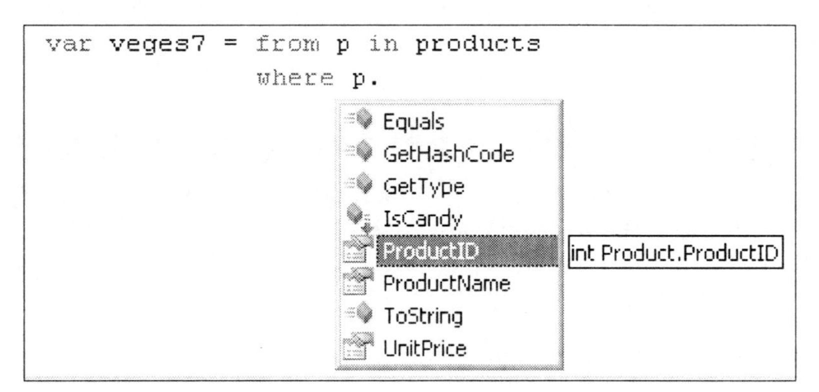

If there is a typo in the syntax (as is the case in this statement: `where p.productName.Contains("vegetable"))`, the compiler will tell you exactly where the mistake is is and why it is wrong. There won't be any run-time error such as "invalid SQL statement". The following image shows the error message when there is a typo in the syntax:

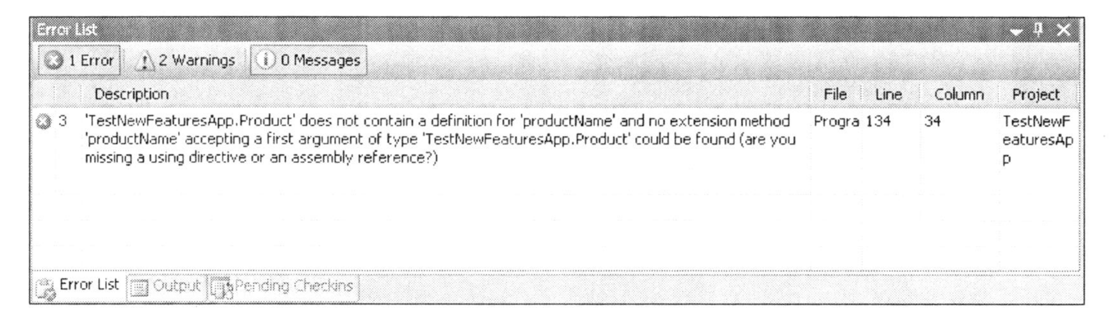

As you can see, you can write a LINQ statement in the query syntax, much like when you are working with a database in Query Analyzer. However, the .NET common language runtime (CLR) has no notion itself of the query syntax. Therefore, at compile time, query expressions are translated to something that the CLR does understand: **method calls**. Under the covers, the compiler takes the query syntax expressions and translates them into explicit method invocation code that utilizes the new LINQ Extension Method and lambda expression language features in C# 3.0.

For example, the `candyOrVeges` query expression will be translated to this method invocation call:

```
products.Where(p => p.ProductName.Contains("candy") || p.ProductName.
Contains("vegetable")).OrderByDescending(p => p.UnitPrice).
ThenBy(p=>p.ProductID).Select(p=>new { p.ProductName, p.UnitPrice })
```

In general, query syntax is recommended over method syntax because it is usually simpler, and more readable. However, there is no semantic difference between method syntax and query syntax.

Built-in LINQ operators

As we have seen in the previous sections, there are no semantic differences between method syntax, and query syntax. In addition, some queries, such as those that retrieve the number of elements matching a specified condition, or those that retrieve the element that has the maximum value in a source sequence, can be expressed only as method calls. These kinds of methods are sometimes referred to as **.NET Standard Query Operators** and include as `Take`, `ToList`, `FirstOrDefault`, `Max` and `Min`.

In addition to those methods that can only be expressed as method calls, all the extension methods that can be used in either query syntax, or method syntax are also defined as standard query operators such as `select`, `where`, and `from`. So, the .NET Standard Query Operators contain all of the LINQ-related methods.

A complete list of these operators can be found at Microsoft MSDN library for class `System.Linq.Enumerable`.

To have a quick look at all those operations, in Visual Studio 2008, open the `program.cs` file, and type in **System.Linq.Enumerable**. Then, type in a dot after **Enumerable**. You will see the whole list of operators in the intellisense menu.

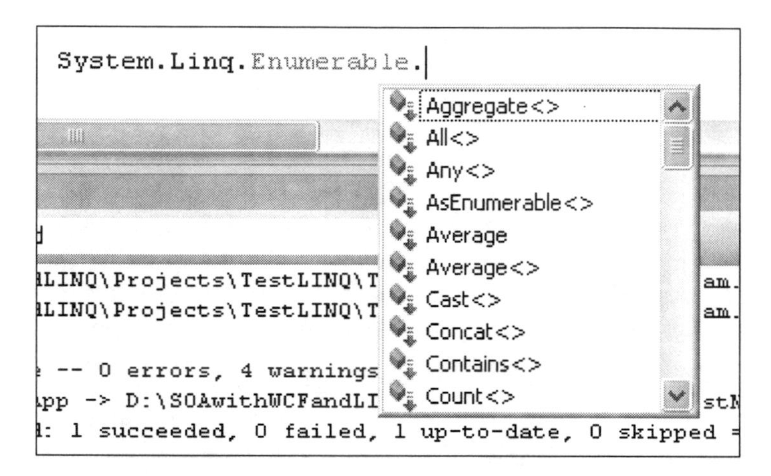

The methods in this static class provide an implementation of the standard query operators for querying data sources that implement `IEnumerable<(Of <(T>)>)`. The standard query operators are general-purpose methods that follow the LINQ pattern and enable you to express traversal, filter, and projection operations over data in any .NET-based programming language.

The majority of the methods in this class are defined as extension methods that extend `IEnumerable<(Of <(T>)>)`. This means that they can be called like an instance method on any object that implements `IEnumerable<(Of <(T>)>)`.

Note that this class was called `System.Query.Sequence`, and it was renamed to `System.Linq.Enumerable` just before Visual Studio 2008 was released, in February 2008. However, the old name was still used in much of the LINQ documentation, even in the official C# 3.0 Specification document. So, whenever you see the namespace `System.Query` or the class `Sequence`, or the namespace `System.Dlinq`, just substitute it with `System.Linq.Enumerable`, or `System.Data.Linq`. In the release version of .NET 3.5, there is no such thing as `System.Query`, or `System.Dlinq`.

Summary

In this chapter, we have learned new features related to LINQ, including the new data type `var`, object and collection initializers, extension methods, lambda expressions, LINQ syntax, and query expressions. Now that we have the required knowledge for LINQ, we are ready to try LINQ to SQL, which will be discussed in the next chapter.

The key points covered in this chapter include:

- The new data type `var` gives extra flexibility when defining new variables
- The Automatic Property feature can be used to define simple properties
- Initial values can be assigned to a new object, and collection variables by using Object initializer and Collection initializer
- Actual types will be created for anonymous types at compile time
- Extension methods can be used to extend the public contract of an existing CLR type, without having to subclass or recompile the original type
- Lambda expression is just another way of writing anonymous methods in a more concise, functional syntax
- Many LINQ-specific extension methods have been pre-defined in .NET framework 3.5
- All .NET Standard LINQ Query Operators are defined in the static class, `System.Linq.Enumerable`
- LINQ query syntax can be used to make expressions in method syntax SQL-like, but there is no semantic difference between the method syntax and the query syntax
- Some LINQ queries can only be expressed in method calls

10

LINQ to SQL: Basic Concepts and Features

In the previous chapter, we learned new features of C# 3.0 including LINQ. In this chapter and the next, we will explain how to use LINQ to query a database, or in other words, how to use LINQ to SQL in C#. After reading these two chapters, we will have a good understanding of LINQ to SQL, so that we can rewrite the data access layer of our WCF service with LINQ to SQL, to securely, and reliably communicate with the underlying database.

In this chapter, we will cover the basic concepts and features of LINQ to SQL, which include:

- What ORM is
- What LINQ to SQL is
- What LINQ to Entities is
- Comparing LINQ to SQL with LINQ to Objects and LINQ to Entities
- Modeling the Northwind Database in LINQ to SQL
- Querying and updating a database with a table
- Deferred execution
- Lazy loading and eager loading
- Joining two tables
- Querying with a view

In the next chapter, we will cover the advanced concepts and features of LINQ to SQL, such as stored procedure support, inheritance, simultaneous updating, and transaction processing.

ORM—Object-Relational Mapping

LINQ to SQL is considered to be one of Microsoft's new ORM products. So before we start explaining LINQ to SQL, let us first understand what ORM is.

ORM stands for **Object-Relational Mapping**. Sometimes it is called O/RM, or O/R mapping. It is a programming technique that contains a set of classes that map relational database entities to objects in a specific programming language.

Initially, applications could call specified native database APIs to communicate with a database. For example, `Oracle Pro*C` is a set of APIs supplied by Oracle to query, insert, update, or delete records in an Oracle database from C applications. The `Pro*C` pre-compiler translates embedded SQL into calls to the Oracle runtime library (SQLLIB).

Then, ODBC (Open Database Connectivity) was developed to unify all of the communication protocols for various RDBMS. ODBC was designed to be independent of programming languages, database systems, and operating systems. So with ODBC, one application can communicate with different RDBMS by using the same code, simply by replacing the underlying ODBC drivers.

No matter which method is used to connect to a database, the data returned from a database has to be presented in some format in the application. For example, if an `Order` record is returned from the database, there has to be a variable to hold the `Order` number, and a set of variables to hold the `Order` details. Alternatively, the application may create a class for the `Orders`, and another class for `Order` details. When another application is developed, the same set of classes may have to be created again, or if it is designed well, they can be put into a library, and re-used by various applications.

This is exactly where ORM fits in. With ORM, each database is represented by an ORM context object in the specific programming language, and database entities such as tables are represented by classes, with relationships between these classes. For example, the ORM may create an `Order` class to represent the `Order` table, and an `OrderDetail` class to represent the `Order Details` table. The `Order` class will contain a collection member to hold all of its details. The ORM is responsible for the mappings and the connections between these classes and the database. So, to the application, the database is now fully-represented by these classes. The application only needs to deal with these classes, instead of with the physical database. The application does not need to worry about how to connect to the database, how to construct the SQL statements, how to use the proper locking mechanism to ensure concurrency, or how to handle distributed transactions. These databases-related activities are handled by the ORM.

The following diagram shows the three different ways of accessing a database from an application. There are some other mechanisms to access a database from an application, such as JDBC, and ADO.NET. However, to keep the diagram simple, they have not been shown here.

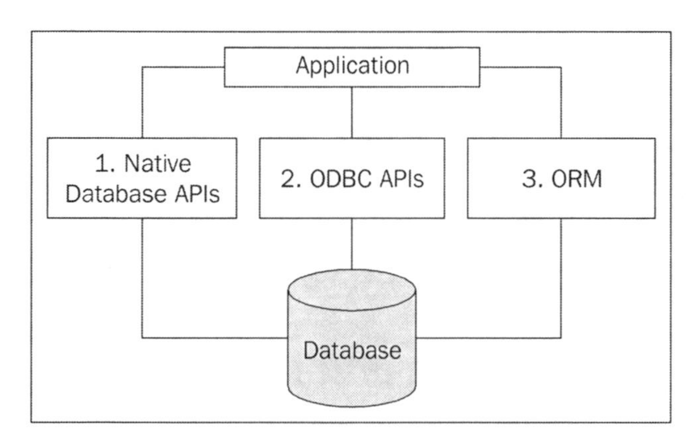

LINQ to SQL

LINQ to SQL is a component of the .NET framework 3.5 that provides a run-time infrastructure for managing relational data as objects.

In LINQ to SQL, the data model of a relational database is mapped to an object model expressed in the programming language of the developer. When the application runs, LINQ to SQL translates the language-integrated queries in the object model into SQL, and sends them to the database for execution. When the database returns the results, LINQ to SQL translates the results back to objects that you can work with in your own programming language.

LINQ to SQL fully supports transactions, views, stored procedures, and user-defined functions. It also provides an easy way to integrate data validation and business logic rules into your data model, and supports single table inheritance in the object model.

LINQ to SQL is one of Microsoft's new ORM products and competes with many existing ORM products for the .NET platform, such as open source products `NHibernate` and `NPersist`, and commercial products `LLBLGen` and `WilsonORMapper`. LINQ to SQL has many overlaps with other ORM products, but because it is designed and built specifically for .NET and SQL Server, it has many advantages over other ORM products. For example, it takes the advantages of all of the LINQ features, and it fully supports SQL Server stored procedures. You get all of the relationships (foreign keys) for all of the tables, and the fields of each table just become properties of its corresponding object. You even have the intellisense popup when you type in an entity (table) name, which will list all of the table's fields in the database. Also, all the fields and the query results are strongly-typed, which means that you will get a compilation error instead of a runtime error if you have misspelled the query statement or have cast the query result to a wrong type. In addition, because it is part of the .NET framework, you don't need to install and maintain any third-party ORM product in your production or development environments.

Under the hood of LINQ to SQL, ADO.NET `SqlClient` adapters are used to communicate with the actual SQL Server databases. We will show how to capture the generated SQL statements in runtime later in this book.

The following diagram shows the use of LINQ to SQL in a .NET application:

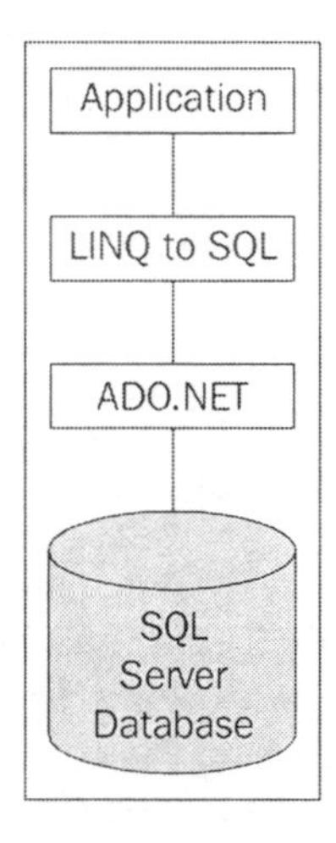

We will explore detailed LINQ to SQL features in the following two chapters, and use LINQ to SQL in our WCF services later in this book.

Comparing LINQ to SQL with LINQ to Objects

In the previous chapter, we used LINQ to query in-memory objects. Before we dive further into the world of LINQ to SQL, we first need to look at the relationships between LINQ to SQL and LINQ to Objects.

Some key differences between LINQ to SQL and LINQ to Objects are:

- LINQ to SQL needs a Data Context object. The DataContext object is the bridge between LINQ and the database. LINQ to Objects doesn't need any intermediate LINQ provider or API.
- LINQ to SQL returns data of type `IQueryable<T>` whereas LINQ to Objects returns data of type `IEnumerable<T>`.
- LINQ to SQL queries are translated to SQL by way of Expression Trees, which allow them to be evaluated as a single unit, and translated to appropriate and optimal SQL Statements. LINQ to Objects queries do not need to be translated.
- LINQ to SQL queries are translated to SQL calls and executed on the specified Database while LINQ to Objects queries are executed in the local machine memory.

The similarities shared by all aspects of LINQ are the syntax. They all use the same SQL-like syntax and share the same groups of standard query operators. From the language syntax perspective, working with a database is the same as working with in-memory objects.

LINQ to Entities

For LINQ to SQL, another product that you will want to compare it with is the **.NET Entity Framework**. Before comparing LINQ to SQL with Entity Framework, let's first explain what Entity Framework is.

ADO.NET Entity Framework (EF) was first released with Visual Studio 2008 and .NET framework 3.5 Service Pack 1. So far, many people view EF as just another ORM product from Microsoft, although by design, it is supposed to be much more powerful than just an ORM tool.

With Entity Framework, developers work with a conceptual data model—an Entity Data Model, or EDM—instead of the underlying databases. The conceptual data model schema is expressed in the **Conceptual Schema Definition Language** (**CSDL**), the actual storage model is expressed in the **Storage Schema Definition Language** (**SSDL**), and the mapping between the two is expressed in the **Mapping Schema Language** (**MSL**). A new data-access provider, `EntityClient`, is created for this new framework. But under the hood, the ADO.NET data providers are still being used to communicate with the databases. The following diagram, which has been taken from the July 2008 issue of the MSDN Magazine, shows the architecture of Entity Framework:

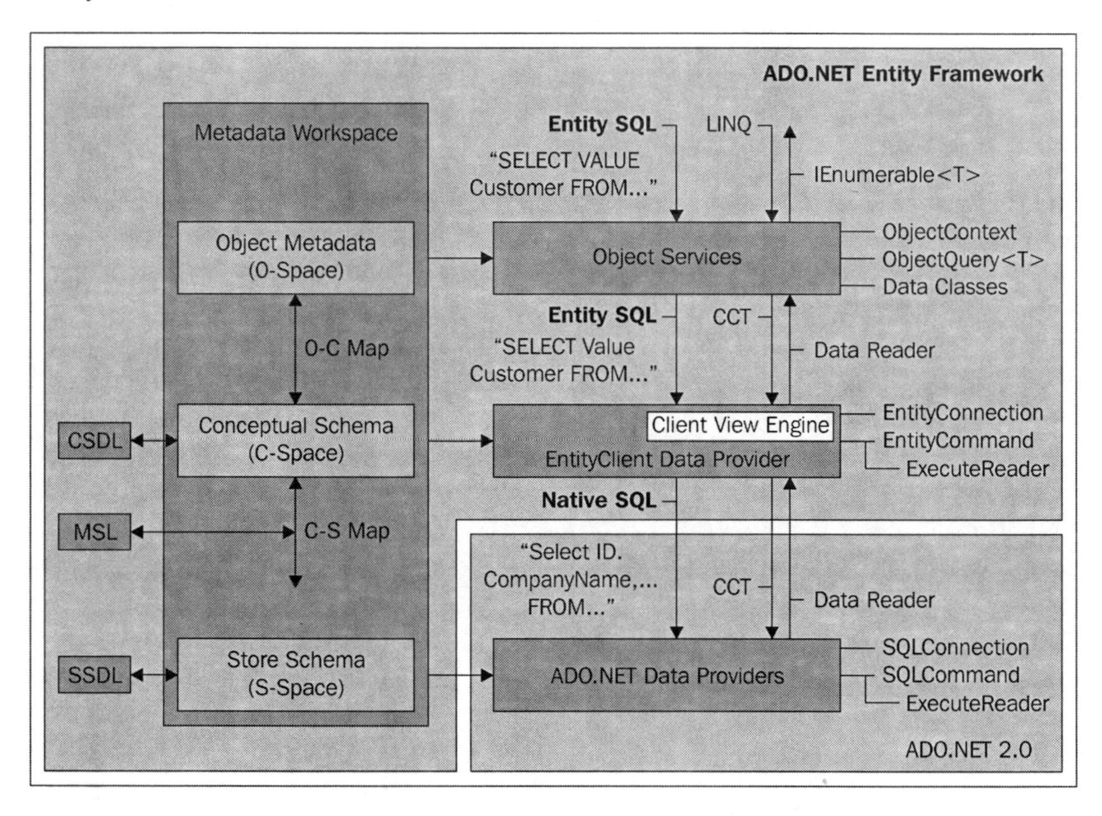

From the diagram, you can see that LINQ is one of the query languages that can be used to query against Entity Framework Entities. LINQ to Entities allows developers to create flexible, strongly-typed queries against the Entity Data Model (EDM) by using LINQ expressions and standard LINQ query operators. This is just the same as what LINQ to SQL can do, although LINQ to Entities supports more features than LINQ to SQL, such as multiple-table inheritance, and it also supports many other mainstream RDBMS databases such as Oracle, DB2, and MySQL in addition to Microsoft SQL Server.

Comparing LINQ to SQL with LINQ to Entities

As described earlier, LINQ to Entities applications work against a conceptual data model (EDM). All mappings between the languages and the databases go through the new `EntityClient` mapping provider. The application no longer connects directly to a database, or sees any database-specific constructs. The entire application operates in terms of the higher-level EDM.

This means that you can no longer use the native database query language. Not only will the database not understand the EDM model, but also current database query languages do not have the constructs required to deal with the elements introduced by the EDM, such as inheritance, relationships, complex-types, and so on.

On the other hand, for developers who do not require mapping to a conceptual model, LINQ to SQL enables developers to experience the LINQ programming model directly over existing database schema.

LINQ to SQL allows developers to generate .NET classes that represent data. Rather than map to a conceptual data model, these generated classes map directly to database tables, views, stored procedures, and user defined functions. Using LINQ to SQL, developers can write code directly against the storage schema using the same LINQ programming pattern as was previously described for in-memory collections, Entities, or the Data Set, as well as for other data sources such as XML.

Compared to LINQ to Entities, LINQ to SQL has some limitations, mainly because of its direct mapping against the physical relational storage schema. For example, you can't map two different database entities into one single C# or VB object, and if the underlying database schema changes, this might require significant client application changes.

So, in a summary, if you want to work against a conceptual data model, use LINQ to Entities. If you want to have a direct mapping to the database from your programming languages, use LINQ to SQL.

The following table lists some of the features supported by these two data access methodologies:

Features	LINQ to SQL	LINQ to Entities
Conceptual Data Model	No	Yes
Storage Schema	No	Yes
Mapping Schema	No	Yes
New Data Access Provider	No	Yes
Non-SQL Server Database Support	No	Yes
Direct Database Connection	Yes	No
Language Extensions Support	Yes	Yes
Stored Procedures	Yes	Yes
Single-table Inheritance	Yes	Yes
Multiple-table Inheritance	No	Yes
Single Entity from Multiple Tables	No	Yes
Lazy Loading Support	Yes	Yes

We will use LINQ to SQL in this book, because we will use it in the data access layer, and the data access layer is only one of the three layers for a WCF service. LINQ to SQL is much less complex than LINQ to Entities, so we can still cover it in the same book with WCF. However, once you have learned how to develop WCF services with LINQ to SQL through this book, and have learned how to use LINQ to Entities through some other means, you can easily migrate your data access layer to using LINQ to Entities.

Creating LINQ to SQL test application

Now that we have explained some of the basic concepts of LINQ to SQL, let us start exploring LINQ to SQL with some real examples. We will apply the skills we are going to learn in the following two chapters to the data access layer of our WCF service, so that from the WCF service we can communicate with the database and LINQ to SQL, instead of the raw ADO.NET data adapter.

First, we need to create a new project to test LINQ to SQL. Just follow these steps to add this test application to the solution:

1. Open the solution **TestLINQ**
2. From the Solution Explorer, right-click on the **Solution** item and select **Add | New Propject...** from the context menu

3. Select **Visual C# | Windows** as the project type, and **Console Application** as the project template, enter **TestLINQToSQLApp** as the (project) **Name**, and **D:\SOAwithWCFandLINQ\Projects\TestLINQ\TestLINQToSQLApp** as the **Location**
4. Click **OK**

Modeling the Northwind database

The next thing to do is to model the Northwind database. We will now drag and drop two tables and one view from the Northwind database into our project, so that later on we can use them to demonstrate LINQ to SQL.

Adding a LINQ to SQL item to the project

To start with, let us add a new item to our project `TestLINQToSQLApp`. The new item added should be of type **LINQ to SQL Classes**, and named **Northwind.dbml** as shown in the following **Add New Item** dialog window:

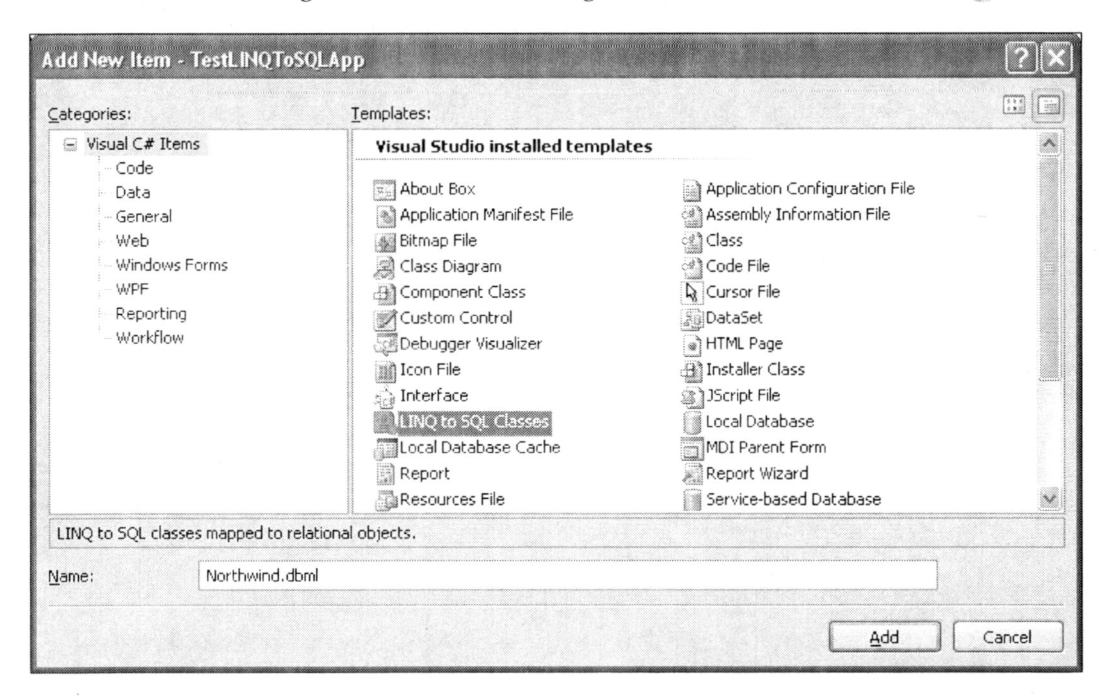

After you click **Add**, the following three files will be added to the project: **Northwind.dbml**, **Northwind.dbml.layout**, and **Northwind.designer.cs**. The first file holds the design interface for the DB model, while the second one is the XML format of the model. Only one of them can remain open inside Visual Studio IDE. The third one is the code for the model, which defines the `DataContext` of the model.

At this point, the Visual Studio LINQ to SQL designer should be open and empty, as shown in the following image:

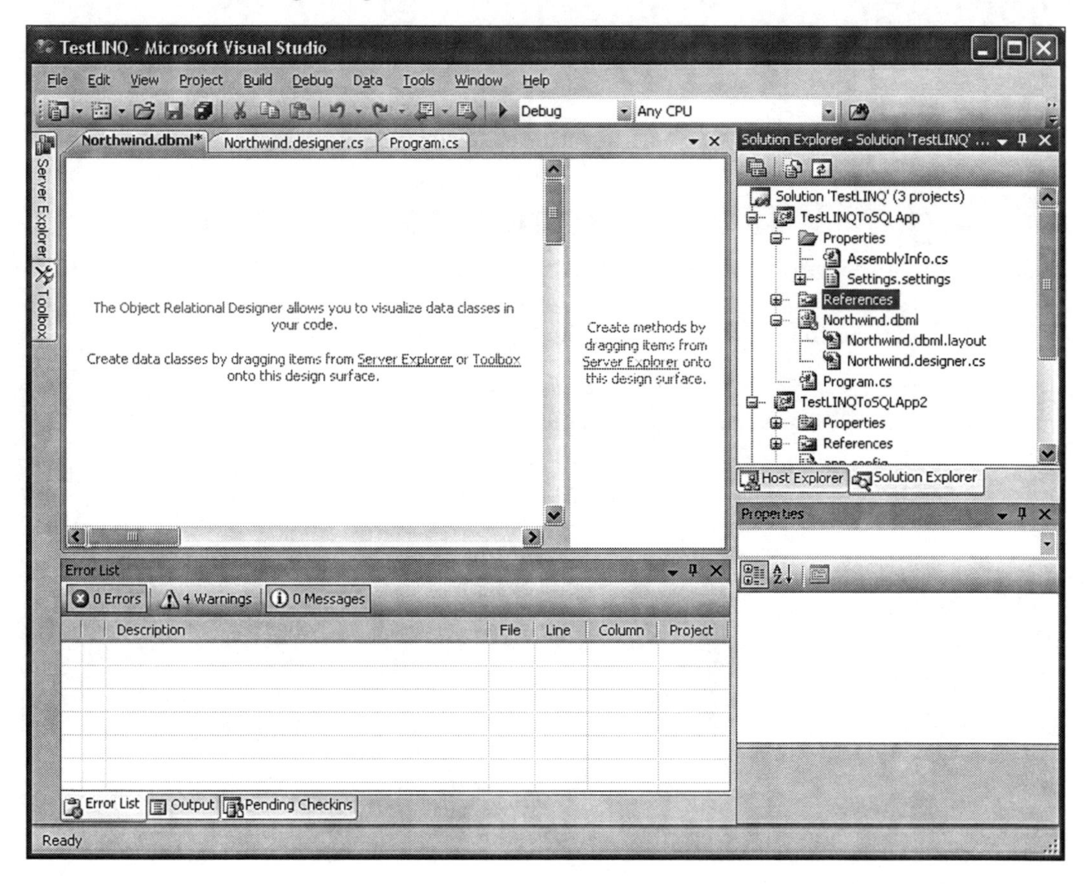

Connecting to the Northwind database

Now, we need to connect to our Northwind sample database, in order to drag and drop objects from the database.

1. Open the **Server Explorer** window from the left most side of the IDE. You can hover your mouse over **Server Explorer** and wait for a second, or click on **Server Explorer** to open it. If it is not visible in your IDE, select menu option **View | Server Explorer,** or press *Ctrl+Alt+S*, to open it.

2. In **Server Explorer**, right-click on **Data Connections**, and select **Add Connection** to open the **Add Connection** dialog box. In this dialog box, specify your server name (including your instance name if this is not a default installation), login information, and choose **Northwind** as the database. You can click **Test Connection** to make sure everything is set correctly.

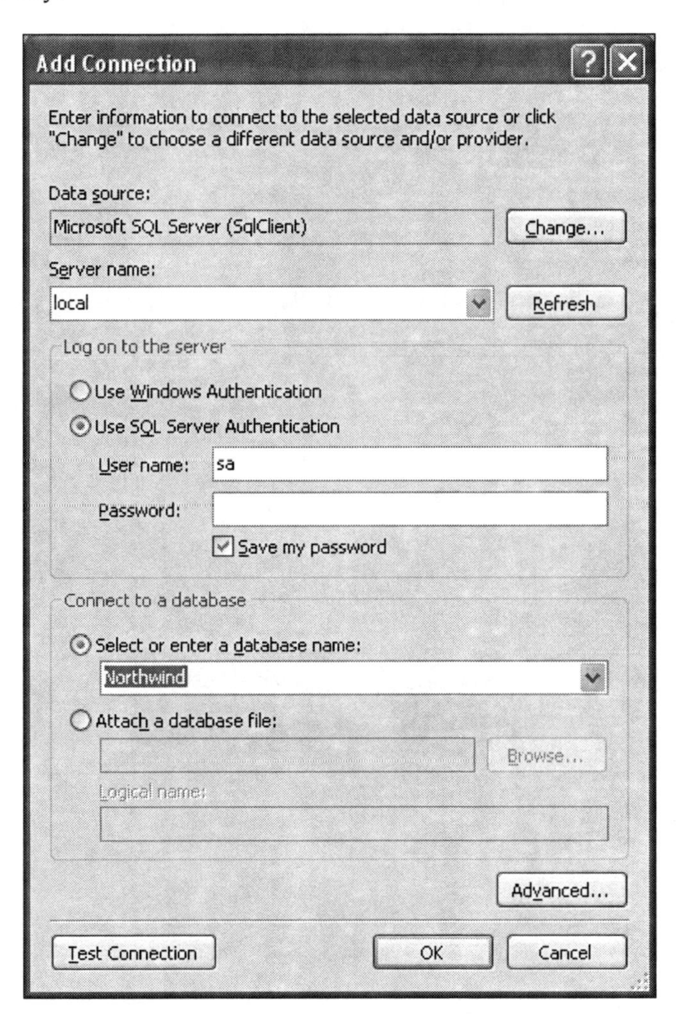

3. Click **OK** to add this connection. From now on, Visual Studio will use this database as the default database for your project. You can look at the new file `Properties\Settings.Designer.cs` for more information.

Adding tables and views to the design surface

The new connection **Northwind.dbo** should appear in the **Server Explorer** now. Next, we will drag and drop two tables and one view onto the LINQ to SQL design pane.

1. Expand the **Connection** until all of the tables are listed, and drag the **Products** to the **Northwind.dbml** design pane. You should then have a screen similar to:

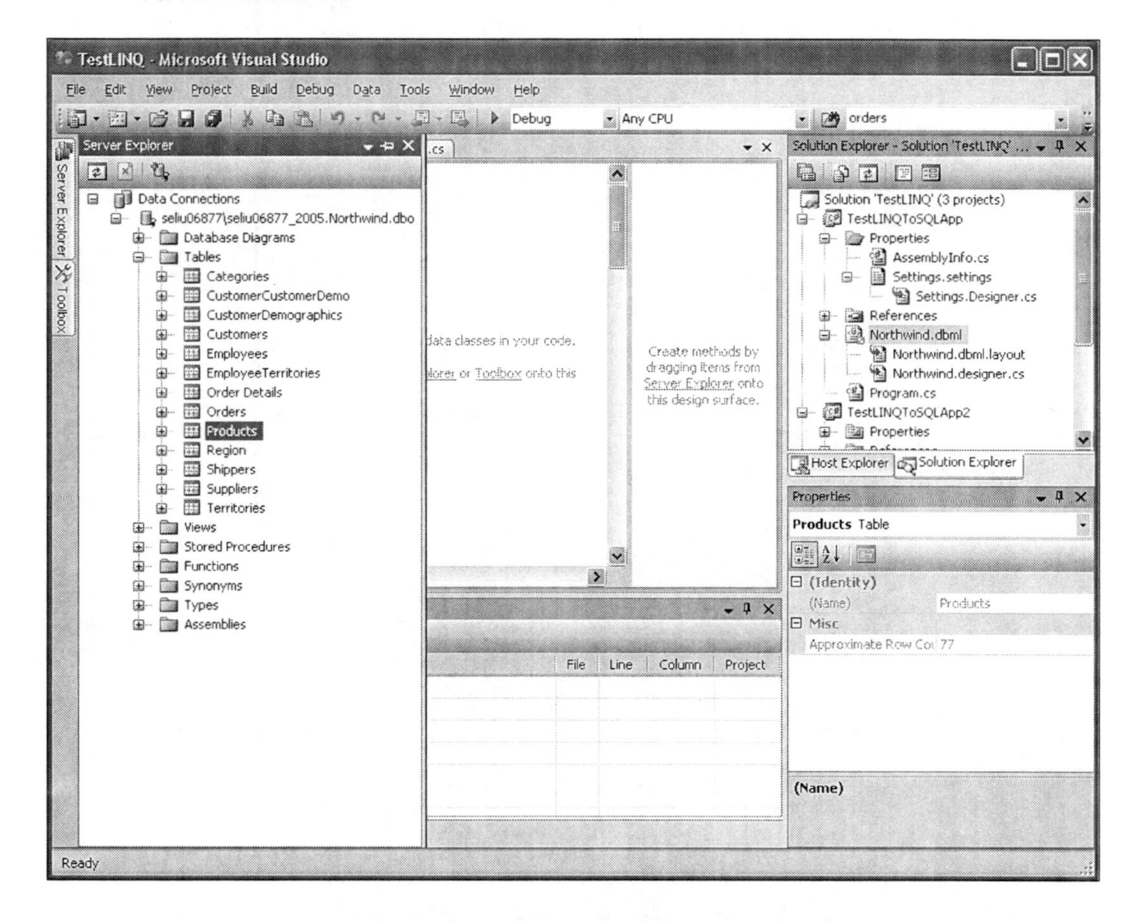

2. Next, drag the **Categories** table from the **Server Explorer** to the **Northwind.dbml** design pane.
3. We will also need to query data using a view. So drag view **Current Product List** from **Server Explorer** to the **Northwind.dbml** design pane.

The `Northwind.dbml` design pane on your screen should now look like the following image:

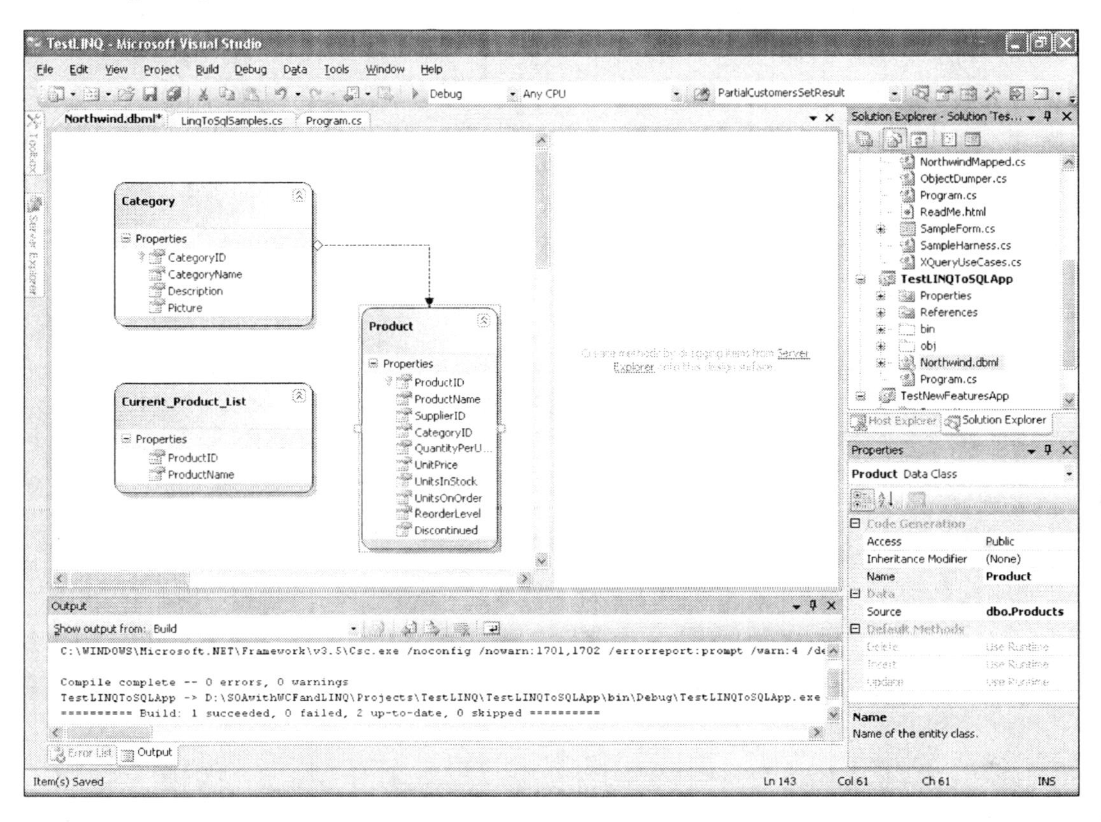

Generated LINQ to SQL classes

If you open file `Northwind.Designer.cs`, you will find that the following classes have been generated for the project:

```
public partial class NorthwindDataContext : System.Data.Linq.
DataContext
public partial class Product : INotifyPropertyChanging,
INotifyPropertyChanged
public partial class Category : INotifyPropertyChanging,
INotifyPropertyChanged
public partial class Current_Product_List
```

In the above four classes, the `DataContext` class is the main conduit through which we'll query entities from the database, as well as apply changes back to it. It contains various flavors of types and constructors, partial validation methods, and property members for all of the included tables. It inherits from the `System.Data.Linq.DataContext` class, which represents the main entry point for the LINQ to SQL framework.

The next two classes are for the two tables that we are interested in. They implement the `INotifyPropertyChanging` and `INotifyPropertyChanged` interfaces. These two interfaces define all of the related property changing, and property changed event methods, which we can extend to validate properties before and after the change.

The last class is for the view. This is a simple class with only two property members. Because we are not going to update the database through this view, it doesn't define any property change or changed event method.

Querying and updating the database with a table

Now that we have the entity classes created, we will use them to interact with the database. We will first work with the `products` table to query and update records, as well as to insert and delete records.

Querying records

First, we will query the database to get some products.

To query a database using LINQ to SQL, we first need to construct a `DataContext` object, like this:

```
NorthwindDataContext db = new NorthwindDataContext();
```

We can then use LINQ query syntax to retrieve records from the database:

```
IEnumerable<Product> beverages = from p in db.Products
                     where p.Category.CategoryName == "Beverages"
                     orderby p.ProductName
                     select p;
```

The preceding code will retrieve all of the products in the `Beverages` category, sorted by product name.

Updating records

We can update any of the products that we have just retrieved from the database, like this:

```
// update one product
Product bev1 = beverages.ElementAtOrDefault(10);
if (bev1 != null)
{
    Console.WriteLine("The price of {0} is {1}. Update to 20.0",
                              bev1.ProductName, bev1.UnitPrice);
    bev1.UnitPrice = (decimal)20.00;
}

// submit the change to database
db.SubmitChanges();
```

We used the `ElementAtOrDefault` method, and not the `ElementAt` method just in case there is no product at element 10. There are 12 beverage products in the sample database, and the 11th (element 10 starting from index 0) is `Steeleye Stout`, whose unit price is 18.00. We changed this price to 20.00, and called `db.SubmitChanges()` to update the record in the database. After you run the program, if you query the product with ProductID **35**, you will find that its price is now **20.00**.

Inserting records

We can also create a new product, and then insert this new product into the database by using the following code:

```
Product newProduct = new Product {ProductName="new test product" };
db.Products.InsertOnSubmit(newProduct);
db.SubmitChanges();
```

Deleting records

To delete a product, we first need to retrieve it from the database, and then call the `DeleteOnSubmit` method, as shown in the following code:

```
// delete a product
Product delProduct = (from p in db.Products
                     where p.ProductName == "new test product"
                     select p).FirstOrDefault();
if(delProduct != null)
    db.Products.DeleteOnSubmit(delProduct);
db.SubmitChanges();
```

Running the program

The file `Program.cs` has been used so far. Note that we declared `db` as a class member, and added one method to it to contain all of the test cases for table operations. We will now add more methods to test other LINQ to SQL functionalities.

```
using System;
using System.Collections.Generic;
using System.Linq;
using System.Text;
using System.Data.Linq;

namespace TestLINQToSQLApp
{
    class Program
    {
        // create data context
        static NorthwindDataContext db = new NorthwindDataContext();

        static void Main(string[] args)
        {
            // CRUD operations on tables
            TestTables();

            Console.ReadLine();
        }

        static void TestTables()
        {
            // retrieve all Beverages
            IEnumerable<Product> beverages = from p in db.Products
                                             where p.Category.
            CategoryName == "Beverages"
                                             orderby p.ProductName
                                             select p;
            Console.WriteLine("There are {0} Beverages",
                                  beverages.Count());

            // update one product
            Product bev1 = beverages.ElementAtOrDefault(10);
            if (bev1 != null)
            {
                Console.WriteLine("The price of {0} is {1}.
                   Update to 20.0", bev1.ProductName, bev1.UnitPrice);
                bev1.UnitPrice = (decimal)20.0;
            }

            // submit the change to database
            db.SubmitChanges();
```

```
            // insert a product
            Product newProduct = new Product { ProductName =
                                     "new test product" };
            db.Products.InsertOnSubmit(newProduct);
            db.SubmitChanges();

            Product newProduct2 = (from p in db.Products
                                   where p.ProductName == "new test product"
                                   select p).SingleOrDefault();
            if (newProduct2 != null)
            {
                Console.WriteLine("new product inserted with product
                                   ID {0}", newProduct2.ProductID);
            }

            // delete a product
            Product delProduct = (from p in db.Products
                                  where p.ProductName == "new test product"
                                  select p).FirstOrDefault();
            if (delProduct != null)
            {
                db.Products.DeleteOnSubmit(delProduct);
            }
            db.SubmitChanges();
        }
    }
}
```

If you run the program now, the output will be:

Deferred execution

One important thing to remember when working with LINQ to SQL is the **deferred execution** of LINQ.

The standard query operators differ in the timing of their execution, depending on whether they return a singleton value or a sequence of values. Those methods that return a singleton value (for example, `Average` and `Sum`) execute immediately. Methods that return a sequence defer the query execution, and return an enumerable object. These methods do not consume the target data until the query object is enumerated. This is known as deferred execution.

In the case of the methods that operate on in-memory collections, that is, those methods that extend `IEnumerable<(Of <(T>)>)`, the returned enumerable object captures all of the arguments that were passed to the method. When that object is enumerated, the logic of the query operator is employed, and the query results are returned.

In contrast, methods that extend `IQueryable<(Of <(T>)>)` do not implement any querying behavior, but build an expression tree that represents the query to be performed. The query processing is handled by the source `IQueryable<(Of <(T>)>)` object.

Checking deferred execution with SQL profiler

There are two ways to check when a query has been executed. The first is:

1. Open Profiler (`All Programs\Microsoft SQL Server 2005(or 2008)\Performance Tools\SQL 2005(or 2008) Profiler`).
2. Start a new trace on the Northwind database engine.
3. Debug the program.

For example, when the following statement is executed, there is nothing in the Profiler:

```
IEnumerable<Product> beverages = from p in db.Products
                        where p.Category.CategoryName == "Beverages"
                        orderby p.ProductName
                        select p;
```

However, when the following statement is being executed, you will see from the profiler that a query has been executed in the database:

```
Console.WriteLine("There are {0} Beverages", beverages.Count());
```

The query executed in the database is like this:

```
exec sp_executesql N'SELECT [t0].[ProductID], [t0].[ProductName],
[t0].[SupplierID], [t0].[CategoryID], [t0].[QuantityPerUnit],
[t0].[UnitPrice], [t0].[UnitsInStock], [t0].[UnitsOnOrder],
[t0].[ReorderLevel], [t0].[Discontinued]
FROM [dbo].[Products] AS [t0]
LEFT OUTER JOIN [dbo].[Categories] AS [t1] ON [t1].[CategoryID] =
[t0].[CategoryID]
WHERE [t1].[CategoryName] = @p0
ORDER BY [t0].[ProductName]',N'@p0 nvarchar(9)',@p0=N'Beverages'
```

The profiler window should look as shown the following image:

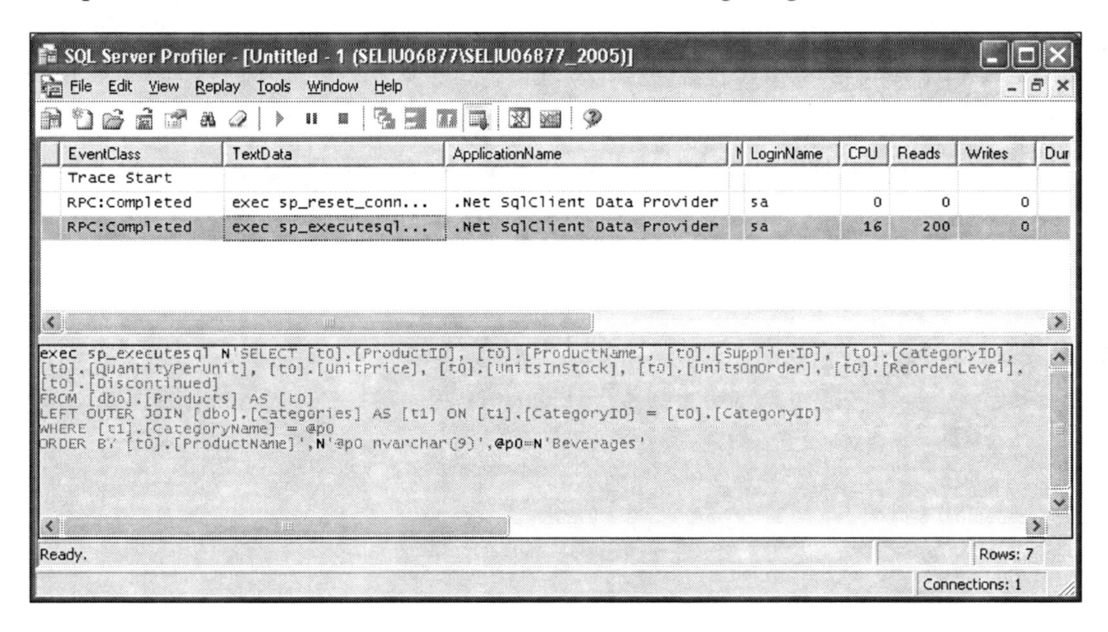

From the Profiler, we know that, under the hood, LINQ actually called `sp_executesql`, and it also used a left outer join to get the categories of products.

Checking deferred execution with SQL logs

Another way to trace the execution time of a LINQ statement is to use the logs. The `DataContext` class provides a method to log every SQL statement it executes. To see the logs, we can first add the following statement to the beginning of the program, immediately after the `Main` statement:

```
db.Log = Console.Out;
```

Then, we can add the following statement immediately after the variable `beverages` is defined, but before its count is referenced:

```
Console.WriteLine("After query syntax is defined, before it is
referenced.");
```

So the first few lines of the program are now:

```
static void Main(string[] args)
{
    // log database query statements to stand out
    db.Log = Console.Out;

    // CRUD operations on tables
    TestTables();

    Console.ReadLine();
}

static void TestTables()
{
    // retrieve all Beverages
    IEnumerable<Product> beverages = from p in db.Products
                where p.Category.CategoryName == "Beverages"
                orderby p.ProductName
                select p;
    Console.WriteLine("After query syntax beverages is defined, before
it is referenced.");
    Console.WriteLine("There are {0} Beverages", beverages.Count());
// rest of the file
```

Now, if you run the program, the output will look like this:

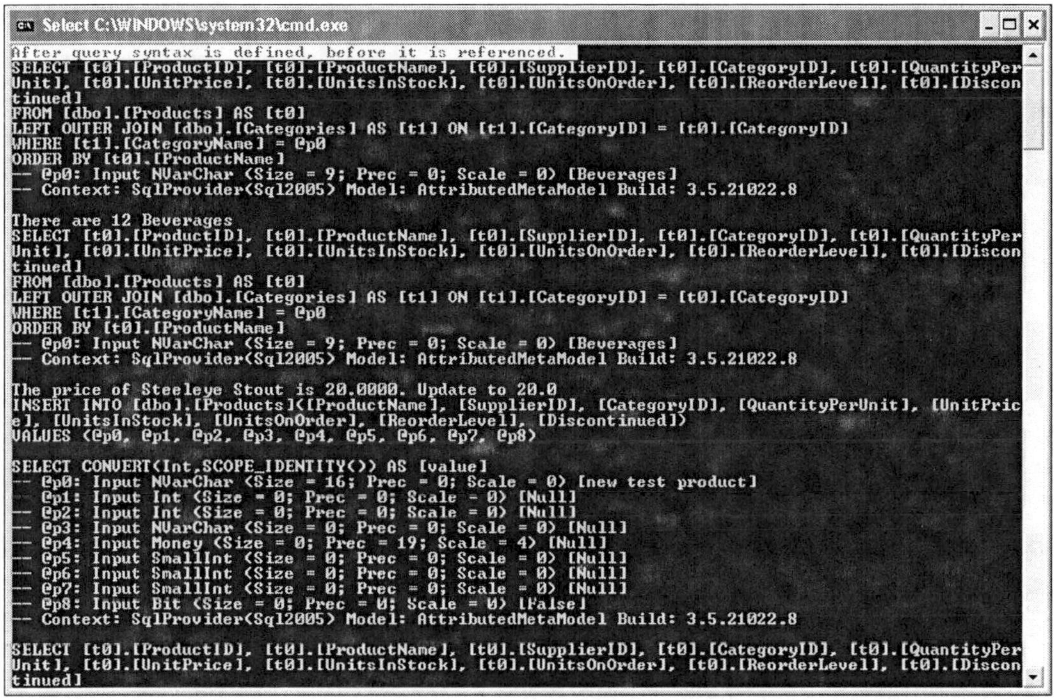

```
Select C:\WINDOWS\system32\cmd.exe
After query syntax is defined, before it is referenced.
SELECT [t0].[ProductID], [t0].[ProductName], [t0].[SupplierID], [t0].[CategoryID], [t0].[QuantityPer
Unit], [t0].[UnitPrice], [t0].[UnitsInStock], [t0].[UnitsOnOrder], [t0].[ReorderLevel], [t0].[Discon
tinued]
FROM [dbo].[Products] AS [t0]
LEFT OUTER JOIN [dbo].[Categories] AS [t1] ON [t1].[CategoryID] = [t0].[CategoryID]
WHERE [t1].[CategoryName] = @p0
ORDER BY [t0].[ProductName]
-- @p0: Input NVarChar (Size = 9; Prec = 0; Scale = 0) [Beverages]
-- Context: SqlProvider(Sql2005) Model: AttributedMetaModel Build: 3.5.21022.8

There are 12 Beverages
SELECT [t0].[ProductID], [t0].[ProductName], [t0].[SupplierID], [t0].[CategoryID], [t0].[QuantityPer
Unit], [t0].[UnitPrice], [t0].[UnitsInStock], [t0].[UnitsOnOrder], [t0].[ReorderLevel], [t0].[Discon
tinued]
FROM [dbo].[Products] AS [t0]
LEFT OUTER JOIN [dbo].[Categories] AS [t1] ON [t1].[CategoryID] = [t0].[CategoryID]
WHERE [t1].[CategoryName] = @p0
ORDER BY [t0].[ProductName]
-- @p0: Input NVarChar (Size = 9; Prec = 0; Scale = 0) [Beverages]
-- Context: SqlProvider(Sql2005) Model: AttributedMetaModel Build: 3.5.21022.8

The price of Steeleye Stout is 20.0000. Update to 20.0
INSERT INTO [dbo].[Products]([ProductName], [SupplierID], [CategoryID], [QuantityPerUnit], [UnitPric
e], [UnitsInStock], [UnitsOnOrder], [ReorderLevel], [Discontinued])
VALUES (@p0, @p1, @p2, @p3, @p4, @p5, @p6, @p7, @p8)

SELECT CONVERT(Int,SCOPE_IDENTITY()) AS [value]
-- @p0: Input NVarChar (Size = 16; Prec = 0; Scale = 0) [new test product]
-- @p1: Input Int (Size = 0; Prec = 0; Scale = 0) [Null]
-- @p2: Input Int (Size = 0; Prec = 0; Scale = 0) [Null]
-- @p3: Input NVarChar (Size = 0; Prec = 0; Scale = 0) [Null]
-- @p4: Input Money (Size = 0; Prec = 19; Scale = 4) [Null]
-- @p5: Input SmallInt (Size = 0; Prec = 0; Scale = 0) [Null]
-- @p6: Input SmallInt (Size = 0; Prec = 0; Scale = 0) [Null]
-- @p7: Input SmallInt (Size = 0; Prec = 0; Scale = 0) [Null]
-- @p8: Input Bit (Size = 0; Prec = 0; Scale = 0) [False]
-- Context: SqlProvider(Sql2005) Model: AttributedMetaModel Build: 3.5.21022.8

SELECT [t0].[ProductID], [t0].[ProductName], [t0].[SupplierID], [t0].[CategoryID], [t0].[QuantityPer
Unit], [t0].[UnitPrice], [t0].[UnitsInStock], [t0].[UnitsOnOrder], [t0].[ReorderLevel], [t0].[Discon
tinued]
```

From the logs, we see that the query is not executed when the query syntax is defined. Instead, it is executed when `beverages.Count()` is being called.

Deferred execution for singleton methods

If the query expression will return a singleton value, the query will be executed as soon as it is defined. For example, we can add this statement to get the average price of all products:

```
decimal? averagePrice = (from p in db.Products
                         select p.UnitPrice).Average();
Console.WriteLine("After query syntax averagePrice is defined, before 
it is referenced.");
Console.WriteLine("The average price is {0}", averagePrice);
```

The output is like this:

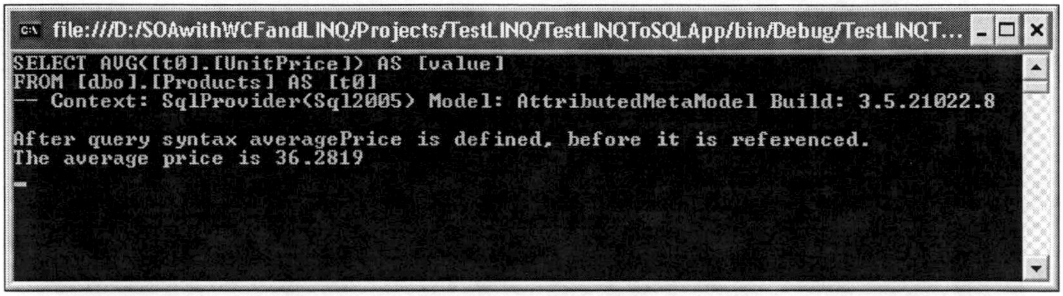

```
file:///D:/SOAwithWCFandLINQ/Projects/TestLINQ/TestLINQToSQLApp/bin/Debug/TestLINQT...
SELECT AVG([t0].[UnitPrice]) AS [value]
FROM [dbo].[Products] AS [t0]
-- Context: SqlProvider(Sql2005) Model: AttributedMetaModel Build: 3.5.21022.8

After query syntax averagePrice is defined, before it is referenced.
The average price is 36.2819
```

From this output, we know that the query is executed at the same time as the query syntax is defined.

Deferred execution for singleton methods within sequence expressions

However, just because a query is using one of the singleton methods such as `sum`, `average`, or `count`, this doesn't mean that the query will be executed as soon as it is defined. If the query result is a sequence, the execution will still be deferred. The following is an example of this kind of query:

```
// deferred execution2
var cheapestProductsByCategory =
    from p in db.Products
    group p by p.CategoryID into g
    select new
    {
        CategoryID = g.Key,
        CheapestProduct =
            (from p2 in g
             where p2.UnitPrice == g.Min(p3 => p3.UnitPrice)
             select p2).FirstOrDefault()
    };

Console.WriteLine("Cheapest products by category:");
foreach (var p in cheapestProductsByCategory)
{
    Console.WriteLine("categery {0}: product name: {1} price: {2}",
p.CategoryID, p.CheapestProduct.ProductName, p.CheapestProduct.
UnitPrice);
}
```

If you run the above query, you will see that it is executed when the result is being printed, and not when the query is being defined. An extract of the results looks like this:

```
file:///D:/SOAwithWCFandLINQ/Projects/TestLINQ/TestLINQToSQLApp/bin/Debug/TestLINQT...
Cheapest products by category:
SELECT MIN([t0].[UnitPrice]) AS [value], [t0].[CategoryID]
FROM [dbo].[Products] AS [t0]
GROUP BY [t0].[CategoryID]
-- Context: SqlProvider(Sql2005) Model: AttributedMetaModel Build: 3.5.21022.8

SELECT TOP (1) [t0].[ProductID], [t0].[ProductName], [t0].[SupplierID], [t0].[Ca
tegoryID], [t0].[QuantityPerUnit], [t0].[UnitPrice], [t0].[UnitsInStock], [t0].[
UnitsOnOrder], [t0].[ReorderLevel], [t0].[Discontinued]
FROM [dbo].[Products] AS [t0]
WHERE ([t0].[UnitPrice] = @x2) AND ((((@x1 IS NULL) AND ([t0].[CategoryID] IS NUL
L)) OR ((@x1 IS NOT NULL) AND ([t0].[CategoryID] IS NOT NULL) AND (@x1 = [t0].[C
ategoryID])))
-- @x1: Input Int (Size = 0; Prec = 0; Scale = 0) [1]
-- @x2: Input Money (Size = 0; Prec = 19; Scale = 4) [4.5000]
-- Context: SqlProvider(Sql2005) Model: AttributedMetaModel Build: 3.5.21022.8

categery 1: product name: Guaraná Fantástica price: 4.5000
SELECT TOP (1) [t0].[ProductID], [t0].[ProductName], [t0].[SupplierID], [t0].[Ca
tegoryID], [t0].[QuantityPerUnit], [t0].[UnitPrice], [t0].[UnitsInStock], [t0].[
UnitsOnOrder], [t0].[ReorderLevel], [t0].[Discontinued]
FROM [dbo].[Products] AS [t0]
WHERE ([t0].[UnitPrice] = @x2) AND ((((@x1 IS NULL) AND ([t0].[CategoryID] IS NUL
L)) OR ((@x1 IS NOT NULL) AND ([t0].[CategoryID] IS NOT NULL) AND (@x1 = [t0].[C
ategoryID])))
-- @x1: Input Int (Size = 0; Prec = 0; Scale = 0) [2]
-- @x2: Input Money (Size = 0; Prec = 19; Scale = 4) [10.0000]
-- Context: SqlProvider(Sql2005) Model: AttributedMetaModel Build: 3.5.21022.8

categery 2: product name: Aniseed Syrup price: 10.0000
```

From this output, you can see that when the result is being printed, it first goes to the database to get the minimum price for each category. Then, for each category, it goes to the database again to get the first product with that price. In a real application, you probably wouldn't want to write such a complex query in your code. So, you would put it in a stored procedure.

Deferred (lazy) loading versus eager loading

In one of the above examples, we retrieved the category name of a product using this expression:

```
p.Category.CategoryName == "Beverages"
```

Even though there is no such field called `categoryname` in the `Products` table, we can still get the category name of a product because there is an association between `Products` and `Category` table. In the **Northwind.dbml** design pane, click on the line that connects the **Products** table and the **Categories** table and you will see all of the properties of the association. Note that its participating properties are `Category.CategoryID -> Product.CategoryID`, meaning that category ID is the key field to link these two tables.

Because of this association, we can retrieve the category for each product, and on the other hand, we can also retrieve products for each category.

Lazy loading by default

However, even with an association, the associated data is not loaded when the query is executed. For example, suppose we retrieve all of the categories like this:

```
var categories = from c in db.Categories select c;
```

Later on, if we need to get products for each category, the database has to be queried again. The following diagram shows the result of executing the query:

```
file:///D:/SOAwithWCFandLINQ/Projects/TestLINQ/TestLINQToSQLApp/bin/Debug/TestLINQT...
SELECT [t0].[CategoryID], [t0].[CategoryName], [t0].[Description], [t0].[Picture
]
FROM [dbo].[Categories] AS [t0]
-- Context: SqlProvider(Sql2005) Model: AttributedMetaModel Build: 3.5.21022.8

SELECT [t0].[ProductID], [t0].[ProductName], [t0].[SupplierID], [t0].[CategoryID
], [t0].[QuantityPerUnit], [t0].[UnitPrice], [t0].[UnitsInStock], [t0].[UnitsOnO
rder], [t0].[ReorderLevel], [t0].[Discontinued]
FROM [dbo].[Products] AS [t0]
WHERE [t0].[CategoryID] = @p0
-- @p0: Input Int (Size = 0; Prec = 0; Scale = 0) [1]
-- Context: SqlProvider(Sql2005) Model: AttributedMetaModel Build: 3.5.21022.8

There are 12 products in category Beverages
SELECT [t0].[ProductID], [t0].[ProductName], [t0].[SupplierID], [t0].[CategoryID
], [t0].[QuantityPerUnit], [t0].[UnitPrice], [t0].[UnitsInStock], [t0].[UnitsOnO
rder], [t0].[ReorderLevel], [t0].[Discontinued]
FROM [dbo].[Products] AS [t0]
WHERE [t0].[CategoryID] = @p0
-- @p0: Input Int (Size = 0; Prec = 0; Scale = 0) [2]
-- Context: SqlProvider(Sql2005) Model: AttributedMetaModel Build: 3.5.21022.8

There are 12 products in category Condiments
```

From this diagram, we know that LINQ first goes to the database to query all of the categories. Then, for each category, when we need to get the total count of products, it goes to the database again to query all of the products for that category.

This is because by default lazy loading is set to `true`, meaning that the loading of all associated data (children) is deferred until the data is needed.

Eager loading with load options

To change this behavior, we can use the `LoadWith` method to tell the `DataContext` to automatically load the specified children during the initial query:

```
// eager loading products of categories
DataLoadOptions dlo2 = new DataLoadOptions();
dlo2.LoadWith<Category>(c => c.Products);
// create another data context, because we can't change LoadOptions of
db
// once a query has been executed against it
NorthwindDataContext db2 = new NorthwindDataContext();
db2.Log = Console.Out;
db2.LoadOptions = dlo2;
var categories2 = from c in db2.Categories select c;
foreach (var category2 in categories2)
{
    Console.WriteLine("There are {0} products in category {1}",
category2.Products.Count(), category2.CategoryName);
}
db2.Dispose();
```

Note that `DataLoadOptions` is in the namespace `System.Data.Linq`. So you have to add a `using` statement to the program:

```
using System.Data.Linq;
```

Also, we have to create a new `DataContext` instance for this test, because we have run some queries in the original db `DataContext`, and it is no longer possible to change its `LoadOptions`.

Now, after the category is loaded, all of its children (products) will be loaded too. This can be confirmed in the following image:

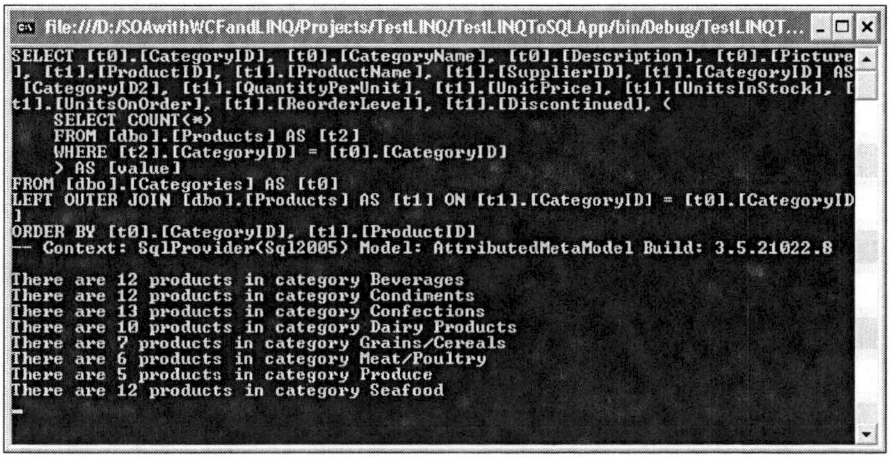

```
file:///D:/SOAwithWCFandLINQ/Projects/TestLINQ/TestLINQToSQLApp/bin/Debug/TestLINQT...
SELECT [t0].[CategoryID], [t0].[CategoryName], [t0].[Description], [t0].[Picture
], [t1].[ProductID], [t1].[ProductName], [t1].[SupplierID], [t1].[CategoryID] AS
 [CategoryID2], [t1].[QuantityPerUnit], [t1].[UnitPrice], [t1].[UnitsInStock], [
t1].[UnitsOnOrder], [t1].[ReorderLevel], [t1].[Discontinued], (
    SELECT COUNT(*)
    FROM [dbo].[Products] AS [t2]
    WHERE [t2].[CategoryID] = [t0].[CategoryID]
    ) AS [value]
FROM [dbo].[Categories] AS [t0]
LEFT OUTER JOIN [dbo].[Products] AS [t1] ON [t1].[CategoryID] = [t0].[CategoryID
]
ORDER BY [t0].[CategoryID], [t1].[ProductID]
-- Context: SqlProvider(Sql2005) Model: AttributedMetaModel Build: 3.5.21022.8

There are 12 products in category Beverages
There are 12 products in category Condiments
There are 13 products in category Confections
There are 10 products in category Dairy Products
There are 7 products in category Grains/Cereals
There are 6 products in category Meat/Poultry
There are 5 products in category Produce
There are 12 products in category Seafood
```

As you can see from this image, all products for all categories are loaded during the first query.

Filtered loading with load options

While `LoadWith` is used to eager load all children, `AssociateWith` can be used to filter the children that are to be loaded. For example, if we only want to load products for categories 1 and 2, we can use this query:

```
// eager loading only certain children
DataLoadOptions dlo3 = new DataLoadOptions();
dlo3.AssociateWith<Category>(c => c.Products.Where(p => p.CategoryID
== 1 || p.CategoryID == 2));
// create another data context, because we can't change LoadOptions of
db
// once query has been executed against it
NorthwindDataContext db3 = new NorthwindDataContext();
db3.LoadOptions = dlo3;
db3.Log = Console.Out;
var categories3 = from c in db3.Categories select c;
foreach (var category3 in categories3)
{
    Console.WriteLine("There are {0} products in category {1}",
category3.Products.Count(), category3.CategoryName);
}
db3.Dispose();
```

Now, if we query all of the categories, and print out the product count for each category, we will find that only the first two categories contain products, and all other categories have no products at all, as seen in the following image:

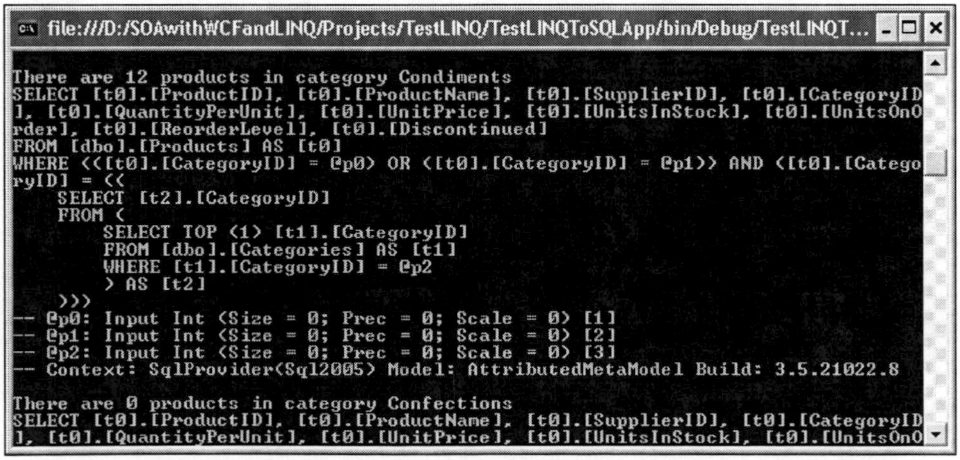

```
file:///D:/SOAwithWCFandLINQ/Projects/TestLINQ/TestLINQToSQLApp/bin/Debug/TestLINQT...
There are 12 products in category Condiments
SELECT [t0].[ProductID], [t0].[ProductName], [t0].[SupplierID], [t0].[CategoryID
], [t0].[QuantityPerUnit], [t0].[UnitPrice], [t0].[UnitsInStock], [t0].[UnitsOnO
rder], [t0].[ReorderLevel], [t0].[Discontinued]
FROM [dbo].[Products] AS [t0]
WHERE ((([t0].[CategoryID] = @p0) OR ([t0].[CategoryID] = @p1)) AND ([t0].[Catego
ryID] = ((
    SELECT [t2].[CategoryID]
    FROM (
        SELECT TOP (1) [t1].[CategoryID]
        FROM [dbo].[Categories] AS [t1]
        WHERE [t1].[CategoryID] = @p2
        ) AS [t2]
    )))
-- @p0: Input Int (Size = 0; Prec = 0; Scale = 0) [1]
-- @p1: Input Int (Size = 0; Prec = 0; Scale = 0) [2]
-- @p2: Input Int (Size = 0; Prec = 0; Scale = 0) [3]
-- Context: SqlProvider(Sql2005) Model: AttributedMetaModel Build: 3.5.21022.8

There are 0 products in category Confections
SELECT [t0].[ProductID], [t0].[ProductName], [t0].[SupplierID], [t0].[CategoryID
], [t0].[QuantityPerUnit], [t0].[UnitPrice], [t0].[UnitsInStock], [t0].[UnitsOnO
```

Combining eager loading and filtered loading

However, from the output above, you can see that this uses lazy loading. If you want the eager loading of products with some filters, you can combine `LoadWith` and `AssociateWith`, as shown in the following code:

```
DataLoadOptions dlo4 = new DataLoadOptions();
dlo4.LoadWith<Category>(c => c.Products);
dlo4.AssociateWith<Category>(c => c.Products.Where(p => p.CategoryID
== 1 || p.CategoryID == 2));
// create another data context, because we can't change LoadOptions of
db
// once q query has been executed
NorthwindDataContext db4 = new NorthwindDataContext();
db4.Log = Console.Out;
db4.LoadOptions = dlo4;
var categories4 = from c in db4.Categories select c;
foreach (var category4 in categories4)
{
    Console.WriteLine("There are {0} products in category {1}",
category4.Products.Count(), category4.CategoryName);
}
db4.Dispose();
```

The output of this query is shown in the following image:

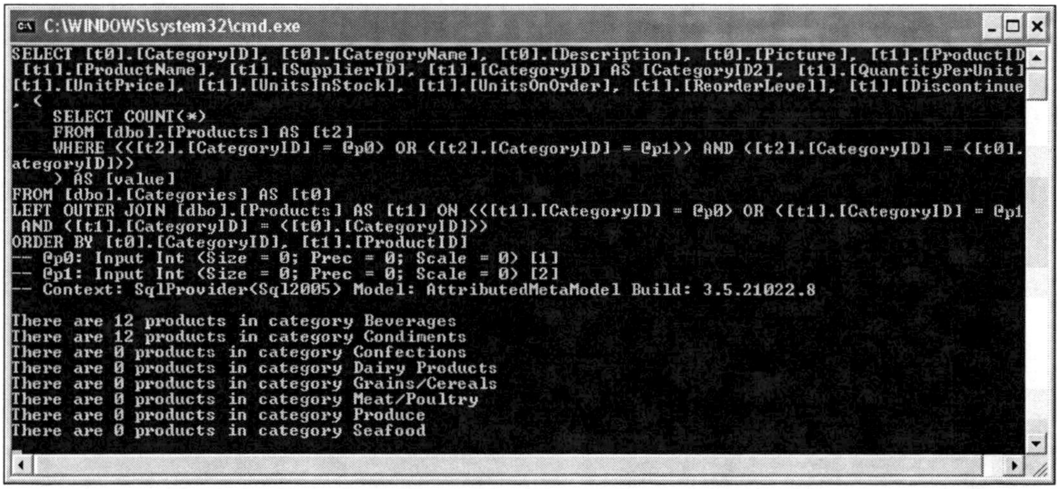

```
C:\WINDOWS\system32\cmd.exe
SELECT [t0].[CategoryID], [t0].[CategoryName], [t0].[Description], [t0].[Picture], [t1].[ProductID
 [t1].[ProductName], [t1].[SupplierID], [t1].[CategoryID] AS [CategoryID2], [t1].[QuantityPerUnit]
[t1].[UnitPrice], [t1].[UnitsInStock], [t1].[UnitsOnOrder], [t1].[ReorderLevel], [t1].[Discontinue
, (
    SELECT COUNT(*)
    FROM [dbo].[Products] AS [t2]
    WHERE (([t2].[CategoryID] = @p0) OR ([t2].[CategoryID] = @p1)) AND ([t2].[CategoryID] = ([t0].
ategoryID]))
    ) AS [value]
FROM [dbo].[Categories] AS [t0]
LEFT OUTER JOIN [dbo].[Products] AS [t1] ON (([t1].[CategoryID] = @p0) OR ([t1].[CategoryID] = @p1
 AND ([t1].[CategoryID] = ([t0].[CategoryID]))
ORDER BY [t0].[CategoryID], [t1].[ProductID]
-- @p0: Input Int (Size = 0; Prec = 0; Scale = 0) [1]
-- @p1: Input Int (Size = 0; Prec = 0; Scale = 0) [2]
-- Context: SqlProvider(Sql2005) Model: AttributedMetaModel Build: 3.5.21022.8

There are 12 products in category Beverages
There are 12 products in category Condiments
There are 0 products in category Confections
There are 0 products in category Dairy Products
There are 0 products in category Grains/Cereals
There are 0 products in category Meat/Poultry
There are 0 products in category Produce
There are 0 products in category Seafood
```

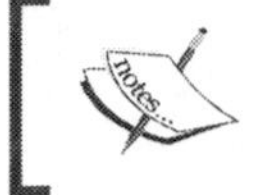

For each field of an entity, you can also set its `Delay Loaded` property to change its loading behavior. This is different from the child lazy/eager loading, as it only affects one property of that particular entity.

Joining two tables

Although associations are a kind of join in LINQ, we can also explicitly join two tables using the keyword `Join`, as shown in the following code:

```
var categoryProducts =
    from c in db.Categories
    join p in db.Products on c.CategoryID equals p.CategoryID into
products
    select new {c.CategoryName, productCount = products.Count()};
foreach (var cp in categoryProducts)
{
    Console.WriteLine("There are {0} products in category {1}",
cp.CategoryName, cp.productCount);
}
```

This is not so useful in the above example, because the tables `Products` and `Categories` are associated with a foreign key relationship. If there is no foreign key association between two tables, this will be particularly useful.

From the following output, we can see that only one query is executed to get the results:

```
C:\WINDOWS\system32\cmd.exe
SELECT [t0].[CategoryName], (
    SELECT COUNT(*)
    FROM [dbo].[Products] AS [t1]
    WHERE ([t0].[CategoryID]) = [t1].[CategoryID]
    ) AS [productCount]
FROM [dbo].[Categories] AS [t0]
-- Context: SqlProvider(Sql2005) Model: AttributedMetaModel Build: 3.5.21022.8

There are Beverages products in category 12
There are Condiments products in category 12
There are Confections products in category 13
There are Dairy Products products in category 10
There are Grains/Cereals products in category 7
There are Meat/Poultry products in category 6
There are Produce products in category 5
There are Seafood products in category 12
```

In addition to joining two tables, you can also:

- Join three or more tables
- Join a table to itself
- Create left, right, and outer joins
- Join using composite keys

Querying a view

Querying a view is the same as querying a table. For example, you can query the view "current product lists" like this:

```
var currentProducts = from p in db.Current_Product_Lists
                      select p;
foreach (var p in currentProducts)
{
    Console.WriteLine("Product ID: {0} Product Name: {1}",
p.ProductID, p.ProductName);
}
```

This will get all of the current products, using the view.

Summary

In this chapter, we have learned what an ORM is, why we need an ORM, and what LINQ to SQL is. We also compared LINQ to SQL with LINQ to Entities, and explored some basic features of LINQ to SQL.

The key points covered in this chapter include:

- An ORM product can greatly ease data access layer development
- LINQ to SQL is one of Microsoft's ORM products that uses LINQ against SQL Server databases
- The built-in LINQ to SQL designer in Visual Studio 2008 can be used to model databases
- You can connect to a database in Visual Studio 2008 Server Explorer, and then drag and drop database items onto the LINQ to SQL design pane
- The class `System.Data.Linq.DataContext` is the main class for LINQ to SQL applications
- LINQ methods that return a sequence, defer the query execution and you can check the timing of the execution of a query with Profiler, or SQL logs

- LINQ query expressions that return a singleton value will be executed as soon as they are defined
- By default, the loading of associated data is deferred (lazy loading). You can change this behavior with the `LoadWith` option
- Associated data results can be filtered with the `AssociateWith` option
- The options `LoadWith` and `AssociateWith` can be combined together to eager load associated data and filter it at the same time
- `The Join` operator can be used to join multiple tables and views
- Views can be used to query a database in LINQ to SQL in the same way as for tables

11
LINQ to SQL: Advanced Concepts and Features

In the previous chapter, we learned some basic concepts and features of LINQ to SQL, such as querying and updating databases with tables and views, and changing loading behaviors by using load options.

In this chapter, we will learn some advanced features of LINQ to SQL such as stored procedure support, concurrency control, and transactional processing. After this chapter, we will rewrite the data access layer of our WCF service to utilize LINQ to SQL technology.

In this chapter, we will cover:

- Calling a stored procedure
- Compiled queries
- Direct SQL
- Dynamic querying
- Inheritance support
- Concurrency control
- Transaction support
- Entity class validation
- Debugging LINQ to SQL programs

Calling a stored procedure

Calling a stored procedure is different from a table or a view, because a stored procedure can have input parameters, output parameters, and it can return multiple result-sets. It can also return different result-sets dynamically, which makes it even harder to interpret the results. The modeling of a stored procedure is also different from modeling a table or view. In the following sections, we will explain how to call a simple stored procedure, how to map the returned result of a stored procedure to an entity class, and how to handle output parameters, return codes, and multiple result-sets.

We will re-use the same application that we used in the previous chapter, and add more testing methods to the program.

Calling a simple stored procedure

First, we will try to call a simple stored procedure. In the sample database, there is a stored procedure called "Ten Most Expensive Products". We will call this stored procedure to get the top ten most expensive products.

Before we can call this stored procedure, we need to model it.

1. Open the `Northwind.dbml` designer.
2. In the **Server Explorer**, expand the node **Stored Procedures**.
3. Drag the stored procedure **Ten Most Expensive Products** to the right-hand panel of the **Northwind.dbml** design window.

This will add the method `Ten_Most_Expensive_Products` to the `NorthwindDataContext` class, and add a new class, `Ten_Most_Expensive_ProductsResult`, as the result data type of the stored procedure.

Now, from the `Program.cs`, we can call this stored procedure as follows:

```
var tenProducts = from p in db.Ten_Most_Expensive_Products()  select
p;
foreach (var p in tenProducts)
{
   Console.WriteLine("Product Name: {0}, Price; {1}", p.TenMostExpensi
veProducts, p.UnitPrice);
}
```

Because we know exactly the return result of the stored procedure, we can also replace the `var` data type with the specific return type, as in the following code:

```
IEnumerable<Ten_Most_Expensive_ProductsResult> tenProducts = from p in
db.Ten_Most_Expensive_Products()  select p;
foreach (Ten_Most_Expensive_ProductsResult p in tenProducts)
{
   Console.WriteLine("Product Name: {0}, Price; {1}", p.TenMostExpensi
veProducts, p.UnitPrice);
}
```

The output will look like the following image:

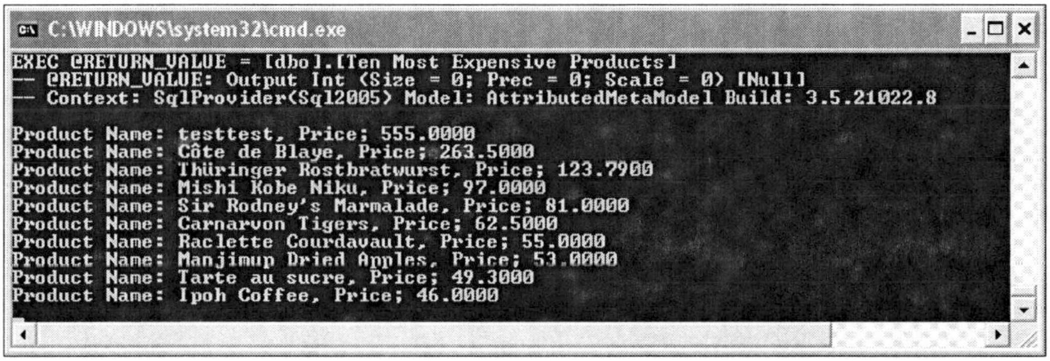

```
C:\WINDOWS\system32\cmd.exe
EXEC @RETURN_VALUE = [dbo].[Ten Most Expensive Products]
-- @RETURN_VALUE: Output Int (Size = 0; Prec = 0; Scale = 0) [Null]
-- Context: SqlProvider(Sql2005) Model: AttributedMetaModel Build: 3.5.21022.8

Product Name: testtest, Price; 555.0000
Product Name: Côte de Blaye, Price; 263.5000
Product Name: Thüringer Rostbratwurst, Price; 123.7900
Product Name: Mishi Kobe Niku, Price; 97.0000
Product Name: Sir Rodney's Marmalade, Price; 81.0000
Product Name: Carnarvon Tigers, Price; 62.5000
Product Name: Raclette Courdavault, Price; 55.0000
Product Name: Manjimup Dried Apples, Price; 53.0000
Product Name: Tarte au sucre, Price; 49.3000
Product Name: Ipoh Coffee, Price; 46.0000
```

Mapping a stored procedure to an entity class

In the above example, LINQ to SQL creates a new type for the return result of the stored procedure. It actually just added the word "Result" after the stored procedure name, to create the name of the return data type. If we know that the return result is a kind of entity, we can tell LINQ to SQL to use that specific entity as the return type instead of creating a new type.

For example, let us create a stored procedure like this:

```
Create PROCEDURE [dbo].[GetProduct]
   (
   @ProductID int
   )
AS
   SET NOCOUNT ON
   Select * from Products where ProductID = @ProductID
```

You can create this stored procedure in Microsoft SQL Server Management Studio, or by right-clicking on the **Stored Procedures** node in the Server Explorer of Visual Studio 2008, and selecting **Add New Stored Procedure** from the context menu.

After the stored procedure has been created, drag and drop it into the **Product** class on the **Northwind.dbml** design pane. Now, LINQ to SQL will use the `Product` class as the return type of this stored procedure. The method for this stored procedure will be as follows:

```
[Function(Name="dbo.GetProduct")]
public ISingleResult<Product> GetProduct([Parameter(Name="ProductID",
DbType="Int")] System.Nullable<int> productID)
{
    IExecuteResult result = this.ExecuteMethodCall(this,
((MethodInfo)(MethodInfo.GetCurrentMethod())), productID);
    return ((ISingleResult<Product>)(result.ReturnValue));
}
```

From the signature of the method, we know that the return type is of the `Product` class.

Interestingly, if you drag and drop the same stored procedure to the right-hand panel of the **Northwind.dbml** design window, instead of the **Product** class, LINQ to SQL will automatically create a new class for the return type. The new method might be as follows:

```
[Function(Name="dbo.GetProduct")]
public ISingleResult<GetProductResult> GetProduct1([Parameter(Name="Pr
oductID", DbType="Int")] System.Nullable<int> productID)
{
    IExecuteResult result = this.ExecuteMethodCall(this,
((MethodInfo)(MethodInfo.GetCurrentMethod())), productID);
return ((ISingleResult<GetProductResult>)(result.ReturnValue));
}
```

The generated return type class `GetProductResult` is almost identical to the `Product` class, except that there are no event handling methods.

Another difference between the `GetProduct` and `GetProduct1` methods is that the product you retrieved using `GetProduct` is within the `DataContext`. So, any changes you made to it will be committed back to the database if you call `db.SubmitChanges()` later. However, the product you retrieved using `GetProduct1` is not within the `DataContext`, and thus won't be committed back to the database if you call `db.SubmitChanges()` later.

Also, when a stored procedure is dropped to an entity class, LINQ to SQL will first check the return result of the stored procedure to make sure it is compatible with the target class. If not, you will get a warning message, and the stored procedure won't be mapped on the model. For example, if you drag and drop the stored procedure **Ten Most Expensive Products** to the **Product** class, you will see a dialog box like this:

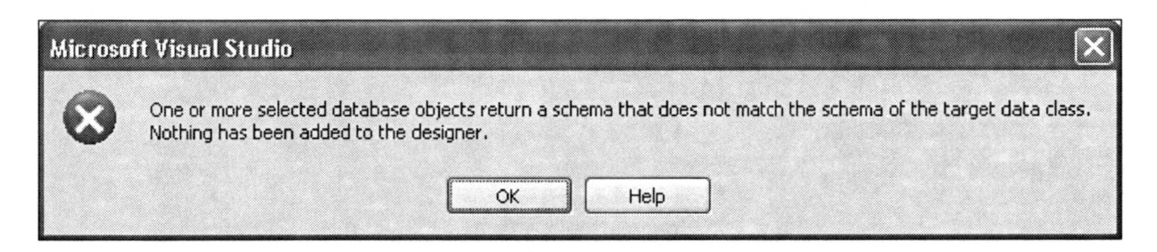

Handling output parameters, return codes, multiple shapes of a single result-set, and multiple result-sets

Now that we have a basic understanding of LINQ to SQL stored procedure processing, we will create a fairly complex stored procedure with an input parameter, an output parameter, a return code, multiple shapes of a single result-set, and multiple result-sets.

Creating a complex stored procedure

Before we explain the LINQ to SQL comprehensive stored procedure support, we need to create a complex stored procedure. We will create a stored procedure called `GetCategoryDetails`. The stored procedure will have one input parameter, `CategoryID`, which will specify which category it is for, and one output parameter `AveProductPrice`, which will return the average price of all the products in that category.

The first result-set of this stored procedure will give some information about the category, depending on the value of another input parameter, `FullOrPartial`. If `FullOrPartial` is `true` (`1`), this result-set will contain all of the columns of the `Categories` table for the requested category. Otherwise, it will contain only the `CategoryID` and `CategoryName` columns of the category.

The second result-set will contain all of the products for the category.

If the input parameter is not a valid category ID, the procedure returns an error code of 10001, and stops. Otherwise, it returns `0` at the end of the stored procedure, to indicate a success.

The SQL to create this stored procedure is:

```
CREATE PROCEDURE [dbo].[GetCategoryDetails]
    @CategoryID int,
    @FullOrPartial bit,
    @AveProductPrice money OUTPUT
AS
    SET NOCOUNT ON
    if not exists (select 1
                        from categories
                        where categoryID = @categoryID)
            return 10001
    if @FullOrPartial = 1
            select * from Categories
            where categoryID = @categoryID
    else
            select categoryID, categoryName from Categories
            where categoryID = @categoryID
    select * from products
    where categoryID = @categoryID
    select @AveProductPrice = avg(UnitPrice)
    from products
    where categoryID = @CategoryID
return 0
```

Modeling the stored procedure

In order to call this complex stored procedure, we first need to add it into the `Northwind.dbml` model. Just drag and drop it from the **Server Explorer** to the right-hand panel of the **Northwind.dbml** design window. If you have created it in the **SQL Management Studio** and can't see it in the **Server Explorer**, try to refresh your **Server Explorer**.

LINQ to SQL designer will create the following method in the class `NorthwindDataContext` within the file, `Northwind.designer.cs`:

```
[Function(Name="dbo.GetCategoryDetails")]
public ISingleResult<GetCategoryDetailsResult> GetCategoryDetails(
[Parameter(Name="CategoryID", DbType="Int")] System.Nullable<int>
categoryID, [Parameter(Name="FullOrPartial", DbType="Bit")] System.
Nullable<bool> fullOrPartial, [Parameter(Name="AveProductPrice",
DbType="Money")] ref System.Nullable<decimal> aveProductPrice)
{
```

```
    IExecuteResult result = this.ExecuteMethodCall(this,
((MethodInfo)(MethodInfo.GetCurrentMethod())), categoryID,
fullOrPartial, aveProductPrice);
    aveProductPrice = ((System.Nullable<decimal>)(result.
GetParameterValue(2)));
    return ((ISingleResult<GetCategoryDetailsResult>)(result.
ReturnValue));
}
```

Note that the variable `aveProductPrice` is passed to the method call `ExecuteMethodCall`, but its actual value doesn't come back after the call. The output value has to be retrieved using `result.GetParameterValue`.

This class is also added to the return result (this is really the first result-set in the stored procedure):

```
public partial class GetCategoryDetailsResult
```

However, this is not what we want. The `GetCategoryDetails` method only returns one result-set, instead of two. We have to customize it for our needs.

Customizing DataContext class for the stored procedure

In the previous sections, we modeled the stored procedure with LINQ to SQL designer, but the retuning result is not correct. In this section, we will customize it.

1. Extend the class `NorthwindDataContext` by adding a new class file called `NorthwindDataContext.cs`.
2. Inside the new class file `NorthwindDataContext.cs`, add the following `using` statements:

```
using System.Data.Linq;
using System.Data.Linq.Mapping;
using System.Reflection;
```

3. Add the following class inside the file `NorthwindDataContext.cs`, for one of the return results:

```
public class PartialCategory
{
    public int CategoryID;
    public string CategoryName;
}
```

This class is parallel to the `NorthwindDataContext` class. Next, we will use this class to define a new method.

4. Change the class definition to the following code (note that it should be changed to a partial class):

```
public partial class NorthwindDataContext
{
   // modified GetCategoryDetails, to overwrite the generated one
   [Function(Name = "dbo.GetCategoryDetails")]
   [ResultType(typeof(PartialCategory))]
   [ResultType(typeof(Category))]
   [ResultType(typeof(Product))]
   public IMultipleResults GetWholeOrPartialCategoryDetails(
        [Parameter(Name="CategoryID", DbType="Int")]
            System.Nullable<int> categoryID,
        [Parameter(Name="FullOrPartial", DbType="Bit")]
            System.Nullable<bool> fullOrPartial,
        [Parameter(Name="AveProductPrice", DbType="Money")]
            ref System.Nullable<decimal> aveProductPrice)
    {
IExecuteResult result = this.ExecuteMethodCall(this,
        ((MethodInfo)(MethodInfo.GetCurrentMethod())), categoryID,
        fullOrPartial, aveProductPrice);
           aveProductPrice = ((System.Nullable<decimal>)(result.
                                        GetParameterValue(2)));
        return ((IMultipleResults)(result.ReturnValue));
    }
}
```

As you can see, we defined a method `GetWholeOrPartialCategoryDetails` to map the results of the stored procedure to different types.

We can also modify the generated method inside of the `Northwind.designer.cs` file to meet our needs. However, it is recommended that we don't do so, because if you modify this file, and it is regenerated later on, you will lose all your changes.

Testing the stored procedure

Now, inside the file `program.cs`, we can add this test method:

```
static void TestComplexStoredProcedure(int categoryID, bool
wholeOrPartial)
{
    decimal? avePrice = 0;
    IMultipleResults result = db.GetWholeOrPartialCategoryDetails(cate
                              goryID, wholeOrPartial, ref avePrice);
    int returnCode = (int)result.ReturnValue;
    if (returnCode == 0)
```

```
        {
            if (wholeOrPartial == true)
            {
                Category wholeCategory = result.GetResult<Category>().
                                                    FirstOrDefault();
                Console.WriteLine("Category name: {0}", wholeCategory.
                                                        CategoryName);
                Console.WriteLine("Category description: {0}",
                                  wholeCategory.Description);
            }
            else
            {
                PartialCategory partialCategory =
                     result.GetResult<PartialCategory>().FirstOrDefault();
                Console.WriteLine("Category name: {0}",
                        partialCategory.CategoryName);
            }
            Console.WriteLine("Average product price: {0}", avePrice);
            IEnumerable<Product> products = result.GetResult<Product>();
            Console.WriteLine("Total products in category: {0}",
                                             products.Count());
        }
        else
        {
            Console.WriteLine("No category is retrieved,
                       return code : {0}", returnCode);
        }
    }
```

Inside the `Main` method, we call the above method three times as follows:

```
// get full category details
TestComplexStoredProcedure (2, true);

// get partail category details
TestComplexStoredProcedure (6, false);

// invalid category ID
TestComplexStoredProcedure (999, true);
```

The first call will return the full category information for category two, including category ID, name, description, and picture. The second call will return only partial information for category six, including category ID, and name. In both of the cases, it will return the products in the category, and the average product price in that category. The third call will print an error message because there is no category with ID 999.

The output is as shown in the following image:

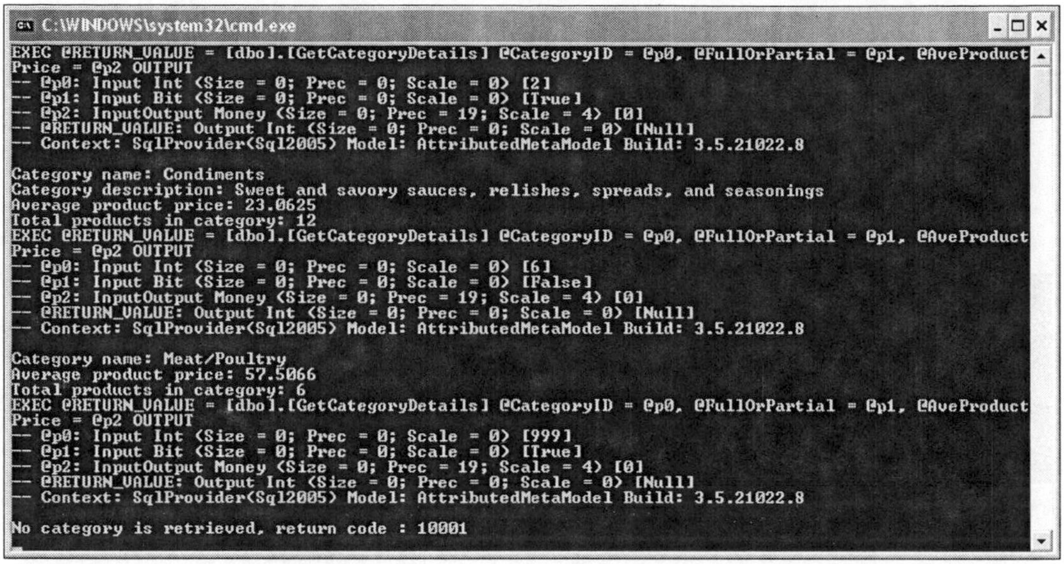

```
C:\WINDOWS\system32\cmd.exe
EXEC @RETURN_VALUE = [dbo].[GetCategoryDetails] @CategoryID = @p0, @FullOrPartial = @p1, @AveProduct
Price = @p2 OUTPUT
-- @p0: Input Int (Size = 0; Prec = 0; Scale = 0) [2]
-- @p1: Input Bit (Size = 0; Prec = 0; Scale = 0) [True]
-- @p2: InputOutput Money (Size = 0; Prec = 19; Scale = 4) [0]
-- @RETURN_VALUE: Output Int (Size = 0; Prec = 0; Scale = 0) [Null]
-- Context: SqlProvider(Sql2005) Model: AttributedMetaModel Build: 3.5.21022.8

Category name: Condiments
Category description: Sweet and savory sauces, relishes, spreads, and seasonings
Average product price: 23.0625
Total products in category: 12
EXEC @RETURN_VALUE = [dbo].[GetCategoryDetails] @CategoryID = @p0, @FullOrPartial = @p1, @AveProduct
Price = @p2 OUTPUT
-- @p0: Input Int (Size = 0; Prec = 0; Scale = 0) [6]
-- @p1: Input Bit (Size = 0; Prec = 0; Scale = 0) [False]
-- @p2: InputOutput Money (Size = 0; Prec = 19; Scale = 4) [0]
-- @RETURN_VALUE: Output Int (Size = 0; Prec = 0; Scale = 0) [Null]
-- Context: SqlProvider(Sql2005) Model: AttributedMetaModel Build: 3.5.21022.8

Category name: Meat/Poultry
Average product price: 57.5066
Total products in category: 6
EXEC @RETURN_VALUE = [dbo].[GetCategoryDetails] @CategoryID = @p0, @FullOrPartial = @p1, @AveProduct
Price = @p2 OUTPUT
-- @p0: Input Int (Size = 0; Prec = 0; Scale = 0) [999]
-- @p1: Input Bit (Size = 0; Prec = 0; Scale = 0) [True]
-- @p2: InputOutput Money (Size = 0; Prec = 19; Scale = 4) [0]
-- @RETURN_VALUE: Output Int (Size = 0; Prec = 0; Scale = 0) [Null]
-- Context: SqlProvider(Sql2005) Model: AttributedMetaModel Build: 3.5.21022.8

No category is retrieved, return code : 10001
```

Compiled query

It is common in many applications to execute structurally-similar queries many times. In such cases, it is possible to increase performance by compiling the query once, and executing it several times in the application with different parameters. This result is obtained in LINQ to SQL by using the `CompiledQuery` class.

The following code shows how to define a compiled query:

```
Func<NorthwindDataContext, string, IQueryable<Product>> fn =
CompiledQuery.Compile((NorthwindDataContext db2, string category) =>
    from p in db2.Products
    where p.Category.CategoryName == category
    select p);
var products1 = fn(db, "Beverages");
Console.WriteLine("Total products in category Beverages: {0}",
products1.Count());
var products2 = fn(db, "Seafood");
Console.WriteLine("Total products in category Seafood: {0}",
products2.Count());
```

As you can see, a compiled query is actually a function. The function contains a compiled LINQ query expression, and can be called just like a regular function.

Direct SQL

LINQ to SQL is a part of the ADO.NET family of technologies. It is based on services provided by the ADO.NET provider model. Therefore, it is possible to mix LINQ to SQL code with existing ADO.NET applications. For example, you can create a `DataContext` using an existing ADO.NET connection.

In some cases, you might find that the query or submit changes facility of the `DataContext` is insufficient for the specialized task that you want to perform. In these cases, it is possible to use the `DataContext` to issue raw SQL commands directly to the database.

The `ExecuteQuery()` method lets you execute a raw SQL query, and converts the result of your query directly into objects.

The `ExecuteCommand()` method lets you directly execute SQL commands against the database.

For example, the following code will retrieve all discontinued products, and update the price for one product:

```
var products = db.ExecuteQuery<Product>(
    "SELECT ProductID, ProductName " +
    "FROM Products " +
    "WHERE Discontinued = 0 " +
    "ORDER BY ProductName;"
);
Console.WriteLine("Total discontinued products :{0}", products.
Count());

int rowCount = db.ExecuteCommand(
   " update products "
   + "set UnitPrice=UnitPrice+1 "
   + "where productID=35");
if (rowCount < 1)
    Console.WriteLine("No product is updated");
else
    Console.WriteLine("Product price is updated");
```

Dynamic query

In addition to using LINQ syntax, we can also build queries dynamically at runtime using `Expressions`. For example, the following code will create two method expressions, one for the `where` clause, and one for the `order by` clause:

```
ParameterExpression param = Expression.Parameter(typeof(Product),
"p");

Expression left = Expression.Property(param, typeof(Product).GetProper
ty("UnitPrice"));
Expression right = Expression.Constant((decimal)100.00, typeof(System.
Nullable<decimal>));
Expression filter = Expression.GreaterThanOrEqual(left, right);
Expression pred = Expression.Lambda(filter, param);

IQueryable products = db.Products;

Expression expr = Expression.Call(typeof(Queryable), "Where",
    new Type[] { typeof(Product) }, Expression.Constant(products),
pred);

expr = Expression.Call(typeof(Queryable), "OrderBy",
    new Type[] { typeof(Product), typeof(string) }, expr, Expression.
Lambda(Expression.Property(param, "ProductName"), param));

IQueryable<Product> query = db.Products.AsQueryable().Provider.CreateQ
uery<Product>(expr);

foreach (var p in query)
    Console.WriteLine("Product name: {0}", p.ProductName);
```

To build the first expression, we first created a `left` expression, and a `right` expression. Then, we used them to create a `filter` expression. The `predicate` expression is then created based on this filter expression.

As the second expression takes the first expression as an argument, it expands the first expression to include an `order by` expression.

The statement with the `CreateQuery` method is the one that creates the query dynamically, according to the expressions that we have created before this statement. And, of course, the query won't get executed until the `foreach` statement is executed.

Before running this program, you need to add the following `using` statement to the beginning:

```
using System.Linq.Expressions;
```

The output of the above code looks as shown in the following image:

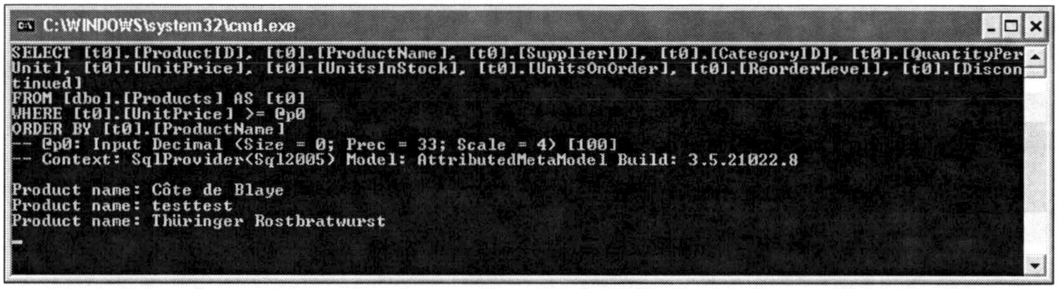

```
C:\WINDOWS\system32\cmd.exe
SELECT [t0].[ProductID], [t0].[ProductName], [t0].[SupplierID], [t0].[CategoryID], [t0].[QuantityPer
Unit], [t0].[UnitPrice], [t0].[UnitsInStock], [t0].[UnitsOnOrder], [t0].[ReorderLevel], [t0].[Discon
tinued]
FROM [dbo].[Products] AS [t0]
WHERE [t0].[UnitPrice] >= @p0
ORDER BY [t0].[ProductName]
-- @p0: Input Decimal (Size = 0; Prec = 33; Scale = 4) [100]
-- Context: SqlProvider(Sql2005) Model: AttributedMetaModel Build: 3.5.21022.8

Product name: Côte de Blaye
Product name: testtest
Product name: Thüringer Rostbratwurst
```

Inheritance

The LINQ to SQL Object Relational Designer (O/R Designer) supports the concept of single-table inheritance as it is often implemented in relational systems. In the following sections, we will explore what single-table inheritance is, and how to use it with LINQ.

LINQ to SQL single-table inheritance

In **single-table inheritance**, there is a single database table that contains fields for both parent information and child information. With relational data, a discriminator column contains the value that determines which class any given record belongs to.

For example, consider a `Persons` table that contains everyone employed by a company. Some people are employees, and some are managers. The `Persons` table contains a column named `EmployeeType` that has a value of `1` for managers and a value of `2` for employees; this is the discriminator column.

In this scenario, you can create a subclass of employees, and populate the class with only records that have an `EmployeeType` value of `2`. You can also remove columns that do not apply, from each of the classes.

In our `Northwind` database, the `Products` table contains all of the products in eight different categories. Suppose that all products share some common properties, and each category also has some unique properties of its own. We can then define a `BaseProduct` entity class for all of the common properties of the products, and define a unique child entity class for each category.

We assume that all products have the following properties:

`ProductID, ProductName, SupplierID, CategoryID, QuantityPerUnit, UnitPrice, UnitsInStock, UnitsOnOrder.`

To simplify the example, we will define only two child entity classes in this example: one for `beverage` products, and another for `sea food` products. We assume that a `beverage` product has one more property of `Discontinued` and a `sea food` product has one more property of `ReorderLevel`.

Modeling the BaseProduct and Beverage classes

We will first model these classes with LINQ to SQL designer.

1. Open the **Server Explorer**, and drag the **Products** table to **Northwind.dbml** design pane. Change the entity class name from **Product1** to **BaseProduct**, and delete its member properties of **Discontinued**, and **ReorderLevel**.
2. Drag another instance of the **Products** table from the **Server Explorer** to the **Northwind.dbml** design pane, and change its name from **Product1** to **Beverage**. Click the the association line between **Category** and **Beverage**, and delete it. Then, delete all of the new table's properties except **Discontinued**.
3. Now, we need to set up the inheritance relationship between the `BaseProduct` and `Beverage` class. Open the **Object Relational Designer Toolbox**, and click the shape **Inheritance**.

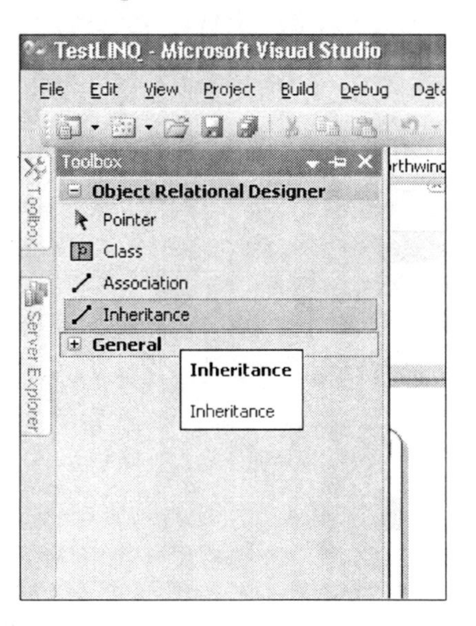

4. While the cursor is changed, click the **Beverage** class, and then click the **BaseProduct** class, to connect them together.
5. Click the newly-created association line between the **BaseProduct** and **Beverage** classes, and set the following properties:

Property	Value	Explanation
Inheritance Default	BaseProduct	a `Product` without a derived class will be of type `BaseProduct`
Base Class Discriminator Value	0	the default product type's discriminator value
Derived Class Discriminator Value	1	the `Beverage` type's discriminator value
Discriminator Property	CategoryID	the column `CategoryID` is used to identify derived classes

The properties of the association between `BaseProduct` and `Beverage` should look like this:

Modeling the Seafood class

Next, we need to model the `Seafood` class. This class will inherit from the `BaseProduct` class, but will have an extra property of `ReorderLevel`.

1. Drag another instance of the **Products** table from the **Server Explorer** to the **Northwind.dbml** design surface, and change its name from **Product1** to **Seafood**.
2. Click the association line between **Category** and **Seafood,** and delete it. Then, delete all of the new table's properties except **ReorderLevel**.
3. Do the same thing as we did for the `Beverage` class, to set up the inheritance relationship between the `BaseProduct` class and the `Seafood` class, except that you need to set the **Derived Class Discriminator Value** to **8**. Actually, this is the only inheritance value you need to set for this class because all of the other three properties (**Inheritance Default**, **Base Class Discriminator Value**, and **Discriminator Property**) have been set previously.

The finished model should be as shown in the following image:

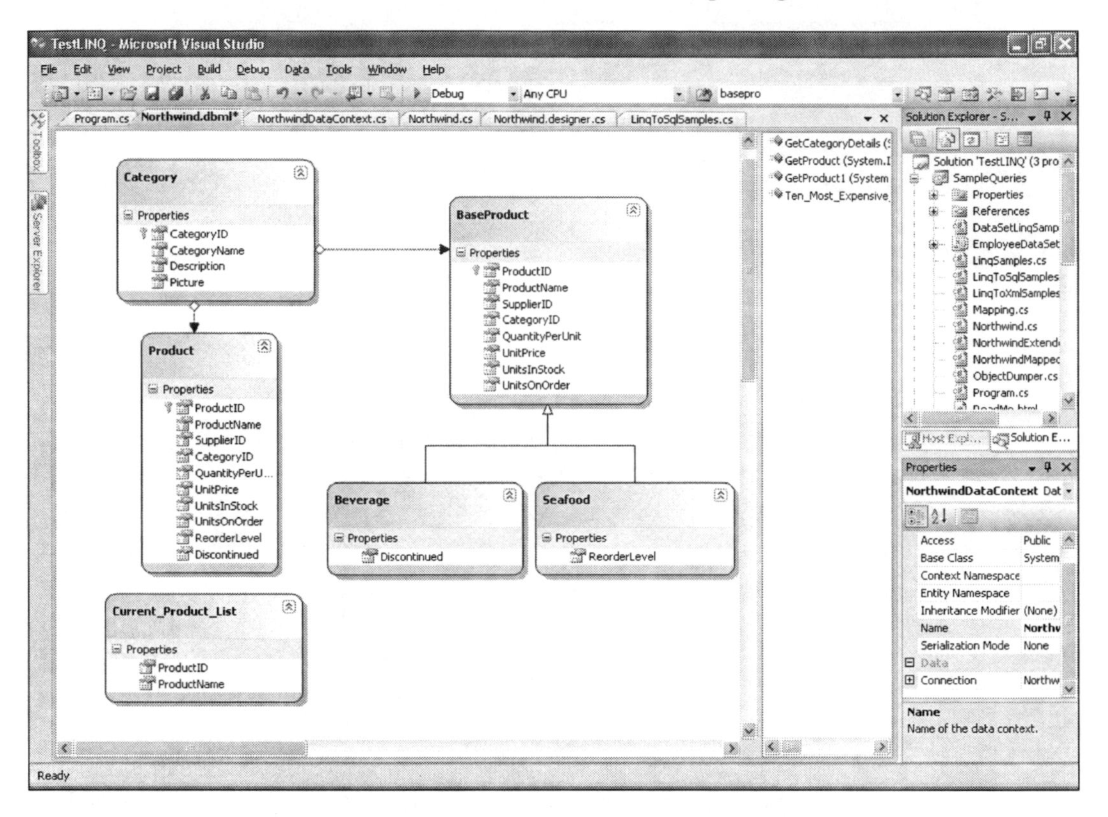

The generated classes with inheritance

Save the model, and open the `Northwind.designer.cs` file. You will find that three classes have been added to the `DataContext`. The first class is the `BaseProduct` class, which has this signature:

```
[Table(Name="dbo.Products")]
[InheritanceMapping(Code="0", Type=typeof(BaseProduct),
IsDefault=true)]
[InheritanceMapping(Code="1", Type=typeof(Beverage))]
[InheritanceMapping(Code="8", Type=typeof(Seafood))]
public partial class BaseProduct : INotifyPropertyChanging,
INotifyPropertyChanged
```

Its class body is almost identical to the `Product` class, except without the properties `ReorderLevel` and `Discontinued`. The three inheritance mapping attributes are generated from the inheritance properties we set in the model.

So, why don't we just use the existing `Product` class as the base class?

Actually, this is OK and realistically it should be the preferred way to use the `Product` class as the base class. However, we have used the `Product` class in all of our previous examples, and if we delete two of its properties, some of those examples might not work. So, we decided to create a new class from the same table for this example only.

The other two classes are for the derived classes; each has only one property:

```
public partial class Beverage : BaseProduct
public partial class Seafood : BaseProduct
```

Testing the inheritance

Now we can write a query to show the inheritance between the `BaseProduct` and the two derived classes.

First, we can retrieve all of the beverage products by using the `is` operator like this:

```
var beverages1 = from b in db.BaseProducts
                 where b is Beverage
                 select b;
```

We can also use the `OfType` operator to retrieve the same products, as follows:

```
var beverages2 = from b in db.BaseProducts.OfType<Beverage>()
            select b;

Console.WriteLine("Total number of beverage products: {0}",
beverages1.Count());
Console.WriteLine("Total number of beverage products: {0}",
beverages2.Count());
```

Run the program, and you will see both queries return **12**.

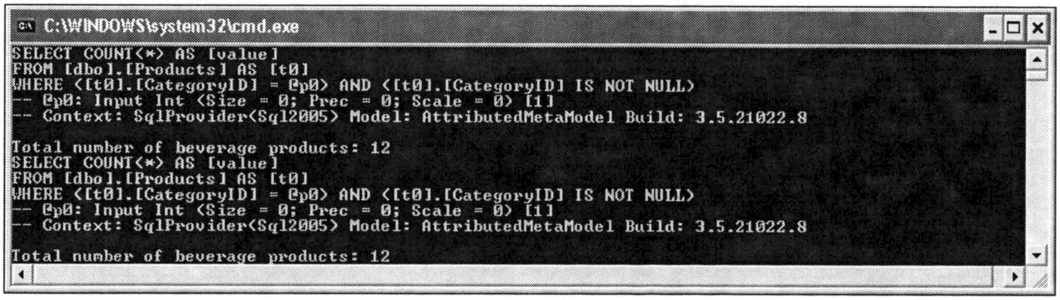

```
C:\WINDOWS\system32\cmd.exe
SELECT COUNT(*) AS [value]
FROM [dbo].[Products] AS [t0]
WHERE ([t0].[CategoryID] = @p0) AND ([t0].[CategoryID] IS NOT NULL)
-- @p0: Input Int (Size = 0; Prec = 0; Scale = 0) [1]
-- Context: SqlProvider(Sql2005) Model: AttributedMetaModel Build: 3.5.21022.8

Total number of beverage products: 12
SELECT COUNT(*) AS [value]
FROM [dbo].[Products] AS [t0]
WHERE ([t0].[CategoryID] = @p0) AND ([t0].[CategoryID] IS NOT NULL)
-- @p0: Input Int (Size = 0; Prec = 0; Scale = 0) [1]
-- Context: SqlProvider(Sql2005) Model: AttributedMetaModel Build: 3.5.21022.8

Total number of beverage products: 12
```

We can also use the `as` operator to search for all the products that are beverages:

```
var beverages3 = from b in db.BaseProducts
            select b as Beverage;

foreach (var b in beverages3)
{
    if (b != null)
    {
        Console.WriteLine("Found a beverage: {0}, it is {1}
            discontinued", b.ProductName, (b.Discontinued?"":"not"));
    }
}
```

In the above code, if there are no products that are beverages, the routine will return null.

In all of the above three queries, `Discontinued` is a property of the returning item, which means it is of the `Beverage` type. Also, all of the `BaseProduct` properties are available, because the returning item's data type is a child of the `BaseProduct` type.

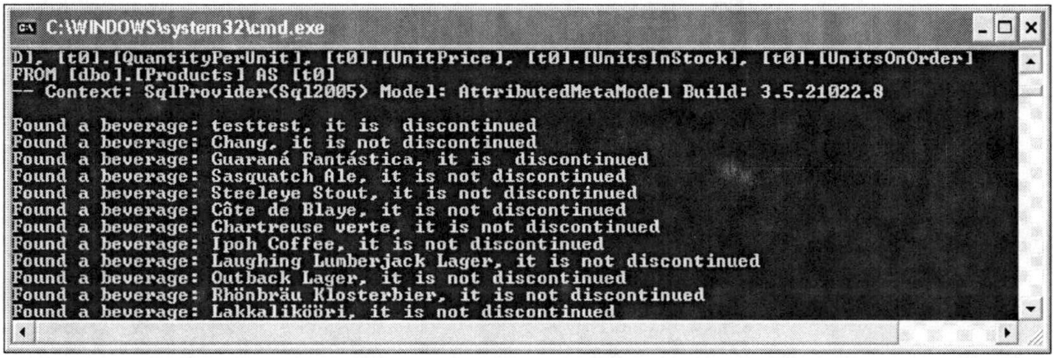

```
C:\WINDOWS\system32\cmd.exe
D], [t0].[QuantityPerUnit], [t0].[UnitPrice], [t0].[UnitsInStock], [t0].[UnitsOnOrder]
FROM [dbo].[Products] AS [t0]
-- Context: SqlProvider(Sql2005) Model: AttributedMetaModel Build: 3.5.21022.8

Found a beverage: testtest, it is  discontinued
Found a beverage: Chang, it is not discontinued
Found a beverage: Guaraná Fantástica, it is  discontinued
Found a beverage: Sasquatch Ale, it is not discontinued
Found a beverage: Steeleye Stout, it is not discontinued
Found a beverage: Côte de Blaye, it is not discontinued
Found a beverage: Chartreuse verte, it is not discontinued
Found a beverage: Ipoh Coffee, it is not discontinued
Found a beverage: Laughing Lumberjack Lager, it is not discontinued
Found a beverage: Outback Lager, it is not discontinued
Found a beverage: Rhönbräu Klosterbier, it is not discontinued
Found a beverage: Lakkalikööri, it is not discontinued
```

Similarly, we can retrieve all `sea food` products, and use its `ReorderLevel` property, as follows:

```
var seafood = from s in db.BaseProducts.OfType<Seafood>()
              select s;

foreach (var s in seafood)
    Console.WriteLine("Product name: {0} Reorder level: {1}",
        s.ProductName, s.ReorderLevel);
```

The output of this is shown in the following image:

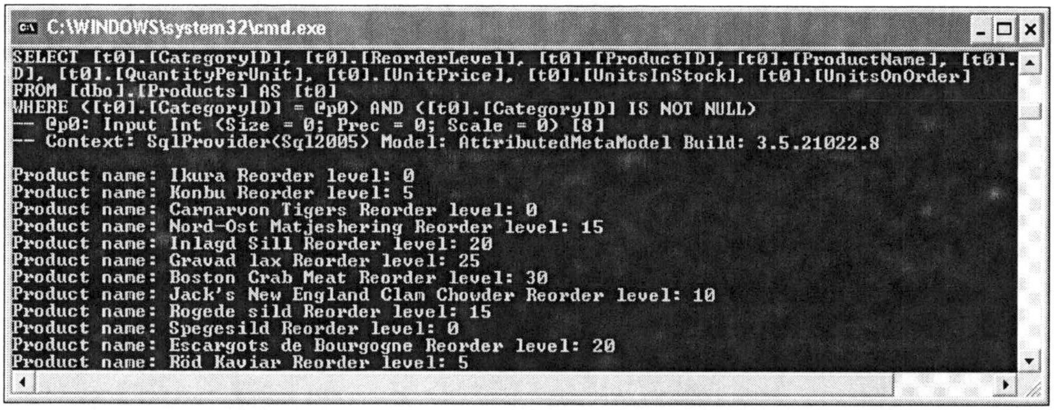

```
C:\WINDOWS\system32\cmd.exe
SELECT [t0].[CategoryID], [t0].[ReorderLevel], [t0].[ProductID], [t0].[ProductName], [t0].
D], [t0].[QuantityPerUnit], [t0].[UnitPrice], [t0].[UnitsInStock], [t0].[UnitsOnOrder]
FROM [dbo].[Products] AS [t0]
WHERE ([t0].[CategoryID] = @p0) AND ([t0].[CategoryID] IS NOT NULL)
-- @p0: Input Int (Size = 0; Prec = 0; Scale = 0) [8]
-- Context: SqlProvider(Sql2005) Model: AttributedMetaModel Build: 3.5.21022.8

Product name: Ikura Reorder level: 0
Product name: Konbu Reorder level: 5
Product name: Carnarvon Tigers Reorder level: 0
Product name: Nord-Ost Matjeshering Reorder level: 15
Product name: Inlagd Sill Reorder level: 20
Product name: Gravad lax Reorder level: 25
Product name: Boston Crab Meat Reorder level: 30
Product name: Jack's New England Clam Chowder Reorder level: 10
Product name: Rogede sild Reorder level: 15
Product name: Spegesild Reorder level: 0
Product name: Escargots de Bourgogne Reorder level: 20
Product name: Röd Kaviar Reorder level: 5
```

Handling simultaneous (concurrent) updates

If two users are updating the same record at the same time, a conflict will occur. There are normally three different ways to handle this conflict. The first method is to let the last update win, so no controlling mechanism is needed. The second one is to use a pessimistic lock, in which case, before updating a record, a user will first lock the record, and then process and update the record. At the same time, all other users will have to wait for the lock to be released in order to start the updating process.

The third and most common mechanism in an enterprise product is the optimistic locking. A user doesn't lock a record for update when the data is retrieved, but when the application is ready to commit the changes, it will first check to see if any other user has updated the same record since that data was retrieved. If nobody else has changed the same record, the update will be committed. If any other user has changed the same record, the update will fail, and the user has to decide what to do with the conflict. Some possible options include overwriting the previous changes, discarding their own changes, or refreshing the record and then reapplying (merging) the changes.

LINQ to SQL supports optimistic concurrency control in two ways. Next, we will explain both of them.

Detecting conflicts using the Update Check property

The first way is to use the `Update Check` property. At design time, this property can be set for a column to be one of these three values:

- `Always`
- `Never`
- `WhenChanged`

For a column, there are three values to remember: the original value before update, the current value to be updated, and the database value when the change is submitted. For example, consider the case where you fetch a product record from the database with a `UnitPrice` of `25.00`, and update it to `26.00`. After you fetched this product, but before you submit your changes back to database, somebody else may have updated this product's price to `27.00`. In this example, the original value of the price is `25.00`, the current value to update is `26.00`, and the database value when the change is submitted is `27.00`.

When the change is submitted to the database, the original value and the database value are compared. If they are different, a conflict is detected.

Now, let us look at these three settings. The first setting of the property `Update Check` is `Always`, which means that the column will always be used for conflict detecting. Whenever a record is being changed, this column will always be checked to see if it has been updated by other users. If it has been, it raises a conflict. This is the default setting of this property. So by default, all columns will be used for conflict detecting.

The second setting, `Never`, means that column will never be used for conflict checking. When a change is submitted to the database, the application will not check the status of this column. So even if this column has been updated by other users, it won't raise an error.

The third setting, `WhenChanged`, is in between the two previous settings. It will be used for conflict detecting, but only if the current process has changed its value. If the current process hasn't changed its value, the application won't care if some other processes have updated its value.

Writing the test code

To show how to use these three settings, we can write the following code:

```
// first user
Console.WriteLine("First User ...");
Product product = (from p in db.Products
```

```
              where p.ProductID == 2
              select p).First();
Console.WriteLine("Original price: {0}", product.UnitPrice);
product.UnitPrice = 26;
Console.WriteLine("Current price to update: {0}", product.UnitPrice);
// process more products

// second user
Console.WriteLine("Second User ...");
NorthwindDataContext db2 = new NorthwindDataContext();
Product product2 = (from p in db2.Products
               where p.ProductID == 2
               select p).First();
Console.WriteLine("Original price: {0}", product2.UnitPrice);
product2.UnitPrice = 26;
Console.WriteLine("Current price to update: {0}", product2.UnitPrice);
db2.SubmitChanges();
db2.Dispose();

// first user is ready to submit changes
Console.WriteLine("First User ...");
try
{
    db.SubmitChanges();
}
catch (ChangeConflictException)
{
    Console.WriteLine("Conflict is detected");
    foreach (ObjectChangeConflict occ in db.ChangeConflicts)
    {
        MetaTable metatable = db.Mapping.GetTable(occ.Object.
GetType());
        Product entityInConflict = (Product)occ.Object;
        Console.WriteLine("Table name: {0}", metatable.TableName);
        Console.Write("Product ID: ");
        Console.WriteLine(entityInConflict.ProductID);
        foreach (MemberChangeConflict mcc in occ.MemberConflicts)
        {
            object currVal = mcc.CurrentValue;
            object origVal = mcc.OriginalValue;
            object databaseVal = mcc.DatabaseValue;
            MemberInfo mi = mcc.Member;
            Console.WriteLine("Member: {0}", mi.Name);
            Console.WriteLine("current value: {0}", currVal);
            Console.WriteLine("original value: {0}", origVal);
            Console.WriteLine("database value: {0}", databaseVal);
        }
    }
}
```

In this example, we first retrieved product `2` and updated its price from `19.00` to `26.00`. Then, we simulated another user to retrieving the same product, and also updated its price to `26.00`. The second user submitted the changes first with no error, but when the first user tried to submit the changes, a conflict was detected because at that time the original value of `19.00` was different from the database value of `26.00`. We can also use `ChangeConflicts` of the `DataContext` to get the list of conflicts.

Testing the conflicts

Now, add the following `using` statements first:

```
using System.Data.Linq.Mapping;
using System.Reflection;
```

Run the program. You will get an output as shown in the following image:

```
C:\WINDOWS\system32\cmd.exe
First User ...
SELECT TOP (1) [t0].[ProductID], [t0].[ProductName], [t0].[SupplierID], [t0].[CategoryID], [t0].[Qua
ntityPerUnit], [t0].[UnitPrice], [t0].[UnitsInStock], [t0].[UnitsOnOrder], [t0].[ReorderLevel], [t0]
.[Discontinued]
FROM [dbo].[Products] AS [t0]
WHERE [t0].[ProductID] = @p0
-- @p0: Input Int (Size = 0; Prec = 0; Scale = 0) [2]
-- Context: SqlProvider(Sql2005) Model: AttributedMetaModel Build: 3.5.21022.8

Original price: 19.0000
Current price to update: 26
Second User ...
Original price: 19.0000
Current price to update: 26
First User ...
UPDATE [dbo].[Products]
SET [UnitPrice] = @p9
WHERE ([ProductID] = @p0) AND ([ProductName] = @p1) AND ([SupplierID] = @p2) AND ([CategoryID] = @p3
) AND ([QuantityPerUnit] = @p4) AND ([UnitPrice] = @p5) AND ([UnitsInStock] = @p6) AND ([UnitsOnOrde
r] = @p7) AND ([ReorderLevel] = @p8) AND (NOT ([Discontinued] = 1))
-- @p0: Input Int (Size = 0; Prec = 0; Scale = 0) [2]
-- @p1: Input NVarChar (Size = 5; Prec = 0; Scale = 0) [Chang]
-- @p2: Input Int (Size = 0; Prec = 0; Scale = 0) [1]
-- @p3: Input Int (Size = 0; Prec = 0; Scale = 0) [1]
-- @p4: Input NVarChar (Size = 18; Prec = 0; Scale = 0) [24 - 12 oz bottles]
-- @p5: Input Money (Size = 0; Prec = 19; Scale = 4) [19.0000]
-- @p6: Input SmallInt (Size = 0; Prec = 0; Scale = 0) [17]
-- @p7: Input SmallInt (Size = 0; Prec = 0; Scale = 0) [40]
-- @p8: Input SmallInt (Size = 0; Prec = 0; Scale = 0) [25]
-- @p9: Input Money (Size = 0; Prec = 19; Scale = 4) [26]
-- Context: SqlProvider(Sql2005) Model: AttributedMetaModel Build: 3.5.21022.8

Conflict is detected
Table name: dbo.Products
Product ID: 2
SELECT [t0].[ProductID], [t0].[ProductName], [t0].[SupplierID], [t0].[CategoryID], [t0].[QuantityPer
Unit], [t0].[UnitPrice], [t0].[UnitsInStock], [t0].[UnitsOnOrder], [t0].[ReorderLevel], [t0].[Discon
tinued]
FROM [dbo].[Products] AS [t0]
WHERE [t0].[ProductID] = @p0
-- @p0: Input Int (Size = 0; Prec = 0; Scale = 0) [2]
-- Context: SqlProvider(Sql2005) Model: AttributedMetaModel Build: 3.5.21022.8

Member: UnitPrice
current value: 26
original value: 19.0000
database value: 26.0000
```

Now, open **Northwind.dbml**, click on the **UnitPrice** member of the **Product** class, change its **Update Check property** to **Never**, and run the program again. You won't see the exception this time, because this column is not used for conflict detecting. The output is as follows (you will need to change its price back to `19.00` before you re-run the program):

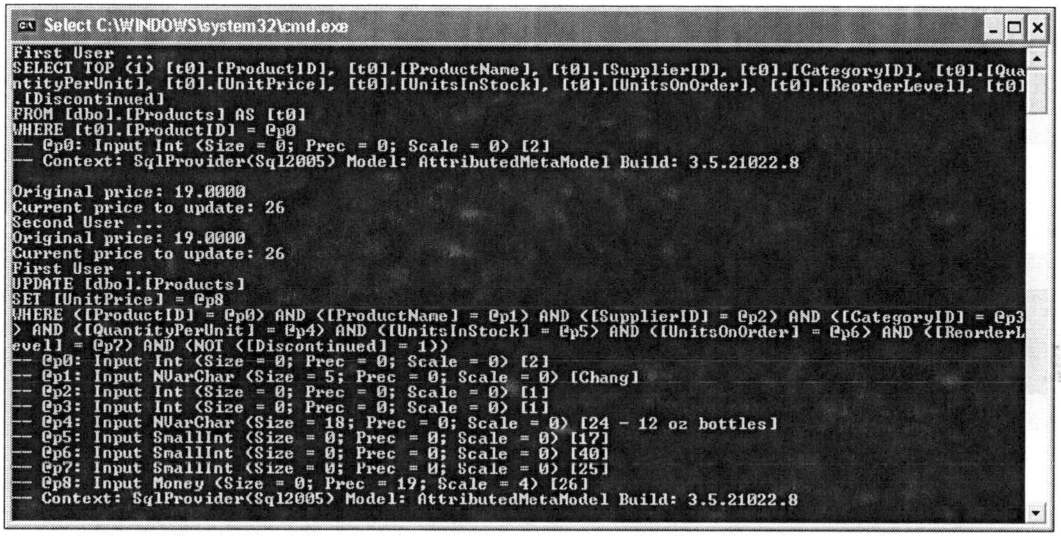

```
Select C:\WINDOWS\system32\cmd.exe
First User ...
SELECT TOP (1) [t0].[ProductID], [t0].[ProductName], [t0].[SupplierID], [t0].[CategoryID], [t0].[Qua
ntityPerUnit], [t0].[UnitPrice], [t0].[UnitsInStock], [t0].[UnitsOnOrder], [t0].[ReorderLevel], [t0]
.[Discontinued]
FROM [dbo].[Products] AS [t0]
WHERE [t0].[ProductID] = @p0
-- @p0: Input Int (Size = 0; Prec = 0; Scale = 0) [2]
-- Context: SqlProvider(Sql2005) Model: AttributedMetaModel Build: 3.5.21022.8

Original price: 19.0000
Current price to update: 26
Second User ...
Original price: 19.0000
Current price to update: 26
First User ...
UPDATE [dbo].[Products]
SET [UnitPrice] = @p8
WHERE ([ProductID] = @p0) AND ([ProductName] = @p1) AND ([SupplierID] = @p2) AND ([CategoryID] = @p3
) AND ([QuantityPerUnit] = @p4) AND ([UnitsInStock] = @p5) AND ([UnitsOnOrder] = @p6) AND ([ReorderL
evel] = @p7) AND (NOT ([Discontinued] = 1))
-- @p0: Input Int (Size = 0; Prec = 0; Scale = 0) [2]
-- @p1: Input NVarChar (Size = 5; Prec = 0; Scale = 0) [Chang]
-- @p2: Input Int (Size = 0; Prec = 0; Scale = 0) [1]
-- @p3: Input Int (Size = 0; Prec = 0; Scale = 0) [1]
-- @p4: Input NVarChar (Size = 18; Prec = 0; Scale = 0) [24 - 12 oz bottles]
-- @p5: Input SmallInt (Size = 0; Prec = 0; Scale = 0) [17]
-- @p6: Input SmallInt (Size = 0; Prec = 0; Scale = 0) [40]
-- @p7: Input SmallInt (Size = 0; Prec = 0; Scale = 0) [25]
-- @p8: Input Money (Size = 0; Prec = 19; Scale = 4) [26]
-- Context: SqlProvider(Sql2005) Model: AttributedMetaModel Build: 3.5.21022.8
```

Detecting conflicts using a version column

The second and a more efficient way provide conflict control is by using a **version column**. If you add a column of type `Timestamp`, or `ROWVERSION`, when you drag this table to the OR/M designer pane, this column will be marked as `IsVersion = True`.

Version numbers are incremented, and timestamp columns are updated every time the associated row is updated. Before the update, if there is a column with `IsVersion=true`, LINQ to SQL will first check this column to make sure that this record has not been updated by any of the other users. This column will also be synchronized immediately after the data row is updated. The new values are visible after `SubmitChanges` finishes.

When there is a column marked `IsVersion=true`, LINQ to SQL will use only this column for conflict detecting. All other columns' `Update Property` will be ignored, even if they have been set to `Always` or `WhenChanged`.

Adding a version column

Now, let us try this in the `Products` table. First, we need to add a new column called `LastUpdateVersion`, which is of type `timestamp`. You can add it within Visual Studio 2008 in the Server Explorer by right-clicking on the table **Products**, and selecting **Open Table Definition**, as shown in the following image:

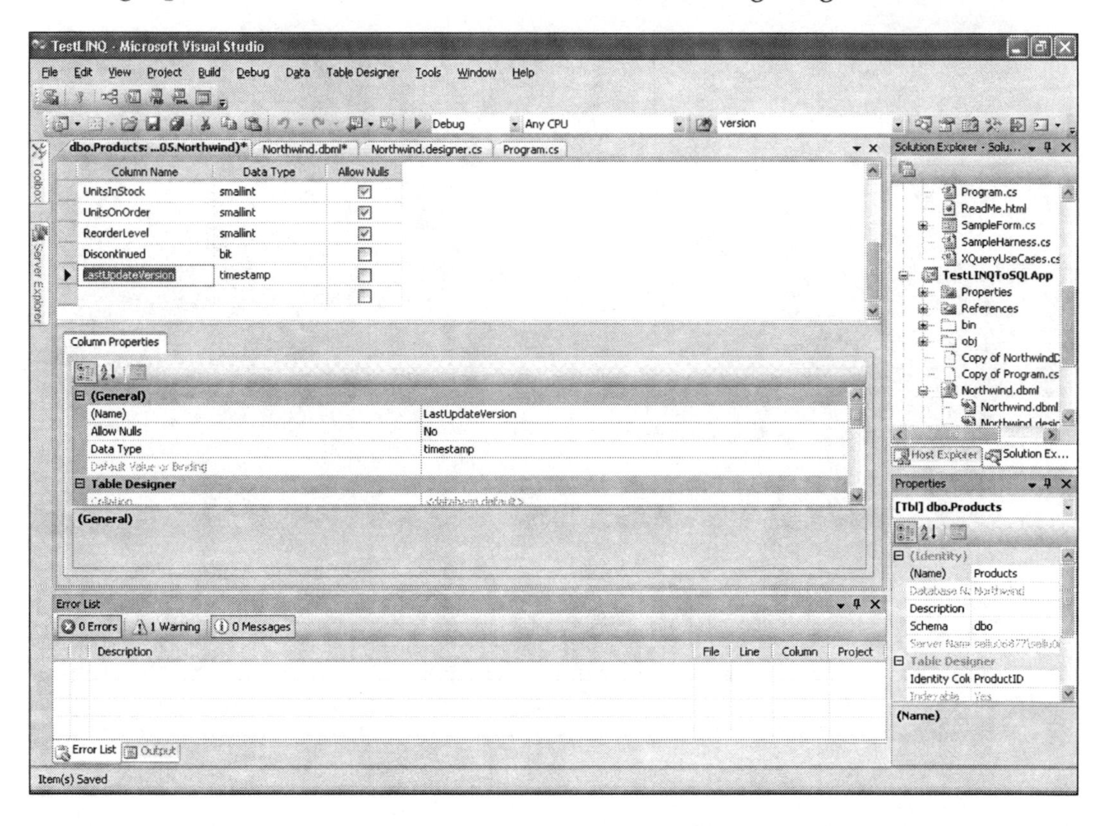

You can also open **SQL Server Management Studio**, and add the column from there.

Modeling the products table with a version column

After saving the changes, drag the **Products** table from the **Server Explorer** to the **Northwind.dbml** design pane, and keep the name **Product1**. This table now has a version controlling column, `LastUpdateVersion`, with properties as shown in the **Properties** dialog box image.

Note that its **Update Check Property** is set to **Never**. Actually, all other members' **Update Check** properties have been set to **Never**, because for this class, only the `LastUpdateVersion` column will be used for conflict detecting.

Open the `Northwind.designer.cs` file, and you will see that the column `LastUpdateVersion` has the following attributes:

```
[Column(Storage="_LastUpdateVersion", AutoSync=AutoSync.Always,
DbType="rowversion NOT NULL", CanBeNull=false, IsDbGenerated=true,
IsVersion=true, UpdateCheck=UpdateCheck.Never)]
public System.Data.Linq.Binary LastUpdateVersion
```

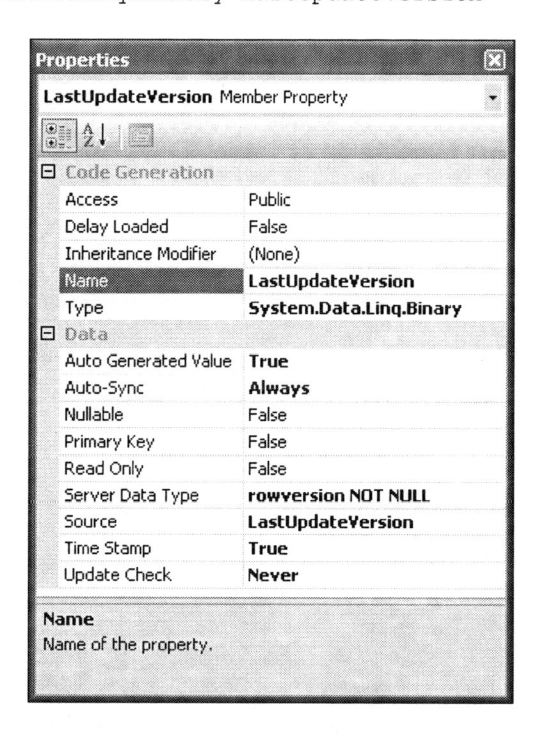

Writing the test code

We can write similar code to test this new version controlling mechanism:

```
// first user
Console.WriteLine("First User ...");
Product product = (from p in db.Products
                   where p.ProductID == 3
                   select p).First();
Console.WriteLine("Original unit in stock: {0}", product.
UnitsInStock);
product.UnitsInStock = 26;
Console.WriteLine("Current unit in stock to update: {0}", product.
UnitsInStock);
// process more products
```

```
// second user
Console.WriteLine("Second User ...");
NorthwindDataContext db2 = new NorthwindDataContext();
Product product2 = (from p in db2.Products
                    where p.ProductID == 3
                    select p).First();
Console.WriteLine("Original unit in stock: {0}", product2.
UnitsInStock);
product2.UnitsInStock = 27;
Console.WriteLine("Current unit in stock to update: {0}", product2.
UnitsInStock);
db2.SubmitChanges();
db2.Dispose();

// first user is ready to submit changes
Console.WriteLine("First User ...");
try
{
    db.SubmitChanges();
}
catch (ChangeConflictException)
{
    Console.WriteLine("Conflict is detected");
    foreach (ObjectChangeConflict occ in db.ChangeConflicts)
    {
        MetaTable metatable =
                          db.Mapping.GetTable(occ.Object.GetType());
        Product entityInConflict = (Product)occ.Object;
        Console.WriteLine("Table name: {0}", metatable.TableName);
        Console.Write("Product ID: ");
        Console.WriteLine(entityInConflict.ProductID);
        foreach (MemberChangeConflict mcc in occ.MemberConflicts)
        {
            object currVal = mcc.CurrentValue;
            object origVal = mcc.OriginalValue;
            object databaseVal = mcc.DatabaseValue;
            MemberInfo mi = mcc.Member;
            Console.WriteLine("Member: {0}", mi.Name);
            Console.WriteLine("current value: {0}", currVal);
            Console.WriteLine("original value: {0}", origVal);
            Console.WriteLine("database value: {0}", databaseVal);
        }
    }
}
```

Testing the conflicts

This time we tried to update `UnitInStock` for product `3`. From the output, we can see a conflict was detected again, when the first user submitted their changes to the database.

```
C:\WINDOWS\system32\cmd.exe
First User ...
SELECT TOP (1) [t0].[ProductID], [t0].[ProductName], [t0].[SupplierID], [t0].[CategoryID], [t0].[Qua
ntityPerUnit], [t0].[UnitPrice], [t0].[UnitsInStock], [t0].[UnitsOnOrder], [t0].[ReorderLevel], [t0]
.[Discontinued]
FROM [dbo].[Products] AS [t0]
WHERE [t0].[ProductID] = @p0
-- @p0: Input Int (Size = 0; Prec = 0; Scale = 0) [3]
-- Context: SqlProvider(Sql2005) Model: AttributedMetaModel Build: 3.5.21022.8

Original unit in stock: 13
Current unit in stock to update: 26
Second User ...
Original unit in stock: 13
Current unit in stock to update: 27
First User ...
UPDATE [dbo].[Products]
SET [UnitsInStock] = @p8
WHERE ([ProductID] = @p0) AND ([ProductName] = @p1) AND ([SupplierID] = @p2) AND ([CategoryID] = @p3
) AND ([QuantityPerUnit] = @p4) AND ([UnitsInStock] = @p5) AND ([UnitsOnOrder] = @p6) AND ([ReorderL
evel] = @p7) AND (NOT ([Discontinued] = 1))
-- @p0: Input Int (Size = 0; Prec = 0; Scale = 0) [3]
-- @p1: Input NVarChar (Size = 13; Prec = 0; Scale = 0) [Aniseed Syrup]
-- @p2: Input Int (Size = 0; Prec = 0; Scale = 0) [1]
-- @p3: Input Int (Size = 0; Prec = 0; Scale = 0) [2]
-- @p4: Input NVarChar (Size = 19; Prec = 0; Scale = 0) [12 - 550 ml bottles]
-- @p5: Input SmallInt (Size = 0; Prec = 0; Scale = 0) [13]
-- @p6: Input SmallInt (Size = 0; Prec = 0; Scale = 0) [70]
-- @p7: Input SmallInt (Size = 0; Prec = 0; Scale = 0) [25]
-- @p8: Input SmallInt (Size = 0; Prec = 0; Scale = 0) [26]
-- Context: SqlProvider(Sql2005) Model: AttributedMetaModel Build: 3.5.21022.8

Conflict is detected
Table name: dbo.Products
Product ID: 3
SELECT [t0].[ProductID], [t0].[ProductName], [t0].[SupplierID], [t0].[CategoryID], [t0].[QuantityPer
Unit], [t0].[UnitPrice], [t0].[UnitsInStock], [t0].[UnitsOnOrder], [t0].[ReorderLevel], [t0].[Discon
tinued]
FROM [dbo].[Products] AS [t0]
WHERE [t0].[ProductID] = @p0
-- @p0: Input Int (Size = 0; Prec = 0; Scale = 0) [3]
-- Context: SqlProvider(Sql2005) Model: AttributedMetaModel Build: 3.5.21022.8

Member: UnitsInStock
current value: 26
original value: 13
database value: 27
```

Transactions support

In the previous section, we learned that simultaneous changes by different users can be controlled by using a version column or the `Update Check` property. Sometimes, the same user may have made several changes, and some of the changes might not succeed. In this case, we need a way of controlling the behavior of the overall update result. This is handled by transaction support.

LINQ to SQL uses the same transaction mechanism as ADO.NET, that is, uses implicit or explicit transactions. It can also participate in an existing ADO.NET transaction to let the outsider code decide on the result of the updates.

Implicit transactions

By default, LINQ to SQL uses an implicit transaction for each `SubmitChanges` call. All updates between two `SubmitChanges` calls are wrapped within one transaction.

For example, in the following code, we are trying to update two products. The second update will fail due to a constraint, so both updates will fail. Nothing will be written to the database.

```
Product prod1 = (from p in db.Products
                 where p.ProductID == 4
                 select p).First();
Product prod2 = (from p in db.Products
                 where p.ProductID == 5
                 select p).First();
prod1.UnitPrice += 1;
// update will fail because UnitPrice can't be < 0
prod2.UnitPrice = -5;
// both updates will fail because they are wihtin one transaction
db.SubmitChanges();
```

The output will look like this :

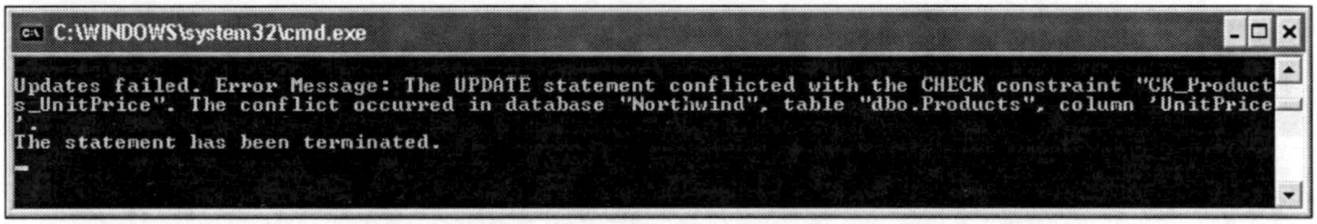

```
C:\WINDOWS\system32\cmd.exe
Updates failed. Error Message: The UPDATE statement conflicted with the CHECK constraint "CK_Products_UnitPrice". The conflict occurred in database "Northwind", table "dbo.Products", column 'UnitPrice'.
The statement has been terminated.
```

Explicit transactions

In addition to implicit transactions, you can also define a transaction scope, to explicitly control the update behavior. All updates within a transaction scope will be within a single transaction, Thus, they will either all succeed or all fail.

For example, in the following code, we started a transaction scope first. Then, within this transaction scope, we updated one product, and submitted the change to the database. However, at this point, the update had not really been committed, because the transaction scope was still not closed. We then tried to update another product, which failed due to the same constraint as mentioned in the previous example. The final result is that neither of these two products have been updated; nor can we say that the first update has been rolled back.

```
using (TransactionScope ts = new TransactionScope())
{
    try
    {
        Product prod1 = (from p in db.Products
                         where p.ProductID == 4
                         select p).First();
        prod1.UnitPrice += 1;
        db.SubmitChanges();

        // now let's try to update another product
        Product prod2 = (from p in db.Products
                         where p.ProductID == 5
                         select p).First();
        // update will fail because UnitPrice can't be < 0
        prod2.UnitPrice = -5;
        db.SubmitChanges();
    }
    catch (System.Data.SqlClient.SqlException e)
    {
        // both updates will fail because they are wihtin one
transaction
        Console.WriteLine("Updates failed. Error Message: {0}",
e.Message);
    }
}
```

Note that `TransactionScope` is in .NET Assembly `System.Transactions`. So you need to add a reference to `System.Transactions` first, and then add the following `using` statement to the `Program.cs` file:

```
using System.Transactions;
```

The output of the program is the same as shown in the previous example, in which an implicit transaction was used.

If you start the program in debugging mode, after the first `SubmitChanges` is called, you can go to SQL Server Management Studio, and query product `4`'s price using the following statement:

```
select UnitPrice from products (nolock) where productID = 4
```

The `nolock` hint is equivalent to `READUNCOMMITTED`, and it is used to retrieve dirty data that has not been committed. With this hint, you can see its price has been increased by the first change. Then, after the second `SubmitChanges` is called, an exception is thrown, and the transaction scope is closed. At this point, if you run the query again, you will see that product `4`'s price is rolled back to its original value.

> After the first call to the `SubmitChanges` method, you shouldn't use the following statement to query the price value of the product:
>
> select UnitPrice from products where productID = 4
>
> If you do so, you will not be able to get back any result. Instead, you will be waiting forever, as it is waiting for the transaction to be committed.

Participating in existing ADO.NET transactions

Because LINQ to SQL is a part of the ADO.NET family, it can also participate in an existing ADO.NET transaction. Regardless of whether the updates are done in the traditional ADO.NET code, or in LINQ to SQL, all of them will be committed at the same time, or all rolled back if any of them fails.

In the following code, we will first update a product using a traditional ADO.NET connection, and then update another product using LINQ to SQL. The second update will fail, making the whole transaction roll back.

```
string connString = "Server=your_db_name\\your_db_instance;initial cat
aLog=Northwind;user=your_user_name;pwd=your_password";

SqlConnection conn = null;
SqlCommand cmd = null;

try
{
    // open the connection
    conn = new SqlConnection(connString);
    conn.Open();

    // Use pre-existing ADO.NET connection to create DataContext:
    NorthwindDataContext db2 = new NorthwindDataContext(conn);

    SqlTransaction trans = conn.BeginTransaction();
    try
    {
        //update first product using ADO.NET
        using (cmd = new SqlCommand())
        {
```

```
            cmd.CommandText = "UPDATE Products SET UnitPrice =
                            UnitPrice+1 WHERE ProductID = 4";
            cmd.Connection = conn;
            cmd.Transaction = trans;
            cmd.ExecuteNonQuery();
        }
        // update second product using LINQ to SQL
        // Share pre-existing ADO.NET transaction:
        db2.Transaction = trans;
        Product prod2 = (from p in db2.Products
                         where p.ProductID == 5
                         select p).First();
        // update will fail because UnitPrice can't be < 0
        prod2.UnitPrice = -5;
        db2.SubmitChanges();
        db2.Dispose();
        //commit the transaction
        trans.Commit();
    }
    catch (Exception e)
    {
        // both updates will fail because they are wihtin one
           transaction Console.WriteLine("Updates failed. Error
           Message: {0}", e.Message);
    }
}
catch (Exception e)
{
    Console.WriteLine("Can not connect to database. Error: {0}",
                                                       e.Message);
}
finally
{
    if (cmd != null)
        cmd.Dispose();
    if (conn != null)
        conn.Dispose();
}
```

There are two things to note in the above code.

1. First, we can't re-use this connection string:

   ```
   global::TestLINQToSQLApp.Properties.Settings.Default.
   NorthwindConnectionString
   ```

   This is because the password has been stripped out from this string.

2. Secondly, the following `using` statement has to be added at the beginning of the `Program.cs` file:

   ```
   using System.Data.SqlClient;
   ```

The output of the program is still the same as shown in the previous examples.

Adding validations to entity classes

Validating data is the process of confirming that the values entered into data objects comply with the constraints in an object's schema, in addition to the rules established for your application. Validating data before you send updates to the underlying database is a good practice that reduces both errors and the potential number of round trips between an application and the database.

The **Object Relational Designer** (O/R Designer) provides partial methods that enable users to extend the designer-generated code that runs during Inserts, Updates, and Deletes of complete entities, and also during and after individual column changes.

These validation methods are all partial methods. Therefore, there is no overhead at all if you don't implement them, because unimplemented partial methods are not compiled into IL.

You can implement a validation method in another partial class. In our example, we can add the following method to the existing `NorthwindDataContext.cs` file:

```
public partial class Product
{
    partial void OnProductNameChanging(string value)
    {
        if (value.IndexOf("@") >= 0)
            throw new Exception("ProductName can not contain @");
    }
}
```

Note that this method should be placed inside the partial class `Product`, and not inside `NorthwindDataContext`.

Now, we can test it using the following code:

```
Product product = (from p in db.Products
                   where p.ProductID == 5
                   select p).First();
try
{
    product.ProductName = "Name @ this place";
    db.SubmitChanges();
}
catch (Exception e)
{
    Console.WriteLine("Update failed. Reason: {0}", e.Message);
}
```

Run this program, and you will get an output as shown in the following image:

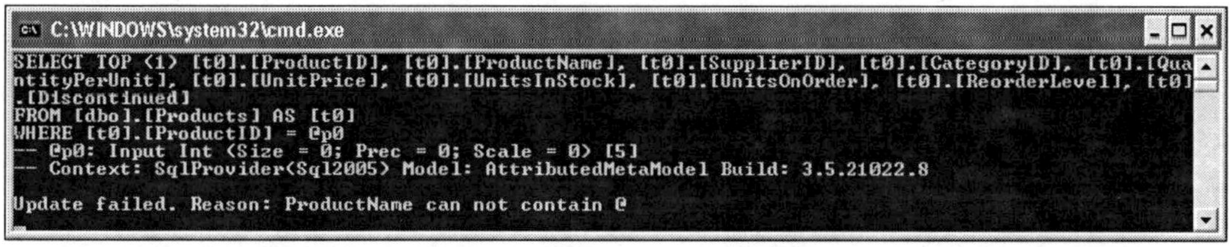

```
C:\WINDOWS\system32\cmd.exe
SELECT TOP (1) [t0].[ProductID], [t0].[ProductName], [t0].[SupplierID], [t0].[CategoryID], [t0].[Qua
ntityPerUnit], [t0].[UnitPrice], [t0].[UnitsInStock], [t0].[UnitsOnOrder], [t0].[ReorderLevel], [t0]
.[Discontinued]
FROM [dbo].[Products] AS [t0]
WHERE [t0].[ProductID] = @p0
-- @p0: Input Int (Size = 0; Prec = 0; Scale = 0) [5]
-- Context: SqlProvider(Sql2005) Model: AttributedMetaModel Build: 3.5.21022.8

Update failed. Reason: ProductName can not contain @
```

You can implement any of the validation methods for any properties, before or after the change.

Debugging LINQ to SQL programs

Within Visual Studio 2008, when debugging a LINQ to SQL program, we can use the traditional either of the **Watch** or **QuickWatch** windows to inspect a variable. For example, after the following line is executed, we can right-click on the **products** variable, and select **QuickWatch ...** or **Add Watch** to see the contents of this variable:

```
var products = from p in db.Products
               where p.CategoryID == 1
               select p;
```

The **QuickWatch** window will look like this:

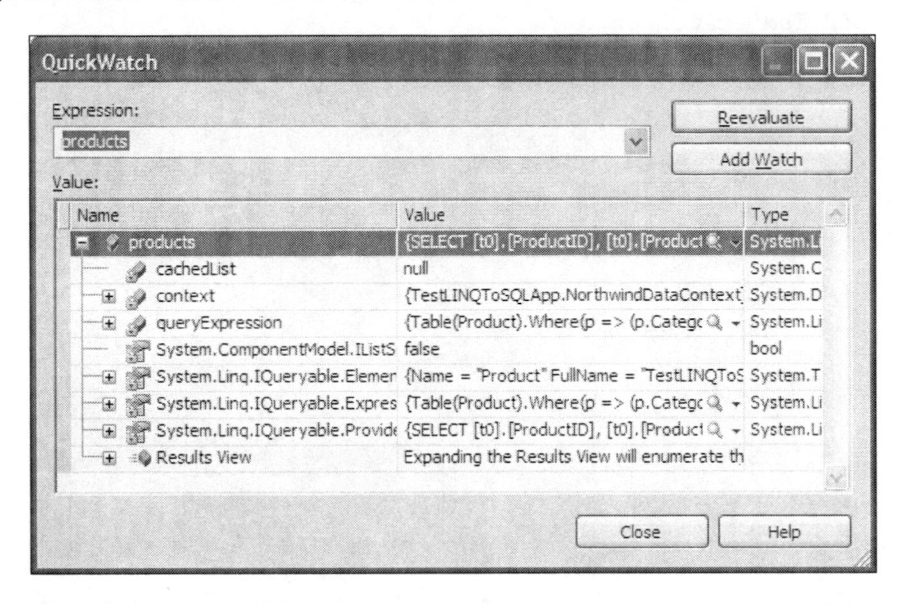

We can also hover our mouse over the **products** variable, and wait for the Quick Info pop-up window to appear, and then inspect it on the fly. The pop-up Quick Info window will appear as shown in the following image:

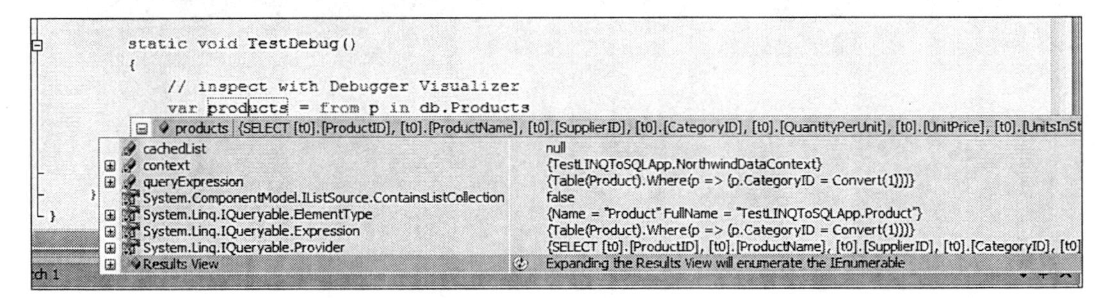

In the **Watch** window, we can inspect the returned result of the variable, its properties, and even its children.

This inspection may trigger a real query to the database. For example, if you let your mouse hover over `db.Products`, and then try to open **Results View**, the database will be queried to get all of the products. In an environment with a big database, this may cause some problems.

Summary

In this chapter, we have learned some advanced features of LINQ to SQL. At this point, we have a good understanding of LINQ to SQL. In the next chapter, we will apply these skills to the data access layer of our WCF service, to connect to databases securely and reliably with LINQ to SQL.

The key points covered in this chapter include:

- LINQ to SQL fully supports stored procedures with return codes, output parameters, and multiple result sets
- Compiled queries can increase the performance of repeatedly-executed LINQ queries
- LINQ to SQL allows SQL queries to the database
- Dynamic Queries can be built at runtime, using Expressions
- LINQ to SQL supports single-table inheritance via the discriminator column
- Concurrent updates can be controlled using an Update Check property or a Version column
- By default, LINQ to SQL updates are within one implicit transaction
- Explicit transactions can be defined for LINQ to SQL updates by using `TransactionScope`
- LINQ to SQL updates can also participate in traditional ADO.NET transactions
- Customized validation code can be added to LINQ to SQL entity classes
- A debugging process may trigger a real query to the database

12
Applying LINQ to SQL to a WCF Service

Now that we have learned all of the new features for C# 3.0, including LINQ and LINQ to SQL, we will use them in the data access layer of a WCF service. We will create a new WCF service, which is very similar to the one we created in the previous chapters, but in this service, we will use LINQ to SQL to connect to the `Northwind` database, to retrieve and update a product.

In the data access layer, we will use LINQ to SQL to retrieve product information from the database, and return it to the business logic layer. You will see that with LINQ to SQL, we will need only one LINQ statement in the `GetProduct` method, and we will no longer need to worry about the database connection, or the actual query statement.

In this chapter, we will also learn how to update a product with LINQ to SQL in the data access layer. We will see how to attach an entity object to LINQ to SQL `DataContext`, and leave all of the update work to LINQ to SQL, and will also see how to control the concurrency of updates with LINQ to SQL.

In this chapter, we will cover:

- Creating the solution using Service Factory
- Modeling the WCF service using Service Factory
- Generating source code for the service
- Modeling the `Northwind` database in LINQ to SQL designer
- Implementing the data access layer using LINQ to SQL
- Implementing the business logic layer
- Implementing the service interface layer

- Modeling the host application and the test client
- Implementing the test client
- Testing the get and update operations of the WCF service
- Testing concurrent updates with LINQ to SQL

Creating the LINQNorthwind solution

From this point on on, in the first few sections of this chapter, we will use Service Factory for creating the solution files, modeling the service, and generating the source code. The steps here are very similar to those discussed in Chapter 7, so we will not have screenshots for every step. You can follow the steps here to quickly create the solution, and refer back to Chapter 7 for detailed instructions if you have any doubts. You can also download the source code for this chapter, if you don't want to repeat all of these steps.

One thing that is different here is that we will add an operation of `UpdateProduct` in this chapter, so that we can test the concurrent updates with LINQ to SQL later on.

To start, follow these steps to create the initial solution files:

1. Start Visual Studio 2008.
2. Select menu option **File | New | Project.....**
3. Select **Guidance Packages | Service Factory: Modeling Edition** as the **Project type**, and **Model Project** as the **Template**.
4. Enter **LINQNorthwind** as the **Name**, and leave the **Location** as the default value (**D:\SOAwithWCFandLINQ\Projects**).
5. Click **OK**.

The **Guidance Packages** project type will be shown only after you have the Guidance Packages installed. You should have installed Guidance Packages in Chapter 7.

6. Change the model project name from **LINQNorthwind** to **LINQNorthwind Models**.

Modeling the data contracts

Next, we will add a data contract model, a `Product` data contract, and a `Product Fault` contract to the model.

1. Add a **Data Contract Model** with the name **ProductService**.
2. Add a **Data Contract** to the model with the name **Product**. This data contract should have the following data members with these data types: `ProductID (Int32)`, `ProductName (String)`, `QuantityPerUnit (String)`, `UnitPrice (Decimal)`, and `Discontinued (Boolean)`.
3. Add a **Fault Contract** to the model with the name **ProductFault**. This fault contract should have one data member: **FaultMessage (String)**.

In this model, we didn't specify the unit price as type `Decimal?`, even though it should really be `Decimal?`. This is because Service Factory doesn't support nullable data types.

Also, we didn't add `LastUpdateVersion` as a data member, even though we need to pass this member to the client to that when the product is passed back, we can check if this product has been updated by other applications. The reason why we didn't include this data member in the model is that Service Factory doesn't support `Binary` data types.

We will adjust these two data members in the data contract in a later section, after we have generated the source code.

The detailed steps, and the final data contract model should be the same as described in Chapter 7. To refresh your memory, your data contract model should look like this:

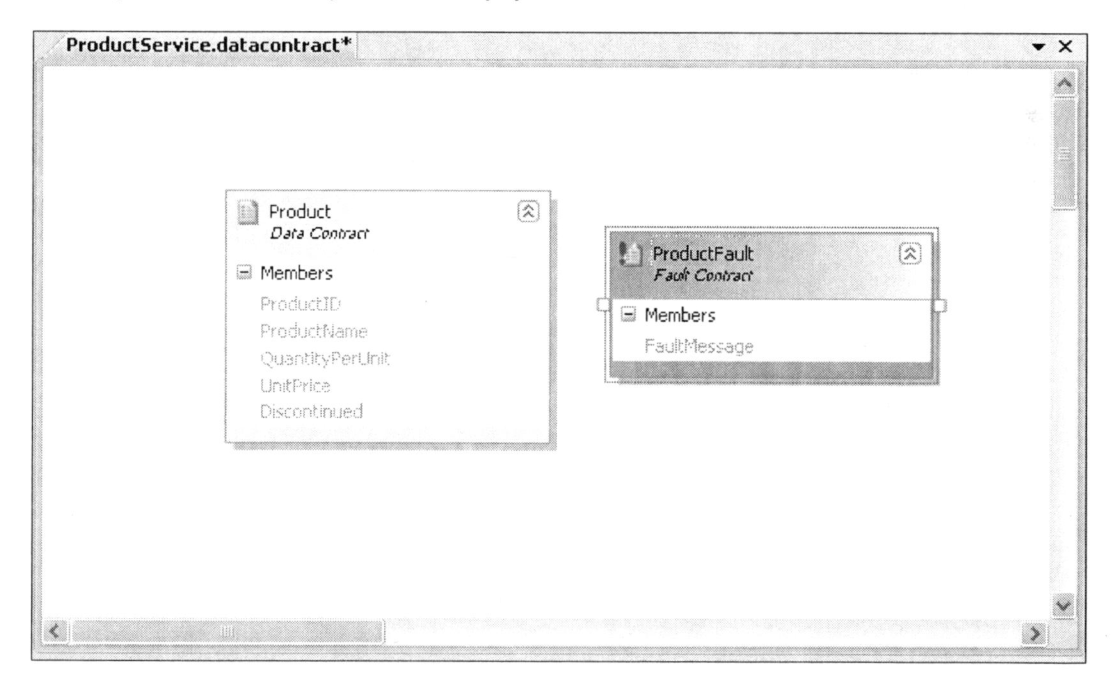

Modeling the service contracts

Now, we will add a service contract model, and add operations to the service model.

1. Add a **Service Contract Model** with the name **ProductService**.
2. Add an **Operation** with the name **GetProduct** to the model.
3. Add two **Message Contracts** with the names **GetProductRequest,** and **GetProductResponse** respectively.
4. Add an **Operation** with name **UpdateProduct**. This operation should have a fault with the name **UpdateProductFault** and of type **ProductFault**.
4. Add two **Message Contracts** with the names **UpdateProductRequest,** and **UpdateProductResponse** respectively. The request message contract should have a data part **Product** that is of type **Product**, and the response contract should have a data part **UpdateResult** that is of type **Boolean**.
5. Add a **Service Contract** with the name **ProductServiceContract**.
6. Add a **Service** with the name **ProductService**.
7. Connect the service, the service contract, the service operations, and the message contracts together.

The service contract model is very similar to the one described in Chapter 7, except that there is one more operation (**UpdateProduct**), and two more message contracts (**UpdateProductRequest** and **UpdateProductResponse**). It should look like this :

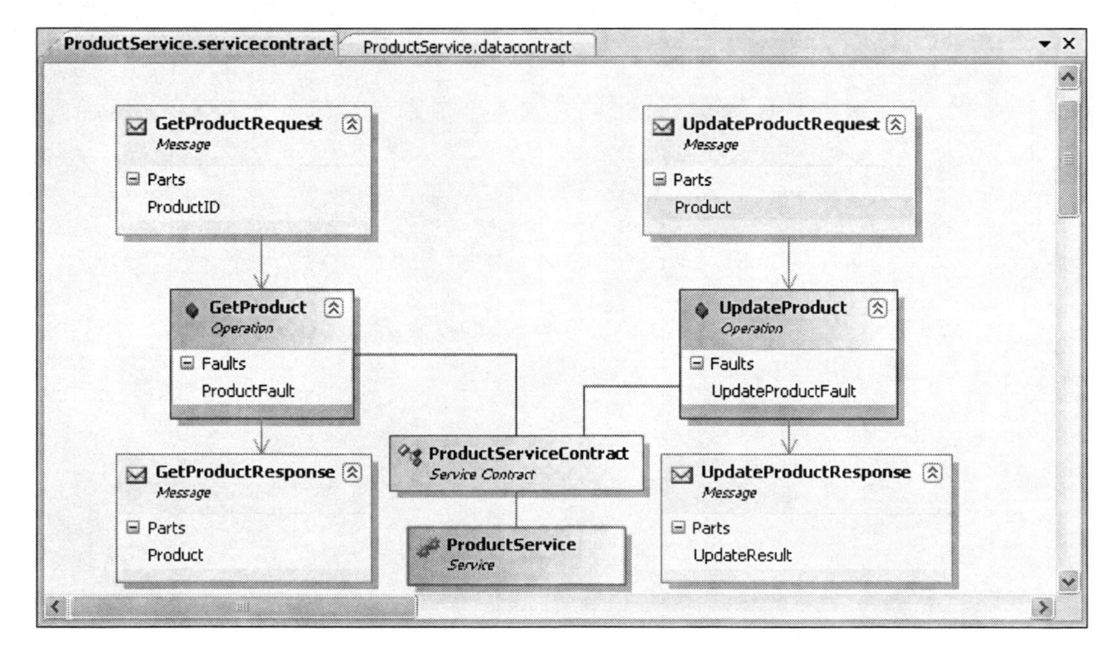

Next, we need to change some values for these contracts. Follow these steps:

1. Specify **Implementation Technologies** for both the data contract and service contract models, just as we did in Chapter 7. As a result, both models should have **WCF Extension** as the implementation technology.
2. Change the property value of **Reply Action** to be the same as the property value of **Action** for both **GetProduct** and **UpdateProduct** operations.
3. Change the property value of **Is Wrapped to be True for both** for **GetProductRequest** and **UpdateProductRequest** messages.
4. Change the service contract model's **Serializer Type** from **XmlSerializer** to **DataContractSerializer**.
5. Order all of the data members for the data contract model.

Again, you can refer to Chapter 7 for detailed instructions and screenshots.

Generating the source code

At this point, we have finished modeling the WCF service. So, we can now generate the source code. Follow these steps to generate the source code for the new WCF service:

1. Add **WCF Implementation Projects** to the solution, with **MyWCF.LINQNorthwind** as the **Project name**. Service Factory should generate ten projects for you, including service interface layer projects, business logic layer projects, and data access layer projects.
2. Link both the service contract and data contract models, to the projects by setting the value of the model's property **Project Mapping Table** to be **MyWCF.LINQNorthwind**.
3. Validate the data contract and the service contract models.
4. Generate source code for all of the projects from the data contract and service contract models.

At this point, you should have the source code generated for the service interface layer projects. The detailed steps are same as described in Chapter 7, so you can refer back to that chapter for more information and screenshots if necessary.

Next, we will implement the data access layer of the service with LINQ to SQL, and then implement the business logic layer of the service. Many steps in the following sections are similar to those described in Chapter 8, with a few differences that we will discuss in detail.

Modeling the Northwind database

For the data access layer, we will use LINQ to SQL instead of the raw ADO.NET data adapters. As you will see in the next section, we will use one LINQ statement to retrieve product information from the database, and the update LINQ statements will handle the concurrency control for us easily and reliably.

As you may recall, to use LINQ to SQL in the data access layer of our WCF service, we first need to add a LINQ to SQL model class to the project. The following steps are very similar to those described in Chapter 10. So, you can refer back to that chapter for more information and screenshots if necessary.

1. In the Solution Explorer, right-click on the project item **MyWCF.LINQNorthwind.DataAccess**, select menu option **Add | New Item...**, and then choose **LINQ to SQL Classes** as the Template, and enter **Northwind.dbml** as the **Class name**.
2. After **Northwind.dbml** has been added to the project, add a connection to the `Northwind` database in the Server Explorer, if a connection to the database is not there.
3. Then, in the Server Explorer, drag the **Products** table onto the **Northwind.dbml** design pane. Rename the entity class from **Product** to **ProductEntity**.
4. The new column **LastUpdateVersion** should be in the **Products** table, as we added it in the previous chapter. If it is not there, add it to the table with a type of **Timestamp**, and recreate the entity class.

Just as in the previous chapters, this will generate a class file called `Northwind.designer.cs`, which contains the data context for the `Northwind` database.

This same file also contains the `ProductEntity` class, which will be shared by all three layers of the WCF service. By design, LINQ to SQL includes all of the entity classes inside this same file. So if you have many entity classes, this file could be very big.

There is a standalone project, **MyWCF.LINQNorthwind.BusinessEntities**, in the solution. As you may recall, this is the project where we define all of the data entities for the WCF service. However, because the entity classes are all contained inside the LINQ to SQL designer class now, this project will contain no more entity classes in the solution. We will leave this project in the solution, but won't use it at all. However, if you think this is confusing, you can delete this project (and all the references to this project) from the solution.

Implementing the data access layer

Now that we have the `Northwind.dbml` added to the project file, we will need to add a new class file to the data access project. We will implement the data access layer inside this new class.

1. Open the **web.config** file in the **MyWCF.LINQNorthwind.Host** project folder. Change the **<connectionStrings/>** element to this:

   ```
   <connectionStrings configSource="connections.config"/>
   ```

2. Add a new XML file **connections.config** to the project **MyWCF. LINQNorthwind.Host**, with the following content:

   ```
   <?xml version="1.0" encoding="utf-8" ?>
   <connectionStrings>
     <add name="NorthwindConnectionString"
          providerName="System.Data.SqlProvider"
          connectionString="server=your_db_server\your_db_instance;
          uid=your_user_name; pwd=your_password;
          database=Northwind;"/>
   </connectionStrings>
   ```

   As you have learned in the previous chapters, you should change this connection string according to your specific database environment, and you can also change it to use a Windows trusted connection, or an SSPI integrated security connection.

3. Add a new class called `ProductDAL` to the data access project.
4. Change the `ProductDAL` class to make it a `public` class.
5. Define `connectionString` variable as a class member like this:

   ```
   string connectionString = ConfigurationManager.ConnectionStrings["
   NorthwindConnectionString"].ConnectionString;
   ```

6. Add a `using` statement to the assembly `System.Configuration`.

You may recall that in Chapter 8, we added a reference to the `BusinessEntities` project, because the data access project will use entities defined in the `BusinessEntities` project. However, in this solution, because all entities will be inside the data access layer within the LINQ to SQL designer class, we no longer need to reference the `BusinessEntities` project from the data access project. So we don't need to add a reference to the `BusinessEntities` project here.

Adding GetProduct to the data access layer

We can now add the `GetProduct` method to the data access layer class `ProductDAL`, like this:

```
public ProductEntity GetProduct(int id)
{
  NorthwindDataContext db = new NorthwindDataContext(connectionString
);
  ProductEntity productEntity = (from p in db.ProductEntities
                 where p.ProductID == id
                 select p).FirstOrDefault();
    return productEntity;
}
```

You will recall that in the previous chapters, for the `GetProduct` method, we had to create an ADO.NET connection, create an ADO.NET command object with that connection, specify the command text, connect to the `Northwind` database, and send the SQL statement to the database for execution. After the result was returned from the database, we had to loop through the `DataReader`, and cast the columns to our entity object one by one.

Here, with LINQ to SQL, as you can see, we only construct one LINQ to SQL statement, and everything else is handled by LINQ to SQL. Not only do we need to write less code, but now the statement is also strongly typed. We won't have a runtime error like "invalid query syntax", or "invalid column name". Also, an SQL Injection attack is no longer an issue, as LINQ to SQL will also take care of this when translating LINQ expressions to underlying SQL statements.

Adding UpdateProduct to the data access layer

In the previous section, we have added the `GetProduct` method to the data access layer. Now, let's add the `UpdateProduct` method to the data acces layer, as follows:

```
public bool UpdateProduct(ProductEntity productEntity)
{
    // check product ID
    NorthwindDataContext db = new
                         NorthwindDataContext(connectionString);
    ProductEntity productEntityInDB = (from p in
                         db.ProductEntities
                                   where p.ProductID ==
                         productEntity.ProductID
```

```
                                        select p).FirstOrDefault();
        db.Dispose();
        // check product
        if (productEntityInDB == null)
        {
            throw new Exception("No product with ID " +
                                productEntity.ProductID);
        }
        // preserve these properties (they should not be updated by
    client)
        productEntity.SupplierID = productEntityInDB.SupplierID;
        productEntity.CategoryID = productEntityInDB.CategoryID;
        productEntity.UnitsInStock = productEntityInDB.UnitsInStock;
        productEntity.UnitsOnOrder = productEntityInDB.UnitsOnOrder;
        productEntity.ReorderLevel = productEntityInDB.ReorderLevel;
        // use another DataCOntext to update the product
        NorthwindDataContext db2 = new
                                NorthwindDataContext(connectionString);
        db2.ProductEntities.Attach(productEntity, true);
        db2.SubmitChanges();
        db2.Dispose();
        return true;
    }
```

Inside this method, we first check to see if the product to be updated is a valid product in our database. If not, processing will stop, and an exception will be thrown.

Then, we assign the database values of columns `SupplierID`, `CategoryID`, `UnitsInStock`, `UnitsOnOrder`, and `ReorderLevel` to associated properties of the product entity that is passed in from the service interface layer. Remember that the data contract doesn't have these properties. So the client won't see them at all. Thus, when the product is passed back to the service, and converted to a product entity, all of these properties will be empty. We need to make sure that we don't change any of them.

However, the `LastUpdateVersion` property will be of the same value as when the client fetches the product, and this value shouldn't be changed by the client. This is very important, because this property is used to control the optimistic update.

Now that the `productEntity` object holds all of the values that we want to commit to the database, we need to create another `DataContext` object, and attach this object to the `DataContext`.

Note that we can't attach it to the original `DataContext`, because one `DataContext` can't have two objects with the same primary key, and there is no way to detach an object from a `DataContext`.

We use the following syntax to attach this object to the `DataContext`:

```
db2.ProductEntities.Attach(productEntity, true);
```

The parameter `true` means that the attached product is the current object to be updated, and `DataContext` should treat all of its properties as having changed.

As you can see, the logic to update a product is the same as in the previous chapters, but this time we implemented it using LINQ to SQL. Just like in the previous `GetProduct` method, here you won't see any activities like managing database connection, or checking update conflicts. All of these issues have been taken care of by the LINQ to SQL engine. We just need to concentrate on the real application logic.

In the previous chapters, if you ever tried to start up two client applications, and update the same product at the same time from each client application, you will have seen that those WCF services don't handle this very well. You will find that some updates have overwritten other updates, making the result unpredictable. To overcome this, you will have to add a lot more code to the `UpdateProduct` method, with ADO.NET.

Now with this piece of code, concurrent update is handled very well by LINQ to SQL. Just as we had learned from the previous LINQ to SQL chapters, the `LastUpdateVersion` column has been used by LINQ to SQL to provide concurrent update control for this service. We don't need to do any more work to gain this. Later in this chapter, we will explain and test how this small piece of code has had concurrent update control embedded, with optimistic locking mechanisms being implemented without any extra effort from us.

Implementing the business logic layer

Now that we have the data access layer ready, we can modify the business logic layer to call this layer.

1. Add a new class file called `ProductLogic.cs`.
2. Change the `ProductLogic` class to be a `public` class.
3. Define the `productDAL` variable as a class member, like this:
   ```
   ProductDAL productDAL = new ProductDAL();
   ```

4. Add the `GetProduct` method as follows:

```
public ProductEntity GetProduct(int id)
{
    return productDAL.GetProduct(id);
}
Add UpdateProduct method like this:
public bool UpdateProduct(ProductEntity productEntity)
{
    return productDAL.UpdateProduct(productEntity);
}
```

This class is very similar to the business logic class in the previous chapters, except that in the previous chapters this project references the `BusinessEntities` project, whereas here it only references the data access project. As we said earlier, this is because the product entity is now embedded inside the data access project LINQ to SQL designer class file, instead of being in a separate `BusinessEntities` project.

Implementing the service interface layer

In the service interface layer, we need to modify a few classes, including the product fault class, the data contract class, and the service implementation classes.

Modifying the ProductFault class

We need to add a new file called `ProductFault.cs` to the project `FaultContracts`. This will be used to create a constructor with one string parameter.

The partial `ProductFault` class should look like this:

```
using System;
using System.Collections.Generic;
using System.Linq;
using System.Text;

namespace MyWCF.LINQNorthwind.FaultContracts
{
    public partial class ProductFault
    {
        public ProductFault(string message)
        {
            this.faultMessage = message;
        }
    }
}
```

Modifying the DataContract class

For the data contract class, we need to make the following changes:

1. Open the file **Product.cs** under the **GeneratedCode** folder in the project **DataContracts**.
2. Change the type of the private variable **unitPrice** from **decimal** to **decimal?**.
3. Change the type of the public property **UnitPrice** from **decimal** to **decimal?**.
4. Add a reference to **System.Data.Linq**.
5. Add a `using` statement like this:
   ```
   using System.Data.Linq;
   ```
6. Add the following `private` variable:
   ```
   private Binary lastUpdateVersion;
   ```
7. Add the following `public` property:
   ```
   [WcfSerialization::DataMember(Name = "lastUpdateVersion",
   IsRequired = true, Order = 5)]
   public Binary LastUpdateVersion
   {
       get { return lastUpdateVersion; }
       set { lastUpdateVersion = value; }
   }
   ```

The reason we have to change the type for the member **UnitPrice** from **decimal** to **decimal?** is that in the database, the column **UnitPrice** is nullable, but in Service Factory, you can't specify a property of an entity class to be a nullable data type.

Also, Service Factory doesn't support the data type `Binary` (`timestamp`), so we have to manually add the `LastUpdateVersion` property to the product data contract.

Modifying the ServiceImplementation class

We also need to change the `ServiceImplementation` project. We will need to add a reference to the `DataAccess` project, add a translator class, modify the data contract class, and implement the `GetProduct` and `UpdateProduct` operations.

Adding references to the project

We need to add two references to the `ServiceImplementation` project.

- Add a reference to the **DataAccess** project. This is because we have to reference the **ProductEntity** class, which is now embedded inside the data access layer LINQ to SQL designer class.

- Add a reference to the **System.Data.Linq** assembly. This is because in this project, we need to translate the **LastUpdateVersion**, which is of type **System.Data.Linq.Binary**.

Adding a translator class

In this solution, we can't ask the Service Factory to create the translator classes. This is because we now have to translate between the data contracts and the data entities defined within the LINQ to SQL designer class, while Service Factory is restricted to translating between the data contracts and the business entities defined within the `BusinessEntities` project.

Because we can't use Service Factory, we have to manually add a translator class to translate between the `ProductEntity` and the `Product` data contract. We will call this translator class `TranslateBetweenProductEntityAndProduct`, and the source code is very similar to the code in the previous chapters, except that now there is one more property to translate—`LastUpdateVersion`.

> The `ProductEntity` class here is the one inside the `DataAccess` layer assembly, and not the one inside the `BusinessEntities` assembly.

The translator class should be as follows:

```
using System;
using MyWCF.LINQNorthwind.DataContracts;
using MyWCF.LINQNorthwind.DataAccess;

namespace MyWCF.LINQNorthwind.ServiceImplementation
{
    public static class TranslateBetweenProductEntityAndProduct
    {
        public static MyWCF.LINQNorthwind.DataAccess.ProductEntity
            TranslateProductToProductEntity(MyWCF.LINQNorthwind.
            DataContracts.Product from)
        {
            MyWCF.LINQNorthwind.DataAccess.ProductEntity to =
                   new MyWCF.LINQNorthwind.DataAccess.ProductEntity();
            to.ProductID = from.ProductID;
            to.ProductName = from.ProductName;
            to.QuantityPerUnit = from.QuantityPerUnit;
            to.UnitPrice = from.UnitPrice;
            to.Discontinued = from.Discontinued;
            to.LastUpdateVersion = from.LastUpdateVersion;
            return to;
```

```
        }
        public static MyWCF.LINQNorthwind.DataContracts.Product
            TranslateProductEntityToProduct(MyWCF.LINQNorthwind.
            DataAccess.ProductEntity from)
        {
            MyWCF.LINQNorthwind.DataContracts.Product to =
                      new MyWCF.LINQNorthwind.DataContracts.Product();
            to.ProductID = from.ProductID;
            to.ProductName = from.ProductName;
            to.QuantityPerUnit = from.QuantityPerUnit;
            to.UnitPrice = from.UnitPrice;
            to.Discontinued = from.Discontinued;
            to.LastUpdateVersion = from.LastUpdateVersion;
            return to;
        }
    }
}
```

Implementing the GetProduct and UpdateProduct operations

Finally, for the WCF service, we need to implement the operations in the service contract. The Service Factory only generates empty operation methods, and we have to write the code by ourselves.

To implement the two `get` and `update` operations, we need to add a new partial class `ProductService.cs` to the project, and customize this to contain the `GetProduct` and `UpdateProduct` methods. The `GetProduct` method is the same as the one in Chapter 8, and the `UpdateProduct` method should be as follows:

```
public override UpdateProductResponse UpdateProduct(UpdateProductRequ
est request)
{
    ProductEntity productEntity;
    productEntity = TranslateBetweenProductEntityAndProduct.TranslateP
roductToProductEntity(request.Product);
    // call business entity layer to update a product
    bool updateResult = false;
    try
    {
        updateResult = productLogic.UpdateProduct(productEntity);
    }
    catch (Exception e)
    {
```

```
            throw new FaultException<ProductFault>(new ProductFault("could
    not update product. Error message:" + e.Message));
        }
        // create a response message
        UpdateProductResponse response = new UpdateProductResponse();
        response.UpdateResult = updateResult;
        // return the response message
        return response;
    }
```

Inside this method, we first translate the `Product` object from the request message to a `ProductEntity` object, and then call the business logic layer to update this project. If there is anything wrong with this update, we throw a `Fault` back to the client. Otherwise, we return a response message back to the client.

As you can see, the source code in the interface layer is almost identical to the code in previous chapters, except for the different references to the `ProductEntity` class.

Creating the host application and the test client

Now that we have the WCF service ready, we need to create a host application to host it, and a test client to test it. We will use the Service Factory to model the Host, and then customize it in subsequent sections. Once we have finished creating the host and test applications, we will test the WCF service. We will see how LINQ to SQL can help us to enhance the WCF service. Note that many steps here are very similar to those described in Chapter 8, so you can refer to that chapter for more information and screenshots if necessary.

Modeling the host application and the test client

First, we need to model the host application, and generate a test client to test the WCF service. We will use this test client to test the normal `get` and `update` operations of the service, and then test the concurrent update control of the service.

Follow these steps to model the host application and the test client:

1. Add a new **Host Model** to the solution model project, with the name **LINQNorthwind**.
2. Add a **New Host Application** to the **LINQNorthwind Host** model, with the name **LINQNorthwindHost**, select **WCF Extensions** as the **Implementation Technology**, and select **MyWCF.LINQNorthwind.Host** as the **Implementation Project**.
3. Add a **New Service Reference** of **LINQNorthwind ProductService** to the **LINQNorthwind** host application, with the name **ProductServiceRef**, and change this reference's **Enable Metadata Publishing** property to **True**.
4. Add a **New Endpoint** for the Host application, with the name **ProductEndpoint**.
5. Validate the model, and generate the Host application from the model.
6. Change the Host website **MyWCF.LINQNorthwind.Host** to use static port number **8080**.
7. Add a **New Client Application** to the Host model with the name **LINQNorthwindClient**, select **WCF Extensions** as the **Implementation Technology**, and select **MyWCF.LINQNorthwind.Client** as the **Implementation Project**.
8. Add a **New Proxy** to the test client, with the name **LINQNorthwindProxy**, and select **ProductEndpoint** for its **Endpoint** property.
9. Validate the model, and generate the client from the model. Don't forget that you will need to start the host application before you can generate the client application code.

Implementing the GetProduct functionality

Now that we have the Host application, and the test client generated, we will customize the client application to test the new WCF service.

First, we would need to customize the test client to call the WCF service to get a product from the database, so that we can test the `GetProduct` operation with LINQ to SQL.

To simplify the process, we will customize the main form just as we did in Chapter 8. So, the main form should be as shown in the following screenshot:

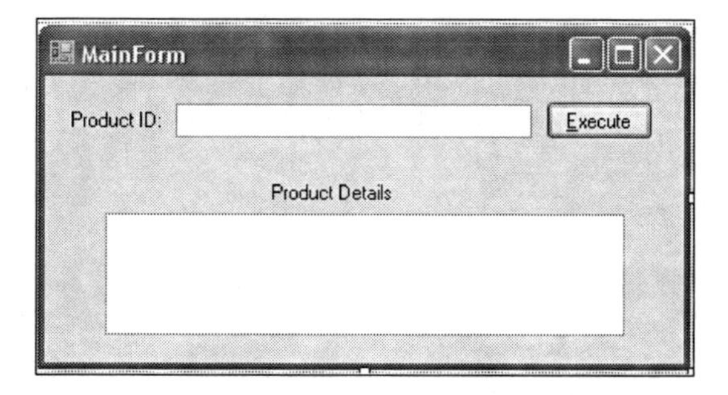

And the event handler of the **Execute** button should be as follows:

```
private void ExecuteButton_Click(object sender, EventArgs e)
{
    ProductServiceContractClient client =
       new ProductServiceContractClient();
    GetProductRequest request = new GetProductRequest();

    string result = "";
    try
    {
        request.ProductID = Int32.Parse(SearchText.Text.ToString());
        Product product = client.GetProduct(request);

        StringBuilder sb = new StringBuilder();
        sb.Append("ProductID:" + product.ProductID.ToString() +
                                                        "\r\n");
        sb.Append("ProductName:" + product.ProductName + "\r\n");
        sb.Append("QuantityPerUnit:" + product.QuantityPerUnit +
                                                        "\r\n");
        sb.Append("UnitPrice:" + product.UnitPrice.ToString() +
                                                        "\r\n");
        sb.Append("Discontinued:" + product.Discontinued.ToString() +
                                                              "\r\n");
        sb.Append("LastUpdateVersion:" + product.lastUpdateVersion.
                                                       ToString());
        result = sb.ToString();
    }
    catch (TimeoutException ex)
    {
        result = "The service operation timed out. " + ex.Message;
    }
    catch (FaultException<ProductFault> ex)
```

```
        {
            result = "ProductFault returned: " + ex.Detail.FaultMessage;
        }
        catch (FaultException ex)
        {
            result = "Unknown Fault: " + ex.ToString();
        }
        catch (CommunicationException ex)
        {
            result = "There was a communication problem. " +
                                  ex.Message + ex.StackTrace;
        }
        catch (Exception ex)
        {
            result = "Other excpetion: " + ex.Message + ex.StackTrace;
        }
        txtResult.Text = result;
    }
```

As you can see, this is almost identical to the code given in Chapter 8, except that the formatting of the property `UnitPrice` is a little different here. This is because LINQ to SQL has defined this property as `System.Nullable<decimal>`, and we have to change the data type of this property in the data contract from `Decimal` to `Decimal?`.

We have also added the `LastUpdateVersion` to the displayed text, so that we know the version of the record in the database.

Before you build this test client, you need to add the following `using` statements to the class:

```
using MyWCF.LINQNorthwind.Client.LINQNorthwindProxy;
using System.ServiceModel;
```

Implementing the UpdateProduct functionality

Next, we need to modify the client program to call the `UpdateProduct` operation of the web service. This method is particularly important to us, because we will use this method to test the concurrent update control of LINQ to SQL. We will also need it to explain the distributed transaction support of WCF in the next chapter. As this functionality was not implemented in Chapter 8, we will explain how to implement it in detail in this section.

First, we need to add some more controls to the form. We will modify the form UI as follows:

1. Open the file **MainForm.cs** in the **MyWCF.LINQNorthwind.Client** project.
2. Add a label with text **Product ID**.
3. Add a textbox named **txtProductID**.
4. Add a button named **updateButton** with text **&Update Price**.
5. Add a label with text **Update Result**.
6. Add a textbox control named **txtUpdateResult**.

The form should now appear as shown in the following screenshot:

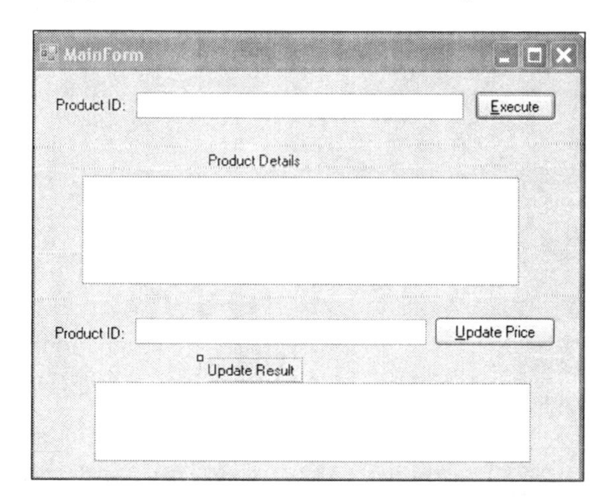

Now, double-click the **Update Price** button, and add the following event handler method:

```
private void updateButton_Click(object sender, EventArgs e)
{
    ProductServiceContractClient client =
       new ProductServiceContractClient();
    GetProductRequest getRequest = new GetProductRequest();
    string result = "";
    try
    {
        // first get the  product from database
        getRequest.ProductID = Int32.Parse(txtProductID.Text.
                                                   ToString());
        Product product = client.GetProduct(getRequest);
        // then update its price by 1
```

```
            product.UnitPrice += 1;

            // submit to database
            UpdateProductRequest updateRequest =
                    new UpdateProductRequest();
            updateRequest.Product = product;
            result = client.UpdateProduct(updateRequest).ToString();
        }
        catch (TimeoutException ex)
        {
            result = "The service operation timed out. " + ex.Message;
        }
        catch (FaultException<ProductFault> ex)
        {
            result = "ProductFault returned: " + ex.Detail.FaultMessage;
        }
        catch (FaultException ex)
        {
            result = "Unknown Fault: " + ex.ToString();
        }
        catch (CommunicationException ex)
        {
            result = "There was a communication problem. " +
                                ex.Message + ex.StackTrace;
        }
        catch (Exception ex)
        {
            result = "Other excpetion: " + ex.Message + ex.StackTrace;
        }

        txtUpdateResult.Text = result;
    }
```

Inside the **Update Price** button even handler listed above, we first get the product from the database, then just update its price by `1`, and submit it back to the database. As you can see, we didn't do anything specific about the concurrent update control of the update, but later we will explain how LINQ to SQL inside the WCF service handles this for us.

As we did in the previous chapters, here too, we will capture all kinds of exceptions and display appropriate messages for them.

Testing the GetProduct and UpdateProduct operations

We can build and run the program to test the `GetProduct` and `UpdateProduct` operations now.

1. On the Client form UI, enter **10** as the product ID in the top **Product ID** text box, and click **Execute** to get the product details. Note that the unit price is now **31.0000**, as shown in following screenshot:

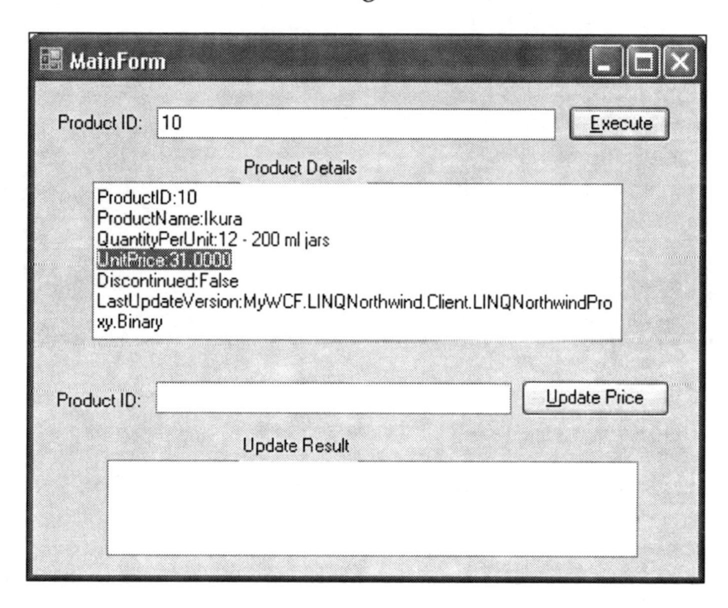

2. Now enter **10** as the product ID in the bottom **Product ID** text box, and click the **Update Price** button to update its price. The **Update Result** should be **True**.

3. Finally, click the **Execute** button again to get the product details for this product, and you will see that the unit price has been updated to **32.0000**.

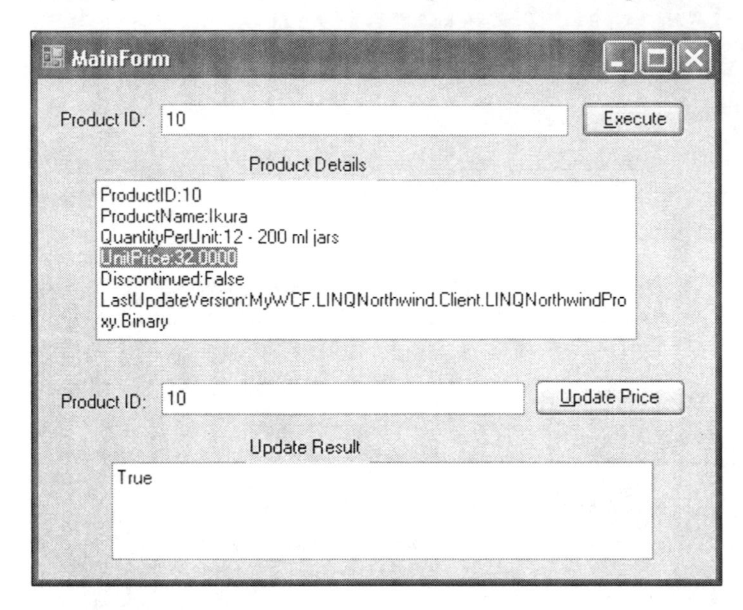

Testing concurrent update manually

We can also test concurrent updates by using the client application.

In this section, we will start two clients and update the same product from these two clients at same time. We will start one of the clients in debugging mode, so we can control the execution time of the update. We will create a conflict between the updates from these two clients so we can test if this conflict is properly handled by LINQ to SQL.

The test sequence will be like this:

1. First client starts.
2. Second client starts.
3. First client reads the product information.
4. Second client reads the same product information.
5. Second client updates the product successfully.
6. First client tries to update the product, and fails.

The last step is where the conflict occurs, as the product has been updated in between the read and the update by the first client.

Thee steps are described in detail below:

1. Start the host application in non-debugging mode.
2. Set a breakpoint on the following line in the `MainForm.cs` file, within the `updateButton_Click` method (line 77):

   ```
   product.UnitPrice += 1;
   ```

3. Start the client application in debugging mode by pressing *F5*. We will refer to this client as the first client.
4. In this first client application, enter **10** in the top **Product ID** text box, and click the **Execute** button to get the product's details. Note that the unit price is **32.0000**.
5. Now, still in this client application, enter **10** in the bottom **Product ID** text box, and click the **Update Price** button. The program should stop at the breakpoint we set earlier, and should be waiting for us to press *F5* to continue.
6. From the Windows Explorer, go to the **LINQNorthwindClient** directory:

   ```
   D:\SOAwithWCFandLINQ\Projects\LINQNorthwind\MyWCF.
   LINQNorthwind\Tests\MyWCF.LINQNorthwind.Client\bin\Debug\
   ```

7. Double-click on the following client executable file to start another client. We will refer to this client as the second client:

   ```
   MyWCF.LINQNorthwind.Client.exe
   ```

8. In the second client application, enter **10** in the bottom **Product ID** text box, and click the **Update Price** button.
9. The second client update is committed to the database, and the **Update Result** value should be **True**. The price of this product has now been increased by 1 in the database, and the **LastUpdateVersion** should also have been updated to a new value.
10. In the second client, enter **10** in the top **Product ID** text box, and click the **Execute** button to get product details. Note that the unit price is now **33.0000**.
11. Go to Visual Studio 2008, and press *F5* to let the first client application continue. This client will first update the product, and then try to commit the update back to the database.
12. The first client update fails with an error message **could not update product. Error message: Row not found or changed**.
13. In the second client, click **Execute** again to get the product's details. You will see that the unit price is still **33.0000**, which means that the first client's update didn't get committed to the database.

The following image is for the second client. You can see the **Update Result** is **True**, and the price after the update is **33.0000**.

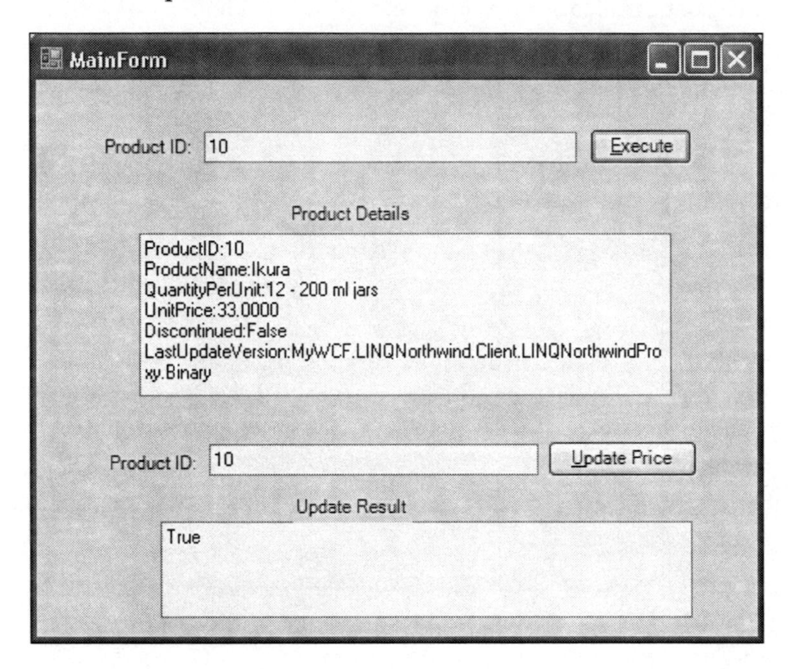

The following image is for the first client. You can see that the price before the update is **32.0000**, and the update fails with an error message.

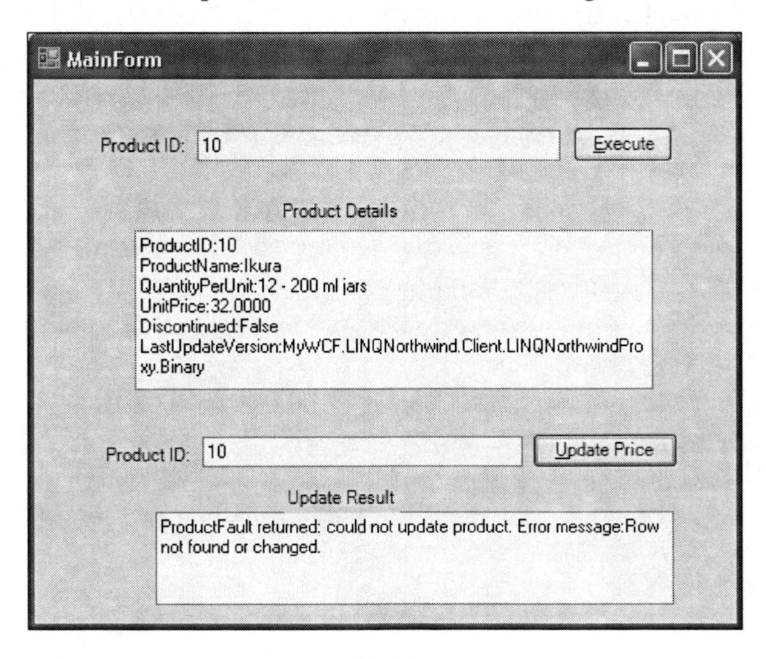

From the test above, we know that the concurrent update is controlled by LINQ to SQL. An optimistic locking mechanism is enforced, and one client's update won't overwrite another client's update. The client that has a conflict will be notified by a fault message.

Concurrent update locking is applied at the record level in the database. If two clients try to update different records in the database, they will not interfere with each other. For example, if you repeat the above steps to update product 10 in one client and 11 in another client, there will be no problem at all.

Testing concurrent update automatically

In the previous section, we tested the concurrent update control of LINQ to SQL, but as you can see, it is very complex, time consuming, and requires many steps. In this section, we will use another way to test it. We will add new functionality to update one product 100 times, and let two clients compete with each other, until one of the updates fails.

This time, we will add another button called `AutoButton`, with the text `Auto Update`, and then add the following `OnClick` event handler for this new button:

```
private void AutoButton_Click(object sender, EventArgs e)
{
    ProductServiceContractClient client =
       new ProductServiceContractClient();
    GetProductRequest getRequest = new GetProductRequest();
    bool bException = true;
    string result = "";
    try
    {
        getRequest.ProductID = Int32.Parse(txtProductID.Text.
                                              ToString());
        for (int i = 0; i < 100; i++)
        {
            // first get the  product from database
            Product product = client.GetProduct(getRequest);
            // then update its price by 1
            product.UnitPrice += 1;
            // submit to database
            UpdateProductRequest updateRequest =
                     new UpdateProductRequest();
            updateRequest.Product = product;
            result = client.UpdateProduct(updateRequest).ToString();
```

```
                txtUpdateResult.Text = "Updated price to " +
                   product.UnitPrice.ToString() + ", result is " + result;
                txtUpdateResult.Refresh();
            }
            bException = false;
        }
        catch (TimeoutException ex)
        {
            result = "The service operation timed out. " + ex.Message;
        }
        catch (FaultException<ProductFault> ex)
        {
            result = "ProductFault returned: " + ex.Detail.FaultMessage;
        }
        catch (FaultException ex)
        {
            result = "Unknown Fault: " + ex.ToString();
        }
        catch (CommunicationException ex)
        {
            result = "There was a communication problem. " +
                                  ex.Message + ex.StackTrace;
        }
        catch (Exception ex)
        {
            result = "Other excpetion: " + ex.Message + ex.StackTrace;
        }
        if (bException)
            txtUpdateResult.Text = result;
    }
```

The concept here is that once this button is clicked, it will keep updating the price of the selected product 100 times, with a price increase of `1.00` with each iteration. If two clients are running, and this button is clicked on both the clients, one of the updates will fail as the other client will also updating the same record.

The sequence of the updates will be as follows:

1. The first client reads the product's details, updates the product, and commits the changes back to the database.
2. The second client reads the product's details, updates the same product, and commits the changes back to the database.

3. At some point, these two sets of processes will cross, so the following events will happen:
    - The first client reads the product's details
    - The first client processes the product in memory
    - The second client reads the product's details
    - The first client finishes processing, and commits the changes back to the database
    - The second client finishes processing, and tries to commit the changes back to the database
    - The second client update fails because it finds that the product has been updated while it (the second client) was still processing the product
    - The second client stops
    - The first client keeps updating the product until it has done so 100 times

Now, follow these steps to finish this test:

1. Build the solution.
2. Run the program twice in non-debugging mode by pressing *Ctrl+F5*. Two clients should be up and running.
3. From each client, enter **3** in the top **Product ID** text box, and click **Execute** to get the product details. Both clients should display the price as **10.0000**.
4. Enter **3** in the bottom **Product ID** box in each client, and click the **Auto Update** button on each client. You should do this in quick succession in each of the clients.

You will see that one of the client update fails while another one is keeping the updates to the end of 100 times. Now the test is very easy, although the result is the same.

The following image shows the results in the successful client. As you can see, the initial price of the product was **10.0000**, but after the updates, it has been changed to **111.0000**. From the source code, we know that this client only updates the price 100 times, with an increase of 1.00 each time, so we know that another client has updated this product once.

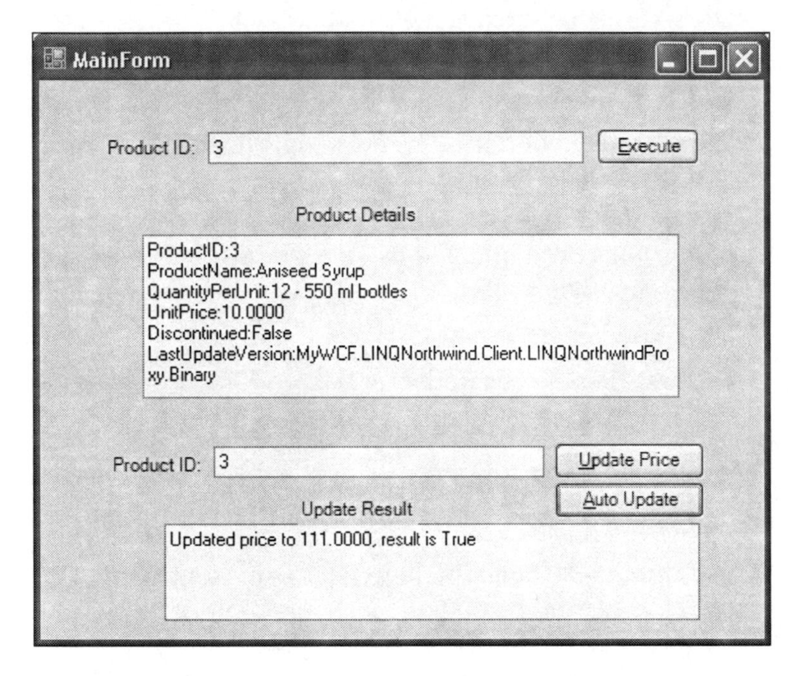

The following image shows the results in the failed client. As you can see, the initial price of the product is **10.000** but when this client tries to update the price, it fails with the error message **Row not found or changed**. From this image, we don't know how many times this client has updated the product successfully before it fails. But from the results in the other client, we know that this client has updated the product only once.

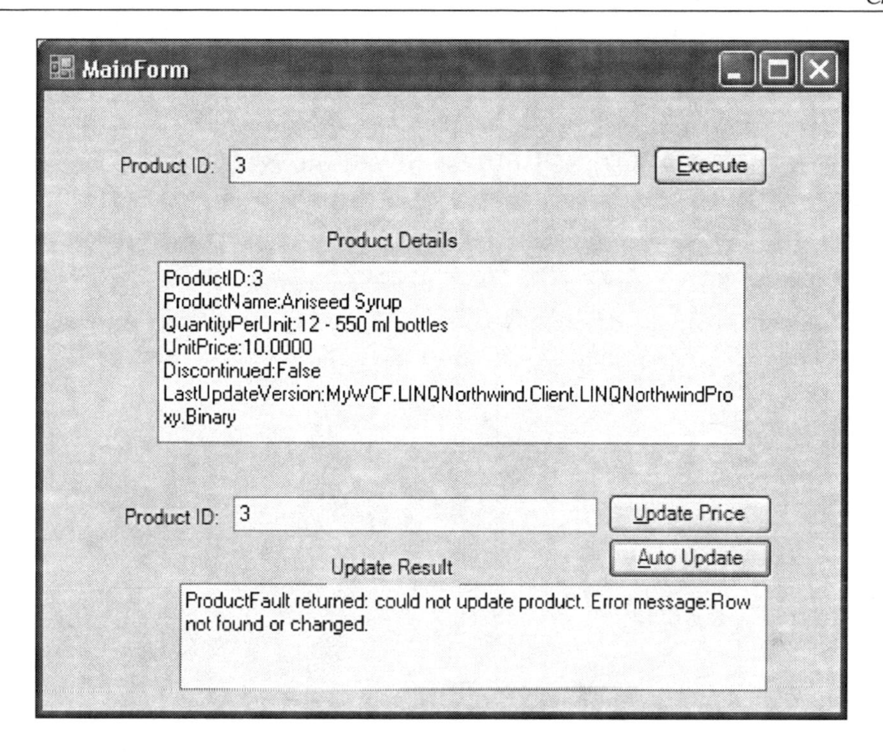

However, if you enter two different product IDs in each client, both client updates will be successful until all 100 updates have been made. This proves that locking is applied on a record level of the database.

Summary

In this chapter, we have used LINQ to SQL to communicate with the database in the data access layer, rather than use the raw ADO.NET APIs. We have used only one LINQ statement to retrieve product information from the database, and as you have seen, the updates with LINQ to SQL prove to be much easier than with the raw ADO.NET data adapters. Now, WCF and LINQ are combined together for our services, so we can take advantage of both technologies.

The key points covered in this chapter include:

- Service Factory can be used to model the service, and generate source code for the service interface layer projects.
- The data access layer should be modeled with LINQ to SQL designer.
- Business entity classes are all located inside the LINQ to SQL designer file, within the data access layer.

- The service interface layer and the business logic layer have to reference the data access layer in order to use the entity classes.
- Client applications still communicate with the service by exchanging messages. The LINQ to SQL objects are not exposed to clients, and the technology used in the data access layer is transparent to the clients.
- When updating the database in the data access layer, the updated entity has to be attached to a fresh LINQ to SQL `DataContext` object.
- Concurrent updates are handled by LINQ to SQL naturally and easily. We just need to add one more column to the database, and LINQ to SQL will do the rest for us.

13 Distributed Transaction Support of WCF

In the chapters so far, we have created a WCF service using LINQ to SQL in the data access layer. Next, we will apply some settings so that this WCF service will be a distributed service, which means that it can participate in distributed client transactions, if there are any. Client applications will control the transaction scope and decide whether a service should commit or rollback its transaction.

In this chapter, we will first verify that the `LINQNorthwind` WCF service that we built in the previous chapter does not support distributed transaction processing. We will then explain how to enhance this WCF service to support distributed transaction processing, and how to configure all related computers to enable distributed transaction support. As a proof, we will propagate a transaction from the client to the WCF service, and verify that all sequential calls to the WCF service are within one single distributed transaction. We will also explain the multiple database support of the WCF service, and discuss how to configure MSDTC and the firewall for the distributed WCF service.

We will cover the following topics in this chapter:

- Creating the solution files
- Testing the transaction behavior of the `LINQNorthwind` WCF service
- Enabling transaction flow in the service bindings
- Modifying the service operation contract to allow transaction flow
- Modifying the service operation implementation to require a transaction scope
- Propagating a transaction from the client to the WCF service
- Testing the multiple database support of the distributed WCF service

- Configuring the Distributed Transaction Coordinator for the distributed WCF service
- Configuring the firewall for the distributed WCF service

Creating the DistNorthwind solution

In this chapter, we will create a new solution based on the `LINQNorthwind` solution. We will copy all of the source code from the `LINQNorthwind` directory to a new directory, and then customize it to suit our needs.

Follow these steps to create the new solution:

1. Create a new directory named `DistNorthwind` under the existing `D:\SOAwithWCFandLINQ\Projects\` directory.
2. Copy all of files under the `D:\SOAwithWCFandLINQ\Projects\LINQNorthwind` directory to the `D:\SOAwithWCFandLINQ\Projects\DistNorthwind` directory.
3. Start Visual Studio 2008.
4. Open the solution **LINQNorthwind** under the **DistNorthwind** directory.
5. In the **Solution Explorer**, rename the solution to **DistNorthwind**. We will leave all of other files as LINQ-something, but renaming the solution is necessary, otherwise we may get confused as to which solution we are working on.
6. Rebuild the **DistNorthwind** solution.

Testing the transaction behaviour of the WCF service

Before explaining how to enhance this WCF service to support distributed transactions, we will first confirm that the existing WCF service doesn't support distributed transactions. In this section, we will test the following scenarios:

1. Create a client to call the service twice in one method.
2. The first service call should succeed and the second service call should fail.
3. Verify that the update in the first service call has been committed to the database, which means that the WCF service does not support distributed transactions.
4. Wrap the two service calls in one `TransactionScope` and redo the test.

5. Verify that the update in the first service call has still been committed to the database, which means the WCF service does not support distributed transactions even if both service calls are within one transaction scope.
6. Add a second database support to the WCF service.
7. Modify the client to update both databases in one method.
8. The first update should succeed and the second update should fail.
9. Verify that the first update has been committed to the database, which means the WCF service does not support distributed transactions with multiple databases.

Creating a client to call the WCF service sequentially

The first scenario to test is that, within one method of the client application, two service calls will be made and one of them will fail. We then verify whether the update in the successful service call has been committed to the database. If it has been, it will mean that the two service calls are not within a single atomic transaction, and will indicate that the WCF service doesn't support distributed transactions.

You can follow these steps to create a client for this test case:

1. In the **Solution Explorer**, right-click on the **Tests** folder under the solution **MyWCF.LINQNorthwind**, and select **Add | New Project ...** from the context menu.
2. Select **Visual C# | Console Application** as the template.
3. Enter **DistributedClient** as the **Name**.
4. Click the **OK** button to create the new client project.

Now, the new test client should have been created and added to the solution. Let's follow these steps to customize this client, so that we can call `ProductService` twice within one method, and test the distributed transaction support of this WCF service:

1. Add a reference `System.ServiceModel` to this `DistributedClient` project.
2. Add a service reference of the product service to this `DistributedClient` project. The namespace of this service reference should be `ProductServiceProxy`, and the URL of the product service should be like this:

   ```
   http://localhost:8080/MyWCF.LINQNorthwind.Host/
   ProductServiceRef.svc
   ```

3. Add the following `using` statements to the `Program.cs` file:

```
using DistributedClient.ProductServiceProxy;
using System.ServiceModel;
```

4. Customize the `Program.cs` file like this:

```
using System;
using System.Collections.Generic;
using System.Linq;
using System.Text;
using DistributedClient.ProductServiceProxy;
using System.ServiceModel;

namespace DistributedClient
{
    class Program
    {
        static void Main(string[] args)
        {
            MultiCallTest();
        }
        static void MultiCallTest()
        {
            ProductServiceContractClient client = new
                        ProductServiceContractClient();
            GetProductRequest getRequest = new GetProductRequest();
            UpdateProductRequest updateRequest =
                    new UpdateProductRequest();

            string exception = "";
            StringBuilder sb = new StringBuilder();
            sb.Append("Prices before update:");
            Product product;
            try
            {
                // update product 30
                // first get the  product from database
                getRequest.ProductID = 30;
                product = client.GetProduct(getRequest);
                sb.Append(product.UnitPrice.ToString() + "    ");

                // then update its price by 1
                product.UnitPrice += 1;

                // submit to database
```

```
        updateRequest.Product = product;
        bool result1 = client.UpdateProduct(updateRequest);

        // update product 31
        // first get the  product from database
        getRequest.ProductID = 31;
        product = client.GetProduct(getRequest);
        sb.Append(product.UnitPrice.ToString() + "\r\n");

        // then update its price
        product.UnitPrice = -10;

        // submit to database -- this update will fail
        updateRequest.Product = product;
        bool result2 = client.UpdateProduct(updateRequest);
    }
    catch (TimeoutException ex)
    {
        exception = "The service operation timed out. "
                                            + ex.Message;
    }
    catch (FaultException<ProductFault> ex)
    {
        exception = "ProductFault returned: " +
                        ex.Detail.FaultMessage;
    }
    catch (FaultException ex)
    {
        exception = "Unknown Fault: " + ex.ToString();
    }
    catch (CommunicationException ex)
    {
        exception = "There was a communication problem. " +
                               ex.Message + ex.StackTrace;
    }
    catch (Exception ex)
    {
        exception = "Other excpetion: " + ex.Message +
                                      ex.StackTrace;
    }

    sb.Append("Prices after update:");
    getRequest.ProductID = 30;
    product = client.GetProduct(getRequest);
    sb.Append(product.UnitPrice.ToString() + "    ");
```

```
                getRequest.ProductID = 31;
                product = client.GetProduct(getRequest);
                sb.Append(product.UnitPrice.ToString() + "\r\n");

                Console.WriteLine(sb.ToString() + exception);
            }
        }
    }
```

In the above test function, we first create a client object to the service, then update the product `30`'s price by 1. We then try to update product `31`'s price to an invalid value. At the end of the method, we display the prices of both products, both before and after the update, so that they can be compared.

We know that the second update will fail due to a database constraint, but what about the first update? Will it be committed to database, or will it be rolled back due to the failure of the second update?

Testing the sequential calls to the WCF service

Let's run the program now, to find out. Set the solution to start with the `Host` and the `DistributedClient`, and then press *F5* or *Ctrl+F5* to run this program. We will get an error message saying "**could not update product**", as shown in the following image:

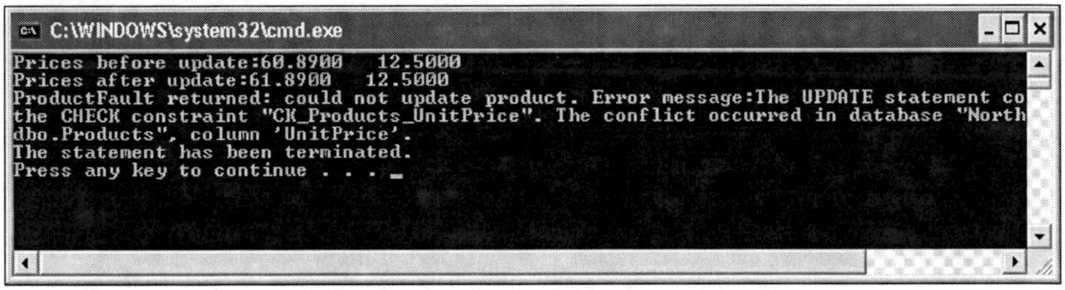

```
C:\WINDOWS\system32\cmd.exe
Prices before update:60.8900   12.5000
Prices after update:61.8900   12.5000
ProductFault returned: could not update product. Error message:The UPDATE statement co
the CHECK constraint "CK_Products_UnitPrice". The conflict occurred in database "North
dbo.Products", column 'UnitPrice'.
The statement has been terminated.
Press any key to continue . . .
```

We know that the exception is due to the second service call, so the second update should not be committed to the database. From the test result, we know this is true (the second product price didn't change). However, from the test result, we also know that the first update in the first service call has been committed to the database (the first product price has been changed). This means that the first call to the service is not rolled back even when a subsequent service call has failed. Therefore, each service call is in a separate standalone transaction. In other words, the two sequential service calls are not within one atomic transaction.

Wrapping the WCF service calls in one transaction scope

But this test is not a complete distributed transaction test. On the client side, we didn't explicitly wrap the two updates in one transaction. We should test to see what will happen if we put the two updates within once transaction scope.

Follow these steps to wrap the two service calls in one transaction scope:

1. Add a reference to `System.Transactions` in the client project.
2. Add a `using` statement to the `Program.cs` file like this:

   ```
   using System.Transactions;
   ```

3. Add a `using` statement to put both updates within one transaction scope. Part of the source code should appear as shown here (we have omitted the try/catch blocks inside this method):

   ```
   static void MultiCallTest()
   {
       ProductServiceContractClient client = new
                ProductServiceContractClient();
       GetProductRequest getRequest = new GetProductRequest();
       UpdateProductRequest updateRequest =
               new UpdateProductRequest();

       string exception = "";
       StringBuilder sb = new StringBuilder();
       sb.Append("Prices before update:");
       Product product;
       using (TransactionScope ts = new TransactionScope())
       {
           // the original try/catch blocks in this method
       }

       sb.Append("Prices after update:");
       getRequest.ProductID = 30;
       product = client.GetProduct(getRequest);
       sb.Append(product.UnitPrice.ToString() + "    ");
       getRequest.ProductID = 31;
       product = client.GetProduct(getRequest);
       sb.Append(product.UnitPrice.ToString() + "\r\n");

       Console.WriteLine(sb.ToString() + exception);
   }
   ```

Run the client program again, and you will find that even though we have wrapped both updates within one transaction scope, the first update is still committed to the database—it is not rolled back, even though the outer transaction on the client side fails and requests all participating parties to roll back.

At this point, we have proved that the WCF service does not support distributed transactions with multiple sequential service calls. Irrespective of whether the two sequential calls to the service have been wrapped in one transaction scope or not, each service call is treated as a standalone separate transaction, and they do not participate in any distributed transaction.

Testing multiple database support of the WCF service

In the previous sections, we tried to call the WCF service sequentially to update records in the same database. We have proved that this WCF service does not support distributed transactions. In this section, we will do one more test, that is, to add a new operation—`UpdateCategoryDesc`—to this WCF service, to update records in another database on another computer, and call this new operation together with the original `UpdateProduct` operation, and then verify whether the two updates to the two databases will be within one distributed transaction.

This new operation is very important for our distributed transaction support test, because the distributed transaction coordinator will only be activated if more than two servers are involved in the same transaction. For test purposes, we can't just update two databases on the same SQL server, even though a transaction within a single SQL server that spans two or more databases is actually a distributed transaction. This is because the SQL server manages the distributed transaction internally; to the user it operates as a local transaction.

We will follow these steps for this test:

1. Modify the data access layer to update a second database.
2. Modify the business logic layer to call the new data access layer methods.
3. Modify the service interface layer to expose a new service contract with two new service operations.
4. Modify the host application to add a new endpoint for the new service interface.
5. Modify the client to call the existing and new WCF service operations to update two databases.
6. One of the updates will fail.

7. Verify that another update is committed to the database, which means that the WCF service does not support distributed transactions, even with multiple databases on different computers.

Modifying the data access layer for the second database support

We will start from the data access layer. We will add a second database support to the data access layer in this section. Follow these steps to add the necessary files to this layer:

1. Discover another machine with the SQL server installed. We will refer to this machine as the remote machine, going forward.
2. Install a Northwind database to this SQL server.
3. Open the **DistNorthwind** solution in Visual Studio 2008.
4. Open the `connections.config` file under the **MyWCF.LINQNorthwind.Host** project.
5. Insert the following line to this file:

   ```
   <add name="RemoteNorthwindConnectionString" providerName="System.
   Data.SqlProvider" connectionString="server=remote_pc_name\
   remote_db_instance;uid=your_db_user_name; pwd=your_db_password;
   database=Northwind;" />
   ```

   This defines a `connection` string to another `Northwind` database on another computer, which we will use in the new operation.

   Remember that you need to change this connection string according to your real database environment, and you can also choose to use either Windows trusted or SSPI security connections.
6. In the **Solution Explorer**, open **Server Explorer**, and add a connection to the remote `Northwind` database.
7. Add a new LINQ to the SQL Class to the **DataAccess** project, with the name `RemoteNorthwind.dbml`.
8. In the **Server Explorer**, drag the **Categories** table from the remote `Northwind` database to the LINQ to SQL designer pane, and rename it to **CategoryEntity**.
9. Add a new class file named `CategoryDAL.cs` to the **DataAccess** project.
10. Customize this new DAL class to look like this:

    ```
    using System;
    using System.Collections.Generic;
    using System.Linq;
    ```

```
using System.Text;
using System.Configuration;

namespace MyWCF.LINQNorthwind.DataAccess
{
    public class CategoryDAL
    {
        string connectionString = ConfigurationManager.ConnectionS
       trings["RemoteNorthwindConnectionString"].ConnectionString;
        public string GetCategoryDesc(int id)
        {
            RemoteNorthwindDataContext db = new RemoteNorthwindDat
                                            aContext(connectionString);
            CategoryEntity categoryEntity =
             (from c in db.CategoryEntities
                                            where c.CategoryID == id
                                            select c).FirstOrDefault();
            db.Dispose();

            return categoryEntity.Description;
        }
        public bool UpdateCategoryDesc(int id, string desc)
        {
            // update a record in a remote database
            RemoteNorthwindDataContext db = new RemoteNorthwindDat
                                           aContext(connectionString);
            CategoryEntity categoryEntity =
             (from c in db.CategoryEntities
                                            where c.CategoryID == id
                                            select c).FirstOrDefault();
            categoryEntity.Description = desc;
            db.SubmitChanges();
            db.Dispose();

            return true;
        }
    }
}
```

As you can see, we have defined two methods in this new class. The first method will get the description of a category from the remote Northwind database, and the second one will update the description of a category in the remote Northwind database.

To simplify the process, we didn't add error handling to these two methods. However, in a real project, error handling should be built in from the very beginning of the coding process.

Modifying the business logic layer for the second database support

In this section, we will customize the business logic layer to support the second database. Follow these steps to customize this layer:

1. Add a new class file **CategoryLogic.cs** to the **BusinessLogic** project.
2. Customize this new class to look like this:

```
using System;
using System.Collections.Generic;
using System.Linq;
using System.Text;
using MyWCF.LINQNorthwind.DataAccess;

namespace MyWCF.LINQNorthwind.BusinessLogic
{
    public class CategoryLogic
    {
        CategoryDAL categoryDAL = new CategoryDAL();
        public string GetCategoryDesc(int id)
        {
            return categoryDAL.GetCategoryDesc(id);
        }
        public bool UpdateCategoryDesc(int id, string desc)
        {
            return categoryDAL.UpdateCategoryDesc(id, desc);
        }
    }
}
```

In this layer, we just delegate the calls to the data access layer. In a real project, there might be lots of logic applied here.

Modifying the service interface layer for the second database support

Now, we can modify the service interface layer to expose two new operations. We need to add three files to the `FaultContracts`, `ServiceContracts`, and `ServiceImplementation` projects. Follow these steps to customize this layer:

1. Add a new class file called `CategoryFault.cs` to the **MyWCF.LINQNorthwind.FaultContracts** project.
2. Customize this new class to look like this:

```
using System;
using System.Collections.Generic;
using System.Linq;
using System.Text;
using WcfSerialization = global::System.Runtime.Serialization;

namespace MyWCF.LINQNorthwind.FaultContracts
{
    /// <summary>
    /// Data Contract Class - CategoryFault
    /// </summary>
    [WcfSerialization::DataContract(Namespace = "http://mycompany.
                                  com", Name = "CategoryFault")]
    public class CategoryFault
    {
        private string faultMessage;

        [WcfSerialization::DataMember(Name = "FaultMessage",
                                 IsRequired = false, Order = 0)]
        public string FaultMessage
        {
            get { return faultMessage; }
            set { faultMessage = value; }
        }
        public CategoryFault(string message)
        {
            this.faultMessage = message;
        }
    }
}
```

3. Add a new interface file named `ICategoryServiceContract.cs` to the **MyWCF.LINQNorthwind.ServiceContracts** project.

4. Customize this new interface to look like this:

```
using System;
using System.Net.Security;
using WCF = global::System.ServiceModel;
using System.ServiceModel;

namespace MyWCF.LINQNorthwind.ServiceContracts
{
    /// <summary>
    /// Service Contract Class - CategoryServiceContract
    /// </summary>
    [WCF::ServiceContract(Namespace = "http://mycompany.com",
     Name = "CategoryServiceContract", SessionMode = WCF::
     SessionMode.Allowed, ProtectionLevel = ProtectionLevel.None)]
    public interface ICategoryServiceContract
    {
        [WCF::FaultContract(typeof(MyWCF.LINQNorthwind.
                       FaultContracts.CategoryFault))]
        [WCF::OperationContract(IsTerminating = false,
         IsInitiating = true, IsOneWay = false, AsyncPattern
         = false, Action = "http://mycompany.com/
         CategoryServiceContract/UpdateCategoryDesc", ReplyAction
         = "http://mycompany.com/CategoryServiceContract/
         UpdateCategoryDesc", ProtectionLevel = ProtectionLevel.
         None)]
        bool UpdateCategoryDesc(int id, string desc);

        [WCF::OperationContract(IsTerminating = false,
        IsInitiating = true, IsOneWay = false, AsyncPattern =
        false, Action = "http://mycompany.com/
        CategoryServiceContract/GetCategoryDesc", ReplyAction
        = "http://mycompany.com/CategoryServiceContract/
        GetCategoryDesc", ProtectionLevel = ProtectionLevel.None)]
        string GetCategoryDesc(int id);
    }
}
```

5. Add a new class file named `CategoryService.cs` to the project **MyWCF.LINQNorthwind.ServiceImplementation**.
6. Customize this new class to look like this:

```
using System;
using System.Collections.Generic;
using System.Linq;
using System.Text;
using MyWCF.LINQNorthwind.BusinessLogic;
```

```
using WCF = global::System.ServiceModel;
using System.ServiceModel;
using MyWCF.LINQNorthwind.FaultContracts;
namespace MyWCF.LINQNorthwind.ServiceImplementation
{
    /// <summary>
    /// Service Class - CategoryService
    /// </summary>
    [WCF::ServiceBehavior(Name = "CategoryService",
        Namespace = "http://mycompany.com",
        InstanceContextMode = WCF::InstanceContextMode.PerSession,
        ConcurrencyMode = WCF::ConcurrencyMode.Single)]
    public class CategoryService : MyWCF.LINQNorthwind.
             ServiceContracts.ICategoryServiceContract
    {
        #region CategoryServiceContract Members
        CategoryLogic categoryLogic = new CategoryLogic();
        public virtual bool UpdateCategoryDesc(int id, string desc)
        {
            bool result;
            try
            {
               result = categoryLogic.UpdateCategoryDesc(id, desc);
            }
            catch (Exception e)
            {
                throw new FaultException<CategoryFault>(
                 new CategoryFault("could not update category.
                 Error message:" + e.Message));
            }
            return result;
        }
        public virtual string GetCategoryDesc(int id)
        {
            return categoryLogic.GetCategoryDesc(id);
        }
        #endregion
    }
}
```

In the **ServiceContracts** and **ServiceImplementation** projects, we just added two service operations to get and update a category description. Here, we didn't introduce any new data contract or message contract, so that we could concentrate on the distributed transaction support test.

Modifying the service host for the second database support

In the previous sections, we modified the WCF service to expose one more service contract with two new operations. Now we need to modify the host application to publish this new service contract.

Follow these steps to publish this new service contract:

1. Add a new text file to the **MyWCF.LINQNorthwind.Host** project, with the name `CategoryService.svc`.
2. Type the following line into this new file:

```
<%@ ServiceHost language="c#" Debug="true" Service="MyWCF.
LINQNorthwind.ServiceImplementation.CategoryService" %>
```

3. Open the file `web.config` and add the following node as a child node of `<serviceBehaviors>`:

```
<behavior name="MyWCF.LINQNorthwind.ServiceImplementation.
                                CategoryService_Behavior">
 <serviceDebug includeExceptionDetailInFaults="false" />
  <serviceMetadata httpGetEnabled="true" />
</behavior>
```

4. Still in the file `web.config`, add the following node as a child node of `<services>`:

```
<service behaviorConfiguration="MyWCF.LINQNorthwind.
     ServiceImplementation.CategoryService_Behavior"
 name="MyWCF.LINQNorthwind.ServiceImplementation.CategoryService">
  <endpoint address="" binding="basicHttpBinding"
                           name="CategoryEndpoint"
   bindingNamespace="http://mycompany.com" contract="MyWCF.
      LINQNorthwind.ServiceContracts.ICategoryServiceContract" />
  <endpoint address="mex" binding="mexHttpBinding" contract=
                                    "IMetadataExchange" />
</service>
```

The above changes will publish the new service contract. You can follow these steps to confirm this:

1. Save all of the files.
2. Rebuild the solution.
3. In the **Solution Explorer**, right-click on the project **MyWCF.LINQNorthwind.Host**.
4. Select **View in Browser** from the context menu.

Now, when the ASP.NET Development Server is be started, and an Internet browser should pop up with the title of **Directory Listing -- /MyWCF.LINQNOrthwind. Host**. Within this browser, two svc files should be listed. Click on the `CategoryService.svc`, and you will see the introduction of this new service and the WSDL link of this service.

Modifying the client for the second database support

At this point, we have the new service implemented and hosted. Now, we can modify the client to test the multi-database support of the WCF service. We will prove that at this point the WCF service does not support distributed transactions among multiple databases. Later in this chapter, after we have enhanced the service, we will see that the WCF service supports distributed transactions among multiple databases.

Follow these steps to modify the client:

1. Start the Host application in the ASP.NET Development Server.
2. In the **Solution Explorer**, right-click on the project **DistributedClient**.
3. Select **Add Service Reference** from the context menu.
4. Select or type the following address in the **Address** list box of the **Add Service Reference** dialog window:

   ```
   http://localhost:8080/MyWCF.LINQNorthwind.Host/
   CategoryService.svc
   ```

   You can also click the **Discover** button to discover this service.
5. Type **CategoryServiceProxy** as the namespace of the service reference.
6. Click **OK** to add the service reference.
7. Open the `Program.cs` file.
8. Add the following `using` statement to the class:

   ```
   using DistributedClient.CategoryServiceProxy;
   ```

9. Add a new method call of **MultiDBTest** to the **Main** method. The **Main** method now should look like this:

   ```
   static void Main(string[] args)
   {
       MultiCallTest();
       MultiDBTest();
   }
   ```

10. Add a new method called **MultiDBTest** to this file:

```
static void MultiDBTest()
{
    ProductServiceContractClient productClient =
            new ProductServiceContractClient();
    GetProductRequest getRequest = new GetProductRequest();
    UpdateProductRequest updateRequest =
            new UpdateProductRequest();
    CategoryServiceContractClient categoryClient =
             new CategoryServiceContractClient();
    string exception = "";
    StringBuilder sb = new StringBuilder();
    sb.Append("Description and price before update:");
    Product product;
    using (TransactionScope ts = new TransactionScope())
    {
        try
        {
            // first get the category desc from database
            sb.Append(categoryClient.GetCategoryDesc(4) + "    ");
            // first get the  product from database
            getRequest.ProductID = 30;
            product = productClient.GetProduct(getRequest);
            sb.Append(product.UnitPrice.ToString() + "\r\n");
            // update category description
            // submit to database
            bool result1 = categoryClient.UpdateCategoryDesc(
                    4,"Description updated at " + DateTime.Now.
                    ToLongTimeString());
            // update product price
            product.UnitPrice = -10;
            // submit to database -- this update will fail
            updateRequest.Product = product;
            bool result2 = productClient.UpdateProduct(
                                  updateRequest);
        }
        catch (TimeoutException ex)
        {
            exception = "The service operation timed out. " +
                                             ex.Message;
        }
        catch (FaultException<ProductFault> ex)
    {
        exception = "ProductFault returned: " + ex.Detail.
```

```
FaultMessage;
            }
            catch (FaultException<CategoryFault> ex)
            {
                exception = "CategoryFault returned: " +
                                      ex.Detail.FaultMessage;
            }
            catch (FaultException ex)
            {
                exception = "Unknown Fault: " + ex.ToString();
            }
            catch (CommunicationException ex)
            {
                exception = "There was a communication problem. " +
                                         ex.Message + ex.StackTrace;
            }
            catch (Exception ex)
            {
                exception = "Other excpetion: " + ex.Message +
                                              ex.StackTrace;
            }
        }

        sb.Append("Description and price after update:");
        sb.Append(categoryClient.GetCategoryDesc(4) + "    ");
        getRequest.ProductID = 30;
        product = productClient.GetProduct(getRequest);
        sb.Append(product.UnitPrice.ToString() + "\r\n");

        Console.WriteLine(sb.ToString() + exception);
    }
```

In this method, we first call the `CategoryService` to update the description of category `4` in the remote Northwind database, then call the `ProductService` to update product `30`'s price to make it an invalid price. We know the second update will fail due to the database CHECK constraint, but what about the first service call? Will the update of the category description be committed to the remote database?

Testing the WCF service with two databases

Now, let's run the program to find out. Again, we will get an error message saying "could not update product", as shown in the following image:

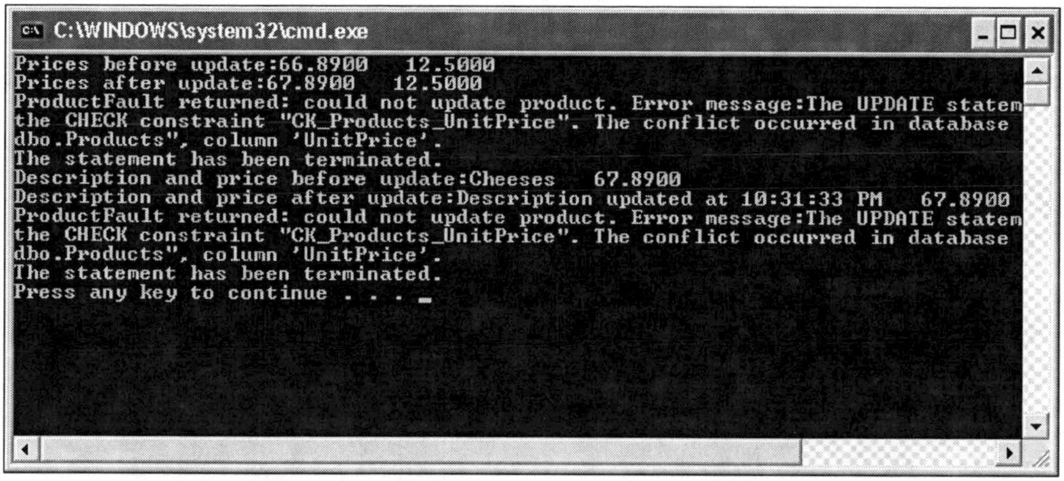

```
C:\WINDOWS\system32\cmd.exe
Prices before update:66.8900    12.5000
Prices after update:67.8900    12.5000
ProductFault returned: could not update product. Error message:The UPDATE statem
the CHECK constraint "CK_Products_UnitPrice". The conflict occurred in database
dbo.Products", column 'UnitPrice'.
The statement has been terminated.
Description and price before update:Cheeses    67.8900
Description and price after update:Description updated at 10:31:33 PM    67.8900
ProductFault returned: could not update product. Error message:The UPDATE statem
the CHECK constraint "CK_Products_UnitPrice". The conflict occurred in database
dbo.Products", column 'UnitPrice'.
The statement has been terminated.
Press any key to continue . . .
```

Just as in the previous test, we know that the exception is due to the second service call, so the second update is not committed to the database. From the test result, we know this is true (product `30`'s price didn't change). However, from the test result, we also know that the first update of the first service call has been committed to the remote database (category `4`'s description has been changed). This means that the first call to the service is not rolled back even when a subsequent service call has failed. Each service call is in a separate standalone transaction. In other words, the two sequential service calls are not within one atomic transaction.

From the output of the program, we also noticed that the price of product `30` has been updated by `1.00` in the first method call (`MultiCallTest`).

Enabling distributed transaction support

In the previous sections, we verified that the WCF service currently does not support distributed transactions, irrespective of whether these are two sequential calls to the same service, or two sequential calls to two different services, either with one database or with two databases.

In the following sections we will explain how to allow this WCF service to support distributed transactions. We will allow this WCF service to participate in the client transaction. From another point of view, we will explain how to flow or propagate a client transaction across the service boundaries so that the client can include service operation calls on multiple services in the same distributed transaction.

Enabling transaction flow in bindings

The first thing that we need to pay attention to is the bindings. As we learned in the previous chapters, the three elements of a WCF service end point are the address, the binding, and the contract (WCF ABC). Although the address has nothing to do with the distributed transaction support, the other two elements do.

For the bindings, we know that WCF supports several different bindings, but not all of these bindings are capable of propagating a transaction across service boundaries. Actually, a transaction can only be propagated from a client application into a WCF service with the following bindings: `NetTcpBinding`, `NetNamedPipeBinding`, `WSHttpBinding`, `WSDualHttpBinding`, and `WSFederationHttpBinding`. In this chapter, we will use `WSHttpBinding` as an example.

However, using a transaction-aware binding doesn't mean that a transaction will be propagated to the service. Actually, the transaction propagation is disabled by default. We have to enable it manually. Unsurprisingly, the attribute to enable transaction flow in the bindings is called `transactionFlow`.

In the following two sections, we will do the following to enable the transaction propagation:

- Use `wsHttpBinding` on both the host and client applications as bindings
- Set the value of the `transactionFlow` attribute to `true` on both the host and client application binding configurations

Enabling transaction flow on the service application

In this section, we will enable transaction flow in bindings for both `ProductService` and `CategoryService`.

1. In the **Solution Explorer**, open the `web.config` file under the folder `D:\...\MyWCF.LINQNorthwind.Host`.
2. Change the following line:

   ```
   <endpoint address="" binding=
                               "basicHttpBinding" name="ProductEndpoint"
   ```

   To this line:

   ```
   <endpoint address="" binding="wsHttpBinding" bindingConfiguration=
    "transactionalWsHttpBinding" name="ProductEndpoint"
   ```

3. Change the following line:

   ```
   <endpoint address="" binding=
                              "basicHttpBinding" name="CategoryEndpoint"
   ```

To this line:

```
<endpoint address="" binding="wsHttpBinding" bindingConfiguration=
 "transactionalWsHttpBinding" name="CategoryEndpoint"
```

4. Add the following node to the `web.config` file inside the node **system.serviceModel** and in parallel with node **services**:

```
<bindings>
  <wsHttpBinding>
     <binding name="transactionalWsHttpBinding"
      transactionFlow="true" receiveTimeout="00:10:00"
      sendTimeout="00:10:00" openTimeout="00:10:00"
      closeTimeout="00:10:00" />
  </wsHttpBinding>
</bindings>
```

In the above configuration file, we changed the bindings for both `ProductService` and `CategoryService` from `basicHttpBinding` to `wsHttpBinding`, and set the attribute `transactionFlow` of the binding to `true`. This will enable distributed transaction support from the WCF service side.

Enabling transaction flow on the client application

Now the service is able to participate in a propagated transaction from the client application, but the client is still not able to propagate a distributed transaction into the service. In this section, we will enable the client to propagate a transaction to the service.

We can modify the client configuration files directly, just as we did for the service host application `web.config` file. However, in this example, we will ask Visual Studio to regenerate the proxy and the configuration files for us.

1. Rebuild the solution.
2. In the **Solution Explorer**, right-click on the Host project, and select **View in Browser** to start the **Host** application.
3. Right-click on the **CategoryServiceProxy** under the **Service References** directory of the **DistributedClient** project.
4. Select **Update Service Reference** from the context menu.
5. Right-click on the **ProductServiceProxy** under the **Service References** directory of the **DistributedClient** project.
6. Select **Update Service Reference** from the context menu.

Once the proxy files have been regenerated, the binding on the client side will be changed from `basicHttpBinding` to `wsHttpBinding`, and the `transactionFlow` attribute will be in the `app.config` file. However, at this time, the value of the `transactionFlow` attribute is set to `false` in the `app.config` file. This is because the code generator didn't find any operation that allows transaction propagation in the service. It might find it to be wasteful to propagate a transaction to a service if this propagated transaction is not going to be used anyway. For now, just leave it as it is, because after we have modified the service operations we will modify this value anyway.

You can build and run the client program now, but the result will be the same as before; that is, the first update is still committed while the second one fails. This is because even though the client transaction is now able to be propagated to the service, the client chooses not to propagate it. And even though the service is now ready to participate in the propagated transaction, no service operation has opted to participate in this transaction. Next, we will explain how to configure service operations to participate in the propagated transaction inside the service, and we will also change the client to really propagate a transaction into the service.

Modifying the service operation contract to allow a transaction flow

As we said in the previous section, the service operation needs to opt in to participate in a distributed transaction. By default, it is opted out.

Two things need to be done in order to allow an operation to participate in a propagated transaction. The first thing is to enable the transaction flow in operation contracts. Follow these steps to enable this option:

1. Open the `IProductServiceContract.cs` file under the **MyWCF.LINQNorthwind.ServiceContracts** project
2. Add a `using` statement such as this:
   ```
   using System.ServiceModel;
   ```
3. Add the following line before the **UpdateProduct** method:
   ```
   [WCF::TransactionFlow(TransactionFlowOption.Allowed)]
   ```
4. Open the `ICategoryServiceContract.cs` file under the `MyWCF.LINQNorthwind.ServiceContracts` project.
5. Add a `using` statement such as this:
   ```
   using System.ServiceModel;
   ```
6. Add the following line before method **UpdateCategoryDesc**:
   ```
   [WCF::TransactionFlow(TransactionFlowOption.Allowed)]
   ```

In the above code, we set the `TransactionFlowOption` of both `UpdateProduct` and `UpdateCategoryDesc` operations to be `Allowed`. This means a transaction can be propagated from the client to these two operations.

The three transaction flow options for a WCF service operation are `Allowed`, `NotAllowed` and `Mandatory`, as shown in the following table:

Option	Description
NotAllowed	A transaction should not be flowed; this is the default value
Allowed	Transaction may be flowed
Mandatory	Transaction must be flowed

Modifying the service operation implementation to require a transaction scope

The second thing we need to do is to specify the `TransactionScopeRequired` behavior for the service operation. This has to be done on the service implementation project.

1. Open the `ProductService.cs` file under the **MyWCF.LINQNorthwind.ServiceImplementation** project.
2. Add a `using` statement such as this:
   ```
   using System.ServiceModel;
   ```
3. Add the following line before the **UpdateProduct** method:
   ```
   [OperationBehavior(TransactionScopeRequired = true)]
   ```
4. Open the `CategoryService.cs` file under the **MyWCF.LINQNorthwind.ServiceImplementation** project.
5. Add a `using` statement such as this:
   ```
   using System.ServiceModel;
   ```
6. Add the following line before the **UpdateCategoryDesc** method:
   ```
   [OperationBehavior(TransactionScopeRequired = true)]
   ```

The `TransactionScopeRequired` attribute means that for the `UpdateProduct` and `UpdateCategoryDesc` methods, the whole service operation will always be executed inside one transaction. If a transaction is propagated from the client application, this operation will participate in this existing distributed transaction. If no transaction is propagated, a new transaction will be created and this operation will be running within this new transaction.

If you are interested, you can examine the ambient transaction inside the WCF service (`Transaction.Current`), and compare it with the ambient transaction of the client, to see if they are the same. You can also examine the `TransactionInformation` property of the ambient transaction object to see if it is a local transaction (`TransactionInformation.LocalIdentifier`), or a distributed transaction (`TransactionInformation.DistributedIdentifier`).

Getting back to our example, we now need to regenerate the service proxy and the configuration files from the client project, because we have changed the service interfaces. However, in your real project, you shouldn't change any service interface; once it goes live, you should version your service, and allow the client applications to migrate to the new versions of the service.

These are the steps to regenerate the configuration and proxy files:

1. Rebuild the solution.
2. In the **Solution Explorer**, right-click on the Host project, and select **View in Browser** to start the Host application.
3. Right-click on the **CategoryServiceProxy** under the **Service References** directory of the **DistributedClient** project.
4. Select **Update Service Reference** from the context menu.
5. Right-click on the **ProductServiceProxy** under the **Service References** directory of the **DistributedClient** project.
6. Select **Update Service Reference** from the context menu.

This time, after you have all of the configuration and proxy files regenerated, you will find that the `transactionFlow` attribute is correctly populated as `true` in the `app.config` file, because the code generator finds that some operations now really allow transaction propagation.

Understanding distributed transaction support of a WCF service

As we have seen now, distributed transaction support of a WCF service depends on the binding of the service, the operation contract attribute, the operation implementation behavior, and the client applications.

The following table shows some possible combinations of the WCF distributed transaction support:

Binding permits transaction flow	Client flows transaction	Service contract opts in transaction	Service operation requires transaction scope	Possible result
True	Yes	Allowed or mandatory	True	Service executes under the flowed in transaction
True or false	No	Allowed	True	Service creates and executes within a new transaction
True	Yes or No	Allowed	False	Service executes without a transaction
True or false	No	Mandatory	True or False	SOAP exception
True	Yes	NotAllowed	True or False	SOAP exception

Testing the distributed transaction support of the WCF service

Now that we have all of the supporting distributed transactions of the service and the client, we will test this service. We will propagate a transaction from the client to the service, test the multiple database support of the WCF service, and discuss the Distributed Transaction Coordinator and Firewall settings for the distributed transactions support of the WCF service.

Propagating a transaction from client to the WCF service

In this section, we will re-run the distributed test client, and verify the distributed transaction support of the enhanced WCF service.

Just press *F5* or *Ctrl+F5* to start the host and client applications. From the source code, we know that in the first method it will try to update two products (`30` and `31`). Both updates are wrapped in one client transaction, which will be propagated into the service, and the service will participate in this distributed transaction. Due to the failure of the second update, the client application will roll back this distributed transaction at the end, and the service should also roll back every update that is within this distributed transaction. So, in the end, the first update should not be committed to the database.

In the second method, it will try to update a category description (category `4`) and a product price (product `30`). Both updates are wrapped in one client transaction, which will be propagated into the service, and the service will participate in this distributed transaction. Due to the failure of the second update, the client application will roll back this distributed transaction at the end, and the service should also roll back every update that is within this distributed transaction. So, in the end, the first update should not be committed to the database.

From the output window, we can see that the first transaction fails due to the database constraint. And we can also see that the prices of both products remain the same, which proves that the first update has been rolled back. The second transaction also fails due to the database constraint. We can also see that both the category description and the product price remain the same, which proves that the first update has been rolled back, too. From this output, we know that both method calls are within a distributed transaction, and the WCF service now fully supports the distributed transaction.

```
C:\WINDOWS\system32\cmd.exe
Prices before update:68.8900   12.5000
Prices after update:68.8900   12.5000
ProductFault returned: could not update product. Error message:The UPDATE statem
the CHECK constraint "CK_Products_UnitPrice". The conflict occurred in database
dbo.Products", column 'UnitPrice'.
The statement has been terminated.
Description and price before update:Description updated at 10:49:40 PM   68.8900
Description and price after update:Description updated at 10:49:40 PM   68.8900
ProductFault returned: could not update product. Error message:The UPDATE statem
the CHECK constraint "CK_Products_UnitPrice". The conflict occurred in database
dbo.Products", column 'UnitPrice'.
The statement has been terminated.
Press any key to continue . . .
```

If you didn't get a similar output as shown here, and instead got one of the following error messages:

- **MSDTC on server 'xxxxxx' is unavailable**
- **Network access for Distributed Transaction Manager(MSDTC) has been disabled**
- **The transaction has already been implicitly or explicitly committed or aborted**

Then it is possible that you haven't set your Distributed Transaction Coordinator or firewall correctly. In this case, you can follow the instructions in the next two sections to configure these settings.

Configuring the Distributed Transaction Coordinator

In the previous section, when we called two services to update two databases on two different computers, a distributed transaction was started. In this case, Microsoft Distributed Transaction Coordinator (MSDTC) was activated to manage this distributed transaction. If MSDTC hadn't been started or configured properly, the distributed transaction would have failed.

To test this, we can disable MSDTC on the remote machine, and try to run the same test to see what happens. You can follow these steps to disable MSDTC on the remote machine:

1. Open **Component Services** from **Control Panel | Administrative Tools** on the remote machine.
2. In the **Component Services** window, expand **Component Services and Computers**, and then right-click on **My Computer**.
3. Select **Properties** from the context menu.
4. On the **My Computer Properties** window, click on the **MSDTC** tab.
5. Click the **Security Configuration** button.
6. Uncheck **Network DTC Access**.

Now, MSDTC on the remote machine is disabled. If you run the client again, you may get this result:

Description and price before update:Description updated at 8:16:46 PM   55.8900

Description and price after update:Description updated at 8:16:46 PM   55.8900

CategoryFault returned: could not update category. Error message:MSDTC on server '[remote_pc_name]' is unavailable.

If you uncheck **Network DTC Access** or **Allow Outbound** in the MSDTC **Security Configuration** window on your local computer where your client application is running, you may get this error message:

Description and price before update:Description updated at 8:16:46 PM   55.8900

Description and price after update:Description updated at 8:16:46 PM   55.8900

CategoryFault returned: could not update category. Error message:Network access for Distributed Transaction Manager (MSDTC) has been disabled. Please enable DTC for network access in the security configuration for MSDTC using the Component Services Administrative tool.

This test tells us that the MSDTC must be enabled for the WCF service to support distributed transactions. Now, change the settings back to the original values so that we can continue our next test. You should have the following settings in your **MSDTC Security Configuration** window for both your local and remote computers (if your remote computer is a Windows 2003 box, you may need to select **No Authentication Required**):

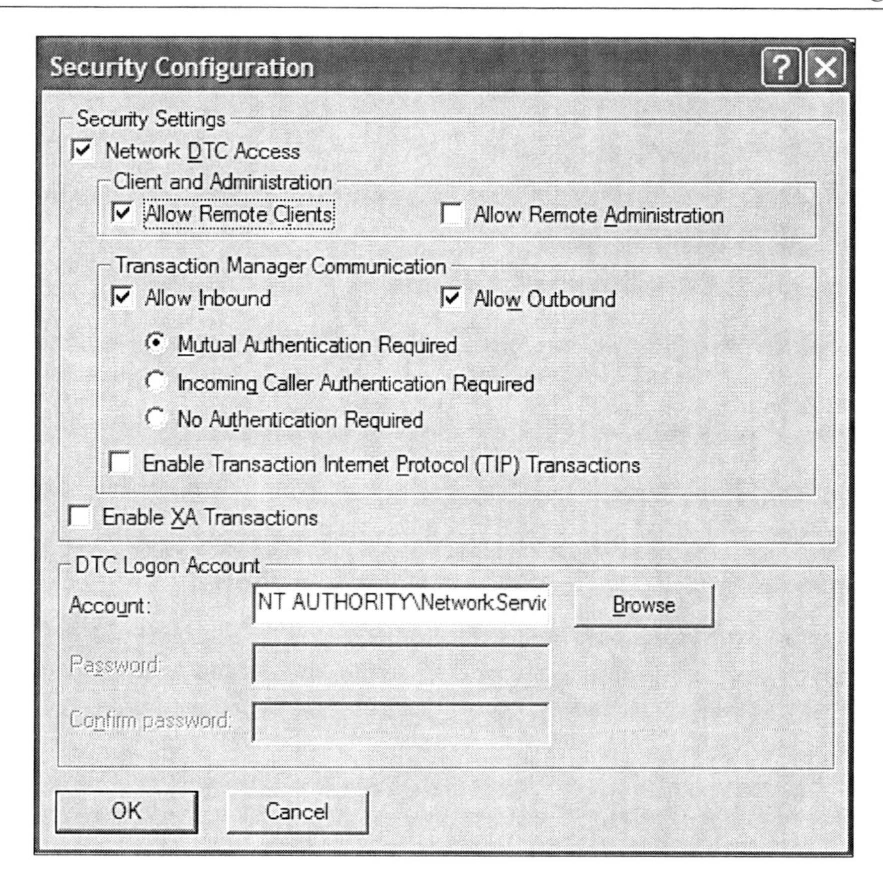

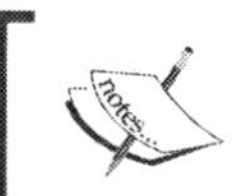

You may have to restart the MSDTC service and your host application after you have changed your MSDTC settings for the changes to take effect.

Configuring the firewall

Even though the Distributed Transaction Coordinator has been enabled, the distributed transaction may still have failed if the firewall is turned on and hasn't been set up properly for MSDTC.

To test this, follow these steps:

1. Open the **Windows Firewall** window from the **Control Panel**.
2. If the firewall is off, turn it on.
3. If **Don't allow exceptions** is checked, you can skip the next two steps.
4. Click on the **Exceptions** tab.
5. Uncheck **(windows\system32\)msdtc.exe**, if it is in the list.

Now, the firewall will block `msdtc.exe`. If you run the client again, you may get this result:

Description and price before update:Description updated at 8:16:46 PM 55.8900

Description and price after update:Description updated at 8:16:46 PM 55.8900

CategoryFault returned: could not update category. Error message:The transaction has already been implicitly or explicitly committed or aborted.

This means that the distributed transaction can't be started due to the firewall blocking `msdtc.exe`. So, to run the distributed transaction, you need to either turn off the firewall, or add `windows\system32\msdtc.exe` to the firewall exception list.

You may need to restart your host application after you have changed your firewall settings. In some cases, you may also have to stop and then restart your firewall for the changes to take effect.

Summary

In this chapter, we have discussed how to enable distributed transaction support for a WCF service. Now, we can wrap sequential WCF service calls within one transaction scope, and flow the distributed transaction into the WCF services. We can also update multiple databases on different computers all within one single distributed transaction.

The key points discussed in this chapter include:

- Only certain bindings allow transactions to flow from the client to the WCF service using the `transactionFlow` attribute
- A WCF service operation contract can opt to participate in a propagated transaction using the `TransactionFlow` attribute

- A WCF service operation can specify its transaction behavior using the `TransactionScopeRequired` attribute
- MSDTC network access must be enabled for distributed transactions support among multiple computers
- The firewall has to be configured to allow `msdtc.exe` for a distributed transaction to succeed

Index

Symbols

A

B

C

D

E

F

G

H

I

J

L

M

N

O

P

Q

S

T

V

W

PACKT
PUBLISHING
Thank you for buying
WCF Multi-tier Services
Development with LINQ

About Packt Publishing

Packt, pronounced 'packed', published its first book "*Mastering phpMyAdmin for Effective MySQL Management*" in April 2004 and subsequently continued to specialize in publishing highly focused books on specific technologies and solutions.

Our books and publications share the experiences of your fellow IT professionals in adapting and customizing today's systems, applications, and frameworks. Our solution based books give you the knowledge and power to customize the software and technologies you're using to get the job done. Packt books are more specific and less general than the IT books you have seen in the past. Our unique business model allows us to bring you more focused information, giving you more of what you need to know, and less of what you don't.

Packt is a modern, yet unique publishing company, which focuses on producing quality, cutting-edge books for communities of developers, administrators, and newbies alike. For more information, please visit our website: `www.packtpub.com`.

Writing for Packt

We welcome all inquiries from people who are interested in authoring. Book proposals should be sent to `author@packtpub.com`. If your book idea is still at an early stage and you would like to discuss it first before writing a formal book proposal, contact us; one of our commissioning editors will get in touch with you.

We're not just looking for published authors; if you have strong technical skills but no writing experience, our experienced editors can help you develop a writing career, or simply get some additional reward for your expertise.

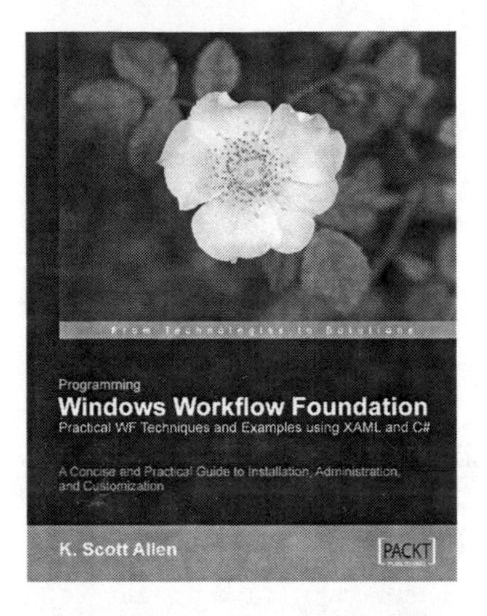

Programming Windows Workflow Foundation

ISBN: 1-904811-21-3 Paperback: 300 pages

A C# developer's guide to the features and programming interfaces of Windows Workflow Foundation

1. Add event-driven workflow capabilities to your .NET applications
2. Highlights the libraries, services and internals programmers need to know
3. Builds a practical "bug reporting" workflow solution example app

---

ASP.NET 3.5 Application Architecture and Design

ISBN: 978-1-847195-50-0 Paperback: 239 pages

Build robust, scalable ASP.NET applications quickly and easily

1. Master the architectural options in ASP.NET to enhance your applications
2. Develop and implement n-tier architecture to allow you to modify a component without disturbing the next one
3. Design scalable and maintainable web applications rapidly
4. Implement ASP.NET MVC framework to manage various components independently

Please check **www.PacktPub.com** for information on our titles

LINQ Quickly

ISBN: 978-1-847192-54-7 Paperback: 250 pages

A Practical Guide to Programming Language Integrated Query with C#

1. LINQ to Objects
2. LINQ to XML
3. LINQ to SQL
4. LINQ to DataSets
5. LINQ to XSD

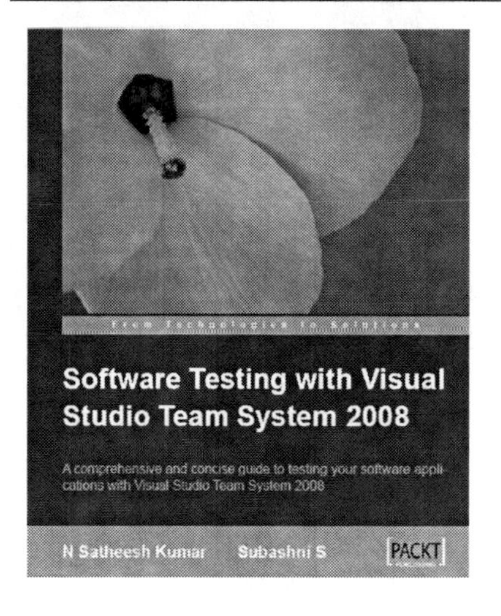

Software Testing with Visual Studio Team System 2008

ISBN: 978-1-847195-58-6 Paperback: 350 pages

A comprehensive and concise guide to testing your software applications with Visual Studio Team System 2008

1. Test your software applications with Visual Studio Team System 2008 and rest assured of its quality
2. Create a structured testing environment for your applications to produce reliable products
3. Comprehensive yet concise guide with a lot of examples and clear explanations
4. No knowledge of software testing is required, only basic knowledge of Visual Studio 2008 operation is expected

Please check **www.PacktPub.com** for information on our titles

Printed in the United States
211920BV00003B/14/P

9 781847 196620